The Future of Translation Technology

Technology has revolutionized the field of translation, bringing drastic changes to the way translation is studied and done. To an average user, technology is simply about clicking buttons and storing data. What we need to do is to look beyond a system's interface to see what is at work and what should be done to make it work more efficiently. This book is both macroscopic and microscopic in approach: macroscopic as it adopts a holistic orientation when outlining the development of translation technology in the last forty years, organizing concepts in a coherent and logical way within a theoretical framework, and predicting what is to come in the years ahead; microscopic as it examines in detail the five stages of technology-oriented translation procedure and the strengths and weaknesses of the free and paid systems available to users. *The Future of Translation Technology* studies, among other issues:

- The Development of Translation Technology
- Major Concepts in Computer-aided Translation
- Functions in Computer-aided Translation Systems
- A Theoretical Framework for Computer-aided Translation Studies
- The Future of Translation Technology

This book is an essential read for scholars and researchers of translational studies and computational linguistics, and a guide to system users and professionals.

Chan Sin-wai, Professor at the School of Humanities and Social Science, The Chinese University of Hong Kong, Shenzhen, has taught and conducted research on translation technology, translation studies, and Chinese-English translation for many years. He has so far authored, edited, compiled, and translated forty-eight academic books, in sixty-two volumes. His book publications in 2016 include *A New Comprehensive Chinese-English Dictionary* (in three volumes), *Routledge Encyclopedia of Translation Technology* and *Routledge Encyclopedia of the Chinese Language*.

Routledge studies in translation technology

Series Editor
Chan Sin-wai

For a full list of titles in this series, please visit https://www.routledge.com/series/RSITT

1 **The Future of Translation Technology**
Towards a World without Babel
Chan Sin-wai

The Future of Translation Technology
Towards a World without Babel

Chan Sin-wai

LONDON AND NEW YORK

First published 2017 by Routledge

2 Park Square, Milton Park, Abingdon, Oxfordshire OX14 4RN
52 Vanderbilt Avenue, New York, NY 10017

Routledge is an imprint of the Taylor & Francis Group, an informa business

First issued in paperback 2019

Copyright © 2017 Chan Sin-wai

The right of Chan Sin-wai to be identified as author of this work
has been asserted by him in accordance with sections 77 and 78
of the Copyright, Designs and Patents Act 1988.

All rights reserved. No part of this book may be reprinted or
reproduced or utilized in any form or by any electronic,
mechanical, or other means, now known or hereafter invented,
including photocopying and recording, or in any information
storage or retrieval system, without permission in writing from the
publishers.

Notice:
Product or corporate names may be trademarks
or registered trademarks, and are used only for identification and
explanation without intent to infringe.

British Library Cataloguing in Publication Data
A catalogue record for this book is available from the British Library

Library of Congress Cataloging-in-Publication Data
Names: Chan, Sin-wai, author.
Title: The future of translation technology : towards a world without
    Babel / by Sin-wai Chan.
Description: Milton Park, Abingdon, Oxon ; New York, NY : Routledge,
    [2017] | Series: Routledge Studies in Translation Technology; 1 |
    Includes bibliographical references and index.
Identifiers: LCCN 2016015991 | ISBN 9781138842045 (hardback) |
    ISBN 9781315731865 (ebook)
Subjects: LCSH: Translating and interpreting—Technological innovations.
Classification: LCC P306.97.T73 C53 2017 | DDC 418/.020285—dc23
LC record available at https://lccn.loc.gov/2016015991

ISBN: 978-1-138-84204-5 (hbk)
ISBN: 978-0-367-40905-0 (pbk)

Typeset in Galliard
by Apex CoVantage, LLC

Contents

List of illustrations		vii
Preface		ix
Acknowledgements		xi
1	The development of translation technology: 1967–2014	1
2	Major concepts in computer-aided translation	30
3	Functions in computer-aided translation systems	68
4	Computer-aided translation: Free and paid systems	167
5	A theoretical framework for computer-aided translation studies	244
6	The future of translation technology	258
	Index	279

Illustrations

Figures

2.1	Screenshot of Dashboard of SDL-Trados 2015	58
2.2	Screenshot of SDL-Trados: 'Progress of Individual Projects'	58
2.3	Screenshot of SDL-Trados: 'Completion of Projects: Today'	59
2.4	Screenshot of SDL-Trados: 'Progress on the Translation of Files'	59
3.1	Editing Interface of Wordfast Anywhere	123
3.2	MadCap Lingo V9	124
4.1	Main Window of Anaphraseus	173
4.2	User Data of ESTeam	178
4.3	Translation Editor of Isometry	184
4.4	User Interface of LogiTerm Web	187
4.5	Project Management Page of Memsource Cloud	191
4.6	Editing Interface of MetaTexis	192
4.7	Translation Editor of MT2007	193
4.8	Editor of OmegaT	197
4.9	SDL TMS 2013	201
4.10	SDL WorldServer	203
4.11	Similis Manager	204
4.12	Similis: Statistics of Translation Tasks	205
4.13	User Interface of Snowman	206
4.14	Screenshot of TMs and Glossaries Management in Wordfast Anywhere	212
4.15	Screenshot of the Login Window in Wordfast Anywhere	213
4.16	Working Document of WordFisher	214
4.17	XTM Cloud	215
4.18	Apertium Translation Interface	223
4.19	Lucy LT KWIK Translator	228
4.20	SDL Automated Translation Solutions	231

viii *Illustrations*

Tables

2.1	Statistics of Languages Support by Seven CAT Systems	51
3.1	Project Wizards of Nine CAT Systems	71
3.2	Designations of Terminology Databases of Nine CAT Systems	80
3.3	Designations of Translation Memory Databases of Nine CAT Systems	84
3.4	Editing Environments of Nine CAT Systems	121
4.1	Comparison between the Costs of Translation Performed by Lingotek Community Translation and Industry Standards (Adapted from Vandenberg 2009: 21)	186
4.2	Most Popular TM tools with Non-TM-users (Adapted from Table 3 in Lagoudaki 2006: 15)	195
4.3	Top 10 Most Widely Used TM Tools (Adapted from Table 7 in Lagoudaki 2006: 20)	195
4.4	Top 10 Most Widely Used TM Tools by other than Windows OS Users (Adapted from Figure 24 in Lagoudaki 2006: 21)	196
4.5	CAT Systems and their MT Links	221
4.6	Online Systems Linked to CAT Systems	222
4.7	Bi-directional Language Pairs Supported in AppTek's TranSphere® MT	224
4.8	Language Pairs for which Uni-directional Translation is Supported in AppTek's TranSphere® MT	224
5.1	A Framework for Computer-aided Translation Studies	247
6.1	Divisions of Translation	259

Preface

This book studies the development of translation technology in the last four decades from a historical, conceptual, functional, and theoretical perspective, as well as how translation technology will move ahead in the years to come, eventually getting to the stage where the Tower of Babel will no longer exist and the entire world will be free from language barriers.

Before we discuss the role of translation technology in the future world of translation, an explanation of the term may be in order. According to Lynne Bowker, author of *Computer-Aided Translation Technology: A Practical Introduction*, translation technology refers to different types of computerized tools used in the translation process. This definition covers the general tools used in computing, such as word processors and electronic resources, and the specific tools used in translating, such as corpus-analysis tools and terminology management systems (Bowker 2002: 5–9). A broader definition of the term is given in *A Dictionary of Translation Technology*, which describes translation technology as 'a branch of translation studies that specializes in the issues and skills related to the computerization of translation' (Chan 2004: 258). In this book, the latter definition is followed, which means that translation technology is considered to cover both computer-aided translation and machine translation tools, and is regarded academically as an integral part of translation studies and professionally as an important component of vocational training for translators.

It is true that the major subject of this book is translation technology, but it should be emphasized that the human factor is also important in all translating activities, either manual or mechanical. In this digital age, all forms of translation are essentially computer-aided translation, with varying degrees of human intervention. Machine translation, which is fully automatic in text generation, needs human intervention at the stage of post-editing and, preferably, also at the pre-translation stage in the form of pre-editing. Computer-aided translation, which is interactive, needs human intervention at all stages of translation. Finally, human translation, which is manual, needs the computer as a means to produce the target text.

As the title of this book suggests, we work towards a world without Babel. Babel, as we know, refers to a story in Genesis of the Bible, which says:

> And the Lord said, 'Behold, they are one people, and they have all one language; and this is only the beginning of what they will do; and nothing

x *Preface*

that they propose to do will now be impossible for them. Come, let us go down, and there confuse their language, that they may not understand one another's speech.' So the Lord scattered them abroad from there over the face of all the earth, and they left off building the city. Therefore its name was called Babel, because there the Lord confused the language of all the earth; and from there the Lord scattered them abroad over the face of all the earth.

(The English Standard Bible, Genesis, 11: 3)

The Tower of Babel can perhaps be regarded as a happy beginning for translators, as it was due to the lack of linguistic sameness that translation was needed to facilitate communication. As we move into the second decade of the twenty-first century, we begin to realize that technology has helped to remove the language barriers that have separated different language communities in the world for a very long time. With the rapid advances in computer science and translation technology, it is quite likely that in the span of a few decades, the Tower of Babel will collapse and we will be able to communicate without any kind of language and cultural barriers.

This book, which explores the issues mentioned above, is divided into six chapters. Chapter 1 provides a chronological and critical analysis of the development of translation technology, mainly computer-aided translation, in different countries and regions since its inception more than forty years ago. Chapter 2 discusses the seven major concepts in translation technology, which have shaped the development of functions in the systems, and the realization of the concepts through these functions. Chapter 3 examines the systems and the functions that are used during the five stages of data management: the initiating, data creation, data processing, data editing, and finalizing stages. Chapter 4 explores various aspects of free and paid computer-aided translation systems. Chapter 5 presents a framework of computer-aided translation studies proposed by the author to show that translation technology has come of age, academically and professionally. Lastly, Chapter 6 looks into the future of translation technology based on the main trends that have emerged in recent decades.

It is hoped that this study on translation technology will shed new light on the nature and application of computer-aided translation and machine translation, thus opening up a new vista for this area.

References

Bowker, Lynne (2002) *Computer-aided Translation Technology: A Practical Introduction*, Ottawa: University of Ottawa Press.

Chan, Sin-wai (2004) *A Dictionary of Translation Technology*, Hong Kong: The Chinese University Press.

Acknowledgements

In completing this book, my gratitude goes to scholars and institutions which invited me to give talks on translation technology in recent years and colleagues at the Centre for Translation Technology, The Chinese University of Hong Kong.

The actual writing of this book and the formation of concepts have been greatly helped by talks and lectures on the various aspects of computer-aided translation that I gave at educational institutions in Taiwan, China, and Hong Kong in the last nine years. These include lectures and speeches delivered at the Department of English Language and Literature of Soochow University in Taiwan, the Department of Foreign Languages of Beihang University, Institute of Computational Linguistics of Peking University, School of Microelectronics and Software of Peking University, the School of Interpreting and Translation Studies of Guangdong University of Foreign Studies, the Faculty of the Humanities and Social Sciences of the Open University of Hong Kong, the School of Chinese of the University of Hong Kong, and the School of Foreign Languages of the University of Shanghai for Science and Technology. I would like to thank them all for their invitations, which helped me to complete this book project sooner than I had expected.

Special mention must be made of the lecture series on computer-aided translation given at Beihang University in Beijing, China. At the invitation of Professor Qian Duoxiu, Chairperson of the Department of Translation and Interpreting at Beihang, I went there in October 2007 for two weeks to deliver a series of lectures on 'Perspectives on Computer-aided Translation'. These lectures form the basis of this book. The finalization of the contents of this book was greatly helped by a public lecture I gave at the Central Library of Hong Kong on 6 December 2008. I would like to express my gratitude to Professor Wong Kwok-pun, former Professor of Translation and Chairman of the Department of Translation of The Chinese University of Hong Kong, who initiated and organized the Central Library talks.

For data collection, data analysis, text translation, and proofreading, my thanks go to my colleagues at the Centre for Translation Technology at The Chinese University of Hong Hong, in particular Miss Florence Li Wing Yee, who devoted so much of her time to this publication project, and Miss Sara Roman Galdran,

xii *Acknowledgements*

who read through the manuscript and made many useful suggestions. For the publication of this book and creation of the Routledge Translation Technology Studies, my gratitude goes to Miss Christina Low, Commissioning Editor of Routledge.

Lastly, I dedicate this book to Proefessor Kenneth Young, Master of C.W. Chu College, The Chinese University of Hong Kong, for his encouragement and support in my academic development.

The author and publishers would like to thank the following copyright holders for permission to reproduce the following material:

"The Development of Translation Technology: 1967–2013" (pp. 3–31) from Chan Sin-wai (ed.) *The Routledge Encyclopedia of Translation Technology.* Published with the permission of Routledge.

"Computer-aided Translation: Major Concepts" (pp. 32–67) from Chan Sin-wai (ed.) *The Routledge Encyclopedia of Translation Technology.* Published with the permission of Routledge.

"A Framework for Computer-aided Translation Studies" (pp. 57–74) from Laurence K.P. Wong and Chan Sin-wai (ed.) *The Dancer and the Dance: Essays in Translation Studies* as Chapter 5: "A Theoretical Framework for Computer-aided Translation Studies". Published with the permission of Cambridge Scholars Publishing.

Figures "Screenshot of Dashboard of SDL-Trados 2015", "Screenshot of SDL-Trados: 'Progress of Individual Projects'", "Screenshot of SDL-Trados: 'Completion of Projects: Today'", "Screenshot of SDL-Trados: 'Progress on the Translation of Files'", "SDL TMS 2013", "SDL WorldServer", and "SDL Automated Translation Solutions" featured in Chapters 2 and 4. Used with kind permission of SDL PLC.

Figures "Editing Interface of Wordfast Anywhere", "Screenshot of TMs and Glossaries Management in Wordfast Anywhere", and "Screenshot of the Login Window in Wordfast Anywhere" featured in Chapters 3 and 4. Used with kind permission of Wordfast LLC.

Figure "MadCap Lingo V9", featured in Chapter 3. Used with kind permission of MadCap Software, Inc.

Figure "Main Window of Anaphraseus", featured in Chapter 4. Used with kind permission of Anaphraseus (Oleg Tsygany).

Figure "User Data of ESTeam", featured in Chapter 4. Used with kind permission of ESTeam AB.

Figure "Translation Editor of Isometry", featured in Chapter 4. Used with kind permission of Finite Field (Toshiya Kazuyoshi).

Figure "User Interface of LogiTerm Web", featured in Chapter 4. Used with kind permission of Terminotix Inc.

Figure "Project Management Page of Memsource Cloud", featured in Chapter 4. Used with kind permission of Memsource.

Figure "Editing Interface of MetaTexis", featured in Chapter 4. Used with kind permission of MetaTexis Software and Services.

Acknowledgements xiii

Figure "Translation Editor of MT2007", featured in Chapter 4. Used with kind permission of Andrew Manson.

Figure "Editor of OmegaT", featured in Chapter 4. Used with kind permission of OmegaT (Marc Prior).

Figures "Similis Manager" and "Similis: Statistics of Translation Tasks" featured in Chapter 4. Used with kind permission of Lingua et Machina.

Figure "User Interface of Snowman", featured in Chapter 4. Used with kind permission of Foshan Snowman Computer Co. Ltd.

Figure "Working Document of WordFisher", featured in Chapter 4. Used with kind permission of Tibor Környei.

Figure "XTM Cloud", featured in Chapter 4. Used with kind permission of XTM International Ltd.

Figure "Apertium Translation Interface", featured in Chapter 4. Used with kind permission of Apertium (Mikel L. Forcada).

Figure "Lucy LT KWIK Translator", featured in Chapter 4. Used with kind permission of Lucy Software and Services GmbH.

While we have made every effort to contact copyright holders of material used in this volume, we would be grateful to hear from any we were unable to contact.

1 The development of translation technology 1967–2014

Introduction

The history of translation technology, or more specifically computer-aided translation (CAT), is short, but its development has been fast (Chan 2015: 3). It is generally recognized that the failure of machine translation in the 1960s as a result of the infamous ALPAC report (1966) led to the emergence of computer-aided translation. The development of computer-aided translation in the course of the last forty-seven years, from its beginning in 1967 to 2014, can be divided into four periods. The first period, which goes from 1967 to 1983, is a period of germination. The second period, covering the years between 1984 and 1992, is a period of steady growth. The third period, from 1993 to 2002, is a decade of rapid growth. The last period, which extends from 2003 to 2014, is a period of global development.

1967–1983: A period of germination

Computer-aided translation, as mentioned above, originated from machine translation, which, in turn, resulted from the invention of the computer. By 1966, when the ALPAC report was published, machine translation had made considerable progress in a number of countries since the invention of the first computer, ENIAC, in 1946. Several events that took place over these two decades are worth noting. In 1947, merely one year after the advent of the computer, Warren Weaver, President of the Rockefeller Foundation, and Andrew D. Booth of Birkbeck College, London University, proposed to make use of the newly invented computer to translate natural languages, becoming the first two scholars who discussed the possibility of incorporating computers into the translation process (Chan 2004: 290–291). In 1949, Warren Weaver wrote a memorandum for peer review outlining the prospects of machine translation, which went down in history as 'Weaver's Memorandum'. In 1952, Yehoshua Bar-Hillel held the first conference on machine translation at the Massachusetts Institute of Technology. Some of the papers that were presented in the conference were compiled by William N. Locke and Andrew D. Booth into an anthology entitled *Machine Translation of Languages: Fourteen Essays*, the first

2 *The development of translation technology*

book on machine translation (Locke and Booth 1955). In 1954, Leon Dostert of Georgetown University and Peter Sheridan of IBM used the IBM701 machine to make a public demonstration of the translation of Russian sentences into English, which marked a milestone in machine translation (Chan 2004: 125–126; Hutchins 1999). Later that year, the inaugural issue of *Mechanical Translation*, the first journal in the field of machine translation, was published by the Massachusetts Institute of Technology (Yngve 2000: 50–51). In 1962, the Association for Computational Linguistics was founded in the United States, and the journal of the association, *Computational Linguistics*, began to be published. It was roughly estimated that by 1965, there were sixteen countries or research institutions engaged in studies on machine translation, including the United States, the former Soviet Union, the United Kingdom, Japan, France, West Germany, Italy, the former Czechoslovakia, the former Yugoslavia, East Germany, Mexico, Hungary, Canada, Holland, Romania, and Belgium (Zhang 2006: 30–34).

The development of machine translation in the United States since the late 1940s, however, fell short of expectations. In 1963, the Georgetown machine translation project was terminated, signifying the end of the largest machine translation project in the United States (Chan 2004: 303). In 1964, the government of the United States set up the Automatic Language Processing Advisory Committee (ALPAC), which comprised seven experts in the field, to enquire into the state of machine translation (ALPAC 1966; Warwick 1987: 22–37). In 1966, the report of the Committee, entitled *Languages and Machines: Computers in Translation and Linguistics*, pointed out that 'there is no immediate or predictable prospect of useful machine translation' (ALPAC 1966: 32) and, as machine translation was twice as expensive as human translation, it failed to meet people's expectations. The Committee thus recommended that resources to support machine translation should be terminated. The report also mentions that 'as it becomes increasingly evident that fully automatic high-quality machine translation was not going to be realized for a long time, interest began to be shown in machine-aided translation' (ALPAC 1966: 25). Therefore, the focus on machine translation shifted to machine-aided translation that was 'aimed at improving human translation, with an appropriate use of machine aids' (ALPAC 1966: iii), and they concluded that 'machine-aided translation may be an important avenue toward better, quicker, and cheaper translation' (ALPAC 1966: 32). The ALPAC report dealt a serious blow to machine translation in the United States, which was to remain stagnant for more than a decade, and it also had a negative impact on the research on machine translation in Europe and Russia. However, this provided an opportunity for machine-aided translation to come into being. All these show that the birth of machine-aided translation is closely related to the development of machine translation.

Computer-aided translation, nevertheless, would not have been possible without the support of related concepts and software. It was no mere coincidence that the idea of a translation memory, which is one of the major concepts and functions of computer-aided translation, emerged during this period. According

The development of translation technology 3

to John Hutchins, the concept of translation memory can be traced back to the period between the 1960s and the 1980s (Hutchins 1998). In 1978, when Alan Melby of the Translation Research Group of Brigham Young University conducted research on machine translation and developed an interactive translation system ALPS (Automated Language Processing Systems), he incorporated the idea of translation memory into a tool known as 'Repetitions Processing', which aimed at finding matched strings (Kingscott 1984: 27–29; Melby 1978; Melby and Warner 1995: 187). In the following year, Peter Arthern, in his paper on the issue of whether machine translation should be used in a conference organized by the European Commission, proposed the method of 'translation by text-retrieval' (Arthern 1979: 93). According to Arthern:

> This information would have to be stored in such a way that any given portion of text in any of the languages involved can be located immediately . . . together with its translation into any or all of the other languages which the organization employs.
>
> (Arthern 1979: 95)

In October 1980, Martin Kay published an article 'The Proper Place of Men and Machines in Language Translation' at the Palo Alto Research Center of Xerox. He proposed to create a machine translation system in which the display on the screen was divided into two windows. The text to be translated would appear in the upper window, while the translation would be composed in the bottom one to allow the translator to edit the translation with the help of simple facilities peculiar to translation, such as aids for word selection and dictionary consultation, which are labeled by Kay as a 'translator amanuensis' (Kay 1980: 9–18). In view of the level of word-processing capacities at that time, his proposal was inspiring to the development of computer-aided translation and exerted a huge impact on its research later on. Kay is generally considered as a pioneer in proposing an interactive translation system.

It can be seen that the idea of translation memory was established in the late 1970s and early 1980s (Bruderer 1975: 258–261, 1977: 529–556). Hutchins believes that the first person to propose the concept of translation memory was Arthern. However, as Melby and Arthern proposed the idea almost at the same time, both could be considered as forerunners. In addition, it should be acknowledged that Arthern, Melby, and Kay made a great contribution to the growth of computer-aided translation in its early days.

The first attempt to deploy the idea of translation memory in a machine translation system was made by Alan Melby and his co-researchers at Brigham Young University, who jointly developed the Automated Language Processing System, or ALPS for short. This system provided access to previously translated segments which were identical (Hutchins 1998: 291). Some scholars classify this type of full match as a function of first-generation translation memory systems (Elita and Gavrila 2006; Gotti, Langlais, Macklovitch, Bourigault, Robichaud, and Coulombe 2005; Kavak 2009). One of the major shortcomings

4 *The development of translation technology*

of this generation of computer-aided translation systems was that sentences with full matching were very small in number, minimizing the reusability of the translation memory and the role of the translation memory database (Wang 2011: 141).

Some researchers around 1980 began to collect and store translation samples with the intention of redeploying and sharing their translation resources. Constrained by the limitations of computer hardware (such as limited storage space), the cost of building a bilingual database was high, and with the immaturity in the algorithms for bilingual data alignment, translation memory technology was forced to remain in a stage of exploration. As a result, a truly commercial computer-aided translation system did not emerge during the sixteen years of this period, and, therefore, translation technology did not have an impact on the translation practice and translation industry (Zachary 1979: 13–28).

1984–1992: A period of steady growth

The eight-year period between 1984 and 1992 is characterized by a steady growth of computer-aided translation and by some developments that took place: corporate operation, in 1984; system commercialization, in 1988; and regional expansion, in 1992 (Marčuk 1989: 682–688).

Company operation

It was during this period that the first computer-aided translation companies, Trados in Germany and Star Group in Switzerland, were founded. These two companies later had a great impact on the development of computer-aided translation.

The German company was founded by Jochen Hummel and Iko Knyphausen in Stuttgart, Germany, in 1984. The name Trados GmbH stood for 'TRAnslation and DOcumentation Software'. This company was set up initially as a language service provider (LSP) to work on a translation project that they had received from IBM. As the company later developed computer-aided translation to help complete the project, the establishment of Trados GmbH is regarded as the starting point of the period of steady growth in computer-aided translation (Garcia and Stevenson 2005: 18–31; http://www.lspzone.com).

Of equal significance was the founding of the Swiss company STAR AG in the same year. STAR, an acronym of 'Software, Translation, Artwork, and Recording', provided manual technical editing and translations with information technology and automation. Two years later, STAR opened its first foreign office in Germany in order to serve the increasingly important software localization market, and started developing two software products, namely GRIPS and Transit, for information management and translation memory, respectively. At the same time, client demand and growing export markets led to the establishment of additional overseas locations in Japan and China. The STAR Group still plays an important role in the translation technology industry (http://www.star-group.net).

The development of translation technology 5

It can be observed that during this early period of computer-aided translation, all companies in the field either were established or operated in Europe. This Eurocentric phenomenon was bound to change in the next period.

System commercialization

The commercialization of computer-aided translation systems began in 1988, when Eiichiro Sumita and Yutaka Tsutsumi of the Japanese branch of IBM released the ETOC ('Easy TO Consult') tool, which was no more than an upgraded electronic dictionary. Consultation of traditional electronic dictionaries was performed based on individual words; it was impossible to search phrases or sentences with more than two words. ETOC, however, offered a flexible solution. When inputting the sentence to be searched into ETOC, the system tried to extract it from its dictionary. If no matches were found, the system carried out a grammatical analysis of the sentence, extracting some substantive words but keeping the empty words and adjectives, which formed the sentence pattern. The sentence pattern was then compared with the bilingual sentences in the dictionary database to find those with a similar pattern, which were displayed for the translator to select. The translator could then copy and paste the sentence onto the Editor, where he was able to revise it to complete the translation. Although the system did not use the term translation memory, and the translation database was still considered a 'dictionary', it had essentially the basic features of today's translation memory tools. The main shortcoming of this system was that, as it needed to perform grammatical analyses, its programming was difficult and its scalability limited. If a new language were to be added, a grammatical analysis module would have to be programmed for the language in question. Furthermore, as the system could only work on perfect matching but not fuzzy matching, it drastically cut down on the reusability of translations (Sumita and Tsutsumi 1988: 2).

Around the time that ETOC was released in Japan, Trados developed TED, a plug-in for text processor tools that was later to become, in its expanded form, the first Translator's Workbench editor, developed by two people and their secretary (Brace 1992a; Garcia and Stevenson 2005). It was also around this time that Trados made the decision to split the company, passing the translation services part of the business to INK in the Netherlands, so that they could concentrate on developing translation software (http://www.translation zone.com).

Two years later, the company also released the first version of MultiTerm as a memory-resident multilingual terminology management tool for DOS, taking the innovative approach of storing all data in a single, freely structured database with entries classified by user-defined attributes (Eurolux Computers 1992: 8; http://www.translationzone.com; Wassmer 2011).

Three years later, in 1991, STAR AG released worldwide Transit 1.0 32-bit DOS version, which had been under development since 1987 and used exclusively for in-house production. Transit, derived from the phrase 'translate it',

6 The development of translation technology

featured the modules that are standard features of today's computer-aided translation systems, such as a proprietary translation editor with separate but synchronized windows for source and target languages, tag protection, a translation memory engine, a terminology management component, and project management features. In the context of system development, the ideas of terminology management and project management began with Transit 1.0. Additional products were later developed for the implementation and automation of corporate product communications, such as TermStar, WebTerm, GRIPS, MindReader, SPIDER, and STAR James (http://www.star-group.net).

Despite the above, the most important event in this period is probably the release of the first commercial system Trados in 1992, which marks the beginning of commercial computer-aided translation systems.

Regional expansion

The year 1992 marks the beginning of the regional expansion of computer-aided translation. This year witnessed some significant advances in translation software achieved in different countries. First, in Germany, Translator's Workbench I and Translator's Workbench II (DOS version of Trados) were launched within the year, with Workbench II being a standalone package with an integrated editor. Translator's Workbench II comprised the TW II Editor (formally TED) and MultiTerm 2. Translator's Workbench II was the first system to incorporate translation memory and alignment facilities into its workstation. Also of considerable significance was the creation, by Matthias Heyn, of Trados's T Align, later known as WinAlign, the first alignment tool on the market. In addition, Trados began to open a network of global offices in a number of locations worldwide, including Brussels, Virginia, the United Kingdom, and Switzerland (Brace 1994; Eurolux Computers 1992; http://www.translationzone.com; Hutchins 1998: 287–307).

Second, in the United States, IBM launched its IBM Translation Manager/2 (TM/2), with the Operating System/2 (OS/2) package, which integrated a variety of translation aids within a so-called 'Presentation Manager' interface. TM/2 comprised an editor of its own and a translation memory feature that used fuzzy search algorithms to retrieve existing material from its translation database. TM/2 could analyse texts to extract terms. TM/2 came with lemmatizers, spelling lists, and other linguistic resources for nineteen languages, including Catalan, Flemish, Norwegian, Portuguese, Greek, and Icelandic. External dictionaries could also be integrated into the system, provided that they were formatted in Standard Generalized Markup Language (SGML). On top of that, TM/2 could be linked to a logic-based machine translation engine (Brace 1992b), becoming perhaps the first hybrid computer-aided translation system (Brace 1993; Wassmer 2011).

Third, in Russia, PROMT Ltd was founded in St. Petersburg by two doctorates in computational linguistics, Svetlana Sokolova and Alexander Serebryakov. At the beginning, the company mainly developed machine translation (MT)

The development of translation technology 7

technology, which has been at the heart of all PROMT products. Later, they began to provide a full range of translation solutions: MT systems and services, dictionaries, translation memory systems, data mining systems, etc. (http://www.promt.com).

Finally, in the United Kingdom, two companies that specialized in translation software production were founded. On the one hand, Mark Lancaster established SDL International, which served as a service provider for the globalization of software (http://www.sdl.com). On the other hand, ATA Software Technology Ltd, a London-based software house specializing in Arabic translation software, was established in 1992 by some programmers and Arabic software specialists. The company later developed a series of MT products (between Arabic and English), such as the MT-TM hybrid system Xpro7, and an online translation engine (http://www.atasoft.com).

1993–2003: A period of rapid growth

The decade that extends from 1993 to 2003 was a period of rapid growth, due largely to (1) the emergence of more commercial systems, (2) the development of more built-in functions, (3) the dominance of Windows operating systems, (4) the support of more document formats, (5) the support of more languages for translation, and (6) the dominance of Trados as a market leader.

The emergence of more commercial systems

Before 1993, there were only three computer-aided translation systems available on the market, namely Translator's Workbench II of Trados, IBM Translation Manager/2, and STAR Transit 1.0. During the ten-year period between 1993 and 2003, about 20 systems were developed for sale, including well-known software, such as Déjà Vu, Eurolang Optimizer (Brace 1994), WordFisher, SDLX, ForeignDesk, Trans Suite 2000, Yaxin CAT, Wordfast, Across, OmegaT, MultiTrans, Huajian, Heartsome, and Transwhiz. This means that there was a six-fold increase in the number of available commercial computer-aided translation systems during this period.

Déjà Vu is the name of a translation memory tool launched by Atril in Spain in 1993. A preliminary version of Déjà Vu, a customizable computer-aided translation system that combined translation memory technology with example-based machine translation techniques, was initially developed by Emilio Benito, founder of Atril, in June to fulfil his own need for a professional translation tool. At first, he worked exclusively with MT systems, but the experiments with machine translation were extremely disappointing. Subsequent experiences with other translation memory tools exposed two main shortcomings: all systems ran under MS-DOS and were capable of processing only plain text files. It was then that Benito began considering the idea of writing his own translation memory software. Déjà Vu 1.0 was first released to the public in November 1993. It provided an interface for Microsoft Word for Windows 2.0, which was regarded

8 The development of translation technology

as the first of its kind. Version 1.1 followed soon afterwards, incorporating several performance improvements and an integrated alignment tool (at a time when alignment tools were sold as expensive individual products) and setting a new standard for the translation tool market (http://www.atril.com). Designed to be a professional translation tool, this system produced acceptable results at an affordable price. In fact, it was a first in many areas: the first translation memory tool for Windows, the first translation memory tool that could be directly integrated into Microsoft Word, the first 32-bit translation memory tool (Déjà Vu version 2.0), and the first affordable professional translation tool.

In the following year, Eurolang Optimizer was developed by Eurolang in France. Its components included a translator's workstation, a pre-translation server with translation memory and terminology databases, and a project management tool for multiple languages and users (Brace 1992b).

In Germany, Trados GmbH announced the release of the new Windows version of Translator's Workbench, which could be used with standard Windows word processing packages via the Windows DDE interface (Brace 1994). In June 1994, Trados included in Translator's Workbench the new MultiTerm Professional 1.5, which featured a fuzzy search engine to deliver successful searches even when words were incorrectly spelt, a dictionary style interface, faster searches through the use of new and highly compressed data algorithms, functions to drag and drop content into the word processor, and an integrated programming language to create powerful layouts (http://www.translationzone. com). Meanwhile, in Hungary, Tibor Környei was developing WordFisher for Microsoft Word macro set. The software was written in the WordBasic language. For translators, it resembled a translation memory programme, but provided a simpler interface in Word (Környei 2000).

In 1995, Nero AG was founded in Germany as a manufacturer of CD and DVD application software. Later, the company set up the division Across Systems GmbH, which developed and marketed a tool with the same name for corporate translation management (CTM). This tool was able to support the project and workflow management of translations (German 2009; Schmidt 2006).

During the first half of 1996, when Windows 95 was in its final stages of beta testing, Atril Development S.L. in Spain began writing a new version of Déjà Vu – not just porting the original code to 32 bits, but adding a large amount of important functionalities that had been suggested by the users. In October, Atril released Déjà Vu beta v2.0. It consisted of a universal editor, Déjà Vu Interactive (DVI), a database maintenance module with an alignment tool, and a full-featured terminology maintenance module (Wassmer 2007: 37–38). Déjà Vu was again the first translation memory tool available for 32-bit Windows and was shipped with a number of filters for DTP packages, including FrameMaker, Interleaf, and QuarkXPress, and provided extensive project management facilities to enable project managers to handle large, multi-file, multilingual projects (Heyn 1996: 15–33).

In 1997, some developments that took place in France and Germany deserve mentioning. In France, CIMOS released Arabic to English translation software,

An-Nakel Al-Arabi, with features that comprised MT, customized dictionaries, and translation memory. Because of its deep sentence analysis and semantic connections, An-Nakeel Al-Arabi could learn new rules and knowledge. CIMOS had previously released other translation software between English and Arabic (MultiLingual 1997). In Germany, Trados GmbH released WinAlign as a visual text alignment tool that became the first fully fledged 32-bit application in Trados. Microsoft decided to base its internal localization memory store on Trados and consequently acquired a share of 20 per cent in the company (http://www.translationzone.com).

The year 1998 marked a milestone in the development of translation technology in China and Taiwan. In Beijing, Beijing Yaxincheng Software Technology Co. Ltd. 北京雅信誠公司 was set up as a developer of translation software, becoming the first computer-aided translation software company in China. In Taipei, the Inventec Corporation released Dr. Eye 98 譯典通 with instant MT, dictionaries, and termbases in Chinese and English (http://www.dreye.com.tw).

In the same year, the activities of SDL and International Communications are worth noting. In the United Kingdom, SDL began to acquire and develop translation and localization software and hardware – both for its own use in client-specific solutions and to be sold as free-standing commercial products. At the end of the year, SDL also released SDLX, a suite of translation memory database tools. SDLX was developed and used in-house at SDL, and therefore was a mature product at its first offering (Hall 2000; MultiLingual 1998). Another British company, International Communications, a localization, translation, and multilingual communications services provider, released ForeignDesk v5.0 with full support of Trados Translator's Workbench 2.0 and WinAlign, S-Tagger. The system was subsequently acquired by Lionbridge Technologies Inc. (known as Massachusetts-based INT'L.com at the transaction), who in November 2001 decided to open-source the ForeignDesk suite free of charge under BSD license.

In June 1999, Beijing YaxinCheng Software Technology Co. Ltd. established Shida CAT Research Centre 實達 CAT 研究中心 (Chan 2004: 338). In the same month, SJTU Sunway Software Industry Ltd. acquired Yaxin CAT, which was one of the most famous computer-aided translation products in China at the moment, from them and released Yaxin CAT v1.0 in August. The release of this software suggested, in a small way, that the development of computer-aided translation was no longer a European monopoly.

In France, the first version of the suite of Wordfast PlusTools was developed with only a few translation memory software packages available. One of the developers was Yves A. Champollion, who later incorporated Wordfast LLC. The first version of Wordfast could be freely downloaded online until 2002, although prior registration was required (http://www.wordfast.net/champollion.net).

In the United States, MultiCorpora R&D Inc. was established as a company dedicated exclusively to providing language technology solutions to enterprises, governments, and language service providers (http://www.multicorpora.com).

10 *The development of translation technology*

In the United Kingdom, following the launch of SDLX, SDL announced their new software: SDL Workbench. Packaged together with SDLX, SDL Workbench memorized the user's translations and automatically offered other possible translations and terminology from that user's translation database within the Microsoft Word environment. In line with its 'open' design, it was able to work with a variety of file formats, including those of Trados and pre-translated RTF files (Multilingual 1998).

The year 2000 proved to be a busy year in the computer-aided translation industry. In China, Yaxin CAT v2.5 Bidirectional (English and Chinese) was released with new features that ranged from 74 topic-specific lexicons with six million terms free-of-charge to project analysis and management, and offered translators the possibility of sharing translation memory online and editing the machine output simultaneously (Chen 2001). In Germany, OmegaT, a free translation memory tool, was publicly released. The key features of OmegaT were basic, and its functionality was very limited. The benefits of this software involved it being free, open-source, and programmed in Java, which enabled it to work on different operating systems (http://www.omegat.org; Prior 2003). In Ireland, Alchemy Software Development Limited announced the acquisition of Corel CATALYST™, which was designed to boost the efficiency and quality of globalizing software products and was used by over 200 software development and globalization companies worldwide (http://www.alchemysoftware.ie). In March, Trados relocated its headquarters to the United States and became a Delaware corporation. In April, SDL International made public the release of SDLX 2.0, which was a new and improved version of SDLX 1.03 (http://www.sdl.com). In addition, they released SDL Webflow for managing multilingual website content (http://www.sdlintl.com). Finally, in France, Wordfast v3.0 was released in September. The on-the-fly tagging and un-tagging of HTML (HyperText Markup Language) files was a major breakthrough in the industry, allowing freelancers to translate HTML pages without worrying about the technical hurdles.

Not much happened in 2001. In Taiwan, Inventec Corporation released Dr. Eye 2001, with new functions like an online search engine, full-text MT from English into Chinese, MT from Japanese into Chinese and a localization plug-in (Xu 2001). In the United Kingdom, SDL International released SDLX 4.0 with real-time translation, a flexible software license, and enhanced capabilities. In the United States, Trados announced the launch of Trados 5 in two flavours, Freelance and Team (http://www.translationzone.com).

In contrast, the year 2002 was full of activities in the industry. During that year, North America observed two major releases. In Canada, MultiCorpora R&D, Inc. released MultiTrans 3, which provided corpus-based translation support and language management solution, and introduced a new translation technology called Advanced Leveraging Translation Memory (ALTM). This model provided past translations in their original context and required virtually no alignment maintenance to obtain superior alignment results. In the United States, Trados 5.5 (Trados Corporate Translation Solution™) was released. In Europe, and more specifically, in the United Kingdom, SDL International

The development of translation technology 11

launched its new SDLX Translation Suite 4 and, later this year, released the elite version of the suite. The SDLX Translation Suite featured a modular architecture consisting of five to eight components: SDL Project Wizard, SDL Align, SDL Maintain, SDL Edit, and SDL TermBase, present in all versions; and SDL Analyse, SDL Apply, and SDLX AutoTrans, only present in the Professional and Elite versions (Wassmer 2003). In Germany, MetaTexis Software and Services released in April the first official version 1.00 of MetaTexis (http://www.metatexis.com). Asia was also a witness of some computer-aided translation advances. In China, Huajian Corporation released Huajian IAT (http://www.hjtek.com); while in Taiwan, Otek launched Transwhiz Power version (client/server structure), which was aimed at enterprise customers (http://www.otek.com.tw). Moreover, in Singapore, Heartsome Holdings Pte. Ltd. was founded to develop language translation technology (Garcia and Stevenson 2006: 77).

North America and Europe were particularly active in translation technology in 2003. MultiCorpora R&D Inc. in Canada released MultiTrans 3.5, which had new and improved capabilities, including increased processing speed of automated searches and network communications speed, improved automatic text alignment for all languages, and optional corpus-based pre-translation. Version 3.5 also offered several new terminology management features, such as support for additional data types, additional filters, batch updates, and added import and export flexibility, as well as full Microsoft Office 2003 compatibility, enhanced Web security, and document analysis capabilities for a wider variety of document formats (MultiLingual 2003). In the United States, Trados 6 was launched in April and Trados 6.5 was launched in October with new features, such as auto-concordance search, Word 2003 support, and access to the Internet translation memory server (Wassmer 2004). In Germany, MetaTexis version 2.0 was released in October with a new database engine. And MetaTexis version 'Net/Office' was released with new features that supported Microsoft PowerPoint and Excel files as well as Trados Workbench, and could be connected with Logoport servers (http://www.metatexis.com). In France, Atril, which was originally founded in Spain but relocated its group business to France in the late 1990s, released Déjà Vu X (Standard, Professional, Workgroup, and Term Sever) (Harmsen 2008); and Wordfast launched Wordfast 4, which could import and translate PDF content (http://www.wordfast.net).

In this period, some developers of MT systems also launched new versions that included a translation memory component, such as LogoVista, An-Nabel Al-Arabi, and PROMT. Each of these systems was created with distinct philosophies in their design, offering their own solutions to problems and issues in the work of translation. This was aptly pointed out by Brace (1994):

> Eurolang Optimizer is based on an ambitious client/server architecture designed primarily for the management of large translation jobs. Trados Workbench, on the other hand, offers more refined linguistic analysis and has been carefully engineered to increase the productivity of single translators and small workgroups.

12 *The development of translation technology*

As aforementioned, PROMT released a new version, PROMT Expert, integrated Trados as a translation memory solution, and a proprietary terminology extraction system (http://www.promt.com). Earlier in 2003, they also launched PROMT XT, which was the first translation software that supported PDF, even before the release of the aforementioned Wordfast 4.

The development of more built-in functions

Computer-aided translation systems of the first and second periods were usually equipped with basic components, such as translation memory, terminology management, and translation editor. In the third period, however, more functions were developed, and more components were gradually integrated into computer-aided translation systems. Of all the new functions developed, tools for alignment, machine translation, and project management were most significant. Trados Translator's Workbench II, for instance, incorporated T Align, later known as WinAlign, into its workstation (http://www.translationzone.com). It was followed by other systems, such as Déjà Vu, SDLX, WordFisher, and Multi-Trans. Machine translation was also integrated into computer-aided translation systems to handle those segments that were not found in the translation memory. IBM's Translation Manager, for example, introduced its Logic-Based Machine Translation (LMT) to run on IBM mainframes and RS/6000 Unix systems (Brace 1993). The function of project management was also implemented by Eurolang Optimizer in 1994 to improve the management of translation memories and terminology databases for multiple languages and users (Brace 1992b).

The dominance of the Windows operating system

All the computer-aided translation systems created before 1993 run exclusively in the DOS or OS/2 operating system, yet in 1993, the versions for Windows, which would later became the dominant stream, were first introduced. IBM and Trados GmbH released the Windows version of TM/2 and of Translator's Workbench, respectively, in mid-1993, and the preliminary version for Windows of Atril's Déjà Vu 1.0 was launched in June. After that, an increasing number of Windows versions came onto the market, including SDLX, ForeignDesk, Trans Suite 2000, Yaxin CAT, Across, MultiTrans, Huajian, and TransWhiz.

The support of more document formats

By 2003, computer-aided translation systems could handle a wide variety of document formats, either directly or with filters, including Adobe InDesign, FrameMaker, HTML, QuarkXPress, Microsoft PowerPoint, Excel, and Word, and even PDF. Trados 6.5, for example, supported all the widely used file formats in the translation community, which allowed translators and translation companies to translate documents in Microsoft Office 2003 Word, Excel, and PowerPoint, Adobe InDesign 2.0, FrameMaker 7.0, QuarkXPress 5, and Page-Maker format, among many others.

The development of translation technology 13

The support of translation of more languages

Translation memory is supposed to be language-independent, but computer-aided translation systems developed in the early 1990s definitely did not support all languages. In 1992, Translator's Workbench Editor, for instance, could handle merely five European languages, namely German, English, French, Italian, and Spanish; whereas IBM Translation Manager/2 already supported 19 languages, including Chinese, Korean, and other OS/2 compatible character code sets. This was largely due to the contribution of Unicode 3.0 in 1999, which provided the basis for the processing, storage, and interchange of text data in any language in all modern software, thereby allowing developers of computer-aided translation systems to gradually overcome the obstacles in language processing. Especially after the release of Microsoft Office 2000, systems with Unicode support mushroomed. Some of these Unicode-based systems are Transit 3.0 in 1999, MultiTerm, and WordFisher 4.2.0, that emerged in 2000, Wordfast Classic 3.34 in 2001, and Tr-AID 2.0 and MultiTrans 3, in 2002.

The dominance of Trados as a market leader

As a forerunner in the field, Trados became a market leader in this period. As observed by Colin Brace, 'Trados has built up a solid technological base and a good market position' in its first decade (Brace 1992a). By 1994, the company had a range of translation software, including Trados Translator's Workbench (Windows and DOS versions), MultiTerm Pro, MultiTerm Lite, and MultiTerm Dictionary. Its technology in translation memory and file format was then widely used in other computer-aided translation systems, and its products were the most popular in the industry. From the late 1990s, a few computer-aided translation tools began to integrate Trados' translation memory into their systems. In 1997, ProMemoria, to give an example, was launched with a translation memory component provided by Trados. In 1998, International Communications released ForeignDesk 5.0 with the full support of Trados Translator's Workbench 2.0, WinAlign, and S-Tagger. In 1999, SDLX supported import and export formats such as Trados and tab-delimited and CSV files. In 2000, Trans Suite 2000 was released with the capacity to process a Trados RTF file. In 2001, Wordfast 3.22 could directly open Trados TMW translation memories (Translator's Workbench versions 2 and 3). In 2003, PROMT XT Export integrated Trados' translation memory. In October 2003, MetaTexis 'Net/Office' 2.0 was released and was able to work with Trados Workbench.

2004–Present: A period of global development

Advances in technology have given added capabilities to computer-aided translation systems. During the last ten years, most old systems have been upgraded on a regular basis, and close to 30 new systems have been released to the market.

14 *The development of translation technology*

This situation has offered a wider range of choices for buyers to acquire systems with different packages, functions, operating systems, and prices.

One of the most significant changes in this period is the addition of new computer-aided translation companies in countries other than those mentioned above. Hungary is a typical example. In 2004, Kilgray Translation Technologies was established by three Hungarian language technologists. The name of the company was made up of the founders' surnames: Kis Balázs (KI), Lengyel István (L), and Ugray Gábor (GRAY). Shortly after, in 2005, the company launched the first version of MemoQ, an Integrated Localization Environment (ILE). MemoQ's first version had a server component that enabled the creation of server projects. Products of Kilgray included MemoQ, MemoQ server, QTerm, and translation memory Repository (http://www.kilgray.com). Another example is Japan, where Rozetta Corporation released TraTool, a translation memory system with an integrated alignment tool, an integrated terminology tool, and a user's dictionary. The product is still commercially available, but no major improvement has been made since its first version (http://www.tratool.com). Yet another example is Poland, where AidTrans Soft launched its AidTransStudio 1.00. Unfortunately, the company was discontinued in 2010 (http://www.thelanguagedirectory.com/translation/translation_software).

New versions of existing computer-aided translation systems with some added new features are worth noting. In the United Kingdom, ATA launched a new Arabic translation memory system, Xpro7, which included an MT function (http://www.atasoft.com). SDL Desktop Products, a division of SDL International, announced the launch of SDLX 2004. Its new features included TMX Certification; seamless integration with Enterprise systems, such as online terminology and multilingual workflow management; adoption of new file formats; synchronized web-enabled TM; and knowledge-based MT (http://www.sdl.com). In the United States, Systran released a new version of Multilizer, which included multiuser translation memory along with a translation memory manager (TMM), a standalone tool for maintaining Multilizer translation memory contents. TMM allowed editing, adding, and deleting translations, and also included a briefcase model for working with translations offline (http://www.multilizer.com). In Ukraine, Advanced International Translations (AIT) started work on a user-friendly translation memory software, later known as AnyMem, which was released in December 2008.

In 2005, translation technology moved further ahead with new versions and new functions. In North America, the Canadian company MultiCorpora released MultiTrans 4, which was built on the foundation of MultiTrans 3.7 and included a new alignment tool that was completely automated (MultiLingual 2005a). Trados, now based in the United States, produced Trados 7 Freelance, which supported 20 additional languages, including Hindi. At an operating system level, Microsoft Windows 2000, Windows XP Home, Windows XP Professional, and Windows 2003 Server were supported. More file formats were now directly supported by TagEditor.

The development of translation technology 15

Meanwhile, in Europe, Lingua et Machina, a French translation tool developer, released Similis v1.4. Similis, which uses linguistic parsers in conjunction with the translation memory, is regarded as the first second-generation translation system. The use of linguistic parsers facilitates the automatic extraction of bilingual terminology from translated documents. Version 1.4 featured compatibility with the Trados translation memory format, text and TMX, and supported a new language, German (MultiLingual 2005b). PROMT, in turn, released @ PROMT 7.0 translation software, which supported the integrated translation memory, the first of its kind among PROMT's products (http://www.promt. com). In the United Kingdom, SDL Desktop Products released the latest version of its translation memory tool SDLX 2005, which expanded the Terminology QA Check and automatically checked source and translations for inconsistent, incomplete, partial, or empty translations, corrupt characters, and consistent regular expressions, punctuation, and formatting. Language support had been added for Maltese, Armenian, and Georgian, and the system could handle more than 150 languages (MultiLingual 2005b). In June 2015, SDL International acquired Trados for £35 million. The acquisition provided extensive end-to-end technology and service solutions for global information assets (http://www. translationzone.com). In October, SDL Synergy was released to the market as a new project management tool.

In Asia, Huajian Corporation in China released in June Huajian Multilingual IAT network version 華建多語 IAT 網絡版 and, in October, Huajian IAT (Russian to Chinese) standalone version (http://www.hjtrans.com). In July, Beijing Orient Yaxin Software Technology Co. Ltd. released Yaxin CAT 2.0, which was a suite including Yaxin CAT 3.5, CAM 3.5, lexicons, translation memory maintenance, and example-based MT. In Singapore, Heartsome Holdings Pte Ltd. launched Heartsome Translation Suite, which was composed of three programs: an XLIFF editor, in which source files were converted to XLIFF format and translated; a TMX editor, which dealt with TMX files; and a dictionary editor, which dealt with TBX files (Garcia and Stevenson 2006: 77). Finally, in Taiwan, Otek released Transwhiz 9.0 for English, Chinese, and Japanese languages (http://www.otek.com.tw).

Significant advances in translation technology were made in 2006, particularly in Europe and in the United States. In February that year, SDL International, based in the United Kingdom, released SDL-Trados 2006, which included new support for Quark, InDesign CS2, and Java (http://www.sdl.com). A few months later, in September, the German company Across Systems GmbH released its Corporate Translation Management 3.5, which marked the start of the worldwide rollout of Across software (MultiLingual 2006a). In the United States, MultiCorpora launched TextBase translation memory concept (http:// www.multicorpora.com). Apple Inc. released in August AppleTrans, a text editor specially designed for translators, featuring an online corpus, which represented 'translation memory', accessible through documents. Lingotek, a language search engine developer from the same country, launched a beta version of a collaborative language translation service that enhanced a translator's efficiency by quickly

16 *The development of translation technology*

finding meaning-based translated material for reuse. Lingotek's language search engine indexed linguistic knowledge from a growing repository of multilingual content and language translations instead of webpages. Users could then access its database of previously translated material to find more specific combinations of words to reuse. Such meaning-based searching helped the translators to maintain a better style, tone, and terminology consistency. Lingotek ran completely on most popular web browsers at that time, including Internet Explorer and Firefox. Lingotek supported Word, Rich Text Format (RTF), Open Office, HTML, XHTML, and Excel formats, thereby allowing users to upload such documents directly into the system. Lingotek also supported existing translation memory files that were TMX-compliant memories, thus allowing users to import TMX files into both private and public indexes (MultiLingual 2006b).

In 2007, Wordfast 5.5 was released in France. It was an upgrade from Wordfast 4 in which Mac support was completely overhauled. This version continued to offer translators the possibility to take part in a collaboration community via a LAN. Each Wordfast license granted users the opportunity to query Wordfast's web-based translation memory and knowledge base, VLTM (http://www.wordfast.net). Nearby, in Germany, a group of independent translators and programmers developed Anaphraseus under the GNU GPL license, a computer-aided translation tool for creating, managing, and using bilingual translation memories. In Hungary, Kilgray Translation Technologies released MemoQ 2.0, focused on networking and, thus, featuring a new resource server. This server not only stored translation memory and termbases, but also offered the possibility of creating server projects that allowed for the easy distribution of work among several translators and ensured productivity at an early stage of the learning curve. Advances on the client side included support for XML and Adobe FrameMaker MIF file formats and improvements for all other supported file formats, support for the Segmentation Rule eXchange standard, auto-propagation of translated segments, better navigation, and over a hundred more minor enhancements (Multilingual 2007a, 2007b). In Russia, MT2007 was developed as a freeware by a professional programmer, Andrew Manson. The main idea was to develop easy-to-use software with extensive features. This software, however, lacked many features that leading systems had. In the United Kingdom, SDL International released in March SDL-Trados 2007, which had features such as a new concept of project delivery and supply chain, new one-central-view dashboard for new project wizard, PerfectMatch, automated quality assurance checker, and full support for Microsoft Office 2007 and Windows Vista.

On the other side of the Atlantic, MultiCorpora launched WordAlign with the so-called 'Advanced Leveraging' function to boast the ability to align text at the individual term and expression level (http://www.multicorpora.com). MadCap Software Inc., a multi-channel content authoring company, developed in May MadCap Lingo, an XML-based, fully integrated Help authoring tool and translation environment. MadCap Lingo offered an easy-to-use interface and complete Unicode support for all left-to-right languages for assisting localization

The development of translation technology 17

tasks. Across Systems GmbH and MadCap Software announced a partnership to combine technical content creation with advanced translation and localization. Shortly after, Alchemy Software Development Ltd. and MadCap Software Inc. announced a joint technology partnership that combined technical content creation with visual translation memory technology.

In 2008, Europe again figured prominently in computer-aided translation software production. In Germany, Across Language Server 4.0 Service Pack 1 was released in April, comprising, in addition to authoring, a number of extensions, such as FrameMaker 8 and SGML support, context matching, and improvements for web-based translations via crossWeb (MultiLingual 2008a). Three months later, Across also introduced its new Language Portal Solution, which would later be known as Across Language Portal, aimed at large-scale organizations and multinational corporations. This system allowed customers to operate at an international scale and implement Web portals for all language-related issues and for all the members of the staff who needed to make use of language resources at any level. In Luxembourg, Wordbee S.A. was founded as a translation software company focusing on web-based integrated computer-aided translation and management solutions (http://www.wordbee.com). In Ireland, Alchemy Software Development, a company in visual localization solutions, released in July Alchemy Publisher 2.0, which combined visual localization technology with translation memory for documentation. It supported standard documentation formats, such as MS Word, XML, application platforms such as Windows 16/22/64x binaries, web-content formats such as HTML, ASP, and all derivative content formats (http://www.alchemysoftware.ie).

During this year, Eastern Europe made considerable progress in computer-aided translation development and commercialization. In March, the Russian PROMT released the version 8.0 with major improvements in the translation engine, an enhanced translation memory system with TMX files import support, and extended language variant support, being able to deal with English (British and American), Spanish (Castilian and Latin American), Portuguese (Portuguese and Brazilian), German (German and Swiss), and French (French, Swiss, Belgian, Canadian) documents (http://www.promt.com). Kilgray Translation Technologies, from Hungary, released in September MemoQ 3.0, which included a new termbase and provided new terminology features. It introduced full support for XLIFF as a bilingual format and offered the visual localization of RESX files. MemoQ 3.0 was available in English, German, Japanese, and Hungarian (http://kilgray.com). In Ukraine, Advanced International Translations (AIT) released in December AnyMem, a translation memory system compatible with Microsoft Word.

In Asia, Yaxin CAT 4.0 was released in China in August with some new features, including a computer-aided project platform for project management and huge databases for handling large translation projects. In Taiwan, Otek released Transwhiz 10 for translating English, Chinese, and Japanese languages, with a fuzzy search engine and a Microsoft Word workstation (http://www.otek.com.tw).

18 *The development of translation technology*

In North America, JiveFusion Technologies, Inc. in Canada officially launched Fusion One and Fusion Collaborate 3.0. The launches introduced a new method of managing translation memories. New features include complete contextual referencing. JiveFusion also integrated Fusion Collaborate 3.0 with TransFlow, a project and workflow management solution by Logosoft (MultiLingual 2008b). In the United States, MadCap Software, Inc. released in February MadCap Lingo 2.0, which included the Darwin Information Typing Architecture standard, Microsoft Word, and a range of standard text and language formats. In September, it released MadCap Lingo 3.0, which included a new project packager function designed to bridge the gap between authors and translators who used other translation memory system software and a new TermBase Editor for creating databases of reusable translated terms.

It was also in 2008 that a South American country came to the fore in the computer-aided translation industry. In Uruguay, Maxprograms launched in April Swordfish version 1.0–0, a cross-platform tool based on the XLIFF 1.2 open standard published by OASIS (http://www.maxprograms.com). In November, the same company released Stingray version 1.0–0, a cross-platform document aligner. The translation memories in TMX, CSV, or Trados TXT format generated by Stingray could be used in most modern computer-aided translation systems (http://www.maxprograms.com).

In the year 2009, Africa joined the game with the development of Autshumato Integrated Translation Environment (ITE) version 1.0, a project funded by the Department of Arts and Culture of the Republic of South Africa. It was released by The Centre for Text Technology (CTexT®) at the Potchefstroom Campus of the North-West University and the University of Pretoria after two years of research and development. Although Autshumato ITE was specifically developed for the eleven official South African languages; it was, in essence, language independent, and could be adapted for translating virtually between any language pair.

In Europe, Wordfast opened the year with the release of Wordfast Translation Studio, a bundled product with Wordfast Classic (for Microsoft Word) and Wordfast Pro (a standalone computer-aided translation platform). With over 15,000 licenses in active use, Wordfast claimed itself the second most widely used translation memory tool (http://www.wordfast.net). In Germany, Across Systems GmbH released in May Across Language Server 5.0, which offered several options for process automation as well as for workflow management and analysis. Approximately 50 connections were available for interacting with other systems (MultiLingual 2009a). In September, STAR Group in Switzerland released Transit NXT (Professional, Freelance Pro, Workstation, and Freelance). The service pack 1 for Transit NXT/TermStar NXT contained additional user interface languages for Chinese, Spanish, Japanese, and Khmer, enhanced alignment usability, support for QuarkXpress 7, and a proofreading function for internal repetitions. In the United Kingdom, SDL had announced in June the launch of SDL-Trados Studio 2009, which included the latest versions of SDL MultiTerm, SDL Passolo Essential, SDL Trados WinAlign, and SDL-Trados

The development of translation technology 19

2007 Suite. New features included Context Match, AutoSuggest, and QuickPlace (http://www.sdl.com). In addition, SDL released in October its enterprise platform SDL translation memory Server 2009, a new solution to centralize, share, and control translation memories (http://www.sdl.com).

In Canada, JiveFusion Technologies Inc. released Fusion 3.1 to enhance its TMX compatibility and the capability to import and export to TMX while preserving complete segment context (MultiLingual 2009b). In the United States, Lingotek introduced software-as-a-service collaborative translation technology that combined the workflow and computer-aided translation capabilities of human and machine translation into one application. Organizations could upload new projects, assign translators (paid or unpaid), check the status of current projects in real time, and download completed documents from any computer with web access (MultiLingual 2009c).

In Asia, Beijing Zhongke LongRay Software and Technology Ltd. Co. released in September the standalone edition of LongRay CAT 3.0, a computer-aided translation system featuring translation memory, alignment, dictionary, and terminology management, amongst other functions (http://www.zklr.com). Two months later, Foshan Snowman Computer Co. Ltd. released Snowman version 1.0 in China (http://www.gcys.cn). Snowman deserves some mentioning for the following reasons: (1) it was new; (2) its green trial version could be downloaded free of charge; (3) it was easy to use, as its interface was user-friendly and the system was easy to operate; and (4) it had the language pair of Chinese and English, catering to the huge domestic market as well as the market abroad.

Most of the activities related to computer-aided translation in 2010 took place in Europe and North America. In Europe, Across Language Server v. 5 Service Pack 1 was released in August and introduced a series of new functionalities and modes of operation, ranging from the classic areas of project management and machine translation to crowdsourcing and authoring assistance. Also in Germany, MetaTexis version 3.0 was released in October, implementing an import filter for Wordfast Pro and Trados Studio translation memories and documents (http://www.metatexis.com). In France, Wordfast LLC released Wordfast Pro 2.4 in July with over 60 enhancements. This system was a standalone environment that featured a highly customizable interface, enhanced batch processing functionality, and increased file format support (http://www.wordfast.net). In October, this company created an application to support translation on the iPhone and iPad in the Wordfast Anywhere environment (http://www.wordfast.net). Atril released in March Team Server, which allowed translators with Déjà Vu Workgroup to work on multinational and multisite translation projects on a LAN or over the Internet, sharing their translations in real-time, thus, ensuring superior quality and consistency. Team Server also provided scalable centralized storage for translation memories and terminology databases. The size of translation repositories and the number of concurrent users were only limited by the server hardware and bandwidth (http://www.atril.com). In October, Atril released Déjà Vu X2 in four editions: Editor, Standard, Professional, and Workgroup. Its new features

20 The development of translation technology

included the DeepMiner data extraction engine, a new StartView interface, and AutoWrite word prediction. In Hungary, Kilgray Translation Technologies released in February MemoQ 4.0, which was integrated with project management functions for project managers who wanted to have more control and enable translators to work in any translation tool; and later that year, the company released MemoQ 4.5, which had a rewritten translation memory engine and improvements to the alignment algorithm (http://www.kilgray.com). In Switzerland, STAR Group released, also in October, Transit NXT Service Pack 3 and TermStar NXT. Transit NXT Service Pack 3 contained the following improvements: support of Microsoft Office 2007, InDesign CS5, QuarkXpress 8, and QuarkXpress 8.1, as well as PDF synchronization for MS Word files. In the United Kingdom, SDL released in March a new subscription level of its SDL-Trados Studio, which included additional productivity tools for translators such as Service Pack 2, enabling translators to plug in to multiple automatic translation tools. The company also did a beta launch of SDL OpenExchange, inviting the developer community to make use of standard open application programming interfaces to increase the functionality of SDL-Trados Studio (Multilingual 2010b). In September, XTM International released XTM Cloud, which was a totally online Software-as-a-Service (SaaS) computer-aided translation tool set and combined translation memory, terminology management, and a fully featured translator workbench within the translation workflow. The launch of XTM Cloud enabled independent freelance translators to have access to XTM for the first time (http://www.xtm-intl.com). In Ireland, Alchemy Software Development Limited released Alchemy Publisher 3.0, which supported all aspects of the localization workflow, including form translation, engineering, testing, and project management. It also provided a connection to an MT engine that was jointly developed by PROMT, so that documentation formats could be translated automatically (http://www.alchemysoftware.ie; http://www.promt.com).

In North America, IBM in the United States released in June the open source version of OpenTM2, which originated from the IBM Translation Manager. OpenTM2 integrated several aspects of the end-to-end translation workflow (http://www.opentm2.org). Partnering with LISA (Localization Industry Standards Association), Welocalize, Cisco, and Linux Solution Group e.V. (LiSoG), IBM aimed to create an open source project that provided a full-featured, enterprise-level translation workbench environment for professional translators. According to LISA, OpenTM2 not only provided a public and open implementation of a translation workbench environment that served as the reference implementation of existing localization industry standards, such as TMX; it also aimed to provide standardized access to globalization process management software (http://www.lisa.org; LISA 2010). The following month, Lingotek upgraded its Collaborative Translation Platform (CTP) to a SaaS product, which combined machine translation, real-time community translation, and management tools (Multilingual 2010a). MadCap Software, Inc. released in September MadCap Lingo v4.0, which had a new utility for easier translation alignment and a redesigned translation editor.

The development of translation technology 21

In South America, Maxprograms in Uruguay released in April Swordfish II, which incorporated Anchovy version 1.0–0 as a glossary manager and term extraction tool, and added support for SLD XLIFF and Microsoft Visio XML Drawings files, amongst others (http://www.maxprograms.com).

The year 2011 witnessed computer-aided translation advances, particularly in Europe. In Luxembourg, the Directorate-General for Translation of the European Commission released in January its one million segments of multilingual translation memory in TMX format in 231 language pairs. Translation units were extracted from one of its large shared translation memories in Euramis (European Advanced Multilingual Information System). This database contained most, but not all, of the documents of the *Acquis Communautaire*, the entire body of European legislation, plus some other documents that were not part of the *Acquis*. Merely one month later, in Switzerland, the STAR Group released the Service Pack 4 for Transit NXT along with TermStar NXT. Transit NXT Service Pack 4 contained the following improvements: support of MS Office 2010, Support of Quicksilver 3.5l, and Preview for MS Office formats. In March, XTM 5.5 was released in the United Kingdom, in both Cloud and On-Premise versions, which contained customizable workflows, a new search and replace feature in Translation Memory Manager, and the redesign of XTM Workbench (http://www.xtm-intl.com). In France, Atril/PowerLing released Déja Vu X2 in May, including a set of new features, such as DeepMiner data mining, a translation engine, SmartView Interface, and a multi-file and multi-format alignment tool (MultiLingual 2011). The following month, Wordfast Classic v6.0 was released, also loaded with new features, such as the ability to share TMs and glossaries with an unlimited number of users, an improved quality assurance tool, an AutoComplete function, and improved support for Microsoft Word 2007/2010 and Mac Word 2011 (http://www.wordfast.net). Around the same time, Kilgray Translation Technologies in Hungary released translation memory Repository, the world's first tool-independent translation memory management system (http://kilgray.com), with an AuditTrail concept implemented in the workflow, which added new improvements like versioning, tracking changes (to show the difference of two versions), X-translate (to show changes on source texts), and Post Translation Analysis on formatting tags (Kilgrary Translation Technologies 2011).

In North America, MultiCorpora R&D Inc. released in May MutliTrans Prism, a translation management system (TMS) for project management, translation memory, and terminology management (MultiCorpora 2011).

In 2012, translation technology proved to continue its march to globalization. In North America, the development of computer-aided translation was fast. In Canada, MultiTrans Prism version 5.5 was released in June. The new version featured a web editing server that extended management control of the translation process and could be fully integrated with content management systems. In September, Terminotix launched LogiTerm 5.2. Some important upgrades included the possibility of indexing TMX files directly in a Bitext

22 *The development of translation technology*

database, a reinforced fuzzy match window, and adjusted buttons (http://terminotix.com/news/newsletter). In December, MultiCorpora added new MT integrations to MultiTrans Prism, allowing the translator to choose between a number of MT providers, such as Systran, Google, and Microsoft (http://www.multicorpora.com).

In Asia, computer-aided translation advances were mostly visible in China. Transn Information Technology Co., Ltd. released TCAT 2.0 as freeware early in the year. New features of this software include the Translation Assistant 翻譯助理 placed at the sidebar of Microsoft Office, pre-translation with translation memory and termbase, and source segment selection by highlighting 自動取句 (http://www.transn.com). In May, Foshan Snowman Computer Co. Ltd. released Snowman 1.27 and Snowman Collaborative Translation Platform 雪人 CAT 協同翻譯平臺 free version. The platform offers a server for a central translation memory and termbase so that all the users can share their translations and terms, and the reviewers can view the translations simultaneously with translators. It also supports online instant communication, document management, and online forums (BBS) (http://www.gcys.cn). In July, Chengdu Urelite Tech Co. Ltd. 成都優譯信息技術有限公司, which was founded in 2009, released Transmate, including the standalone edition (beta), Internet edition, and project management system. The standalone edition, which is freely available for download from the company's website, is targeted at freelancers. This beta release offers basic computer-aided translation functions, such as using a translation memory and terminology during the translation process. It has features such as pre-translation, file-based translation memory creation, bilingual text export, and links to an online dictionary website and Google MT (http://www.urelitetech.com.cn). Heartsome Translation Studio 8.0 was released by the Shenzhen Office of Heartsome in China. Its new features include pre-saving MT results and external proofreading file export in RTF format. The new and integrated interface also allows the user to work in a single unified environment in the translation process (http://www.heartsome.net).

In Japan, Ryan Ginstrom developed and released Align Assist 1.5, which is a freeware system that aligns source and translation files to create a translation memory. The main improvement of this version is the ability to set the format of a cell text (http://felix-cat.com). In October, LogoVista Corporation released LogoVista PRO 2013, which was able to run in Windows 8. More Japanese and English words were included, and it reached a total number of words in dictionaries of 6.47 million (http://www.logovista.co.jp).

In Europe, the developments of computer-aided translation systems are also noteworthy. In the Czech Republic, Memsource Technologies released in January Memsource Editor for translators as a free tool to work with Memsource Cloud and Memsource Server. The Editor is multiplatform and can be currently installed on both Windows and Macintosh (http://www.memsource.com). Merely three months later, Memsource Cloud 2.0 was released by the same company. Memsource Plug-in, the former computer-aided translation component

The development of translation technology 23

for Microsoft Word, was now replaced by the new Memsource Editor, the abovementioned standalone translation editor. Further new improvements offer the opportunity of adding comments to segments, along with an enhanced version control, translation workflow (only in the Team edition), and better quality assurance and segmentation (http://blog.memsource.com). In December, Memsource Technologies released Memsource Cloud 2.8. This new version encrypted all communication by default and included a redesigned menu and tools. Based on the data about previous projects, Memsource can suggest relevant linguistics for a certain translation job (http://www.memsource.com). Simultaneously, in France, Wordfast LLC released Wordfast Pro 3.0. Amongst its new features it includes bilingual review, batch TransCheck, 100 per cent matches filter, split and merge TXML files, reverse source/target, and pseudo-translation (http://www.wordfast.com).

Meanwhile, in Hungary, Kilgray Translation Technologies released in July MemoQ 6.0 with new features, like predictive typing, and several new online workflow concepts, such as FirstAccept (assign job to the first translator who accepted it on the online workflow), GroupSourcing, Slicing, and Subvendor group (http://kilgray.com). In Luxembourg, Wordbee in October designed a new business analysis module for its Wordbee translation management system, which provides a new dashboard where over a hundred real-time reports are generated for every aspect of the localization process (http://www.wordbee. com). In December, the company released MemoQ 6.2 featuring SDL package support, InDesign support with preview, new quality assurance checkers, and the ability to work with multiple machine translation engines at the same time (http://kilgray.com). Before the release of memoQ 6.2, Across Language Server v 5.5 was launched in Germany with enhancements, such as linguistic supply chain management, designed to make project and resources planning more transparent. The new version also supported the translation of texts in various formats and allowed the protection of the translation units to ensure uniform use (http://www.across.net).

In Switzerland, STAR Group released Service Pack 6 for Transit NXT and TermStar NXT. The improvements of Service Pack 6 of Transit NXT contain the support of Windows 8 and Windows Server 2012, QuarkXPress 9.0–9.2, InDesign CS6, integrated OpenOffice spell check dictionaries, and ten additional Indian languages. Finally, in the United Kingdom, XTM International, a developer of XML authoring and translation tools, released in April XTM Suite 6.2. Its updates include full integration with machine translation systems, Asia Online Language Studio, and the content management system XTRF. In October, the company released XTM Suite 7.0 and a new XTM Xchange module in XTM Cloud intended to increase the supply chain. Version 7.0 includes project management enhancements, allowing users to group files, assign translators to specific groups or languages, and create different workflows for different languages (http://www.xtm-intl.com).

During this period, the following trends are of note.

24 The development of translation technology

(1) The systematic compatibility with Windows and Microsoft Office

Out of the 67 currently available systems on the market, there is only one that is unable to run on the Windows operating system. Computer-aided translation systems have to keep up with the advances in Windows and Microsoft Office for the sake of compatibility. Wordfast 5.5, for instance, was released in April 2007, merely three months after the release of Windows Vista; and Wordfast 5.90v was released in July 2010 to support Microsoft Office Word 2007 and 2010.

(2) The integration of workflow control into computer-aided translation systems

Besides reusing or recycling translations of repetitive texts and text-based terminology, systems developed during this period have added functions such as project management, spell check, quality assurance, and content control. Take SDL-Trados Studio 2011 as an example. This version, which was released in September 2011, has a spell checking function for a larger number of languages and PerfectMatch 2.0 to track changes of the source documents. Most of the systems on the market can also perform 'context match', which involves identical matches with identical surrounding segments in the translation document and the translation memory.

(3) The availability of networked or online systems

Due to the rapid development of new information technologies, most computer-aided translation systems during this period are server-based, web-based, and even cloud-based computer-aided translation systems, which have a huge storage of data. By the end of 2012, there were fifteen cloud-based computer-aided translation systems available on the market aimed at individuals or enterprises, such as Lingotek Collaborative Translation Platform, SDL World Server, and XTM Cloud.

(4) The adoption of new formats in the industry

Data exchange between different computer-aided translation systems has always been a difficult issue to handle, as different systems support different formats, such as *dvmdb* for Déjà Vu X and *tmw* for SDL-Trados Translator's Workbench 8.0. These program-specific formats cannot be mutually recognizable, which makes it impossible to share data in the industry. In the past, the Localization Industry Standards Association (LISA) played a significant role in developing and promoting data exchange standards, such as SRX (Segmentation Rules eXchange), TMX (Translation Memory eXchange), TBX (Termbase eXchange), and XLIFF (XML Localization Interchange File Format). It is estimated that

The development of translation technology 25

industry standards compliance is also one of the future directions for better data exchange.

Conclusion

It should be noted that computer-aided translation has been growing rapidly in all parts of the world in the last 47 years since its inception in 1967. Drastic changes have taken place in the field of translation since the emergence of commercial computer-aided translation systems in the 1980s. In 1988, as mentioned above, we only had the Trados system that was produced in Europe. Now we have more than 100 systems developed in different countries, including Asian countries such as China, Japan, and India, and North American countries, such as Canada and the United States. In the 1980s, very few people had any idea about computer-aided translation, let alone translation technology. Now, it is estimated that there are around 200,000 computer-aided translators in Europe, and more than 6,000 large corporations in the world handle their language problems with the use of corporate or global management computer-aided translation systems. At the beginning, computer-aided translation systems only had the standalone editions. Now, there are over seventeen different types of systems on the market.

According to my research, the number of commercially available computer-aided translation systems from 1984 to 2012 is 86. Several observations on these systems can be made. Firstly, about three computer-aided translation systems have been produced every year during the last 28 years. Secondly, due to rapid changes in the market, nineteen computer-aided translation systems failed to survive in the keen competition, and the total number of current commercial systems stands at 67. Thirdly, almost half of the computer-aided translation systems have been developed in Europe, accounting for 49.38%, while 27.16% of them have been produced in America.

All these figures show that translation technology has been on the fast track in the last five decades and will certainly maintain its momentum for many years to come.

References

ALPAC (1966) *Language and Machines: Computers in Translation and Linguistics*, Washington, DC: National Academy of Sciences, National Research Council.

Arthern, Peter J. (1979) 'Machine Translation and Computerized Terminology Systems: A Translator's Viewpoint', B.M. Snell (ed.) *Translating and the Computer: Proceedings of a Seminar*, London: North-Holland Publishing Company, 77–108.

Brace, Colin (1992a) 'Trados: Smarter Translation Software', *Language Industry Monitor* Issue Sept–Oct, Available from http://www.lim.nl/monitor/trados-1.html.

Brace, Colin (1992b) 'From IBM: Translation Manager/2', *Language Industry Monitor* Issue Sep–Oct 1992, Available from http://www.lim.nl/monitor/ibm-tm2-1.html.

26 The development of translation technology

Brace, Colin (1993) 'TM/2: Tips of the Iceberg', *Language Industry Monitor* Issue May–Jun, Available from http://www.mt-archive.

Brace, Colin (1994) 'Bonjour, Eurolang Optimizer', *Language Industry Monitor* Issue Mar–Apr, Available from http://www.lim.nl/monitor/optimizer.html.

Bruderer, Herbert E. (1975) 'The Present State of Machine Translation and Machine-aided Translation', *ALLC Bulletin* 3(3): 258–261.

Bruderer, Herbert E. (1977) 'The Present State of Machine and Machine-assisted Translation', *Overcoming the Language Barrier*, Munich: Verlag Dokumentation, 529–556.

Chan, Sin-wai (2004) *A Dictionary of Translation Technology*, Hong Kong: The Chinese University Press.

Chan, Sin-wai (2015) 'The Development of Translation Technology: 1967–2013', Chan Sin-wai (ed.) *Routledge Encyclopedia of Translation Technology*, London and New York: Routledge, 3–31.

Chen, Gang (2001) 'A Review on Yaxin CAT2.5', *Chinese Science and Technology Translators Journal* 14(2).

Elita, Natalia and Monica Gavrila (2006) 'Enhancing Translation Memories with Semantic Knowledge', *Proceedings of the First Central European Student Conference in Linguistics*, Budapest, Hungary, 29–31 May, 24–26.

The English Standard Version Bible: Containing the Old and New Testaments with Apocrypha (2009), New York: Oxford University Press.

Eurolux Computers (1992) 'Trados: Smarter Translation Software', *Language Industry Monitor* Issue 11(Sept–Oct), Available from http://www.lim.nl.

Garcia, Ignacio and Vivian Stevenson (2005) 'TRADOS and the Evolution of Language Tools: The Rise of the De Facto TM Standard – And Its Future with SDL', *Multilingual Computing and Technology* 16(7).

Garcia, Ignacio and Vivian Stevenson (2006) 'Heartsome Translation Suite', *Multi-Lingual* 17(1): 77, Available from http://www.multilingual.com.

German, Kathryn (2009) 'Across: An Exciting New Computer Assisted Translation Tool', *The Northwest Linguist* 9–10.

Gotti, Fabrizio, Philippe Langlais, Elliott Macklovitch, Didier Bourigault, Benoit Robichaud, and Claude Coulombe (2005) '3GTM: A Third-generation Translation Memory', *Third Computational Linguistics in the North-East (CLiNE) Workshop*, Gatineau, Québec, 26–30.

Hall, Amy (2000) 'SDL Announces Release of SDLX Version 2.0', SDL International, Available from http://www.sdl.com/en/about-us/press/1999/SDL_Announces_Release_of_SDLX_Version_2_0.asp.

Harmsen, R. (2008) 'Evaluation of DVX', Available from http://rudhar.com.

Heyn, Matthias (1996) 'Present and Future Needs in the CAT World', *The Localisation Industry Standards Association Forum Newsletter* 5(3): 15–33.

http://blog.memsource.com.

http://en.wikipedia.org/wiki/XLIFF.

http://felix-cat.com.

http://terminotix.com/news/newsletter.

http://www.alchemysoftware.ie.

http://www.atasoft.com.

http://www.bas.bg.

http://www.colgate.edu.

http://www.cuni.cz.

The development of translation technology   27

http://www.dreye.com.tw.
http://www.gcys.cn.
http://www.heartsome.net.
http://www.hjtek.com.
http://www.hjtrans.com.
http://www.kilgray.com.
http://www.thelanguagedirectory.com/translation/translation_software.
http://www.logovista.co.jp.
http://www.lspzone.com.
http://www.maxprograms.com.
http://www.memsource.com.
http://www.metatexis.com.
http://www.multicorpora.com.
http://www.multilizer.com.
http://www.omegat.org.
http://www.opentm2.org.
http://www.otek.com.tw.
http://www.promt.com.
http://www.sdl.com.
http://www.sdlintl.com.
http://www.star-group.net.
http://www.systransoft.com.
http://www.transbridge.com.tw.
http://www.translationzone.com.
http://www.transtar.com.cn.
http://www.tratool.com.
http://www.unam.mx.
http://www.urelitetech.com.cn.
http://www.wordbee.com.
http://www.wordfast.net.
http://www.xtm-intl.com.

Hutchins, W. John (1998) 'The Origins of the Translator's Workstation', *Machine Translation* 13(4): 287–307.

Hutchins, John (1999) 'The Development and Use of Machine Translation System and Computer-based Translation Tools', Chen Zhaoxiong (ed.) *International Conference on MT & Computer Language Information Processing*, Beijing: Research Center of Computer and Language Engineering, Chinese Academy of Sciences, 1–16.

Kavak, Pinar (2009) 'Development of a Translation Memory System for Turkish to English', Unpublished Master dissertation, Boğaziçi University, Turkey.

Kay, Martin (1980) 'The Proper Place of Men and Machines in Language Translation', Research Report CSL-80-11, Xerox PARC, Palo Alto, CA. Reprinted in *Machine Translation* 12 (1997), Nos., 1–2, pp. 3–23.

Kilgrary Translation Technologies (2011) 'What's New in MemoQ', Available from http://kilgray.com/products/memoq/whatsnew.

Kingscott, Geoffrey (1984) 'ALPS Moves to Improve European Sales for Computer-aided Translation', *Language Monthly* 14: 27–29.

Környei, Tibor (2000) 'WordFisher for MS Word: An Alternative to Translation Memory Programs for Freelance Translators?' *Translation Journal* 4(1), Available from http://accurapid.com/journal/11wf.htm.

28   *The development of translation technology*

LISA (2010) 'IBM and the Localization Industry Standards Association Partner to Deliver Open-Source Enterprise-Level Translation Tools', Available from http://www.lisa.org/OpenTM2.1557.0.html.

Locke, William Nash and Andrew Donald Booth (eds.) (1955) *Machine Translation of Languages: Fourteen Essays*, Cambridge, MA: MIT Press.

Marčuk, Jurij N. (1989) 'Machine-aided Translation: A Survey of Current Systems', Istvan S. Batori, Winfried Lenders, and Wolfgang Putschke (eds.) *Computational Linguistics: An International Handbook on Computer-oriented Language Research and Applications*, Berlin and New York: De Gruyter, 682–688.

Melby, Alan K. (1978) 'Design and Implementation of a Machine-assisted Translation System', Paper Read at the *Seventh International Conference on Computational Linguistics* held in Bergen, Norway, 14–18 August.

Melby, Alan K. and Terry C. Warner (1995) *The Possibility of Language: A Discussion of the Nature of Language, with Implications for Human and Machine Translation*, Amsterdam and Philadelphia: John Benjamins Publishing Company.

MultiCorpora Inc. (2011) 'MultiCorpora Launches New Translation Management System', Available from MultiCorpora's website at http://www.multicorpora.com/news/multicorpora-launches-new-translation-management-system.

MultiLingual Newsletter (1997) 'CIMOS Releases Arabic to English Translation Software', *MultiLingual Newsletter* 20 December, Available from http://multilingual.com/newsDetail.php?id=422.

MultiLingual Newsletter (1998) 'SDL Announces Translation Tools', *MultiLingual Newsletter* 23 September.

MultiLingual Newsletter (2003) 'MultiCorpora R&D Releases MultiTrans 3.5', *MultiLingal Newsletter* 17 October.

MultiLingual Newsletter (2005a) 'MultiCorpora Announces the Release of MultiTrans 4', *MultiLingual Newsletter* 31 August.

MultiLingual Newsletter (2005b) 'SDL Announces SDL Workbench and Product Marketing Executive', *MultiLingual Newsletter* 22 Feburary.

MultiLingual Newsletter (2006a) 'Across Rolls out New Version 3.5', *MultiLingual Newsletter* 20 November.

MultiLingual Newsletter (2006b) 'Lingotek Announces Beta Launch of Language Search Engine', *MultiLingual Newsletter*, Available from http://multilingual.com/newsDetail.php?id=5168.

MultiLingual Newsletter (2007a) 'Kilgray Releases Version 2.0 of MemoQ', *MultiLingual Newsletter* 25 January.

MultiLingual Newsletter (2007b) 'Quality Assurance Module Available for MemoQ', *MultiLingual Newsletter* 4 April.

MultiLingual Newsletter (2008a) 'Across Language Server 4.0 SP1', *MultiLingual Newsletter* 21 April.

MultiLingual Newsletter (2008b) 'Fusion One and Fusion Collaborate 3.0.', *MultiLingual Newsletter* 28 November.

MultiLingual Newsletter (2009a) 'Across Language Server V.5', *MultiLingual Newsletter* 13 May.

MultiLingual Newsletter (2009b) 'Fusion 3.1', *MultiLingual Newsletter* 19 March.

MultiLingual Newsletter (2009c) 'Lingotek Launches Crowdsourcing Translation Platform', *MultiLingual Newsletter*, Available from http://multilingual.com/newsDetail.php?id=7103.

MultiLingual Newsletter (2010a) 'Collaborative Translation Platform 5.0.' *Multi-Lingual Newsletter* 27 July.

MultiLingual Newsletter (2010b) 'SDL Trados Studio', *MultiLingual Newsletter* 10 March.

MultiLingual Newsletter (2011) 'Déjà Vu X2', *MultiLingual Newsletter* 24 May.

Prior, Marc (2003) 'Close Windows. Open Doors', *Translation Journal* 7(1), Available from http://accurapid.com/journal/23linux.htm.

rz.uni-sb.de.

Schmidt, Axel (2006) 'Integrating Localization into the Software Development Process', *PC World* Issue Mar.

Sumita, Eiichiro and Yutaka Tsutsumi (1988) 'A Translation Aid System Using Flexible Text Retrieval Based on Syntax-matching', *Proceedings of The Second International Conference on Theoretical and Methodological Issues in Machine Translation of Natural Languages*, Pittsburgh, PA: Carnegie Mellon University, Available from http:// www.mt-archive.info/TMI-1988-Sumita.pdf.

Wang, Zheng 王正 (2011) 〈翻譯記憶系統的發展歷程與未來趨勢〉 ('The Development of Translation Memory Systems and the Future Trends'), 《編譯論叢》 (*Compilation and Translation Review*) 4(1): 133–160.

Warwick, Susan (1987) 'An Overview of Post-ALPAC Developments', Margaret King (ed.) *Machine Translation Today: The State of the Art*, Edinburgh: Edinburgh University Press, 22–37.

Wassmer, Thomas (2003) 'SDLX TM Translation Suite 2003,' *Translation Journal* 7(3).

Wassmer, Thomas (2004) 'TRADOS 6.5.', *MultiLingual Computing and Technology* 15(1): 61.

Wassmer, Thomas (2007) 'Comparative Review of Four Localization Tools: Déjà Vu, MULTILIZER, MultiTrans and TRANS Suite 2000 and Their Various Capabilites', *MultiLingual Computing & Technology* 14(3): 37–42.

Wassmer, Thomas (2011) 'Dr. Tom's Independent Software Reviews', Available from http://www.localizationworks.com/DRTOM/Trados/TRADOS.html.

Xu, Jie (2001) 〈Dr. Eye 2001 譯典通5大非凡功能〉 ('Five Amazing Functions of Dr. Eye 2001'),《廣東電腦與電訊》 (*Computer and Telecom*) 3.

Yngve, Victor H. (2000) 'Early Research at M.I.T. in Search of Adequate Theory', W. John Hutchins (ed.) *Early Years in Machine Translation*, Amsterdam and Philadelphia: John Benjamins Publishing Company, 39–72.

Zachary, Wayne W. (1979) 'A Survey of Approaches and Issues in Machine-aided Translation Systems', *Computers and the Humanities* 13(1): 13–28.

Zhang, Zheng 張政 (2006) 《計算機翻譯研究》 (*Studies on Machine Translation*), Beijing: Tsinghua University Press.

2 Major concepts in computer-aided translation

Introduction

When the term 'computer-aided translation' is mentioned, we often associate it with the functions that a computer-aided translation system can offer, such as toolbars, icons, and hotkeys; the built-in tools that we can use, such as online dictionaries and browsers; and the computational hitches that we often encounter when working on a computer-aided translation project, such as chaotic codes. However, what is more important is to see beyond the surface of computer-aided translation to consider the major concepts that shape the development of functions in translation technology.

Concepts, which are relatively stable, govern or affect the way functions are designed and developed, and functions, which are fast-changing, realize, in turn, the concepts through the tasks they perform. As a major goal of machine translation is to help human translators, a number of functions in computer-aided translation systems have been created to enable machine processing of the source with minimal human intervention. Concepts, moreover, are related to what translators want to achieve in translating. We have identified seven major concepts which are of particular importance in computer-aided translation: simulativity, emulativity, productivity, compatibility, controllability, customizability, and collaborativity. These concepts are arranged in this order for easier memorization by their acronym, SEPCCCC. Simply put, translators want to have a controllable (*controllability*) and customizable (*customizability*) system that is compatible with file formats and language requirements (*compatibility*) and behaves as well as (*simulativity*) or even better than (*emulativity*) a human translator to allow them to work together (*collaborativity*) to produce quality translations (*productivity*) (Chan 2015: 32–67).

Simulativity

The first concept of computer-aided translation is simulativity, which concerns the manner and ability of a computer-aided translation system to model the behaviour of a human translator by means of its functions, such as the use of concordancers in text analysis to model the ability of comprehension on the

Major concepts in computer-aided translation 31

part of the human translator and the creation of a number of quality assurance tools to follow the way checking is performed by a human translator.

There are a number of ways to illustrate man–machine simulativity.

Goal of translation

The first is about the ultimate goal of translation technology. All forms of translation, including machine translation, computer-aided translation, and human translation, aim at obtaining high-quality translations. In the case of machine translation, the goal of a fully automatic high-quality translation (FAHQT) is to be achieved with the use of a machine translation system without human intervention. In the case of computer-aided translation, the same goal is to be achieved with a computer-aided translation system that simulates the behaviour of a human translator through man–machine interaction.

Translation procedure

A comparison of the procedures of human translation with those of computer-aided translation shows that the latter simulates the former in a number of ways. In manual translation, various translation procedures have been proposed by translation scholars and practitioners, ranging from two-stage to eight-stage models, depending on the text type and the purposes of the translation. In machine translation and computer-aided translation, the process is known as technology-oriented translation procedure.

Two-stage model

In human translation, the first type of translation procedure involves a two-stage model, which consists of a stage of source text comprehension and a stage of target text formulation.

It is a model for human translators with the ability of comprehension. As a computer-aided translation system does not have the ability of comprehension, it cannot model after human translation according to this two-stage model. It can, however, work on a two-stage translation with the use of its system dictionary, particularly in the case of a language-pair-specific system. Another two-stage model of computer-aided translation is a terminology-based system.

Three-stage models

The second type of translation procedure involves a three-stage model. This section covers five variations of this model proposed by Eugene Nida and Charles Taber (1969), Wolfram Wilss (1982), Roger Bell (1991), Basil Hatim and Ian Mason (1997), and Jean Delisle (1988), respectively. A three-stage example-based computer-aided translation system is shown to illustrate the simulation of human translation by computer-aided translation.

32 *Major concepts in computer-aided translation*

(I) MODEL BY EUGENE NIDA AND CHARLES TABER

The first model of a three-stage translation procedure, involving the three phases of analysis, transfer, and restructuring, was proposed by Eugene Nida and Charles Taber (1969/1982: 104). They intended to apply elements of Chomsky's transformational grammar to provide Bible translators with some guidelines when they translated ancient source texts into modern target texts, which are drastically different in both language and structure. Nida and Taber describe this three-stage model as a translation procedure in which 'the translator first analyses the message of the source language into its simplest and structurally clearest forms, transfers it at this level, and then restructures it to the level in the receptor language which is most appropriate for the audience which he intends to reach' (Nida and Taber 1969: 484). Analysis is described by these two scholars as 'the set of procedures, including back transformation and componential analysis, which aim at discovering the kernels underlying the source text and the clearest understanding of the meaning, in preparation for the transfer' (Nida and Taber 1969/1982: 197). Transfer, on the other hand, is described as the second stage, in which 'the analysed material is transferred in the mind of the translator from language A to language B' (1969/1982: 104). Restructuring is the final stage, in which the results of the transfer process are transformed into a 'stylistic form appropriate to the receptor language and to the intended receptors'.

In short, analysis, the first stage, is to analyse the source text; transfer, the second stage, is to transfer the meaning; and restructuring, the final stage, is to produce the target text.

(II) MODEL BY WOLFRAM WILSS

The second three-stage model was proposed by Wolfram Wilss (1982), who regards the translation procedure as a linguistic process of decoding, transfer, and encoding.

(III) MODEL BY ROGER BELL

Another three-stage model of note is that by Roger Bell, whose translation procedure framework is divided into three phases: the first phase involves source text interpretation and analysis; the second, the translation process; and the third, text reformulation. The last phase, in turn, takes into consideration three factors: the writer's intention, the reader's expectation, and the target language norms (Bell 1991).

(IV) MODEL BY BASIL HATIM AND IAN MASON

The model proposed by Basil Hatim and Ian Mason is a more sophisticated three-stage model, which involves the three steps of source text comprehension,

Major concepts in computer-aided translation 33

transfer of meaning, and target text assessment. At the source text comprehension level, text parsing, specialized knowledge, and intended meaning are examined. At the meaning transfer level, consideration is given to the lexical, grammatical, and rhetorical meaning. At the target text assessment level, attention is paid to text readability, target language conventions, and adequacy of purpose.

(V) MODEL BY JEAN DELISLE

The fourth model of a three-stage translation procedure was proposed by Jean Delisle (1988: 53–69), who believes that there are three stages in the development of translation equivalence: comprehension, reformulation, and verification. According to Delisle, 'comprehension is based on decoding linguistic signs and grasping meaning, reformulation is a matter of reasoning by analogy and rewording concepts, and verification involves back-interpreting and choosing a solution' (1988: 53).

Parallel to human translation, a three-stage model in computer-aided translation is the example-based system. The input text goes through the translation memory and glossary databases to generate fuzzy matches and translations of terms before getting the target text.

Four-stage model

The third type of translation procedure consists of a four-stage model. A typical example is given by George Steiner (1975/1992), who believes that the four stages of the translation procedure are: knowledge of the author's time, familiarization with the author's sphere of sensibility, original text decoding, and target text encoding.

For computer-aided translation, a four-stage model is exemplified by Yaxin for a webpage translation. In the first stage, a Chinese webpage is input; in the second stage, the webpage is processed with the multilingual maintenance platform; during the third stage, it is processed with the terminology database; finally, in the closing stage, a bilingual webpage is generated.

Five-stage model

The fourth type of translation procedure is a five-stage one, as proposed by Omar Sheikh Al-Shabab (1996: 52). In this model, the first and second stages involve editing and interpreting the source text, respectively; the third involves interpreting in a new language; the fourth, formulating the translated text; and the fifth, editing the formulation.

In computer-aided translation, a five-stage model is normally practiced. At the first stage, or initiating stage, tasks such as setting computer specifications, logging into a system, creating a profile, and creating a project file are performed. At the second stage, the data preparation stage, the tasks involve data collection,

34 *Major concepts in computer-aided translation*

data creation, and the creation of terminology and translation memory databases. At the third stage, the data processing stage, the tasks include data analysis, using system and non-system dictionaries, using concordancers, pre-translating, data processing by computer-aided translation systems with human intervention or by machine translation systems without human intervention, or data processing by localization systems. At the fourth stage, the data editing stage, the work is divided into two types. One type is data editing for computer-aided translation systems, which concerns interactive editing and the editing environments, matching, and methods used in computer-aided translation. Another type is data editing for machine translation systems, which comprises post-editing and the methods used in human translation. At the last or fifth stage, the finalizing stage, the work involves mainly updating databases.

It can be seen that though there are both five-stage models in human translation and computer-aided translation and the tasks involved are different, the concept of simulativity is at work at almost all stages.

Eight-stage model

The fifth type of translation procedure is an eight-stage one, as proposed by Robert Bly (1983). Bly, who is a poet, suggests an eight-stage procedure for the translation of poetry: (a) set down a literal version; (b) find out the meaning of the poem; (c) make it sound like English; (d) make it sound like American; (e) catch the mood of the poem; (f) pay attention to sound; (g) ask a native speaker to go over the version; and (h) make a final draft with some adjustments.

In computer-aided translation, there is no eight-stage model. But other than the five-stage model mentioned above, there is also a seven-stage model.

The seven stages of computer-aided translation go from sample text collection to termbase creation, translation memory database creation, source text selection, data retrieval, source text translation, and finally, data updating.

All in all, we can say that when compared to human translation, computer-aided translation is simulative, following some of the stages in human translation.

Emulativity

There are obviously some functions which are performable by a computer-aided translation system, but not by a human translator. Emulativity in translation technology should cover both computer-aided translation and machine translation, as hybridity has become the norm in the field. Both computer-aided translation and machine translation simulate human translation, but they also emulate human translation in a number of areas, some of which are discussed below.

Alt-tag translation

This function of machine translation engines allows the user to understand the meaning of text embedded within images (Joy 2002). The images on a website

Major concepts in computer-aided translation 35

are created by IMG tag (inline image graphic tag), and the text that provides an alternative message to viewers who cannot see the graphics is known as ALT tag, which stands for 'alternative text'. Adding an appropriate ALT tag to every image within one's website will make a huge difference to its accessibility. As translators, our concern is the translation of the alternative text, as images are not to be translated anyway.

Chatroom translation

Machine translation has the function to translate the contents of a chatroom, known as 'chat translation' or 'chatroom translation'. Chat translation systems are commercially available for the translation of the contents of the chatroom on the computer. As a chat is part of conversational discourse, all the theoretical and practical issues relating to conversational discourse can be applied to the study of chat translation. It should be noted that this kind of online jargon is drastically different from what we have in other modes of communication.

The function of chatroom translation is available in some systems, such as Fluency, as one of the resources. This function has to be purchased and enabled in the Fluency Chat Server to allow clients to be connected to this closed system for internal communications. For standalone version users, the function of chatroom translation will be provided by Fluency Chat Server provided by its company, Western Standard through connection to the Internet.

Clipboard translation

Clipboard translation involves copying text to the clipboard from any Windows application so it can be translated by a machine translation system. The translated text can then be pasted on the original or any other location. One of the systems that translates clipboards is Atlas.

Conversion between metric and British Imperial systems

A function that can be easily handled by machine translation but not so easily by human translation is the conversion of weight, volume, length, or temperature from the metric to the British Imperial system and vice versa. Fluency, for example, can do the metric/British conversion and display the target text box with the converted units.

Currency conversion

There are a few computer-aided translation systems that can perform currency conversion. For instance, Currency Converter, a function in Fluency, can access the Internet to retrieve the conversion rates, then convert a certain amount in a currency into the currency used in the target language. The number of currencies

36 *Major concepts in computer-aided translation*

that can be handled by a system can be relatively large. Fluency, for example, supports the conversion of currencies of around 220 countries.

Email translation

Email translation refers specifically to the translation of emails by an MT system (Matsuda and Kumai 1999; Rooke 1985: 105–115). The first online and real-time email translation was achieved in 1994 by the CompuServe service, which provided translation service of emails between English and French, German, or Spanish. Email translation has become a very important part of daily communication ever since, and most web translation tools include functions to translate emails. Nonetheless, as emails are usually conversational and often written in an informal or even ungrammatical way, they are difficult for mechanical processing (Fais and Ogura 2001; Han, Gates, and Levin 2006). One of the computer-aided translation systems that translates emails is Atlas.

Foreign language translation

One of the most important purposes of using translation software is to translate a source text whose language is unfamiliar to the target user, so as to make the recipient understand its content in a more familiar language. It is found that a majority of the commercial MT systems are designed for translations among Indo-European languages or major languages with a large number of speakers or users. Software for automatic translation between major languages and minor languages, on the other hand, is relatively small in number (Brandwood 1956: 111–118; Kertesz 1974: 86–104; Liu 1984: 46–57; Lufkin 1966: 9–15; Zagar 2005: 37–40).

Gist translation

Another area where machine translation differs fundamentally from human translation is gist translation, which refers to a translation output that expresses only a condensed version of the source text message. The purpose of this type of rough translation is to provide some essential information of the content of the text, so that the user can decide whether it is necessary to translate it in full or not (Resnik 1997).

Highlight and translate

This function allows the user to highlight a part of the text and translate it into the designated language. The highlighted text is translated on its own without affecting the rest of the text.

Instant transliteration

This refers to an MT function that is able to transliterate the words of a text in a certain Romanization system (Bilac and Tanaka 2005: 402–413; Ekbal, Naskar,

Major concepts in computer-aided translation 37

and Bandyopadhyay 2006; Goto, Kato, Uratani, and Ehara 2003; Knight and Graehl 1997, 1998; Kuo, Li, and Yang 2006; Li, Zhang, and Su 2004: 159–166; Lin and Chen 2002; Lin, Wu, and Chang 2004: 177–186). In the case of Chinese, for instance, the Hanyu Pinyin Romanization system for simplified characters is used mostly in mainland China, whereas the Wade-Giles Romanization system for traditional characters is used in Taiwan (Lee and Chang 2003: 96–103).

Mouse translation

This feature involves translating sentences on a webpage or application by simply clicking the mouse. Atlas is an example of systems that provide mouse translation.

Online translation

This is the translation of a text by an online MT system that is available at all times on demand from users. With the use of online translation services, the functions of information assimilation, message dissemination, language communication, translation entertainment, and language learning can be achieved (Clements 1996: 220–221; Flanagan 1995, 1996: 192–197, 1997; Gaspari 2004: 68–74; McCarthy 2004; Mellebeek, Khasin, van Genabith, and Way 2005; O'Neill-Brown 1996: 222–223; Zervaki 2002).

Pre-translation

Machine translation is regarded as pre-translation on two counts. The former involves preparatory work on the texts to be translated, including checking the spelling, compiling dictionaries, and adjusting the text format. The latter is taken to be a draft translation of the source text, which can be further revised by a human translator.

Sentence translation

Unlike human translation, which works at a textual level, machine translation performs sentential translation. In other words, machine translation works on a sentence-by-sentence basis. This type of translation facilitates the work of post-editing and other methods that are frequently used in translation practice to produce effective target sentences.

Web translation

This refers to the translation of information on a webpage from one language into another. Web translation tools are, therefore, a type of computer-aided translation tool that translates information on a webpage from one language into another. They serve three functions: (1) assimilation, to transmit information to the user; (2) dissemination, to make messages comprehensible; and

38 *Major concepts in computer-aided translation*

(3) communication, to enable people with different language backgrounds to communicate with each other.

Productivity

As translation technology is a field of entrepreneurial humanities, productivity is of great importance. Productivity in computer-aided translation, in particular, is achieved through the use of technology, collective translation, recycling translations, reusing translations, professional competence, profit-seeking, labour-saving, and cost-saving (Bowker 2005: 13–20).

Using technology to increase productivity

The use of technology to increase productivity needs no explanation. As early as 1980, when Martin Kay discussed the proper place of men and machines in language translation, he said:

> Translation is a fine and exacting art, but there is much about it that is mechanical and routine and, if this were given over to a machine, the productivity of the translator would not only be magnified but his work would become more rewarding, more exciting, more human.
>
> (Kay 1980: 1)

All computer-aided translation systems aim to increase translation productivity. In terms of the means of production, all translation nowadays can be considered computer-aided translation, as virtually no one would be able to translate without making use of a computer.

Collective translation to increase productivity

Gone are the days when bilingual competence, pen and paper, and printed dictionaries made a translator. Gone are the days when a single translator did a long translation project all by himself. It is true that in the past, translation was mainly done singly and individually. Translation was also done in a leisurely manner. At present, translation is done largely through teamwork, and translators are commonly linked by a server-based computer-aided translation system. In other words, translation is done in a collective manner.

Recycling translations to increase productivity

In the context of computer-aided translation, the concept of recycling is understood as the use of exact matches that are automatically extracted from a translation memory database. To increase productivity, this practice of recycling translations is widely followed. Networked computer-aided translation systems are used to store centralized translation data, which is created and distributed

Major concepts in computer-aided translation   39

among translators. As this is the case, translators do not have to produce their own translations. They can simply draw from and make use of the translations stored in the bilingual database to form their translation of the source text. Translation is therefore produced by selection.

Reusing translations to increase productivity

To reuse a translation in computer-aided translation is to appropriate terms and expressions stored in the term database and translation memory database (Craig, Dorr, Lin, Pavel, and Hajic 2006). It should be noted that, in literary translation, translators produce translations in a creative manner. In practical translation, however, translators reuse and recycle previously translated segments, as the original texts are often repetitive. Currently, over 90 per cent of the translation projects lie in the area of practical translation. Computer-aided translation is ideal for repetitive practical writings, for translators do not have to translate any sentence that they have translated before. In fact, the more they translate, the less they will have to translate. Computer-aided translation, therefore, reduces the time that a translator needs to complete a certain task by eliminating duplicate work (Merkel 1993: 139–149). Some systems, such as Across, allow the user to automatically reuse existing translations from the translation memory. It can be seen that, also in translation, the rules 'reduce, reuse, recycle' are three effective ways of increasing profitability (de Ilarraza, Mayor, and Sarasola 2000).

Professional competence to increase productivity

Translators have to work with the help of translation technology. The use of computer-aided translation tools, which aim at supporting translators and not at replacing them, has actually been extended to almost every type of translation work. It ensures that translation quality is maintained as 'all output is human input'. As far as the use of tools is concerned, professional translation is technological. In the past, translators used only printed dictionaries and references, yet nowadays there are a wide range of resources available to translators, such as electronic concordancers, speech technology, online terminology systems, and automatic checkers.

Translation competence or knowledge and language skills are not enough today. It is more realistic to talk about professional competence, which includes linguistic, cultural, translation, translator, and technological competences. Professional competence is important for translators, as it affects their career development. A remark made by Timothy Hunt is worth noting: 'Computers will never replace translators, but translators who use computers will replace translators who don't' (Sofer 2009: 88). What is happening in the field of translation technology shows that Hunt's remark may not be far off the mark. In the 1980s, very few people had any ideas about translation technology or computer-aided translation. Now, SDL alone has more than 180,000 computer-aided translators,

40 *Major concepts in computer-aided translation*

and the total number of computer-aided translators in the world is likely to be several times higher than the SDL translators.

Seeking profit to increase productivity

Translation is in part vocational, in part academic. In the training of translators, there are courses on translation skills to foster their professionalism, and there are courses on translation theories to enhance their academic knowledge. However, there are very few courses on translation as a business or as an industry. It should be noted that translation in recent decades has increasingly become a field of entrepreneurial humanities as a result of the creation of the project management function in computer-aided translation systems. This means that translation is now a field of humanities which is entrepreneurial in nature. Translation as a commercial activity has to increase productivity to increase profits.

Saving labour to increase productivity

Computer-aided translation systems help to increase productivity and profits through saving labour by eliminating repetitive translation tasks, such as reusing past translations. Computer-aided translation tools support translators by freeing them from boring work and letting them concentrate on what they can do best over machines, i.e., handling semantics and pragmatics. Generally, this leads to a broader acceptance by translators. The role of a translator, therefore, has changed drastically in the modern age of digital communication. Rather than simply translating the document, a computer-aided translator has to engage in other types of work, such as authoring, pre-editing, interactive editing, post-editing, termbase management, translation memory database management, text alignment, and manual alignment verification. It is estimated that, with the use of translation technology, a single translator can complete the work that would originally be borne by six translators (Vallianatou 2005).

Saving costs to increase productivity

Computer-aided translation is also cost-saving. It helps to keep the overhead cost down, as what has been translated needs not to be translated again. It helps to better plan budgets.

Other issues relating to cost should also be taken into account, namely (i) the actual costs of translation tools and their periodic upgrades; (ii) the licensing policy of the system, which is about the ease of transferring licenses between computers or servers, the incurrence of extra charges for client licenses, the lending of licenses to freelance vendors, and the eligibility for free upgrades; (iii) the cost that is required for support, maintenance, or training; (iv) the affordability of the system for the translators; and (v) the user-friendliness of the system to the computer technicians and translators, which affects the cost of production.

Major concepts in computer-aided translation 41

Compatibility

The concept of compatibility in translation technology must be considered in terms of file formats, operating systems, translation memory databases, terminology databases, and languages supported by different systems.

Compatibility of file formats

One of the most important concepts in translation technology is the type of data that needs to be processed, which is indicated by its format, being shown by one or several letters at the end of a filename. Filename extensions usually follow a period (dot) and indicate the type of information stored in the file. A look at some of the common file types and their file extensions shows that in translation technology, text translation is but one type of data processing, though it is the most popular one.

There are two major types of formats: general documentation types and software development types.

General documentation types

(A) TEXT FILES

All computer-aided translation systems that use Microsoft Word as a text editor can process all formats recognized by Microsoft Word. For Microsoft Word 2000–2003, text files were saved and stored as *.doc* (document text file/word processing file); for Microsoft Word 2007 and later versions, documents are saved and stored as *.docx* (Document text file) or *.dotx* (Microsoft Word 2007 Document Template). Other types of text files include *.txt* (Text files), *.txml* (WordFast files), and *.rtf* (Rich Text files).

All automatic and interactive translation systems can process text files, provided that the text processing system has been installed in the computer before the processing begins. Some computer-aided translation systems that are able to translate text files, as well as other formats, include: Across, AidTransStudio, Anaphraseus (formerly known as OpenWordfast), AnyMem (*.docx* or higher), Araya, Autshumato Integrated Translation Environment (ITE), CafeTran, Déjà Vu, Esperantilo, Felix, Fluency, Fortis, Fusion, GlobalSight, Google Translator Toolkit, Heartsome Translation Suite, Huajian IAT, Lingo, Lingotek, MadCap Lingo, MemoQ, MEMOrg, Memsource, MetaTexis, MultiTrans, OmegaT, OmegaT+, Pootle, SDL-Trados, Similis, Snowman, Swordfish, TM-database, Transit, Wordfast, WordFisher, XTM, and Yaxin.

(B) WEBPAGE FILES

HyperText Markup Language (HTML) is a markup language used by web browsers to interpret and compose text, images, and other material into visual or audible webpages. HTML defines the structure and layout of a webpage or

42 Major concepts in computer-aided translation

document by using a variety of tags and attributes. HTML documents are stored as .asp (Active Server Pages), .aspx (Active Server Page Extended), .htm (Hypertext Markup Language), .html (Hypertext Markup Language Files), .php (originally known as Personal Home Page, and now, Hypertext Preprocessor), .jsp (JavaServer Pages), .sgml (Standard Generalized Markup Language File), .xml (Extensible Markup Language file), and .xsl (Extensible Stylesheet Language file) file formats, which were available since late 1991. Due to the popularity of webpages, web translation has been an important part of automatic and interactive translation systems. Many systems provide comprehensive support for the localization of HTML-based document types. Webpage localization is interchangeable with web translation or web localization (Dube and Rice 2000; Savourel 2001).

Systems that are able to handle HTML include Across, AidTransStudio, Alchemy Publisher, Araya, Atlas, CafeTran, CatsCradle, Déjà Vu, Felix, Fluency, Fortis, GlobalSight, Google Translator Toolkit, Heartsome Translation Suite, Huajian IAT, Lingo, Lingotek, LogiTerm, MemoQ, MemOrg, MetaTexis, MultiTrans, Okapi Framework, OmegaT, OmegaT+, Open Language Tools, Pootle, SDL-Trados, Similis, Snowman, Swordfish, TM-database, Transit, Transolution, TransSearch, and XTM.

(C) MICROSOFT PDF FILES

Portable Document Format (PDF), whose extension is .pdf, is a universally accepted file interchange format developed by Adobe in the 1990s. The software that allows PDF files to be transferred between different types of computers is Adobe Acrobat. In the context of the translation process, a PDF source file can keep the document format, which might require editing to make the file look more like the original, or can be converted to an .rtf file for data processing by a computer-aided translation system.

Alchemy Publisher, CafeTran, Lingo, Similis, and Snowman are examples of systems that can translate Adobe PDF files and save them as Microsoft Word documents.

(D) MICROSOFT OFFICE POWERPOINT FILES

Microsoft PowerPoint is a presentation program that enables users to create all kinds of presentations, from basic to complex slide shows, which consist of slides that may contain text, images, and other media. The extensions of the different versions of Microsoft Office PowerPoint are: .ppt (general file extension), .pps (PowerPoint Slideshow), and .pot (PowerPoint template) for Microsoft PowerPoint 2000–2003; .pptx (Microsoft PowerPoint Open XML Document), .ppsx (PowerPoint Open XML Slide Show), .potx (PowerPoint Open XML Presentation Template), and .ppsm (PowerPoint 2007 Macro-enabled Slide Show) for Microsoft PowerPoint 2007 and later versions.

Major concepts in computer-aided translation 43

Some computer-aided translation systems that can handle PowerPoint files are Across, AidTransStudio, Alchemy Publisher, CafeTran, Déjà Vu, Felix, Fluency, Fusion, GlobalSight, Lingotek, LogiTerm, MadCap Lingo, MemoQ, Memsource, MetaTexis, SDL-Trados, Swordfish, TM-database, Transit, Wordfast, XTM, and Yaxin.

(E) MICROSOFT EXCEL FILES

The extensions used by the different versions of Microsoft Excel include *.xls* (spreadsheet) and *.xlt* (template) for Microsoft Excel 2000–2003; and *.xlsx* (Microsoft Excel Open XML Document), *.xltx* (Excel 2007 spreadsheet template), and *.xlsm* (Excel 2007 macro-enabled spreadsheet) for Microsoft Excel 2007 and later versions.

Across, AidTransStudio, Déjà Vu, Felix, GlobalSight, Lingotek, LogiTerm, MemoQ, MEMOrg, MetaTexis, MultiTrans, Snowman, Wordfast, and Yaxin are some of the computer-aided translation systems that can handle Excel files.

(F) MICROSOFT ACCESS FILES

Not many computer-aided translation systems can deal with Microsoft Access files, characterized by the *.accdb* (Access 2007–2010) file extension. The best example is Déjà Vu.

(G) IMAGE FILES

The processing of image data, mainly graphics and pictures, is important in computer-aided translation. Image data can be stored as *.bmp* (bitmap image file), *.jpg* (Joint Photographic Experts Group), and *.gif* (Graphics Interchange Format). One of the computer-aided translation systems that is capable of translating images is CafeTran.

(H) SUBTITLE FILES

One of the most popular subtitle file extensions on the market is *.srt* (SubRip Text). OmegaT is the best example of a computer-aided translation system that supports subtitle files.

(I) ADOBE INDESIGN FILES

Adobe InDesign is a desktop publishing program. Alchemy Publisher and Any-Mem are able to translate the documents created by InDesign without the need of any third party software. However, for Alchemy Publisher, *.indd* files must be exported to an *.inx* format before they can be processed. Other computer-aided translation systems that support Adobe InDesign files include Across, Déjà Vu, Fortis, GlobalSight, Heartsome Translation Suite, MemoQ, MultiTrans, Okapi Framework, SDL-Trados, Swordfish, Transit, and XTM.

44 *Major concepts in computer-aided translation*

(J) ADOBE FRAMEMAKER FILES

Adobe FrameMaker is an authoring and publishing solution for XML. FrameMaker files, characterized by the extensions *.fm*, *.mif*, and *.book*, can be opened directly by a translation system if Adobe FrameMaker has been previously installed.

Some examples of computer-aided translation systems that can translate Adobe FrameMaker files include Across, CafeTran, Déjà Vu, Fortis, GlobalSight, Heartsome Translation Suite, Lingo, Lingotek, MadCap Lingo, MemoQ, MetaTexis, MultiTrans, SDL-Trados, Swordfish, Transit, Wordfast, XTM, and Alchemy Publisher, which requires a PPF created by Adobe FrameMaker before translating and supports FrameMaker 5.0, 6.0, 7.0, 8.0, 9.0, FrameBuilder 4.0, and FrameMaker + *sgml*.

(K) ADOBE PAGEMAKER FILES

Systems that support Adobe PageMaker 6.5 and 7 files include Déjà Vu, GlobalSight, MetaTexis, and Transit.

(L) AUTOCAD FILES

AutoCAD, developed by Autodesk, Inc. and first released in December 1982, is a software application for computer-aided design (CAD) and drafting that supports both 2D and 3D formats. This software is now used internationally and regarded as the most popular drafting tool for a range of industries, most commonly architecture and engineering.

CafeTran, Transit, and TranslateCAD are some of the computer-aided translation systems that support AutoCad documents.

(M) DTP TAGGED TEXT FILES

DTP stands for Desktop Publishing. A popular desktop publishing system is QuarkXPress.

Computer-aided translation systems that support desktop publishing files include Across, CafeTran, Déjà vu, Fortis, GlobalSight, MetaTexis, MultiTrans, SDL-Trados, and Transit.

(N) LOCALIZATION FILES

Localization files include those with the standardized format for localization *.xliff* (XML Localisation Interchange File Format) files, *.ttx* (XML font file format) files, and *.po* (Portable Object).

Some computer-aided translation systems that can process XLIFF files are Across Language Server, Araya, CafeTran, Esperantilo, Fluency, Fortis, GTranslator, Heartsome Translation Suite, Lingotek, MadCap Lingo, MemoQ, Okapi Framework, Open Language Tools, Poedit, Pootle, Swordfish, Transolution, Virtaal, and XTM.

Major concepts in computer-aided translation 45

Software development types

(A) JAVA PROPERTIES FILES

Java Properties files are simple text files that are used in Java applications. The file extension of Java Properties Files is *.properties.*

Déjà Vu, Fortis, Heartsome Translation Suite, Lingotek, Okapi Framework, OmegaT+, Open Language Tools, Pootle, Swordfish, and XTM support Java Properties files.

(B) OPENOFFICE.ORG/STAROFFICE

StarOffice, of the Star Division, was a German company that ran from 1984 to 1999. It was succeeded by OpenOffice.org, an open-source version of StarOffice owned by Sun Microsystems, from 1999 to 2009, and by Oracle Corporation from 2010 to 2011. Currently it is known as Apache OpenOffice. The extension of the OpenOffice format is *.odf* (OpenDocument Format).

Some computer-aided translation systems that are able to process this type of file are AidTransStudio, Anaphraseus, CafeTran, Déjà Vu, Heartsome Translation Suite, Lingotek, OmegaT, OmegaT+, Open Language Tools, Pootle, Similis, Swordfish, Transolution, and XTM.

(C) WINDOWS RESOURCE FILES

These are simple script files containing startup instructions for an application program, usually a text file containing commands that are compiled into binary files such as *.exe* and *.dll*. Windows resource files' extensions include *.rc* (Record Columnar File) and *.resx* (NET XML Resource Template).

Across, Déjà Vu, Fortis, Lingotek, MetaTexis, and Okapi Framework can handle this kind of file.

Compatibility of operating systems

One of the most important factors that determine the course of development of computer-aided translation systems is their compatibility with the current operating systems on the market. It is therefore essential to examine the major operating systems running from the beginning of computer-aided translation in 1988 to the present, which include, among others, Microsoft Windows and Macintosh OS.

Microsoft operating systems

In the world of computing, Microsoft Windows has always been the dominant operating system. From 1981 to 1995, the x86-based MS-DOS (Microsoft Disk Operating System) was the most commonly used system, especially for IBM PC compatible personal computers. Trados's Translator's Workbench II, developed

46 *Major concepts in computer-aided translation*

in 1992, is a typical example of a computer-aided translation system working on DOS.

DOS was supplemented by Microsoft Windows 1.0, a 16-bit graphical operating environment, released on 20 November 1985 (Windows 2012). In November 1987, Windows 1.0 was succeeded by Windows 2.0, which was available until 2001. Déjà Vu 1.0, released in 1993, was one of the first systems compatible with Windows 2.0. Windows 2.0 was later supplemented by Windows 286 and Windows 386.

Then, on 22 May 1990, came Windows 3.0, succeeding Windows 2.1x. Windows 3.0, featuring a graphical environment, was the third major release of Microsoft Windows. With a significantly revamped user interface and other technical improvements, Windows 3 became the first widely successful version of Windows and a rival to Apple's Macintosh and the Commodore Amiga on the GUI front. It was followed by Windows 3.1x. During its lifespan from 1992 to 2001, Windows 3.1x introduced various enhancements to the still MS-DOS-based platform, including improved system stability, expanded support for multimedia, TrueType fonts, and workgroup networking. Trados's Translator's Workbench, released in 1994, was a system that was adaptable to Windows 3.1x.

A part of Windows and DOS, OS/2 was also one of the operating systems that supported computer-aided translation systems, especially in the late 1980s and early 1990s.

Apple operating systems

Mac OS (1984–2000) and OS X (from 2001) are two series of graphical user interface-based operating systems developed by Apple Inc. for their Macintosh line of computer systems. Mac OS was first introduced in 1984 with the original Macintosh, and this series was terminated in 2000. OS X, first released in March 2001, is a series of Unix-based graphical interface operating systems. Both series share a general interface design but have very different internal architectures.

Only one computer-aided translation system, AppleTrans, was specifically designed for OS X. Its initial release was announced in February 2004 and the latest updated version was version 1.2 (v.38) released in September 2006, which runs on Mac OS X 10.3 or later.

Another computer-aided translation system, Wordfast Classic, was sometimes upgraded in its support of the latest text processor running on Mac OS X, such as Wordfast Classic 6.0, which is compatible with MS Word 2011 for Mac.

Other computer-aided translation systems that can run on either Mac OS or OS X are cross-platform software, rather than software developed particularly for Mac. Examples of cross-platform computer-aided translation tools are java-based applications, such as Autshumato, Heartsome, OmegaT, Open Language Tools, and Swordfish. In addition, all cloud-based systems can be run on Mac OS and OS X, including Wordbee, XTM Cloud, Google Translator Toolkit, Lingotek Collaborative Translation Platform, Memsource Cloud, and WebWordSystem.

Major concepts in computer-aided translation 47

IBM operating system

OS/2 is a series of computer operating systems, initially created by Microsoft and IBM, then later developed by IBM exclusively. Its name stands for 'Operating System/2'.

Until 1992, the early computer-aided translation systems ran either on MS-DOS or OS/2. For example, IBM Translation Manager/2 (TM/2) was released in 1992 and ran on OS/2. ALPS's translation tool also ran on OS/2. But OS/2 had a much smaller market share compared with Windows in the early 1990s. Computer-aided translation system developers therefore gradually shifted from OS/2 and MS-DOS to Windows or discontinued the development of OS/2 and MS-DOS compatible systems. By the end of the 1990s, most computer-aided translation tools ran mainly on Windows, although some developers still offered operating system customization services upon request. OS/2 4.52 was released in December 2001. IBM ended its support to OS/2 on 31 December 2006.

Compatibility of databases

Compatibility of translation memory databases

TMX (Translation Memory eXchange), created in 1998, is widely used as an interchange format between different translation memory formats. TMX files are XML (eXtensible Markup Language) files whose format was originally developed and maintained by OSCAR (Open Standards for Container/Content Allowing Reuse) of the Localization Industry Standards Association (LISA). The latest official version of the TMX specification, version 1.4b, was released in 2005. In March 2011, LISA was declared insolvent; as a result its standards were moved under the Creative Commons license and the standards specification relocated. The technical specification and a sample document of TMX can be found on the website of The Globalization and Localization Association.

TMX has been widely adopted and is supported by more than half of the current computer-aided translation tools on the market. The total number of computer-aided translation systems that can import and export translation memories in TMX format is thought to be 54, including Across, Alchemy Publisher, Anaphraseus, AnyMem, Araya, Atlas, Autshumato, CafeTran, Crowdin, Déjà Vu, EsperantiloTM , Felix, Fluency, Fortis, Fusion, GE-CCT, GlobalSight, Google Translator Toolkit, Heartsome, Huajian IAT, Lingotek, LogiTerm, LongRay CAT, MadCap Lingo, MemoQ, Memsource, MetaTexis, MT2007, MultiTrans, OmegaT, OmegaT+, Open Language Tools, OpenTM2, OpenTMS, PROMT, SDL-Trados, Snowball, Snowman, Swordfish, Systran, Text United, The Hongyahu, TM-database, Transit, Translation Workspace, Transwhiz, TraTool, WebWordSystem, Wordbee, WordFast Classic and Wordfast Pro, XTM, Yaxin CAT, and 翻訳ブレイン (Translation Brain).

48   *Major concepts in computer-aided translation*

Compatibility of terminology databases

Compatibility of terminology databases is best illustrated by TermBase eXchange (TBX), which covers a family of formats for representing the information in a high-end termbase in a neutral intermediate format, complying with the Terminological Markup Framework (TMF) (Melby 2012: 19–21).

TBX is an international standard as well as an industry standard. The industry standard version differs from the ISO standard only by having different title pages. LISA, the host organization for OSCAR that developed Termbase Exchange, was dissolved in February 2011. In September 2011, the European Telecommunications Standards Institute (ETSI) took over the maintenance of the OSCAR standards. ETSI has established an interest group for translation/localization standards and a liaison relationship with the International Organization for Standardization (ISO) so that TBX can continue to be published as both an ISO and an industry standard.

There are many types of termbases in use, ranging from huge termbases operated by governments, to smaller termbases maintained by translation service providers and individual translators, passing through medium-size termbases maintained by corporations and non-governmental organizations. The problem addressed by the designers of term exchange was that existing termbases are generally not interoperable. They are based on different data models that use a variety of data categories. And even if the same data category is used for a particular piece of information, the name of the data category and the values allowed for the data category may be different.

Compatibility of rules

Segmentation rules exchange

Segmentation Rules eXchange (SRX) is an XML-based standard that was maintained by LISA until it became insolvent in 2011. This standard is now maintained by the Globalization and Localization Association (GALA).

Segmentation Rules eXchange provides a common way to describe how to segment text for translation and other language-related processes. It was created when it was realized that translation memory exchange leverage is lower than expected in certain instances due to differences in how tools segment text. Segmentation Rules eXchange is intended to enhance the translation memory exchange so that translation memory data that is exchanged between applications can be used more effectively. Having the segmentation rules that were used when a translation memory was created will increase the leverage that can be achieved when deploying the translation memory data.

Compatibility with the languages supported

As computer-aided translation systems cannot identify languages, language compatibility is, therefore, an important concept in translation technology. There are

Major concepts in computer-aided translation 49

a large number of languages and sub-languages in the world, totalling 6,912. But the number of major languages that computers can process is relatively small. It is therefore important to know whether the languages that require machine processing are supported by a system or not.

With the aid of Unicode, most of the languages in the world can be handled by popular computer-aided translation tools. Unicode is a computing industry standard for the consistent encoding, representation, and handling of text that is expressed in most of the world's writing systems.

There are basically two major types of language and sublanguage codes. Some systems, such as OmegaT and XTM, use two or three letters for language codes and language-and-region codes (2+2 letters), which can be selected from a drop-down list. OmegaT follows the ISO 639 Code Tables in its code list. French, for example, is coded *fr* with the language-and-region code for French (Canada) as *fr-CA*.

The following is a list of languages supported by Wordfast Classic and XTM, two of the nine computer-aided translation systems chosen for analysis in this chapter.

Wordfast Classic

Wordfast can be used to translate any of the languages supported by Microsoft Word. The number of languages supported by Microsoft is 91, with a number of sub-languages for some major languages.

[*Afro-Asiatic*] Arabic (Algeria), Arabic (Bahrain), Arabic (Egypt), Arabic (Iraq), Arabic (Jordan), Arabic (Kuwait), Arabic (Lebanon), Arabic (Libya), Arabic (Morocco), Arabic (Oman), Arabic (Qatar), Arabic (Saudi Arabia), Arabic (Syria), Arabic (Tunisia), Arabic (U.A.E.), Arabic (Yemen), Hebrew, Maltese

[*Altaic*] Azeri (Cyrillic), Azeri (Latin), Japanese, Korean, Turkish

[*Austro-Asiatic*] Vietnamese

[*Austronesian*] Indonesian, Malay (Brunei Darussalam), Malaysian

[*Basque*] Basque

[*Dravidian*] Kannada, Malayalam, Tamil, Telugu

[*Indo-European*] Afrikaans, Albanian, Armenian, Assamese, Belarusian, Bengali, Bulgarian, Byelorussian, Catalan, Croatian, Czech, Danish, Dutch, Dutch (Belgian), English (Australia), English (Belize), English (Canadian), English (Caribbean), English (Ireland), English (Jamaica), English (New Zealand), English (Philippines), English (South Africa), English (Trinidad), English (U.K.), English (U.S.), English (Zimbabwe), Faroese, Farsi, French (Belgian), French (Cameroon), French (Canadian), French (Congo), French (Cote d'Ivoire), French (Luxembourg), French (Mali), French (Monaco), French (Reunion), French (Senegal), French (West Indies), Frisian (Netherlands), Gaelic (Ireland), Gaelic (Scotland), Galician, German, German (Austria), German (Liechtenstein), German (Luxembourg), Greek, Gujarati, Hindi, Icelandic, Italian, Kashmiri, Konkani, Latvian, Lithuanian, Macedonian (FYRO), Marathi, Nepali, Norwegian (Bokmol), Norwegian (Nynorsk),

50   *Major concepts in computer-aided translation*

Oriya, Polish, Portuguese, Portuguese (Brazil), Punjabi, Rhaeto-Romance, Romanian, Romanian (Moldova), Russian, Russian (Moldova), Sanskrit, Serbian (Cyrillic), Serbian (Latin), Sindhi, Slovak, Slovenian, Sorbian, Spanish (Argentina), Spanish (Bolivia), Spanish (Chile), Spanish (Colombia), Spanish (Costa Rica), Spanish (Dominican Republic), Spanish (Ecuador), Spanish (El Salvador), Spanish (Guatemala), Spanish (Honduras), Spanish (Nicaragua), Spanish (Panama), Spanish (Paraguay), Spanish (Peru), Spanish (Puerto Rico), Spanish (Spain), Spanish (Traditional), Spanish (Uruguay), Spanish (Venezuela), Swedish, Swedish (Finland), Swiss (French), Swiss (German), Swiss (Italian), Tajik, Ukrainian, Urdu, Welsh

[*Kartvelian*] Georgian

[*Niger-Congo*] Sesotho, Swahili, Tsonga, Tswana, Venda, Xhosa, Zulu

[*Sino-Tibetan*] Burmese, Chinese, Chinese (Hong Kong SAR), Chinese (Macau SAR), Chinese (Simplified), Chinese (Singapore), Chinese (Traditional), Manipuri, Tibetan

[*Tai-Kadai*] Laotian, Thai

[*Turkic*] Tatar, Turkmen, Uzbek (Cyrillic), Uzbek (Latin)

[*Uralic*] Estonian, Finnish, Hungarian, Sami Lappish

XTM

The languages available in XTM are 157, not including varieties within a single language. These languages are as follows:

[*Afro-Asiatic*] Afar, Amharic, Arabic, Hausa, Hebrew, Maltese, Oromo, Somali, Sudanese Arabic, Syrian, Tigrinya

[*Altaic*] Azeri, Japanese, Kazakh, Korean, Mongolian, Turkish

[*Austro-Asiatic*] Khmer, Vietnamese

[*Austronesian*] Fijian, Indonesian, Javanese, Malagasy, Malay, Maori, Nauru, Samoan, Tagalog, Tetum, Tonga

[*Aymaran*] Aymara

[*Bantu*] Kikongo

[*Basque*] Basque

[*Constructed Language*] Esperanto, Interlingua, Volapk

[*Dravidian*] Kannada, Malayalam, Tamil, Telugu

[*English Creole*] Bislama

[*Eskimo-Aleut*] Greenlandic, Inuktitut, Inupiak

[*French Creole*] Haitian Creole

[*Hmong-Mien*] Hmong

[*Indo-European*] Afrikaans, Armenian, Assamese, Asturian, Bengali, Bihari, Bosnian, Breton, Bulgarian, Byelorussian, Catalan, Corsican, Croatian, Czech, Danish, Dari, Dhivehi, Dutch, English, Faroese, Flemish, French, Frisian, Galician, German, Greek, Gujarati, Hindi, Icelandic, Irish, Italian, Kashmiri, Konkani, Kurdish, Latin, Latvian, Lithuanian, Macedonian, Marathi, Montenegrin, Nepali, Norwegian, Occitan, Oriya, Pashto, Persian,

Major concepts in computer-aided translation 51

Polish, Portuguese, Punjabi, Rhaeto-Romance, Romanian, Russian, Sanskrit, Sardinian, Scottish Gaelic, Serbian, Sindhi, Singhalese, Slovak, Slovenian, Sorbian, Spanish, Swedish, Tajik, Ukrainian, Urdu, Welsh, Yiddish
[*Kartvelian*] Georgian
[*Ngbandi-based Creole*] Sango
[*Niger-Congo*] Chichewa, Fula, Igbo, Kinyarwanda, Kirundi, Kiswahili, Lingala, Ndebele, Northern Sotho, Sesotho, Setswana, Shona, Siswati, Tsonga, Tswana, Twi, Wolof, Xhosa, Yoruba, Zulu
[*Northwest Caucasian*] Abkhazian
[*Quechuan*] Quechua
[*Romanian*] Moldavian
[*Sino-Tibetan*] Bhutani, Burmese, Chinese, Tibetan
[*Tai-Kadai*] Laothian, Thai
[*Tupi*] Guarani
[*Turkic*] Bashkir, Kirghiz, Tarar, Turkmen, Uyghur, Uzbek
[*Uralic*] Estonian, Finnish, Hungarian

Several observations can be made from the languages supported by the current eleven systems.

(1) The number of languages supported by language-specific systems is small, as they need to be supplied with language-specific dictionaries to function well. Yaxin, for instance, is best for English-Chinese translation, covering two languages, while most non-language-specific systems support around or above 100 languages.
(2) For the seven systems developed in Europe, the United Kingdom, and the United States, which include Across, Déjà Vu, MemoQ, OmegaT, SDL-Trados, Wordfast, and XTM, the Indo-European languages take up around 51.89 per cent, while the percentages of the non-Indo-European languages are 48.11 per cent. Table 2.1 shows the details.

Table 2.1 Statistics of Languages Supported by Seven CAT Systems

Name of theSystem	Number of Languages Supported	Number of Language Families Supported	Number and Percentage of Indo-European Languages	Number and Percentage of Non-Indo-European Languages
Across	121	18	61 (50.41%)	60 (49.59%)
Déjà Vu	132	21	66 (50%)	66 (50%)
MemoQ	102	16	54 (52.94%)	48 (47.06%)
OmegaT	90	14	48 (53.33%)	42 (46.67%)
SDL-Trados	115	18	62 (53.91%)	53 (46.09%)
Wordfast	91	13	54 (59.34%)	37 (40.66%)
XTM	157	26	68 (43.31%)	89 (56.69%)

52   *Major concepts in computer-aided translation*

Controllability

One of the main differences between human translation and computer-aided translation lies in the degree of control over the source text (Gommlich 1989: 72–79). In human translation, there is no need, or rather, it is not the common practice, to control how and what the author should write. But in computer-aided translation, control over the input text may not be inappropriate, as the output of an unedited or uncontrolled source language text is generally far from satisfactory (Adriaens and Macken 1995: 123–141; Allen and Hogan 2000: 62–71; Arnold, Balkan, Humphreys, Meijer, and Sadler 1994; Hurst 1997: 59–70; Lehtola, Tenni, and Bounsaythip 1998: 16–29; Mitamura 1999: 46–52; Murphy, Mason, and Sklair 1998; Nyberg, Mitamura, and Huijsen 2003: 245–281; Ruffino 1985: 157–162).

In computer-aided translation, the concept of controllability is regarded as the use of controlled language and the method of pre-editing.

Controllability by the use of controlled language

An effective means of achieving controllability in translation technology is by the use of a controlled language. The idea of controlled language was created, partly at least, as a result of the problems with natural languages that are full of complexities, ambiguities, and robustness (Nyberg, Mitamura and Huijsen 2003: 245–281). A strong rationale for controlled language is that a varied source text generates a poor target text, while a controlled source text produces a quality target text (Bernth 1999). Controlled language is, therefore, considered necessary (Caeyers 1997; Hu 2005: 364–372).

Controlled language, in brief, refers to a type of natural language developed for specific domains with a clearly defined restriction on controlled lexicons, simplified grammars, and style rules to reduce the ambiguity and complexity of a text so as to make it easier to be understood by users and non-native speakers and processed by machine translation systems (Chan 2004: 44; Lux and Dauphin 1996: 193–204).

Control over the three stages of a translation procedure, which include the stages of input of the source text, transfer, and target text generation, is generally regarded as a safe guarantee of quality translation. Control of the source text is in the form of controlled authoring, which makes the source text easier for computer processing (Allen 1999; Chan 2004: 44; van der Eijk and van Wees 1998: 65–70; Zydron 2003). The text produced in this way is a 'controlled language text' (Melby 1995: 1). There must also be control over the transfer stage, thus providing an output of a machine translation system that is known as 'controlled translation' (Carl 2003: 16–24; Gough and Way 2004: 73–81; Rico and Torrejon 2004; Roturier 2004; Torrejon 2002: 107–116), or alternatively as a 'controlled target language text' (Chan 2004: 44). In short, a controlled text is more easily processed by machine translation systems to produce a quality output.

Major concepts in computer-aided translation   53

Goals and means of controlled language

Controlled language is used by both humans and computers. The goals of using controlled language are to make the source text easier to read and understand. These goals are to be achieved both at the lexical and sentential levels.

At the lexical level, controlled language is about the removal of lexical ambiguity and the reduction in homonymy, synonymy, and complexity. This is to be achieved by one-to-one correspondence in the use and translation of words, known as one-word one-meaning. An example is to use only the word 'start' but not similar words such as 'begin', 'commence', 'initiate', and 'originate'. The second method is to use the preferred language, such as the use of American English but not British English. The third method is to have a limited basic vocabulary (Bjarnestam 2003; Chen and Wu 1999; Probst and Levin 2002: 157–167; Wasson 2000: 276–281), which can be illustrated by the use of a controlled vocabulary of 3,100 words in aircraft-maintenance documentation at the European Association of Aerospace Industries (AECMA) in 1980 (AECMA 1995).

At the sentential level, controlled language consists of the removal of syntactical ambiguity, the simplification of sentence structures, limitations on sentence length, and constraints on voice, tense, and other grammatical units. To do all these, there are a limited number of strictly stipulated writing rules to follow. The European Association of Aerospace Industries, for instance, had 57 writing rules. Short sentences are preferred over long and complex sentences, and there is also a limit on the number of words in a sentence. For procedural texts, there should be no more than 20 words. For descriptive texts, the number is 25. There are also rules governing grammatical well-formedness (Loong 1989: 281–297), restricted syntax, the use of passive construction in procedural texts, and structural clarity by the use of parallel structures. At the supra-sentential level, there is a limit of six sentences in a paragraph, a maximum number of clauses in a sentence, and separate sentences are used for sequential steps in procedural texts.

Controlled language checkers

Controlled language cannot be maintained manually; it relies on the use of different kinds of checkers, which are systems that ensure that a text conforms to the rules of a particular controlled language (Fouvry and Balkan 1996: 179–192). The automatic rewriting system, which is specially developed for controlled language, rewrites texts automatically into controlled language without changing the meaning of the sentences in the original in order to produce a high-quality machine translation. There are also controlled language checkers, or software that helps an author determine whether a text conforms to the approved words and writing rules of a particular controlled language.

Checkers can in turn be divided into two types: in-house controlled language checkers and commercial controlled language checkers. In-house controlled language checkers include the PACE (Perkins Approved Clear English) of Perkins

54 *Major concepts in computer-aided translation*

Engines Ltd., the Controlled English of Alcatel Telecom, and the Boeing Simplified English Checker of the Boeing Company (Wojcik and Holmback 1996: 22–31). For commercial controlled language checkers, there are a number of popular systems. The LANTmaster Controlled Checker, for example, is a controlled language checker developed by LANT in Belgium. It is based on work done for the METAL (Mechanical Translation and Analysis of Languages) machine translation project. It is also based on the experience of the Simplified English Grammar and Style Checker (SECC) project (Adriaens 1994; Adriaens and Macken 1995: 123–141). The MAXit Checker is another controlled language software developed by Smart Communications Incorporation to analyse technical texts written in controlled or simplified English with the use of more than 8,500 grammar rules and artificial intelligence to check the clarity, consistency, simplicity, and global acceptance of the texts. The Carnegie Group also produced the ClearCheck, which performs syntactic parsing to detect such grammatical problems as ambiguity (Andersen 1994: 227).

Advantages and disadvantages of controlled language

The advantages of controlled language translation are numerous, including high readability, better comprehensibility, greater standardization, easier computer processing, greater reusability, increased translatability, enhanced consistency, improved customer satisfaction, improved competitiveness, greater cost reduction in global product support, and enhanced communication in global management.

Nonetheless, there are a number of disadvantages in using controlled language, the most significant of which are expensive system construction, high cost of maintenance, time-consuming authoring, and restrictive checking processes.

Controlled language in use

As the advantages of using controlled language outweigh its disadvantages, companies started to use it as early as the 1970s. Examples of business corporations which used controlled languages include Caterpillar Fundamental English (CFE) of Caterpillar Incorporated in 1975 (Kamprath, Adolphson, Mitamura, and Nyberg 1998: 51–61; Lockwood 2000: 187–202), Smart Controlled English of Smart Communications Ltd. in 1975, Douglas Aircraft Company in 1979, the European Association of Aerospace Industries (AECMA) in 1980, the KANT Project at the Center for Machine Translation, Carnegie Mellon University in 1989 (Allen 1995; Carbonell, Mitamura and Nyberg 1992: 225–235; Mitamura and Nyberg 1995: 158–172; Mitamura, Nyberg, Baken, Cramer, Ko, Svoboda, and Duggan 2002: 244–247; Mitamura, Nyberg, and Carbonell 1994: 232–233; Nyberg, Kamprath, and Mitamura 1998; Nyberg and Mitamura 1992: 1069–1073; Nyberg and Mitamura 2000: 192–195; Nyberg, Mitamura, and Carbonell 1997), PACE of Perkins Engines Ltd. in 1989, ScaniaSwedish in Sweden in 1995 (Almqvist and Hein 1996: 159–164; Hein 1997), General Motors in 1996, Ericsson English in Sweden in 2000, Nortel Standard English in the United Kingdom in 2002, and Oce Technologies English in the Netherlands in 2002.

Controlled language in computer-aided translation systems

The concept of controlled language is developed by controlled authoring tools in computer-aided translation systems. Authoring tools are used to check and improve the quality of the source text. There is an automatic rewriting system which is usually used as a tool to realize controlled authoring. One of the computer-aided translation systems that performs controlled authoring is Star Transit. This open-source system provides automatic translation suggestions from the translation memory database from a speedy search engine and can integrate with several authoring systems.

Customizability

Customizability, etymologically speaking, is the ability to be customized. More specifically, it refers to the ability of a computer or a computer-aided translation system to adapt itself to the needs of the user. Customizing a general-purpose machine translation system is an effective way to improve machine translation quality.

Editorial customization

Pre-editing is in essence a process of customization. Pre-editing is 'the process of preparing a source language for translation by a machine translation system' (Chan 2004: 178). The main purpose of pre-editing is to discover and amend any lexical, phrasal, or typographical errors that may cause problems to machine processing of the input text so as to get a quality output text (Quah 2006: 11). Changes are made based on one's knowledge of data management. Pre-editing is, therefore, the act of producing a text to optimize machine translation performance for better readability and computational processing by the removal of lexical and syntactical ambiguity and complexity (Chan 2004: 178). To pre-edit, it is required to have pre-editing tools, which often include means for the control of input language, such as the reduction of ambiguities and the simplification of text structures to facilitate machine translation.

Changes are made to the source text to ensure that it is textually, lexically, grammatically, rhetorically, semantically, and syntactically correct, and it is easier for a computer-aided translation system to process the data. A quality source text, it must be emphasized, generates a quality translation. The customization of machine translation systems, which is a much neglected area, is necessary and essential, as most software on the market is for general use and not for specific domains. Customizing a general-purpose machine translation system is an effective way to improve machine translation quality. Practically, system customization can be considered part of the work of pre-editing, as the words and expressions are pre-edited to facilitate the production of a quality translation.

The degree of customization depends on the goals of translation, as well as the circumstances and the type of text to be translated. These considerations

56 *Major concepts in computer-aided translation*

will have implications on resources, such as time and labour. Localization is also an important factor to be considered. Very often, what is stored in a database prepared by translators of a specific region may not be usable in another region. In this case, efforts are needed to prepare new databases to deal with regional variations in terminology and translation memory.

Language customization

It is true that there are many language combinations in computer-aided translation systems, allowing the user to choose any pair of source and target languages when creating a project. However, many users work only with a limited set of source and target languages. XTM, a cloud-based system, allows the user to set language combinations through the 'Data' section. In the language combinations section, the project administrator or user can reduce and customize the available languages to be used and set the language combinations for the entire system as well as specific language combinations for individual customers (XTM Manual 2012: 15).

Language customization in XTM, for example, can be conducted on the 'Customize' tab, where there are three options for the user to modify and use language combinations. The first option is 'system default language combinations', which refers to the full set of unmodified language combinations. The second option is 'system defaults with customized language combinations', which in turn refers to the full set of language combinations in which the user may have customized some parameters. The third option is 'customized language combinations only', which includes only the language combinations that the user has customized. It is possible to add or delete the source and target languages in the selected customized option.

Lexicographical customization

Lexicographical customization is best shown in the creation of custom dictionaries for each customer, rather than in the dictionaries for spell checking. This means that multiple translators working on projects for the same customer will use the same custom dictionaries.

Linguistic customization

As far as linguistic customization is concerned, there are basically two levels of customization: lexical customization and syntactical customization.

Lexical customization

Lexical customization consists of customizing a machine translation system by preparing a customized dictionary, in addition to the system dictionary, before translating. This removes the uncertainties in translating ambiguous words or word combinations. It must be pointed out, however, that the preparation of a customized dictionary is an enormous task, involving a huge amount of work in database creation, maintenance, and database updating.

Syntactical customization

Syntactical customization, on the other hand, involves adding sentences or phrases to the database to translate texts with many repetitions. Syntactical customization is particularly important when there is a change of location for translation consumption. The translation memory databases built up in Hong Kong for the translation of local materials, for example, may not be suitable for the production of translations targeted at non-Hong Kong readers, such as those in mainland China.

Resource customization

Website customization

Some computer-aided translation systems allow the user to create resource profile settings. Each profile in Fluency, for example, has four customized uniform resource locators (URLs) associated with it. URLs are the Internet addresses of information. Each document or file on the Internet has a unique address for its location. Fluency allows the user to have four URLs of one's preference, two perhaps for specialized sites and two general sites.

Machine translation system customization

Some systems are connected to installed machine translation systems, the terminology databases of which can be customized for the generation of output, thus achieving terminological consistency in the target text.

Collaborativity

Collaborativity is about continuously working and communicating with all parties relating to a translation project, from the client to the reviewer, in a shared work environment to generate the best benefits of team work. Computer-aided translation is a modern mode of translation production that works best in team translation. In the past, and decreasingly at present, individual translation has been the norm. However, at present, and increasingly in the future, team translation is and will be the standard practice.

A number of systems, such as Across and Wordfast, allow users to interact with each other through a translation memory server and share translation memory assets in real-time.

Translation is about management, and the translation business operates on projects. Translation technology is, therefore, about project management, about how work is to be completed by translation teams. With the use of translation technology, the progress of translation work is under control and completed

58 *Major concepts in computer-aided translation*

with higher efficiency. The best example to illustrate this point is project collaboration, which allows translators and project managers to easily access and distribute projects, as well as monitor easily the progress of these projects.

The translation work in the present digital era is done almost entirely online with the help of a machine translation or computer-aided translation systems. This can be illustrated with SDL-Trados 2007 Synergy, which is a computer-aided translation system developed by SDL International and generally considered as the most popular translation memory system on the market at that time.

Below is the dashboard of SDL-Trados 2015.

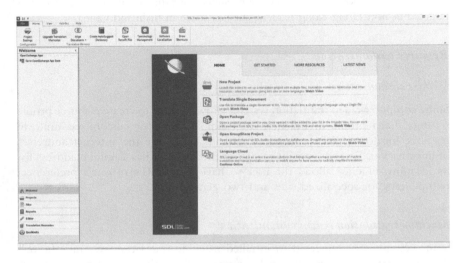

Figure 2.1 Screenshot of Dashboard of SDL-Trados 2015

Figure 2.2 Screenshot of SDL-Trados: 'Progress of Individual Projects'

Major concepts in computer-aided translation 59

Figure 2.3 Screenshot of SDL-Trados: 'Completion of Projects: Today'

Name	Status	Date Due	Created At	Type	Locat..	Server
translator02.pptx	**In Progress**	**10/04/2014 18:00:00**	**03/04/2014 14:10:35**	**Single file project**	**C:\User..**	
SamplePhotoPrinter.doc_en-US..	In Progress	14/04/2014 18:00:00	21/03/2014 15:36:43	Single file project	C:\User..	
Project 24	In Progress	[none]	18/03/2014 15:48:59	Standard Studio project	C:\User..	
Project 23	In Progress	[none]	18/03/2014 15:46:54	Standard Studio project	C:\User..	
Proz April	In Progress	[none]	18/03/2014 15:19:08	Standard Studio project	C:\User..	
SamplePhotoPrinter.doc_en-US..	In Progress	[none]	28/02/2014 16:36:44	Single file project	C:\User..	
2012-08-27-SPECIFICATION-C..	In Progress	[none]	20/02/2014 15:08:04	Single file project	C:\User..	
Project 22	In Progress	[none]	15/01/2014 09:52:40	Standard Studio project	C:\User..	
FL Mailerjan09v1.html_en-US_it-I..	In Progress	[none]	07/01/2014 16:28:15	Single file project	C:\User..	
Project 21	In Progress	[none]	07/01/2014 16:04:05	Standard Studio project	C:\User..	
Proz membership Eng.rtf_en-US..	In Progress	[none]	07/01/2014 15:55:11	Single file project	C:\User..	
Project 20	In Progress	[none]	05/12/2013 17:24:49	Standard Studio project	C:\User..	
Proz membership Eng.doc_en-U..	In Progress	[none]	05/12/2013 17:21:22	Single file project	C:\User..	
SamplePhotoPrinter.doc_en-US..	In Progress	[none]	28/11/2013 17:31:13	Single file project	C:\User..	
globe.docx_it-IT_en-GB	In Progress	[none]	25/11/2013 14:20:19	Single file project	C:\User..	
Group Share 2014 PB_en-US_it-..	In Progress	15/11/2013 08:40:22	13/11/2013 09:58:01	Studio package	C:\User..	
Project 19	In Progress	[none]	11/11/2013 23:45:25	Standard Studio project	C:\User..	
HP Printer page.htm_en-US_it-IT	In Progress	[none]	08/11/2013 21:32:10	Single file project	C:\User..	
Project 2	In Progress	[none]	08/11/2013 21:21:13	Standard Studio project	C:\User..	
Project 1	In Progress	[none]	07/11/2013 21:46:06	Standard Studio project	C:\User..	
retest.docx_en-US_it-IT	In Progress	[none]	07/11/2013 19:04:57	Single file project	C:\User..	

Figure 2.4 Screenshot of SDL-Trados: 'Progress on the Translation of Files'

Workflow of a translation project

To start a project, the first stage of the workflow is the creation of a termbase and a translation memory database. In other words, when the project manager has any publications, files, or webpages to translate, he or she will send them either to the in-house translators in a department or unit, or to freelancers for processing. They will create translation units and term databases from these pre-translated documents and save these databases in the SDL-Trados 2007 Server. This is the first stage of the workflow.

60 *Major concepts in computer-aided translation*

After the creation of a translation memory and a termbase, the project manager can then initiate the translation project and monitor its progress with the use of SDL-Trados 2007 Synergy. He or she can assign and distribute source files to in-house or freelance translators by email. Translators can then perform the translation by (i) reusing the translation memories and terms stored in the databases, and (ii) adding new words or expressions to the translation memory and termbase. When the translation is completed, the translators send their translated files back to the project manager on or before the due date. When the project manager receives the translated files, he or she updates the project status, finalizes the project, and marks it as 'complete'.

To make sure that SDL-Trados 2007 Synergy runs smoothly, a technical support unit may be necessary to maintain the SDL-Trados server.

A translation team usually consists of the following members.

Project manager

A project manager is a professional in the field of project management. The responsibilities of a project manager include the following:

(1) Plan, execute, and close projects. When planning a project, the project manager works on the overall resources and budget of the project, whereas when executing a project, the project manager can add or import customers or subcontract projects.
(2) Create clear and attainable project objectives.
(3) Build the project requirements.
(4) Manage cost, time, and scope of projects.

Terminologist

A terminologist is the professional who manages terms in the terminology database. There are two types of terminologists: (1) customer-specific terminologists, who can only access the terminology of one customer; and (2) global experts, who can access all the terms in the systems for all customers.

Conclusion

This chapter is possibly the first attempt to analyse the concepts that have governed the growth of functionalities in computer-aided translation systems. As computer science and related disciplines advance, more concepts will be introduced and more functions will be developed. However, it is believed that most of the concepts discussed in this chapter will last for a long time.

References

Adriaens, Geert (1994) 'Simplified English Grammar and Style Correction in an MT Framework: The LRE SECC Project', *Translating and the Computer 16*, London: The Association for Information Management, 78–88.

Adriaens, Geert and Lieve Macken (1995) 'Technological Evaluation of a Controlled Language Application: Precision, Recall and Convergence Tests for SECC', *Proceedings of the 6th International Conference on Theoretical and Methodological Issues in Machine Translation (TMI-95)*, Leuven, Belgium, 123–141.

AECMA (1995) *A Guide for the Preparation of Aircraft Maintenance Documentation in the International Aerospace Maintenance Language — Issue 1*, Brussels, Belgium: AECMA.

Allen, Jeffrey (1995) *Review of the Caterpillar KANT English-French MT System*, Internal Technical Report, Peoria, IL: Technical Information Department, Caterpillar Inc.

Allen, Jeffrey (1999) 'Adapting the Concept of "Translation Memory" to "Authoring Memory" for a Controlled Language Writing Environment', *Translating and the Computer 20*, London: The Association for Information Management.

Allen, Jeffrey and Christopher Hogan (2000) 'Toward the Development of a Postediting Module for Raw Machine Translation Output: A Controlled Language Perspective', *Proceedings of the 3rd International Workshop on Controlled Language Applications*, Seattle, Washington, DC, the United States of America, 62–71.

Almqvist, Ingrid and Anna Sågvall Hein (1996) 'Defining ScaniaSwedish — Controlled Language for Truck Maintenance', *Proceedings of the 1st International Workshop on Controlled Language Applications (CLAW-96)*, Leuven, Belgium, 159–164.

Al-Shabab, Omar Sheikh (1996) *Interpretation and the Language of Translation: Creativity and Convention in Translation*, London: Janus Publishing Company.

Andersen, Peggy (1994) 'ClearCheck Demonstration', *Proceedings of the 1st Conference of the Association for Machine Translation in the Americas: Technology Partnerships for Crossing the Language Barrier (AMTA-1)*, Columbia, MD, the United States of America, 227.

Arnold, Doug J., Lorna Balkan, R. Lee Humphreys, Seity Meijer, and Louisa Sadler (1994) *Machine Translation: An Introductory Guide*, Manchester and Oxford: NCC Blackwell.

Bell, Roger T. (1991) *Translation and Translating: Theory and Practice*, London and New York: Longman.

Bernth, Arendse (1999) *Tools for Improving E-G MT Quality*, Yorktown Heights: IBM T.J. Watson Research Center.

Bilac, Slaven and Hozumi Tanaka (2005) 'Direct Combination of Spelling and Pronunciation Information for Robust Back-transliteration', *Proceedings of the 6th International Conference on Intelligent Text Processing and Computational Linguistics (CICLing-2005)*, Mexico City, Mexico, 402–413.

Bjarnestam, Anna (2003) 'Internationalizing a Controlled Vocabulary Based Search Engine for Japanese', *Proceedings of the Localization World Conference 2003*, Seattle, Washington, DC, the United States of America.

Bly, Robert (1983) *The Eight Stages of Translation*, Boston: Rowan Tree Press.

Bowker, Lynne (2005) 'Productivity vs Quality? A Pilot Study on the Impact of Translation Memory Systems', *Localization Focus* 4(1): 13–20.

Brandwood, Leonard (1956) 'The Translation of a Foreign Language by Machine', *Babel* 2(3): 111–118.

Caeyers, Herman (1997) 'Machine Translation and Controlled English', *Proceedings of the 2nd Workshop of the European Association for Machine Translation: Language Technology in Your Organization?* University of Copenhagen, Copenhagen, Denmark, 91–103.

62 Major concepts in computer-aided translation

Carbonell, Jaime G., Teruko Mitamura, and Eric H. Nyberg (1992) 'The KANT Perspective: A Critique of Pure Transfer (and Pure Interlingua, Pure Statistics, . . .)', *Proceedings of the 4th International Conference on Theoretical and Methodological Issues in Machine Translation of Natural Languages: Empiricist vs Rationalist Methods in MT (TMI-92)*, Montreal, Quebec, Canada, 225–235.

Carl, Michael (2003) 'Data-assisted Controlled Translation', *Proceedings of the Joint Conference Combining the 8th International Workshop of the European Association for Machine Translation and the 4th Controlled Language Applications Workshop: Controlled Language Translation (EAMT-CLAW-2003)*, Dublin City University, Ireland, the United Kingdom, 16–24.

Chan, Sin-wai (2004) *A Dictionary of Translation Technology*, Hong Kong: The Chinese University Press.

Chan, Sin-wai (2015) 'Computer-aided Translation: Major Concepts', Chan Sin-wai (ed.) *Routledge Encyclopedia of Translation Technology*, London and New York: Routledge, 32–67.

Chen, Kuang-Hua and Chien-Tin Wu (1999) 'Automatically Controlled-vocabulary Indexing for Text Retrieval', *Proceedings of the International Conference on Research in Computational Linguistics (ROCLING-XII)*, Taipei, Taiwan.

Clements, David (1996) 'The Value of Online MT in the Age of the "Cyber Society"', *Proceedings of the 2nd Conference of the Association for Machine Translation in the Americas: Expanding MT Horizons (AMTA-2)*, Montreal, Quebec, Canada, 220–221.

Craig, Murray G., J. Bonnie Dorr, Jimmy Lin, Pecina Pavel, and Jan Hajic (2006) 'Leveraging Reusability: Cost-effective Lexical Acquisition for Large-scale Ontology Translation', *Proceedings of the Joint Conference of the International Committee on Computational Linguistics and the Association for Computational Linguistics (COLING/ACL-2006)*, Sydney, Australia.

de Ilarraza, Arantxa Diaz, Aingeru Mayor, and Kepa Sarasola (2000) 'Reusability of Wide-coverage Linguistic Resources in the Construction of Multilingual Technical Documentation', *Proceedings of the International Conference on Machine Translation and Multilingual Applications in the New Millenium (MT-2000)*, University of Exeter, England, the United Kingdom.

Delisle, Jean (1988) *Translation: An Interpretive Approach*, tr. Patricia Logan and Monica Creery, Ottawa and London: University of Ottawa Press.

Dube, Daniel W. and John D. Rice (2000) 'XML and the Localisation Process', *Translating and the Computer 22*, London: The Association for Information Management.

Ekbal, Asif, Supid Kumar Naskar, and Sivaji Bandyopadhyay (2006) 'A Modified Joint Source Channel Model for Transliteration', *Proceedings of the Joint Conference of the International Committee on Computational Linguistics and the Association for Computational Linguistics (COLING/ACL-2006)*, Sydney, Australia.

Fais, Laurel and Kentaro Ogura (2001) 'Discourse Issues in the Translation of Japanese Email', *The 5th Pacific Association for Computational Linguistics Conference (PACLING-2001)*, Fukuoka, Japan.

Flanagan, Mary A. (1995) 'MT in the Online Environment: Challenges and Opportunities', *Proceedings of MT Summit V: Machine Translation Conference, Exhibition and Tutorial*, Luxembourg.

Flanagan, Mary A. (1996) 'Two Years Online: Experiences, Challenges, and Trends', *Proceedings of the 2nd Conference of the Association for Machine Translation in the*

Major concepts in computer-aided translation 63

Americas: Expanding MT Horizons (AMTA-2), Montreal, Quebec, Canada, 192–197.

Flanagan, Mary A. (1997) 'Online Translation: MT's New Frontier', *Translating and the Computer 19*, London: The Association for Information Management.

Fouvry, Frederik and Lorna Balkan (1996) 'Test Suites for Controlled Language Checkers', *Proceedings of the 1st International Workshop on Controlled Language Applications*, Katholieke Universiteit, Leuven, Belgium, 179–192.

Gaspari, Federico (2004) 'Enhancing Free On-line Machine Translation Services', M. Lee (ed.) *Proceedings of the 7th Annual CLUK Research Colloquium*, University of Birmingham, Birmingham, the United Kingdom, 68–74.

Gommlich, Klaus (1989) 'The Control Potential of a Computer-aided Translation System', *Linguistische Studien* 196: 72–79.

Goto, Isao, Naoto Kato, Noriyoshi Uratani, and Terumasa Ehara (2003) 'Transliteration Considering Context Information Based on the Maximum Entropy Method', *Proceedings of MT Summit IX*, New Orleans, LA, the United States of America.

Gough, Nano and Andy Way (2004) 'Example-based Controlled Translation', *Proceedings of the 9th Workshop of the European Association for Machine Translation: Broadening Horizons of Machine Translation and Its Applications, Foundation for International Studies*, Malta, 73–81.

Han, Benjamin, Donna Gates, and Lori S. Levin (2006) 'Understanding Temporal Expressions in Emails', *Proceedings of the Human Language Technology Conference—Annual Meeting of the North American Chapter of the Association for Computational Linguistics (HLT-NAACL-2006)*, New York, the United States of America.

Hein, Anna Sagvall (1997) 'Scania Swedish—A Basis for Multilingual Translation', *Translating and the Computer 19*, London: The Association for Information Management.

http://www.alchemysoftware.ie/index.html.

http://www.helicon.co.at/aboutus.html.

http://www.internetworldstats.com/stats.htm.

http://www.lisa.org/Glossary.

http://www.passolo.com.

http://www.schaudin.com.

http://www2.multilizer.com/company.

Hu, Qingping 胡清平 (2005)〈受控語言及其在漢英機器翻譯裏的應用前景〉('Controlled Language and Its Prospective Application in Chinese-English Machine Translation'), Luo Xuanmin 羅選民 (ed.) 《語言認識與翻譯研究》(*Language, Cognition and Translation Studies*), Beijing: Foreign Language Press, 364–372.

Hurst, Matthew F. (1997) 'Parsing for Targeted Errors in Controlled Languages', Ruslan Mitkov and Nicolas Nicolov (eds.) *Recent Advances in Natural Language Processing*, Amsterdam and Philadelphia: John Benjamins Publishing Company, 59–70.

Joy, Lorna (2002) 'Translating Tagged Text-Imperfect Matches and a Good Finished Job', *Translating and the Computer 24*, London: The Association for Information Management.

Kamprath, Christine, Eric Adolphson, Teruko Mitamura, and Eric H. Nyberg (1998) 'Controlled Language Multilingual Document Production: Experience with Caterpillar Technical English', *Proceedings of the 2nd International*

64 *Major concepts in computer-aided translation*

Workshop on Controlled Language Applications (*CLAW-98*), Language Technologies Institute, Carnegie Mellon University, Pittsburgh, PA, the United States of America, 51–61.

Kay, Martin (1980) 'The Proper Place of Men and Machines in Language Translation', *Research Report CSL-80-11*, Xerox Palo Alto Research Center, Palo Alto, CA, the United States of America.

Kertesz, Francois (1974) 'How to Cope with the Foreign-language Problems: Experience Gained at a Multidisciplinary Laboratory', *Journal of the American Society for Information Science* 25(2): 86–104.

Knight, Kevin and Jonathan Graehl (1997) 'Machine Transliteration', *Proceedings of the Conference of the Association for Computational Linguistics (ACL)*.

Knight, Kevin and Jonathan Graehl (1998) 'Machine Transliteration', *Computational Linguistics* 24(4): 599–612.

Kuo, Jin-Shea, Haizhou Li, and Ying-Kuei Yang (2006) 'Learning Transliteration Lexicons from the Web', *Proceedings of the Joint Conference of the International Committee on Computational Linguistics and the Association for Computational Linguistics (COLING/ACL-2006)*, Sydney, Australia.

Lee, Chun-Jen and Jason S. Chang (2003) 'Acquisition of English-Chinese Transliterated Word Pairs from Parallel-aligned Texts Using a Statistical Machine Transliteration Model', *Proceedings of the Human Language Technology and North American Chapter of Association of Computational Linguistics 2003* (*HLT/NAACL-2003*), Edmonton, Alberta, Canada, 96–103.

Lehtola, Aarno, Jarno Tenni, and Catherine Bounsaythip (1998) 'Controlled Language – An Introduction', *Proceedings of the 2nd International Workshop on Controlled Language Applications*, Carnegie Mellon University, Pittsburgh, PA, the United States of America, 16–29.

Li, Haizhou, Zhang Min, and Su Jian (2004) 'A Joint Source-channel Model for Machine Transliteration', *Proceedings of the 42nd Annual Meeting of the Association for Computational Linguistics (ACL-2004)*, Barcelona, Spain, 159–166.

Lin, Tracy, Wu Jian-Cheng, and Jason S. Chang (2004) 'Extraction of Name and Transliteration in Monolingual and Parallel Corpora', Robert E. Frederking and Kathryn B. Taylors (eds.) *Machine Translation: From Real Users to Research*, Berlin: Springer Verlag, 177–186.

Lin, W.-H. and H.-H. Chen (2002) 'Backward Transliteration by Learning Phonetic Similarity', *Proceedings of the 6th Conference on Natural Language Learning* (*CoNLL-2002*), Taipei, Taiwan.

Liu, Yongquan 劉湧泉 (1984) 〈外漢機器翻譯中的中介成分體系〉('The Intermediary Componential System in Machine Translation Systems for Foreign Languages and Chinese'), Liu Yongquan et al. 劉湧泉等 (eds.) 《中國的機器翻譯》 (*Machine Translation in China*), Shanghai: Knowledge Press, 46–57.

Lockwood, Rose (2000) 'Machine Translation and Controlled Authoring at Caterpillar', Robert C. Sprung (ed.) *Translating into Success: Cutting-edge Strategies for Going Multilingual in a Global Age*, Amsterdam and Philadelphia: John Benjamins Publishing Company, 187–202.

Loong, Cheong Tong (1989) 'A Data-driven Control Strategy for Grammar Writing Systems', *Machine Translation* 4(4): 281–297.

Lufkin, J.M. (1966) 'Human Versus Machine Translation of Foreign Languages', *The Incorporated Linguists* 5: 9–15.

Major concepts in computer-aided translation 65

Lux, Veronika and Eva Dauphin (1996) 'Corpus Studies: A Contribution to the Definition of a Controlled Language', *Proceedings of the 1st International Workshop on Controlled Language Applications (CLAW-96)*, Leuven, Belgium, 193–204.

Matsuda, Junichi and Hiroyuki Kumai (1999) 'Transfer-based Japanese-Chinese Translation Implemented on an E-mail System', *Proceedings of MT Summit VII: MT in the Great Translation Era*, Singapore.

McCarthy, Brian (2004) 'Does Online Machine Translation Spell the End of Take-home Translation Assignments?' *CALL-EJ Online* 6(1).

Melby, Alan K. (1995) *The Possibility of Language: A Discussion of the Nature of Language, with Implications for Human and Machine Translation*, Amsterdam and Philadelphia: John Benjamins Publishing Company.

Melby, Alan K. (2012) 'Terminology in the Age of Multilingual Corpora', *The Journal of Specialized Translation*, 18: 7–29.

Mellebeek, Bart, Anna Khasin, Josef Van Genabith, and Andy Way (2005) 'Improving Online Machine Translation Systems', *Proceedings of MT Summit X*, Phuket, Thailand.

Merkel, Magnus (1993) 'When and Why Should Translations Be Reused', *Papers from the XIII AAKKI Symposium*, Vaasa, Finland, 139–149.

Mitamura, Teruko (1999) 'Controlled Language for Multilingual Machine Translation', *Proceedings of MT Summit VII: MT in the Great Translation Era*, Singapore, 46–52.

Mitamura, Teruko and Eric H. Nyberg (1995) 'Controlled English for Knowledge Based MT: Experience with the KANT System', *Proceedings of the 6th International Conference on Theoretical and Methodological Issues in Machine Translation (TMI-95)*, Leuven, Belgium, 158–172.

Mitamura, Teruko, Eric H. Nyberg, and Jaime G. Carbonell (1994) 'KANT: Knowledge-based, Accurate Natural Language Translation', *Proceedings of the 1st Conference of the Association for Machine Translation in the Americas: Technology Partnerships for Crossing the Language Barrier (AMTA-1)*, Columbia, MD, the United States of America, 232–233.

Mitamura, Teruko, Eric H. Nyberg, Kathy Baker, Peter Cramer, Jeongwoo Ko, David Svoboda, and Michael Duggan (2002) 'The KANTOO MT System: Controlled Language Checker and Lexical Maintenance Tool', Stephen D. Richardson (ed.) *Machine Translation: From Research to Real Users*, Berlin and New York: Springer Verlag, 244–247.

Murphy, Dawn, Jane Mason, and Stuart Sklair (1998) 'Improving Translation at the Source', *Translating and the Computer 20*, London: The Association for Information Management.

Nida, Eugene A. and Charles R. Taber (1969/1982) *The Theory and Practice of Translation*, Leiden: E.J. Brill.

Nyberg, Eric H., Christine Kamprath, and Teruko Mitamura (1998) 'The KANT Translation System: From R&D to Large-Scale Deployment', *LISA Newsletter* 2(1): 1–7.

Nyberg, Eric H. and Teruko Mitamura (1992) 'The KANT System: Fast, Accurate, High-quality Translation in Practical Domains', *Proceedings of the 14th International Conference of Computational Linguistics (COLING-92)*, Nantes, France, 1069–1073.

Nyberg, Eric H. and Teruko Mitamura (2000) 'The KANTOO Machine Translation Environment', John S. White (ed.) *Envisioning Machine Translation in the Information Future*, Berlin: Springer Verlag, 192–195.

66   Major concepts in computer-aided translation

Nyberg, Eric H., Teruko Mitamura, and Jaime G. Carbonell (1997) 'The KANT Machine System: From R&D to Initial Deployment', *LISA Workshop on Intergrating Advanced Translation Technology*, Seattle, Washington, DC, the United States of America.

Nyberg, Eric H., Teruko Mitamura, and Willem-Olaf Huijsen (2003) 'Controlled Language for Authoring and Translation', Harold L. Somers (ed.) *Computers and Translation: A Translator's Guide*, Amsterdam and Philadelphia: John Benjamins Publishing Company, 245–281.

O'Neill-Brown, Patricia (1996) 'Online Machine Translation', *Proceedings of the 2nd Conference of the Association for Machine Translation in the Americas: Expanding MT Horizons (AMTA-2)*, Montreal, Quebec, Canada, 222–223.

Probst, Katharina and Lori S. Levin (2002) 'Challenges in Automated Elicitation of a Controlled Bilingual Corpus', *Proceedings of the 9th International Conference on Theoretical and Methodological Issues in Machine Translation (TMI-2002)*, Keihanna, Japan, 157–167.

Quah, Chiew Kin (2006) *Translation and Technology*, Basingstoke and New York: Palgrave Macmillan.

Resnik, Philip (1997) 'Evaluating Multilingual Gisting of Web Pages', *Proceedings of the AAAI Symposium on Cross-language Text and Speech Retrieval*, Stanford University, CA, the United States of America.

Rico, Celia and Enrique Torrejon (2004) 'Controlled Translation as a New Translation Scenario — Training the Future User', *Translating and the Computer 26*, London: The Association for Information Management.

Rooke, Robert (1985) 'Electronic Mail', Catriona Picken (ed.) *Translation and Communication: Translating and the Computer 6*, London: The Association for Information Management, 105–115.

Roturier, Johann (2004) 'Assessing Controlled Language Rules: Can They Improve Performance of Commercial Machine Translation Systems?' *Translating and the Computer 26*, London: The Association for Information Management.

Ruffino, J. Richard (1985) 'The Impact of Controlled English on Machine Translation', Patricia E. Newman (ed.) *American Translators Association Conference — 1985*, Medford and New Jersey: Learned Information, Inc., 157–162.

Savourel, Yves (2001) *XML Internationalization and Localization*, Indianapolis: SAMS Publishing.

Sofer, Morry (2009) *The Translator's Handbook*, Rockville: Schreiber Publishing.

Steiner, George (1975/1992) *After Babel: Aspect of Language and Translation*, 2nd edition, Oxford: Oxford University Press.

Torrejón, Enrique (2002) 'Controlled Translation: A New Teaching Scenario Tailor-made for the Translation Industry', *Proceedings of the 6th Workshop of the European Association for Machine Translation: Teaching Machine Translation*, Manchester, England, the United Kingdom, 107–116.

Vallianatou, Fotini (2005) 'CAT Tools and Productivity: Tracking Words and Hours', *Translation Journal* 9(4).

van der Eijk, Pim and Jacqueline van Wees (1998) 'Supporting Controlled Language Authoring', *Proceedings of the 3rd Workshop of the European Association for Machine Translation: Translation Technology: Integration in the Workflow Environment*, Geneva, Switzerland, 65–70.

Wasson, Mark (2000) 'Large-scale Controlled Vocabulary Indexing for Named Entities', *Proceedings of the 6th Applied Natural Language Processing Conference*, Seattle, Washington, DC, the United States of America, 276–281.

Major concepts in computer-aided translation   67

Wilss, Wolfram (1982) *The Science of Translation: Problems and Methods*, Tubingen: Gunter Narr Verlag.

Windows (2012) 'A History of Windows', *Windows*.

Wojcik, Richard H. and Heather Holmback (1996) 'Getting a Controlled Language Off the Ground at Boeing', *Proceedings of the 1st International Workshop on Controlled Language Applications (CLAW-96)*, Katholieke Universiteit Leuven, Belgium, 22–31.

Zagar, Galvão Elena (2005) 'Translating into the Foreign Language: Using Website "Internationalization" as a Pedagogic Tool', *International Journal of Translation* 4: 37–40.

Zervaki, Thei (2002) 'Online Free Translation Services', *Translating and the Computer 24*, London: The Association of Information Management.

Zydron, Andrzeg (2003) 'Xml: tm—Using XML Technology to Reduce the Cost of Authoring and Translation', *Translating and the Computer 25*, London: The Association for Information Management.

3 Functions in computer-aided translation systems

Introduction

The functions in a computer-aided translation tool are instructions or commands given to the system so that it performs the actions the user wants it to perform. Functions are developed according to some of the concepts mentioned in the previous chapter. However, concepts or goals in translation technology cannot be achieved without the support of an adequate amount of data. All actions in translation technology are data-based and data-driven. It is, therefore, logical to divide the entire process of translation in terms of data into an initiating stage, a data preparation stage, a data processing stage, a data editing stage, and a finalizing stage, putting the functions under the stage to which they belong. This function-based approach is ideal to understand which functions are available and when should they be applied within the process of translation. It allows us to identify functions for starting up a computer-aided translation system with some specifications and creating new projects, or opening old projects, during the first stage; functions for data collection and data creation, during the second stage; functions for data analysis, data formats, data mining, data reuse, and data application, in the third stage; functions for data editing, in the fourth stage; and functions for data updating and data delivery, in the finalizing stage.

The following discussion about the functions of computer-aided translation systems will be based on the nine most popular translation software on the market, namely, SDL-Trados Studio 2014 and XTM v7.3, from the United Kingdom; Across and OmegaT 3.0, from Germany; Déjà Vu X2, from Spain; MemoQ 6.2, from Hungary; Wordfast Classic V6, from the United States; and Snowman V.1.33 and Yaxin V3.5, from China. The choice of these systems is based on the following considerations. First, they cover three major continents where popular computer-aided translation systems are developed and used: Europe, America, and Asia. Second, they present different specifications for different types of users. For instance, Wordfast Classic and Yaxin are standalone systems for ad hoc translators, whereas SDL-Trados Studio 2014 and Fluency are aimed at corporate users, and XTM is designed for cloud-based system subscribers.

Initiating stage

The initiating stage is the first of the five stages in the process of computer-aided translation. The functions of this stage are wizards for the creation of projects, translation memory databases, and terminology databases.

Using a computer meeting the specifications of a computer-aided translation system

For standalone and server-based systems

Before using the software, it is necessary for the user to have a computer that meets the system requirements of the software, such as requirements on the operating systems (such as Windows XP or above), processor (such as 1.6 GHz), RAM (such as 1 GB, 4 GB), and hard drive space (such as 200 MB, 400 MB).

For cloud-based systems

For cloud-based systems, the user needs to subscribe and obtain a license to be able to use their service. Licensing, as in the case of XTM (User Manual 2011: 13), depends on the type of account purchased. Named users, for instance, are freelancers and small-group accounts. The number of users is specified in the subscription agreement. Concurrent users are for language-service-providers (LSP). XTM Suite accounts allow a number of licensed users to be connected with the system at any time.

For cloud-based systems, the user needs a web address to access the system and a web browser (such as Firefox 3.6.x or Microsoft Internet Explorer 6.0, 7.0, or 8.0) to access the Internet.

Installing and logging into a system

For standalone and server-based systems

The next step involves the installation and activation of the system. For standalone and server-based systems, installation is usually completed through downloading the system from its official webpage. The user has to purchase a license from the webpage of the system, which will be sent to the user via email. The activation of a license is usually performed with some function keys, such as the License Management function in Wordfast Pro. Then, the user goes to the login page and enters the account ID, user ID, and password to access the system.

For cloud-based systems

When logging into a cloud-based system for the first time, the user will be asked to activate the computer. Then the user will receive an email with a link.

70 Functions in computer-aided translation systems

Upon clicking on the link, the system will confirm the registration of the user's computer. Then the user will be redirected to a page to change his password.

A number of measures have been designed to control access to the system. Take the cloud-based XTM system as an example. It makes settings tabs to control who logs into a system in a corporate environment.

Logon concepts

A. LOGON ATTEMPTS

The number of attempts allowed for logon is specified. When invalid attempts exceed the specified number, the account will be locked and the user will not be able to access the system.

B. LOGON PERIOD

If the user does not log into their account during the period of days specified, then the account will be locked.

C. LOGON PASSWORD

(i) Password duration   A system may specify the period for user passwords to be valid.

(ii) Reuse of previous passwords   A system can specify the number of previous passwords that cannot be used as the current password.

(iii) Password length   This specifies the number of characters required in the password.

(iv) Excluded passwords   Words such as 'User', 'Guest', 'Admin', 'Sys', 'Test', 'Pass', 'Super', or the first or last name of the user should not be used as or in a password.

(v) Password strength   There are three levels of password strength which define the mixture of characters in the password. Characters are split into four groups: (1) upper-case letters, (2) lower-case letters, (3) numbers, and (4) non-alphanumeric symbols. The password strength is 'simple' when characters from at least one group are used; 'medium', when characters from at least two of the groups are used; and 'strong', when characters from at least three of the groups are used.

Creating a profile

The first task in using a computer-aided translation system is to create a profile and put in profile settings, which normally include 'User Name' and 'Startup Options'.

Functions in computer-aided translation systems 71

Creating a project and setting specifications

When the system is ready for use, the user needs to create a profile through the 'Project Wizard', which is considered the easiest way, or 'Create New Project' by following the steps. The names of project wizards of the nine selected systems and their file extensions are given in Table 3.1.

The wizards usually contain a sequence of dialogues, including (1) Project Setup, (2) Translation Documents, (3) Translation Memories, and (4) Termbases. The following is a discussion of 'Project Setup'.

Project setup

The project information dialogue box allows the user to specify the properties of the project created, which usually include:

(A) PROJECT NAME

This is to specify a unique project name in the designated box. In some systems, such as MemoQ 6.2, it is not possible to change the name of the project after the user has created it.

(B) PROJECT LANGUAGES

This is to select the source text language and the target language pairing. The user selects and enters the source and target languages from the languages supported. It is not possible to change the languages selected after the creation of the project.

Table 3.1 Project Wizards of Nine CAT Systems

Name of the System	Name of the Project Wizard	File Extension of the Project
Across	Project Wizard	Nil (project name is shown in crossBoard)
Déjà Vu X2	New Project Wizard	*.dvprj*
MemoQ 6.2	New memoQ Project Wizard	*.mprx*
OmegaT	Create New Project	*.project*
SDL-Trados Studio 2014	Project Creation Wizard	*.sdlproj*
Snowman 1.3	New Project (新建項目)	*.stp*
Wordfast Classic 6.03t	Create Project	Nil
XTM	Project	Nil
Yaxin CAT 4.0	Create Project	Nil

72 *Functions in computer-aided translation systems*

Computer-aided translation systems normally cannot detect languages. Language detection is done by the human user. However, there are systems, such as Fluency, which have the function of automatic language detection in several languages.

In the language settings, regional variations of the selected source and target languages must be selected. For instance, if the selected 'Source Language' is 'English', the user can then select 'Region: United States' to indicate that the source text is in American English. If the selected 'Target Language' is 'Chinese', the user can then select 'Region: Hong Kong', to indicate that the translation will be in the variation of Hong Kong Chinese. Some languages present a large number of regional variations. XTM, for example, offers twenty-one variations for Spanish apart from Spanish in Spain, including Spanish in Argentina, Bolivia, Chile, Colombia, Costa Rica, Cuba, Dominican Republic, Ecuador, El Salvador, Guatemala, Honduras, Latin America, Mexico, Nicaragua, Panama, Paraguay, Peru, Puerto Rico, Uruguay, United States of America, and Venezuela.

It goes without saying that the language pair or pairs that the user selects must be supported by the system. The number of languages supported by existing systems and the number of languages available for selection vary from system to system.

(C) PROJECT DOMAIN

This is to specify a particular domain for the translation, such as education, sciences, medicine, etc., which can help finding or sorting translation units and terminology in the future.

(D) CLIENT

This is to specify the client of the translation job, which will allow the translator to identify the source of a translation unit and import, export, and manage the translation memory or translation units accordingly.

(E) PROJECT LOCATION

This is for the user to specify a location for the project files that a computer-aided translation system generates, such as C Drive.

(F) PROJECT FILES

This is the box to add all the files associated with the project.

(G) PROJECT CREATOR

This is to specify the name of the project creator, which can be changed later if necessary.

Functions in computer-aided translation systems 73

(H) PROJECT CREATION DATE

This is the system date set in the operating system, which cannot be modified by the user.

(I) PROJECT COMPLETION DATE

This is the date when the project is to be completed. It is known variously as 'Due Date'.

All the project settings can be edited by opening the edit project dialogue box, as in the case of Fluency. The user can add files, remove files, and edit the filters. Click 'Save' to finish the editing.

Data preparation stage

Data collection and data creation are the two main parts of the data preparation stage. Data collection is manually done, whereas data creation relies on the use of computers, scanners, and speech recognition systems. Computers, together with keyboards, are used to key in documents and copy files and webpages; scanners are used to create electronic texts from printed documents; and speech recognition systems are used to produce electronic texts from verbal utterances.

Data collection

The collection of relevant data to be stored in a computer processing system is the first step in the translation process. Relevant data refer to materials relating to the projects to be conducted on fields to be covered.

Data creation

Creation of electronic files

Data creation in the context of computer-aided translation involves the production of electronic files with the use of tools such as computers, scanners, and speech recognition systems, which are not intrinsic components of computer-aided translation tools, as well as the creation of terminology and translation memory databases with the use of tools or functions within the translation system.

Computers

It goes without saying that only electronic files can be mechanically processed. One of the most popular and simple ways of creating or capturing electronic

74   Functions in computer-aided translation systems

texts for computer processing is the copy-and-paste method. Copying takes place in the interface of a computer system through the use of the key-combinations of Ctrl+C, or by using some other method, such as by the use of a context menu or a toolbar button. Once data has been stored into the area of memory referred to as the clipboard, one can paste the contents of the clipboard into the desired destination using the key combinations Ctrl+V, or other methods dependent on the system.

Another method is to key in printed, handwritten, stenographed, and transcribed texts into the computer to transfer it to an electronic format (Chen and Lee 2000; Tsai 2006). Handwritten texts, especially those in cursive script, are totally unrecognizable to a computer. In fact, the writing systems of the natural languages in the world are, in general, problematic for algorithmic recognition. For texts written in shorthand, keyboarding is about the most reliable way of inputting stenographed texts. Though there have been as many as 43 systems, the most widely known form of shorthand was the Pitman shorthand method, originally developed by Isaac Pitman in 1837. Its popularity, however, has been increasingly superseded in the United Kingdom by Teeline Shorthand, a recommended system of the National Council for the Training of Journalists in New Zealand, and in the United States by the method developed by J.R. Gregg in 1888. For this type of text, it is necessary to find a person who knows the system to transcribe shorthand into longhand through typing to create a digital text. The key-in method is also applied to the transcription of recordings or audio information.

To key in a text is one of the most frequently used methods in e-text creation. This inputting method, however, is time-consuming and error-prone. To proofread a typed text also takes a long time and needs considerable effort (Kugler 1995: 109; Langlais, Foster and Lapalme 2000: 135–141).

Scanners

Scanning is another of the data-capturing methods in computer-aided translation. Some systems include a built-in scanning or Optical Character Recognition (OCR) function to turn paper-based texts into digital texts (Kolak and Resnik 2005; Miller, Boisen, Schwartz, Stone, and Weischedel 2000: 316–324; Nagata 2000).

The quality of scanning is related to the condition of the document to be scanned. Poorly handwritten documents or documents which are faded, blurred, or creased normally generate poor results.

Speech recognition systems

Speech recognition systems are used to produce the source language text. The success of speech translation is closely related to speech recognition through the use of speech technology and some speech recognition systems (Arranz, Comelles, and Farwell 2005; Arranz, Comelles, Farwell, Nadeu, Padrell, Febrer,

Functions in computer-aided translation systems 75

Alexander, and Peterson 2004: 7–16; Fletcher 1997; Gao, Erdogan, Li, Goel, and Picheny 2001: 503–506; Guo 2002: 337; IBM Speech Recognition Group 1985; Lee, Hon, and Reddy 1990: 35–45; Lee, Lo, and Ching 2002: 259–265; Lowerre and Reddy 1980: 340–360; Morii, Niyada, Fujii, and Hoshimi 1985: 866–869; Nakamura, Markov, Jitsuhiro, Zhang, Yamamoto, and Kikui 2004). It also hinges on speech processing, speech synthesis, and speech generation. The entire process of translating a spoken text from one language into another is speech translation (Bangalore and Riccardi 2000: 52–59; Lazzari 2000), which requires the use of speech translation systems (Bernth 2003: 1–7; Block, Schachtl, and Gehrke 2000: 394–410), and there are works on the evaluations of these systems (Blanchon, Boitet, and Besacier 2004; Cavar, Kussner, and Tidhar 2000: 597–610; Koehn, Axelrod, Mayne, Callison-Burch, Osborne, and Talbot 2005; Lee and Roukos 2004; Mouldovan, Pasca, Harabagiu, and Surdeanu 2002: 33–40; Somers and Sugita 2003).

Speech recognition systems are used to input verbally into the computer to create electronic texts (Barnett, Corrada, Gao, Gillik, Ito, Lowe, Manganaro, and Peskin 1996: 2191–2194). This technology, also known as Automatic Speech Recognition (ASR), allows a computer to identify the words that a person speaks into a microphone or telephone. There are basically three kinds of speech: isolated words, connected speech, and continuous speech. To enhance the effectiveness of speech recognition, it would be ideal to use isolated-word speech, segmenting each word from the next by silence. This is easier for speech recognition, but it sounds unnatural and is operationally difficult and annoying to listen to. An intermediate level of speech recognition is connected speech, which consists of words strung together. The last level is continuous speech, whose words are all connected without silence between them (Chow, Dunham, Kimball, Krasner, Kubala, Makhoul, Roucos, and Schwartz 1987: 89–92).

To many, a most convenient inputting method would be to voice in a text instead of keying it in. The use of speech as an inputting method is important in several ways. First, speech input is natural because it requires neither special equipment, but a microphone, nor special training or abilities. Second, speech input is convenient, as it allows fast and comfortable communication at a rate of 120 to 210 English words per minute without encumbering the hands or eyes. Third, speech input is universal because nearly everybody can speak, except those who are vocally handicapped.

Ideally, a computer should be able to recognize with 100 per cent accuracy all words that are intelligibly spoken by any person, independent of vocabulary size, noise, speaker's characteristics and accent, or channel conditions. Moreover, it would be ideal to achieve this in real-time too. The main issue in speech recognition is thus the search for the best hypothesized word sequence when given an input feature sequence. Speech recognition is, nonetheless, hindered by noisy environments, such as a noisy factory floor, people talking simultaneously, and a poor telephone connection, and decoding is difficult

76 Functions in computer-aided translation systems

due to segmentation (deciding where one word ends and the next begins) and variability (variations in how an individual word can be pronounced – loud or soft, fast or slow, with rising or falling intonation).

Importing source text/document

Another way of text creation is to import source document or source text into the source text pane. There are two ways to do text importation: loading it from the file menu or copying and pasting it. In the former, a source text, provided that it is part of a file, can be selected, loaded, and imported into the source text pane. In the latter, the text can be copied from one location and pasted onto the source text pane.

Creation of terminology databases

In computer-aided translation, terminology refers to the terms in the source language created from project-based documents (Aráujo 2000; Bowker 2006a, 2006b; Gillam, Ahmad, Dalby, and Coz 2002; Maia 2003: 43–53; Pearson 2000: 92–105; Quirion and Lanthier 2006: 107–118; Sager 1998a: 255–258, 1998b: 258–262; Zauberga 2005: 107–116). In Across, it is defined as 'the total stock of concepts and the respective terms in a subject area' (Manual 2012: 457). Glossary, on the other hand, refers to the translated terms in the target language. Definition, lastly, describes or defines the terms.

Terminology can also be interpreted in a larger context to refer to the study of the body of specialized words relating to a particular subject which are processed electronically. Terminology in translation technology covers a multitude of areas, such as terminology recognition (Bolshakova 2001; Okazaki and Ananiadou 2006; Sui 2002: 318–322), terminology acquisition (Ahmad 1995: 51–76; Kumar and Banu 2004), terminology extraction (Aha and Gupta 2004; Chantrier 2005; Mohit and Narayanan 2003; Nakagawa 2004; Piao, Sun, Rayson, and Qi 2006; Smith 2003; Vintar 2001: 121–132; Yamaoto, Matsumoto, and Kitamura 2001: 87–94; Zielinski 2005), the creation of a so-called 'terminology bank' (Cabré Castellvi 2006: 93–106; Nkwenti-Azeh 1998: 249–251 Yu, Zan, Liu, and Wen 2002: 45–51), terminology processing (McDonald and Brew 2004: 17–24; Oh, Lee, and Choi 2000; Wacholder, Klavans, and Evans 2000: 302–309), terminology management (Austermühln 2001: 102–123; Bernardi, Bocsák, and Porsiel 2005: 41–49; Briscoe 2004; Chiu and Jernudd 2002: 95–114; Jaekel 2000: 159–171; Jones 1999; Wright and Budin 1997; Zielinski 2005), and the systems used for terminology management (Ball 2003; Bowker 2002a: 77–91; Pux 2003; Sestier 2001). All the above are constituent parts of 'terminology translation' (Fang, Hao and Nishino 2006).

The creation of databases, in the context of computer-aided translation, is based on project-specific texts or documents of a period adequate for the preparation of a comprehensive terminology and a translation memory database.

Functions in computer-aided translation systems 77

Terminology also refers to the study of the body of specialized words relating to a particular subject, which are processed electronically to be used in computer-aided translation.

There are several ways to create a terminology database. For instance, a computer-aided translation system can analyse a project and automatically extract words and short phrases from it. By displaying them in order of frequency, important terms and expressions are easily spotted, while non-relevant ones can be eliminated.

Term extraction tools

There are term extraction tools within the computer-aided translation systems in the form of both term managers, as well independent term creation tools, not linked to any particular computer-aided translation system (Bowker 2003: 49–65; Thurmair 2003). Terms can, thus, be extracted by the use of tools, within or without translation software.

(A) SYSTEM TERMINOLOGY CREATION TOOLS

The terms extracted and stored form terminology databases, otherwise known as 'term banks' or 'terminology banks'. These databases contain translations of single words or short phrases and are used to translate all the input terms and improve the quality of fuzzy matches. The way terms in a translation system are handled is known as terminology management, which refers specifically to the documentation, storage, manipulation, and presentation of a specialized terminology or glossary in a computer-aided translation system. There are terminology management systems for the user to create, maintain, and search for terms in bilingual or multilingual databases.

(B) INDEPENDENT TERMINOLOGY CREATION TOOLS

As aforementioned, there are also tools that can be used separately to create terminology databases. One of these tools, WordSmith, enables the user to find out how words are used in certain texts. This application offers a 'Wordlist' function that generates wordlists in alphabetical and frequency order, enabling the user to compare texts lexically. It also provides statistics, such as the total number of words, the length of the words, and the number of sentences.

Functions for operating terminology databases

(A) ADD AND SAVE

This function allows the user to add new entries. There are also functions to quick-add entry terms, such as 'Add Term – Quick' in XTM.

78 *Functions in computer-aided translation systems*

In order to add a term to a terminology database while working within an editing environment, the user must select the word and choose the function key 'Add Term'. The chosen word will then appear in the 'Source' field. To enter a translation for the term, the user can either type the translation in the 'Target' field, or select the translated term in the target segment supplied by the system, click 'Choose Selected', and subsequently click 'Save Term'.

During interactive computer-aided translation, translators can add new terms into termbases in synchrony. The disadvantage for SDL-Trados, a popular computer-aided translation system, is that there is only one termbase set as the default termbase, which accepts the adding of new terms. Suppose that the translator opens two termbases: Termbase A as the default one and Termbase B, the non-default one. If he/she wants to add new terms into Termbase B, he/she has to re-set the default termbase as Termbase B. However, in the later translation work, Termbase A would provide more translation suggestions than Termbase B. The translator therefore has to discard the newly set default termbase and change back to Termbase A.

(B) EXTRACT AND SAVE

Some systems, such as SDL-Trados MultiTerm, feature tools that can automatically identify all the potential terms in a corpus and subsequently present a list of candidates to the user for verification. SDL-Trados MultiTerm has functions of extraction and storage. SDL MultiTerm 7 Extract, for instance, performs automatic monolingual and bilingual term extraction with manual options. The approved extracted terms can then be transferred on-the-fly (while the computer is running) to an SDL MultiTerm termbase to be verified by a terminologist or domain expert.

(C) EXTRACT AND CONVERT

SDL MultiTerm Convert helps to establish termbases. Convert can change terminology data in seven file formats to MultiTerm XML format, namely MultiTerm 5 (*.mtw*), Olif XML (*.xml*), SDL Termbase Online/Desktop (*.tdb* and *.mdb*), Spreadsheet or Exchange (*.txt* and *.csv*), and Microsoft Excel (*.xls*) format. Compared to Wordfast, which only accepts TXT files, SDL MultiTerm Convert assists users to enlarge the termbase more quickly and efficiently.

(D) EXPORT

This function allows the user to export terminology databases.

(E) IMPORT

This function allows the user to import terminology.

(F) REPORT

Some systems, such as Across, can create a terminology report.

(G) SEARCH

The Search bar offers various options for finding entries and terms.

(i) Alphabetic search for terminology starting with a certain letter or number;
(ii) all search for all existing terms in alphabetic order;
(iii) filter selection in search filters to do quick filter, user-defined filter, or filter set;
(iv) wildcard search to find terms with the same roots;
(v) fuzzy search for similar terms;
(vi) entry search with the entry ID;
(vii) concordance search for the context and translation of the corresponding words; and
(viii) search the selected word in Google.

(H) TRANSLATE

Some systems, such as Déjà Vu X, also provide tools to automatically translate the lexicons, thus instantly generating terminology databases from existing projects. The final translated lexicons can be easily validated, making the implantation of standard terminology a feasible task.

Terminology database structure

A terminology database usually has the following fields:

(1) *Term*, which refers to the term in the source language;
(2) *Glossary*, which refers to the translation of the term in the target language;
(3) *Definition*, a description or definition of the term;
(4) *Locale*, which refers to the locale of the source term;
(5) *Domain*, which refers to the domain of the source term;
(6) *Project*, which refers to the project which the term is associated with;
(7) *Client*, which refers to the client for the term in question;
(8) *Part of Speech*, the part of speech that the term belongs to;
(9) *Term Type*, the type of term (abbreviation, acronym, etc.) with values as specified by TBX-Basic;
(10) *Source*, the source of the gloss/definition; and
(11) *Note*, which indicates any additional information about the term.

80 *Functions in computer-aided translation systems*

Features of terminology databases

By making use of the materials stored in terminology databases, translators can benefit from computer-aided translation tools in the following:

(1) Terminological consistency, which means that the same term is always used with the same sense, and the same object or action is always described by the same term.
(2) Access rights to terminology databases can be limited. Customer-specific terminologists can only access the terminology of one customer, while global experts can access all the terms in the system for all customers. The access rights include 'add terminology', 'export terminology', 'import terminology', 'modify terminology', and 'view terminology'.
(3) Some systems allow the use of multiple terminology databases. Wordfast Classic, for example, has three simultaneous glossaries.

Storage of terminology databases

Different systems use different names to designate their terminology databases. Table 3.2 shows the files extensions of the eleven selected systems.

Size of terminology databases

The maximum size of a terminology database varies from system to system. For Wordfast, it is voluntarily limited to 250,000 entries. For most systems, the size of terminology databases is close to unlimited.

Table 3.2 Designations of Terminology Databases of Nine CAT Systems

Name of the System	*Name of the Terminology Database Function*	*File Extension of the Terminology Database*
Across 5.5	crossTerm	Nil
Déjà Vu X2	Lexicon	*.dvtdb*
Fluency Translation Suite 2013	Personal Terminology	*Nil*
MemoQ 6.2	Term Bases	*.mtb*
OmegaT 2.6	Glossary	*.txt*
SDL-Trados Studio 2011	SDL-Trados MultiTerm	*.sdltb*
Snowman 1.3	Project Dictionary 項目詞典	*.txt*
WordfastClassic 6.0	Glossary	*.txt*
XTM Cloud	Terminology	Nil
Yaxin CAT 4.0	Terminology 詞庫	.yxd

Functions in computer-aided translation systems 81

Creating translation memory databases

The process of creating a translation memory database goes through the stages of segmentation and alignment, involving the use of tools, such as concordancers and aligners.

Segmentation

Segmentation consists of sentence separation in machine translation or computer-aided translation (Xu, Zens, and Ney 2005: 280–287). The purpose of segmentation is to divide a text into easily manageable segments. A segment is a predefined unit of a source text that can be aligned with its corresponding translation in a machine translation system or a computer-aided translation tool. This is a function that splits the source text into segments using the rules and exceptions that the user has previously set for the project's source language. This function also allows the user to join the sentences based on corresponding translations.

Some languages are easier to segment than others. Chinese, which has no interval marks or word boundaries between two successive characters or phrases in a Chinese sentence, is particularly difficult to segmentate (Huang 1997; Wang, Deng, and Zou 2006; Yu, Zhu, and Duan 2000: 125–132). That explains the large number of publications on issues related to Chinese automatic segmentation (Hou and Sun 1996: 68–72; Li, Yi, Yang, and Sun 2002: 329–333; Qu W. 2002: 118; Sun M. 2001: 20–40; Sun and T'sou 1995: 40–46).

Most computer-aided translation systems consider the full stop as a symbol that ends a segment. However, as full stops can also be used in abbreviations, they may be the cause of invalid segmentations. To avoid this, the user can add abbreviations to the translation memory so that they are recognized in the text and do not affect normal segmentation.

Alignment

Segmentation is followed by alignment. Whereas segmentation involves breaking down a text into small units, such as sentences, alignment involves matching the source and target texts segment by segment, resulting in translation pairs or units. Alignment can, therefore, be defined as 'a process of matching up a source text and the target text segment by segment into translation pairs' (Chan 2004: 8). These pairs will be stored in a database, the translation memory, making it possible to reuse previously translated segments in future translations.

There are five levels of alignment: word, phrase, sentence, paragraph, and text alignment. Word alignment refers to the alignment of a source-text word with its translation in a target text in a translation memory system (Ayan and Dorr 2006; Cherry and Lin 2003: 88–95; Goutte, Yamada, and Gaussier 2004:

82   *Functions in computer-aided translation systems*

502–509; Kashioka 2005; Lin and Cherry 2003; Lü, Zhao, Li, and Yang 2001: 108–115; Sun, Jin, Du, and Sun 2000: 110–116; Taskar, Simon, and Dan 2005; Wu and Wang 2004: 262–271). Phrase alignment, as indicated in the name itself, refers to the alignment of a phrase in the source text with its equivalent in the target text (de Gispert, Marino, and Crego 2004; Deng and Byrne 2005; Ion, Ceauşu, and Tufiş 2006; Kim, Yoon, and Ra 2004: 306–317; Watanabe, Imamura, and Sumita 2002: 188–198; Zhang and Vogel 2005: 294–301). Sentence alignment involves the alignment of a source-text sentence with its translation in a target text in a translation memory system (Barzilay and Elhadad 2003; Chuang, You, and Chang 2002: 11–30; Moore 2002: 135–144; Nelken and Shieber 2006; Pang, Knight, and Marcu 2003: 102–109; Zhao, Zechner, Vogel, and Waibel 2003). Paragraph alignment consists in the alignment of phrases in the source text with their equivalents in the target text. Finally, text alignment concerns the alignment of bilingual texts so that the paragraphs, sentences, and words are all identified (Oakes and McEnery 2000: 1–37; Ribeiro, Lopes, and Mexia 2000: 30–39; Simard, Foster, Hannan, Macklovitch, and Plamondon 2000: 38–64). In all levels, alignment tools or functions are required for the creation of bilingual text databases where sentences (or phrases) of source texts are linked to corresponding text segments of a target language (Deng and Byrne 2006; Ittycheriah and Roukos 2005; Ma X. 2006; Zhang, Ma, and Isahara 2005).

The alignment workflow involves six steps: (1) creation of a new alignment project in the alignment box; (2) addition of source files and target files; (3) alignment of the source and target files; (4) manual verification of the alignment; (5) saving of the alignment project and exporting the alignment results; and (6) when working on a new project, importing the alignment results into a workbench. An alignment tool, such as the Alignment Editor in SDL-Trados 2011, allows the user to post-process or manipulate the segment pairs by combining, reassigning, deleting, or changing the aligned contents.

Translation memory

The definition of translation memory is not a complicated issue. A definition of translation memory is provided by the Expert Advisory Group on Language Engineering Standards, EAGLES, and reads as follows: 'a multilingual text archive containing segmented, aligned, parsed, and classified multilingual texts, allowing storage and retrieval of aligned multilingual text segments against various search conditions' (EAGLES 1996). A translation memory database, therefore, refers to an electronic file or database that contains aligned pairs of source and target language segments. This database is built by sending sentence pairs to it when a translator is translating, by importing pairs from external databases, and by aligning separate source and target text files. The database that is formed is known as a translation memory database (Fabricz 2005: 34–36).

Some important concepts about translation memories will be provided below:

(A) FEATURES OF TRANSLATION MEMORY DATABASES

A translation memory database, which is created either as a project file to be used in a specific project or as a standalone file to be used with a specific project as well as other related projects, has the following features. First, it is a reusable bilingual database. Second, it has exact or fuzzy matches. For each new segment to be translated, the system scans the database for a previous source segment that matches the new segment exactly (exact match) or approximately (fuzzy match). Third, it contains possible usable translations from exact and fuzzy matches. Fourth, the translator has the choice of accepting, modifying, or rejecting the suggested translations. Fifth, it is a sentence storehouse, as it is a database that stores sentences already translated in a translation memory system. Sixth, it can be shared by a number of users over a local area network, as in the case of Wordfast. Seventh, it is an exchange database because according to the OSCAR agreement, which was an agreement for a common interchange format developed by Open Standards for Container/Content Allowing Reuse (OSCAR) of the Localization Industry Standards Association (LISA), translation memory exchange is allowed, and this is known as Translation Memory Exchange (TMX), the standard format in the industry. Some systems, such as Wordfast Classic, have the function of 'Export to TMX' to create a TMX eport of the current translation memeory database. Eighth, it can be propagated. Some systems, such as XTM, have the function of translation memory propagation, which means if a translator translates a segment that is repeated later in the same document or in another document in the same project, the system will automatically insert the translation in the repeated segment. This applies to fuzzy matches and multiple translators working on the same document.

(B) STRUCTURE OF A TRANSLATION MEMORY DATABASE

A translation memory database usually has the following 11 fields: (1) *Source*, which refers to the source segment; (2) *Target*, which refers to the target segment; (3) *Source Locale*, which refers to the locale of the source segment; (4) *Target Locale*, which refers to the locale of the target segment; (5) *Domain*, which refers to the domain of the source text; (6) *Project*, which refers to the project with which the text is associated; (7) *Client*, which refers to the client for the text in question; (8) *Creation Date*, which is the date when the translation memory was saved; (9) *Change Date* is the date when this memory was last changed; (10) *Property Type*, which refers to properties that the user wants to relate to this text, such as product title and file type; and (11) *Note*, which refers to any additional information about the segment.

84   *Functions in computer-aided translation systems*

Table 3.3 Designations of Translation Memory Databases of Nine CAT Systems

Name of the System	Name of the Translation Memory Function	File Extension of the Translation Memory Database
Across 5.5	crossTank	import: *tmx* export: *tmx* 1.4
Déjà Vu X2	Translation Memory	*.dvmdb*
MemoQ 6.2	Translation Memories	Import: *.csvc, tmx* Export: csv
OmegaT 2.6	Fuzzy Matches	*.tmx*
SDL-Trados Studio 2013	Translation Memories	*.sdltm* Import: *.tmx, tmz.gz, sdlxliff, .ttx.* Export: *.tmx, tmz.gz*
Snowman 1.3	項目記憶庫 (Project Translation Memory Database)	Import: *.tmx, stm, xls*
Wordfast Classic 6.0	Translation Memory	Nil
XTM	TM	Nil
Yaxin CAT 4.0	記憶庫	Nil

(C)   STORAGE OF TRANSLATION MEMORY DATABASES

Different designations for translation memory databases have been used by different computer-aided translation systems in data storage, such as *crossTank* in Across, which is defined as a central databank for the storage of translated sentences or translation units.

Table 3.3 provides a list of names for translation memory databases in different systems.

(D)   SIZE OF TRANSLATION MEMORY DATABASES

The size of translation memory databases varies from system to system. Wordfast Classic, for example, can store up to 1,000,000 units per single translation memory. The user can create and maintain as many translation memories as the user wants, in as many languages as the user wants.

(E)   TYPES OF TRANSLATION MEMORY

There are different types of translation memory, some of which are introduced below.

Functions in computer-aided translation systems 85

(1) Background translation memory This is one of the three types of translation memories offered by Wordfast; the other two being Translation Memory (TM) and Very Large Translation Memory (VLTM).

A background translation memory is a read-only translation memory, which Wordfast will scan for an exact match before scanning the translation memory in use. If both the background translation memory and the current translation memory yield translation units with the same match rate, the former's translation units will be displayed. It is worth noting, however, that Wordfast's user can specify or change the order of preference for the three types of translation memories within the system (User Manual of Wordfast Classic Version 6.0 2013: 29). A background translation memory can be created by selecting a translation memory database other than the active translation memory. It provides exact matches but not fuzzy matches.

(2) File-based translation memory This refers to a type of translation memory which is based on a group of files in a computer-aided translation system.

(3) Master translation memory This refers to a big translation memory ranging from 100,000 to 1,000,000 translation units.

(4) Server-based translation memory This refers to a type of translation memory that is based on a group of databased tables on a database server in a network environment. This kind of translation memory has led to the creation of the Alchemy's Language Exchange, which 'empowers a company's translation and localization teams to share server-based translation memory resources, within networked and international environments, on a global level' (http:// www.alchemysoftware.ie).

(5) Very Large Translation Memory The Very Large Translation Memory (VLTM) is a type of translation memory in Wordfast, which also features a background translation memory and a regular translation memory (Champollion 2006). According to the definition given by Wordfast, the VLTM is 'the first public, open, unrestricted, free, anonymous TM server that serves matches from a set of large TMs'. To enable the VLTM, the computer must be connected to the Internet with the user's workgroup ID. The language pair specifications will then be displayed. The user can choose between 'See Only Workgroup TUs' or 'Use Only for Concordance Search' and can also specify or change the translation memory order.

There are three options for the VLTM. If the users activate their VLTM without a workgroup ID, they will only receive translation units from the VLTM. Alternatively, if they use the VLTM with a workgroup ID and a password, they will be able to read and write in the VLTM while preserving confidentiality. Finally, if they put in the word 'Donor' in the workgroup ID, their translation memory databases will not be confidential, as they will donate their translations to the VLTM.

86 *Functions in computer-aided translation systems*

(6) Working translation memory This refers to a small translation memory which has all the translation units close to the text. To prepare this database, a computer-aided translation system segments the text into translation units according to the segmentation strategies of the product. Subsequently, it retrieves the translation units and places all matches above the pre-set threshold value into the working translation memory.

It is important that there is translation memory compatibility among different systems. The tabular translation memory format of Wordfast, for example, allows for the integration of Trados, SDLX, or Déjà Vu translation memory files.

Security

Security in the context of translation is computational and administrative. Administrative security, as in the case of Wordfast, refers to the assignment of specific rights and privileges to individual translators or linguistic teams by the project manager.

This is a function that by default provides the most basic user-based security feature of tracking any user's activities. Every process that any user performs in Déjà Vu X is associated with his or her computer or login name. The project owner can also enable the advanced security features that limit users to working in only one language combination and prevent them from performing any activities other than translation.

A secure environment can be created by using the options in a computer-aided translation system for configuring the security to the user's needs.

Data processing stage

Data processing is about the computational treatment of data. In other words, it concerns the handling of data in different formats and languages.

Import of files

As there are so many formats for machine processing, computer-aided translation systems usually have file filters to make sure that the file or files that the user wants to translate in a variety of formats can be processed by the system according to some file filtering rules.

Data analysis

When the filtering process is done, the next step in a translation project involves analysing how many words need to be translated and how many can be pre-translated using a translation memory. The function of analysis is a standard feature in a translation system, such as Analysis Expert in Alchemy Publisher.

Functions in computer-aided translation systems 87

It goes without saying that analysis is important in both human and machine translation. The use of concordancers has facilitated greatly the work of analysis. Generally and computationally, it is necessary to conduct source analysis (Bernth and McCord 2000: 89–99; Mitamura, Baker, Svoboda, and Nyberg 2003; Nyberg, Mitamura, Svoboda, Ko, Baker, and Micher 2003), text analysis (Hou M. 2001: 204–210; Taylor and Baldry 2001: 277–305; Wonsever, and Minel 2001; Yarowsky, Ngai, and Wicentowski 2001: 109–116), natural language analysis (Ishikawa and Sugimura 1992: 55–66), and translation analysis (Isabelle, Dymetman, Foster, Jutras, Macklovitch, Perrault, Ren, and Simard 1993: 201–217). More specifically and linguistically, it is necessary to perform linguistic analysis (Chen G. 2000: 63–71; Feng Z. 1994: 79–121), including morphological (Goldwater and McClosky 2005; Tatsuo and Matsumoto 2000: 232–238; Yarowsky and Wicentowski 2000), semantic (Atserias, Castellón, Civit, and Rigau 2000; Bestgen 2006: 5–12; Choi, Wiemer-Hastings, and Moore 2001; Feng Z. 2004: 467–565; Nastase and Szpakowicz 2005: 303–314; Paolillo 2004; Reeder 2006), syntactical (Gelbukh, Sidorov, Han, and Hernández-Rubio 2004: 240–244; Paolillo 2004), and sentential analyses (Tang, Ji, Nie, and Yang 2004: 41–44). Automatic linguistic analysis is generally considered as a basis for quality translation. What need to be studied are the units and tools of analysis.

It has been generally recognized that 'concordancing' is an effective way of analysing the source text (Ulrych 1997: 421–435). Works have been written on three different concordancers, i.e., Multiconcord, ParaConc, and WordSmith, and also on three types of linguistic concordancers, i.e., Bilingual, Multilingual, and Parallel (Barlow 1992, 1996, 2004; Comess 2002: 307–326; King and Woolls 1996: 459–466; Langlois 1996: 34–42; Woolls 1997; Woolls 2000: 116–133). Concordancing is the first stage of the technology-oriented translation procedure where statistical and lexical information of the source text are given in a systematic manner.

Tools to help data processing

Dictionaries and concordancers are used to gather the information we need to process data. Dictionaries can be project-based dictionaries, prepared by the user or provider; built-in system dictionaries, provided by the developer; and other non-system dictionaries available to the user. Concordancers, in turn, can be monolingual, for source analysis, or bilingual and multilingual, for finding the translations of terms and expressions.

Dictionaries and translation

Bilingual or multilingual dictionaries are a necessary evil for translators (Chan 2004). These dictionaries provide clear explanations and equivalents to the expressions that the translator does not know. Furthermore, they enlarge a translator's active vocabulary and give him or her potential equivalents to produce the optimal

88 Functions in computer-aided translation systems

equivalents (Varantola 1998: 179–192). The same holds true for computer-aided translation (Gliozzo and Strapparava 2006).

Before we discuss the role of dictionaries in translation technology, an explanation of the differences among dictionaries, glossaries, and terminologies may be in order. According to the *Webster's Third New International Dictionary*, 'a dictionary is a reference book containing words usually alphabetically arranged along with information about their forms, pronunciations, functions, etymologies, meanings, and syntactical and idiomatic uses' (Gove 1971: 627); 'a glossary is a collection of terms limited to a special area of knowledge'; and 'a terminology is a collection of technical or special terms or expressions used in a business, art, science, or special subject' (Gove 1971: 967). A bilingual or multilingual dictionary is, therefore, a collection of known meanings of words in two or more language; a bilingual or multilingual glossary is a list of bilingual or multilingual translations, respectively, of keywords and phrases in specialized areas; whereas a bilingual or multilingual terminology is a vocabulary of technical terms used in a particular field, subject, science, or art. It is clear that in computer-aided translation usage, the terms 'glossary' and 'terminology' are commonly interchangeable.

It is true that some computer-aided translation systems, such as Snowman, are linked to browsers for access to online dictionaries. The choice of a dictionary, however, has to be made with prudence, based on the reputation of the source, the eminence of the editor, and the quality of the equivalents provided.

The dictionaries available to the translator can be divided into different categories. They can be classified according to the coverage of contents, into general dictionaries, such as *Oxford Dictionary English* (Stevenson 2010), and specialized dictionaries, such as *The Penguin Dictionary of Economics* (Bannock, Baxter and Davis 1998). They can also be divided by their function, for instance, etymological dictionaries and pronunciation dictionaries. A typical example of the former is *Klein's Comprehensive Etymological Dictionary of the English Language (Unabridged)* (Klein 1971), and of the latter, *Cambridge English Pronouncing Dictionary* (Jones 2011). Dictionaries can also be divided by language, such as the monolingual dictionary of the *Xiandai Hanyu cihai* 《現代漢語辭海》 (*A Dictionary of Contemporary Chinese*) (Editorial Committee 2003), the bilingual dictionary of *Xin shidai YingHan da cidian* 《新時代英漢大詞典》 (*New Age English-Chinese Dictionary*) (Zhang B. 2004), and the *Multilingual Dictionary of IT Security: English-German-French-Spanish-Italian* (Vollnhals 1999). Dictionaries can be categorized according to the medium, e.g., electronic dictionaries, paper dictionaries, and online dictionaries. Another method of classification is according to the period, such as the Middle English dictionary *A Concise Dictionary of Middle English* (Mayhew and Skeat 2004) or the historical principles dictionary of *The Shorter Oxford English Dictionary* (Stevenson 2007). Dictionaries can further be divided according to presentation, such as the alphabetical dictionary of *Longman Dictionary of English Language and Culture* (Longman 2003), the classified dictionary of

Functions in computer-aided translation systems 89

the *HanYing fenlei Chatu cidian* 《漢英分類插圖詞典》 (*A Classified and Illustrated Chinese-English Dictionary*) (Compiling Group 1981), the reverse dictionary of *Hanying niyin cidian* 《漢英逆引詞典》 (*A Reverse Chinese-English Dictionary*) (Yu Y. 1986), and the visual dictionary of the *Merriam-Webster's Visual Dictionary* (Corbeil and Archambault 2006). Another categorization involves the size, such as an abridged dictionary, concise dictionary, or pocket dictionaries. Finally, dictionaries can be divided according to the target users, examples of which are the elementary and advanced learner's dictionary of *Niujing gaojie YingHan shuangjie cidian* 《牛津高階英漢雙解詞典》 (*The Oxford Advanced Learners English-Chinese Dictionary*) (Hornby 2013); or according to the theme, such as the thesaurus dictionary of *Bartlett's Roget's Thesaurus* (Barlett 2003) and the synonym dictionary of *Pocket Oxford Dictionary and Thesaurus* (Hawker 2008).

Parts of a dictionary entry

Dictionaries are composed of entries, which in turn contain different parts. These parts are introduced below in alphabetical order.

Abbreviation: Abbreviations are used as a space-saving device in a dictionary to represent frequently used words, such as words for varieties of languages (e.g., BrE for British English), countries (e.g., N.Z. for New Zealand), and fields (e.g., *mus* for music).

Citation source: This refers to the reference from which a citation is quoted in an entry.

Cross-reference: A cross-reference highlights another entry holding relevant information, or some other part of the dictionary where this may be found. It helps users find the word they want, or find other useful information about it.

Date of Definition: This refers to the change of meanings over time by indicating the definitions of an entry according to certain chronological order.

Definition: This is a description of the meaning of the headword in a particular sense. It helps users understand the word.

Entry subdivision: The subdivision is meant to break up an entry into sections or subsections, according to the dictionary sense, making it easier for the user to read and find what is being sought.

Example phrase: The examples illustrate how the word is used in a phrase.

Frequency data: This shows how common the headword is in a general corpus. The order by which definitions are arranged is an indication of the frequency of the entry.

Gloss: This is an informal explanation of a certain word or phrase.

Grammar marker: This is to use a code to indicate grammatical features, such as the countable/uncountable character of nouns or the transitivity of verbs. It helps users use the word correctly.

90 *Functions in computer-aided translation systems*

Headword: A headword/character is a word or term, often in a distinctive type, placed at the beginning of an entry. The main function of a headword is to help users find the word or term they want.

Homograph number: This is a superscript number that is placed on a headword to indicate homographs. It tells the user to look for other identical headwords.

Illustration: Illustrations, in the forms of pictures, diagrams, and graphs, are meant to facilitate the comprehension of certain terms through visual aids.

Inflected form: Inflected forms give other grammatical forms of the same headword, indicating how to use the word correctly.

Linguistic label: A linguistic label is a code that refers to the style, register, domain, and regional variety of the headword and helps users use the expression in the correct context.

Multiword unit: This refers to the idiomatic multiword expressions containing the headword, which include idioms, set expressions, compound words, etc.

Notes on alternate expressions: This part provides notes on the use of other expressions for the highlighted word(s).

Notes on collocation: This part provides notes on collocations of common words.

Notes on countries: These notes identify important countries and explain their significance in the context of the immediate text.

Notes on culture: These notes explain the cultural elements in the text.

Notes on events: These notes identify important events and explain their significance in the context of the immediate text.

Notes on geography: These notes explain the geographical elements in the text.

Notes on grammar: These notes provide grammatical information on entries.

Notes on landmarks: These notes identify important physical units and explain their significance in the context of the immediate text.

Notes on language: This is to provide information on languages of the world.

Notes on literature: These notes provide information on literature and related issues.

Notes on nationalities: These notes provide information on races and nationalities.

Notes on organizations: These notes identify important organizations and explain their significance in the context of the immediate text.

Notes on personalities: These notes identify important personalities and explain their significance as far as the immediate text is concerned.

Notes on usage: This part shows how the headword is used in order to help users avoid confusion in the usage or meaning of the word. It provides a broad background for the user to have a better understanding of the word, or the cultural differences between the source language and the target language terms, in the case of bilingual dictionaries.

Functions in computer-aided translation systems 91

Part-of-speech marker: This marker indicates the part of speech of the headword with a code.

Phonetic transcription: This shows how the headword is pronounced according to the International Phonetic Alphabet (IPA).

Run-on: This refers to a lemma morphologically related to the headword, listed at the end of an entry with no further information given about it. It simply tells the user that the word exists.

Sense indicator: This is a kind of 'signpost' to indicate a specific sense of the headword.

Structure: This is a type of syntactic complementation or construction that is needed in order to be able to use the expression correctly.

Subdivision counter: In this part, a number or letter is used to indicate the start of a new section or subsection to show a sense of the word.

Sub-headword: This is a lemma that is morphologically related to the headword.

Translation: The translation part provides a target language equivalent for the source language item, so that the target language user can understand the headword easier.

Variant form: This part gives an alternative spelling of the headword or a slight variation in the form of an expression.

Types of meanings in dictionaries

Dictionaries have a lot to do with semantics, the study of meaning, or the way in which meaning in a language is structured. In lexicography and translating, meaning is about the most important factor in interlingual transfer. Eugene A. Nida even goes so far as to say that 'translating means translating meaning' (Nida 1985: 119–125).

In lexicography and translation, it is necessary to distinguish between different types of meanings. Apart from denotation, it is important to know the additional meanings that a word or a phrase has beyond its core meaning, including the affective, emotive, social, and collocational meanings. Meaning, however, is not studied in isolation, but in a certain context, which is very important in translation and falls in the realm of pragmatics.

Associative meaning refers to all the meanings that one can think of when a word or an expression is read or heard. Associations aroused by the word have little to do with its basic meaning. For instance, when the word 'birthday' is mentioned, one thinks of presents and parties, while the word 'Chinese New Year' brings the associations of holidays, luck, money, and festivity. Associative meanings are often culture-bound, i.e., linked to historical terms, personalities, or legends (Chan 2004: 15). Dictionaries do not give the associative meanings of a word.

Cognitive meaning concerns the cognitive relationship between a word and the reality to which it refers. It is also known as 'denotative meaning' and

92 *Functions in computer-aided translation systems*

'referential meaning'. It is, nevertheless, difficult to establish what cognitive meaning is and define it by referring it to physical properties. Most adjectives and adverbs do not have cognitive meanings.

Collocational meaning consists of the associations that a word acquires on account of the meanings of the words which tend to occur.

Combinatory meaning is a type of lexical meaning that results from the combination of words.

Connotative meaning refers to the associations related to a word.

Contextual meaning is the meaning that is derived from the context, such as the meaning of a word within a particular sentence, or the meaning of a sentence within a particular paragraph. Contextual meaning is of great importance for translators.

Core meaning is the most basic meaning of the word.

Degradation of meaning, also known as 'deterioration' or 'degeneration' of meaning, refers to the degradation in the course of time of a neutral or appreciative word to a word with a derogatory meaning.

Denotative meaning is the central or core meaning of a lexical item, relating a word or phrase to phenomena in the real world or in a fictional world. It is often equivalent to cognitive meaning and conceptual meaning (Schogt 1988: 65–71).

Designative meaning refers to the meanings obtained from designations.

Elevation concerns the situation in which words that originally have derogatory or neutral meanings develop favourable meanings in the course of time.

Emotive meaning refers to the charge of feeling carried by a particular word or expression in a given utterance or text (Nida 1964: 70–119).

Evaluative meaning concerns words that bear implications of either approval or disapproval.

Extension concerns things that a word can be extended to apply to. For instance, extensions of animal could be dog, cow, tiger, etc. In translation, it is important to stick to the entity that the word refers to, not its extensions.

Fuzzy meaning concerns the indetermination involved in the analysis of several linguistic items which have invariant cores with variant expressions. The linguistic hedges of fuzzy words are often difficult to make.

Generalization is a form of semantic change and what is more commonly known as changes of meaning, extending in the course of time the more specific meaning of a word to a generalized one. Generalization takes place whenever a word is used with a new referent or in a new sentence function (Ke 1992: 24–26).

Homonym is a word with the same spelling or sound as another but different meaning. There are two types of homonyms: homographs and homophones. A homograph is a type of homonym that shares spelling with another but has a different meaning; homophones have the same sound but are spelt differently.

Functions in computer-aided translation systems   93

Lexical gap is said to be present if a word in one language does not seem to have a counterpart in another language. Lexical gaps can usually be filled by paraphrases.

Literal meaning refers to the surface meaning of a word or an expression.

Narrowing of meaning concerns the narrowing of the denotational scope of a lexeme. This often takes place when part of the denotational domain of a lexeme is being taken up or usurped by the extension of the scope of another lexeme, resulting in lexical specialization.

Primary meaning is the meaning of a word at its creation, or the meaning that usually comes to mind when the word is said in isolation.

Prosodic meaning is determined by the way the sentence is said. Stress and intonation can bring out the change in emphasis, informing us of what information in the sentence is 'given' and what is 'new'.

Referential meaning refers to the objective relationship between a word and the reality it denotes (Nida 1964: 70–119).

Reflected meaning is the meaning that arises in cases of multiple conceptual meanings, when one sense of a word forms part of our response to another sense (Zaky 2000).

Semantic change, also known as 'change of meaning', refers to the change and creation of new meanings of a lexical item. It may take several forms: generalization, specialization/narrowing of meaning, elevation, degradation, antonomasia, and transference.

Shades of meaning concern words with identical denotational meanings that may differ in shades of meaning.

Social meaning is the meaning that a piece of language conveys about the social circumstances of its use. Social meanings are determined to a great extent by the paralinguistic and non-linguistic conditions under which the utterances take place. The tone of voice, the facial expression, and the gestures are, therefore, important clues for getting the social meaning behind the words. Social meaning is also a way of telling the social class to which participants of a speech event belong.

Creating translation equivalents from dictionary meanings

Translation is more than a string of dictionary equivalents. It is certain that translation equivalents are produced through the use of dictionaries. These equivalents, however, cannot be understood in the mathematical meaning of identity, but only in terms of proximity. The main task of a translator is to select the 'optimal equivalent' from a variety of 'potential equivalents' that can be found in the target language. Dictionaries, therefore, should be seen as a reference work from which one can choose a large number of potential equivalents.

Absolute equivalence designates the situation in which there is only one translation equivalent for a certain source language term. According to K. Balasubramanian, 'Absolute equivalence requires that the lexical unit be identical in all the three components of lexical meaning, viz., designation, connotation and range of application and occur in all the typical contexts in which SL lexical unit occurs' (Balasubramanian 1988: 13–20). Some examples of absolute equivalents are as follows: numerals, such as 'one' 一 and 'ten' 十; ordinals, such as 'first' 第一 and 'tenth' 第十; parts of the body, such as 'head' 頭, 'eyes' 眼, and 'heart' 心; measurements, such as 'yard' 丈 and 'kilometre' 公里/千米; weights, such as 'kilogramme' 公斤/千克; chemical elements, such as 'fluorine' 氟, 'radium' 鐳, and 'titanium' 鈦; and geographical terms, such as 'mountain' 山 and 'sky' 天空.

Connotative equivalence is a kind of translation equivalence that occurs when words in the source and target languages trigger similar associations in the minds of speakers of the two languages (Koller 1995: 191–222).

Cultural equivalence refers to an approximate translation where a source language cultural word is translated by a target language cultural word. Cultural equivalence refers to the matching of a source language culture-specific term with a corresponding target language term, which can fully and effectively convey the original meaning and image. The more effective use of cultural equivalents in translation is explanatory rather than emotional, particularly for uninformed and not much interested readerships. Cultural equivalents mean to give a general impression and are inaccurate in many details, due to the fact that cultural terms are, per se, peculiar to one language community (Briere 1988: 34–39; Loehlin 1962: 140–141; Reyburn 1969: 158–167; Reyburn 1970: 26–35; Sarcevic 1985: 127–133).

Definitional equivalent: This is to define a source term in the translation. Two things have to be noted: (1) no definition can give all the information, and (2) the information provided must be relevant.

Denotative equivalence occurs when words in the source and target languages refer to the same entity in the real world (Koller 1995: 191–222).

Descriptive equivalence consists of providing an explanation or giving an account of the source language expression in the target language text. Descriptive equivalents are normally used as footnotes, as they are too long to fit in the target text.

Explanatory equivalence involves equivalents that are explanatory, normally in the form of footnotes, in translating expressions in the source text.

Multiple equivalence refers to the translations of a term that has different contextual meanings by using various designations in the translated text (Chan 1991: 79–85).

Natural equivalence concerns the semantic translation of a source-language word initially transliterated by a Romanization system.

Official equivalence involves those equivalents provided by official or semi-official organizations, which are known as 'official equivalents'. The names

Functions in computer-aided translation systems 95

of prominent politicians are usually translated by government translators and used in all official documents.

Phonological equivalence concerns the use of equivalents that involve the production of similar sounds between the source text and the target text. This type of equivalent is important in the translation of onomatopoeic words and in the use of cadence, stress, and rhythm in poetry translation.

Poetic equivalence is reflected by some dictionaries, which include quotable lines in poetry. Poetic equivalents are expressions which creatively render lines in poetry and, thus, allow the voice of the translator to be heard.

Pragmatic equivalence produce a kind of correspondence between the pragmatic meaning of the source and target text in order to generate the pragmatic force of the source text in the target text (Baker 1992: 217–260; Koller 1995: 191–222).

Provisional equivalence, otherwise known as a translation label, is usually marked by inverted commas, which can later be discreetly withdrawn or accepted. Provisional equivalents provide a provisional designation for the source language term in the target text but settle on something more faithful to its meaning in the original at a later stage.

Single equivalence is the situation in which one equivalent, known as a 'single equivalent', for a source expression is used throughout the translation. This method is normally adopted for the translation of terms that comprise a conglomeration of concepts. The advantage of this method is the consistency of usage, yet part of the meanings of the term may be concealed.

Dictionaries in computer-aided translation systems

During data processing or translation, a computer-aided translation system uses dictionaries to analyse words to create the output or target text. Dictionaries used in data processing are of two major categories: system dictionaries and non-system dictionaries. System dictionaries refer to dictionaries or glossaries in computer-aided translation systems for users to use or build. Non-system dictionaries refer to dictionaries or glossaries independent of computer-aided translation systems. Both types of dictionaries are essential for system users.

(A) SYSTEM DICTIONARIES

The number of dictionaries or glossaries in a computer-aided translation system is varied. There are systems that have three dictionaries. Atlas, for instance, has a default Standard Dictionary, which is in use at all times, default Technical Dictionaries for different technical fields, and User Dictionaries, which are created by the user to include terms and translation memory data that cannot be

96   *Functions in computer-aided translation systems*

found in the above dictionaries. Atlas allows the user to create up to 1,000 dictionaries, and the user can select a number of them to suit specific translation projects (http://www.fujitsu.com/global/services/software/translation/atlas). Some computer-aided translation tools allow the user to define user-specific settings that are applied while working within the system. Fortis Dictionary Window, for example, has five options: (1) Show Term, (2) Show Abbreviation, (3) Show Alternative, (4) Show Synonym, and (5) Show Idx (Index). Show Term is ticked by default. Fluency, on the other hand, displays the translations of all the terms in the dictionary of a specific language pair when translating a sentence in the source language.

(B)   NON-SYSTEM DICTIONARIES

At the stage of text transfer, both monolingual and bilingual dictionaries are used to supplement what is not covered by the glossaries prepared from source texts and to provide potential equivalents from bilingual dictionaries and parallel corpora. Two types of tools are used at this stage: online dictionaries and bilingual corpora.

An online dictionary is one that is available via a computer network. There are basically three types of online dictionaries: single-unit online dictionaries, multiple-unit online dictionaries, and bilingual dictionaries. A typical example of a single-unit British English online dictionary is the Oxford English Dictionary Online (http://oxforddictionaries.com), while that of American English is Merriam-Webster Online (http://www.merriam-webster.com). Oxford English Dictionary Online is available to subscribers. It has been updated quarterly with revisions since the year 2000, and it is, therefore, the most up-to-date British English dictionary on the Internet.

There are a number of multiple-unit dictionaries on the Internet, one of which is dictionary.com (http://dictionary.reference.com), which claims that 'it is the largest and most trusted free dictionary free on the web' and provides the functions of audio pronunciation, provision of synonyms, word of the day, example sentences, word origin, and word games. Another function of dictionary.com is translation, which is performed by Dictionary.com Translator. Another popular free online multiple-unit dictionary is Yourdictionary.com (http://www.yourdictionary.com), which provides the users with 'definitions, thesaurus entries, spelling, pronunciation, and etymology results' for the words they search. Another multiple-unit dictionary that is useful is OneLook.com (http://www.onelook.com).

Concordancers

Concordancers are another type of tool aimed at translators and used to extract information from the data of a corpus (Pearson 1996: 85–95). It is always useful for translators to keep a domain-specific corpus to get bilingual data for use in translation. Bilingual corpora allow translators to study existent

Functions in computer-aided translation systems 97

translations; study language usage in translation; analyse the linguistic features in translation through the quantification of lexical and syntactical features; study the application of translation methods, by showing how to develop, test, refine, and verify them; study the treatment of cultural terms; study how decisions in translations are made; reveal decision-making processes in specific translation contexts or situations; study domain-specific concepts by familiarizing translators with concepts of a certain domain; study how words are used in a certain context, which helps when performing a terminological search; study what strategies have previously been used; study previously employed translation strategies; review text-type and stylistic conventions, some of which are hugely different, such as poetry and netspeak; study how translators behave through the provision of information on translator behavior; show how translators process and use language; show how translators overcome difficulties and constraints in translation practice; allow teachers to teach more effectively by validating their own intuitions; illustrate their explanations with corpus evidence; strengthen manual analysis with computer analysis, which can be supplemented by manual analysis; choose the best equivalent through comparison with the collected data, providing contextual clues to meaning and usage; choose the best equivalent for a particular translation context; and, finally, compile task-specific dictionaries, enabling the compilation of domain-specific glossaries.

Concordancing in computer-aided translation can be conducted with two types of tools: system concordancers and independent concordancers.

System concordancers

A system concordancer displays the latest source and target language phrases in the translation memory, which includes the linguistic stem of the chosen word. This allows translators to see how the word was previously translated. XTM is one of the many systems with a built-in concordancer.

Independent concordancers

Concordancers can be monolingual, bilingual, and multilingual. Monolingual concordancers are aimed at the study of the source text, whereas bilingual and multilingual concordancers are focused on the target text. As translators usually work on a single language pair at one time, bilingual concordancers are used more frequently than multilingual concordancers.

Bilingual concordancers, such as ParaConc, are tools that provide a list of words and translation equivalents from a bilingual corpus. A bilingual concordancer finds and displays the translation of each passage that satisfies the query. It establishes the links between corresponding segments of translated texts. They are designed to be used for contrastive corpus-based language research and for training and analysis related to translation studies. It is possible to identify several useful functions for translators: (1) it provides information on bilingual word

98 *Functions in computer-aided translation systems*

usage; (2) it helps to prepare a translation memory dictionary; (3) it helps to prepare a project-specific bilingual dictionary; and (4) it also defines the scope of the vocabulary (Langlois 1996: 34–42).

Types of data processing

With the increasing number of ready-to-use dictionaries and concordancers available to translators, data processing is now possible. There are three major types of data processing:

(1) *Translation*, which goes through the stages of pre-translation and translation. Computer-aided translation systems are used for pre-translation and translation and machine translation systems are for automatic translation. As machine translation will be discussed in Chapter 4 in conjunction with computer-aided translation, in the form of hybrid systems, it will not be discussed here.
(2) *Localization* involves the use of independent or built-in localization systems to create localized software or webpages.
(3) *Multimodal Transfer* involves the use of systems to produce different forms of image presentations to complete the task of translation.

Translation

Translation is the most common form of data processing. With the use of computer-aided translation systems, the translation work can be divided into two stages: pre-translation and translation.

Pre-translation phase

The use of previously translated material to translate subsequent documents is known as pre-translation (Bédard 1991: 19–20). The function of pre-translation exists in a number of systems with different designations.

In the case of very repetitive texts, it is preferable to automatically process the project and insert the appropriate translations, thereby saving a significant amount of time and effort. This highly configurable batch process is called 'pre-translate'. It involves Déjà Vu X, for instance, examining the text that is to be translated and scanning the translation memory for matches of each segment. Déjà Vu will select the best translation – either an (appropriately indicated) guaranteed exact, exact, or fuzzy match – for each sentence, and insert it in the corresponding location, leaving the translator with the task of reviewing and editing the translation rather than starting from scratch.

Pre-translation should not be confused with pseudotranslation, which is generally regarded as a specialized process in which a 'dummy' translation with

Functions in computer-aided translation systems 99

target-language specific characters is performed, and the dummy file is exported to the target user to verify that the special characters of the target language can be displayed appropriately in the original file format.

Systems with the function of pre-translation include crossTank (Across), which has the function of automatic pre-translation of repeated sentences or phrases in the central database. A typical example of a computer-aided translation tool with the function of pseudotranslation is Déjà Vu.

(A) MATCHING

One of the functions that is used in the pre-translation stage and later in the translation stage is matching, the first step in translating a source text. Matching is one of the most important factors that determines how much translation needs to be done with the use of editing platforms. Matching used to be context-free and done entirely on the single sentence level. But matching is becoming more context-based.

It is generally understood that 100% matching is known as exact match, whereas less than 100% matching is considered a fuzzy match. However, none of them is a context match. Recently, the idea of 'perfect match' or 'greatest match' has been introduced to refer to more than 100% matching, which is based on co-text or context and a new form of in-context matching. The best match is not simply identical in the input and stored sentences, but also in the sentences that go before and after the input and stored sentences. If all three input sentences match with three stored sentences in line, an in-context perfect match is retrieved.

(1) More than 100% match In-context matches are considered as matches with more than 100% matching. Déjà Vu uses the term 'Guaranteed Matching', which is a function that provides a guaranteed match that indicates that the context comparison has already been carried out, ensuring that the translation is as accurate and appropriate as the original translation. With this feature, there is an immediate reduction in the total review time and costs, along with a significant boost in translation productivity and consistency. XTM uses the term 'In Context Exact (ICE) Matches', which is defined as 'a 100% leveraged in-context match where the previous and next segments of the translation memory are the same as previous and next segment in the document' (XTM Manual 2012: 91). 'Perfect Match', in turn, is a component of SDL that distinguishes between in-context and out-of-context 100% sentence matches, and ensures that the 100% matches are within context before they are applied to any given translation project.

(2) 100% Match Several designations have been used by different systems to name exact matches. XTM, for example, uses '100% Leveraged Matches'. According to its manual, 'a 100% leveraged match is an exact match but in a different context. This means that the match needs to be reviewed by the

100 *Functions in computer-aided translation systems*

translator' (Manual 2012: 91). 'Leveraged Match' is another term used in XTM to refer to the situation in which 'a sentence or phrase in a translation memory is the same phrase in a different context as the sentence or phrase the translator is currently working on'. This term is interchangeable with 100% leveraged matches.

(3) Less than 100% match Less than 100% matching is regarded as fuzzy matching (Lin and Chen 2006). According to XTM, a fuzzy match 'refers to the situation when a sentence or phrase in a translation memory is similar (but not a 100% match) to the sentence or phrase the translator is currently working on' (Manual 2012: 91). Fuzzy matches are further divided into three groups: 75–84%, 85–94%, and 95–99%, with the fuzzy matching starting at 74%.

Fuzzy matching in Déjà Vu performs two functions. The first is 'assemble', which involves examining the translation memory databases to take relevant fragments or sentences with a similar structure to produce a translation from material that is embedded in other sentences. The second is 'auto-assemble', which automatically examines the translation databases and takes relevant fragments or sentences with a similar structure to produce a translation from material that is embedded in other sentences.

Translation phase: Translating with computer-aided translation systems

Computer-aided translation systems are widely used in the business world (Boitet 1995: 131–134, 1996; Elliston 1979: 149–158). More than 6,000 large corporations in the world handle their language problems with computer-aided translation systems. The European Union, for example, has entrusted half of its multilingual translation work to machine translation or computer-aided translation systems with great success. It can be seen that more and more international or national corporations have adopted computer-aided translation tools for language documentation purposes.

In a more global context, large translation system suppliers, such as SDL, have a number of corporate users, including Daimler Chrysler, Yamaha, Ernst & Young, IBM, Siemens, Dresdner Bank, Adobe, Lucent Technologies, Xerox, Kelly, Microsoft, Symantec, Interwoven, Oracle, Credit Suisse Group, and Merrill Lynch.

In a more local context, as in the case of China, Yaxin, the first company in the country to supply computer-aided translation systems, has clients in the government sector, which include: Sate Administration for Industry and Commerce, Central Compilation and Translation Bureau, International Department, Central Committee of CPC, *Liberation Army Daily*, The Chinese Academy of Agricultural Sciences, Institute of Scientific and Technical Information of China, China Academy of Launch Vehicle Technology, and the China Aerospace Science and Technology Corporation.

The use of machine translation systems in translation will be discussed in Chapter 4, where different hybrid systems are introduced.

Some issues involved in the use of computer-aided translation systems are discussed below.

(A) ACQUISITION OF COMPUTER-AIDED TRANSLATION SYSTEMS

The acquisition or selection of a reliable and user-friendly system that meets the needs of a translator is an important issue. According to John Hutchins, computer-aided translation-related software is being released on a weekly basis, including both brand new systems and upgrades. A number of issues have to be considered when acquiring a system for personal or organizational use.

To buy or not to buy

To buy or not to buy a computer-aided translation system is a hard decision to make. Several questions can be asked: (1) How often do you use a computer-aided translation system? (2) Do you often work on the same type of text? (3) Do you intend to work as a member of a translation team? If possible, it is always advisable to download a trial version to see if it fits one's purpose. In any case, there should not be any illegal downloading of computer-aided translation systems.

Which system to buy

Which system to buy is again not an easy decision to make (Coughlin 1990: 455–457). Generally, it would be better and safer to get a system from a reputable company. This system should be one which is popular in the industry, the latest version of the product, and supported by research and development.

Which version to buy

Generally, there are three different versions of a certain system available: (1) a stand-alone version, which serves as a personal translation workstation of a translator and is less expensive and, therefore, good for students and learners to familiarize themselves with computer-aided translation functions; (2) a professional version, which serves as a personal workstation as well as a platform for the user to serve as a member of a translation team linked by network; and (3) a network version, which serves as a translation management system in a corporate or business setting.

(B) ADVANTAGES OF USING COMPUTER-AIDED TRANSLATION SYSTEMS

There are a number of advantages in using computer-aided translation systems that will be discussed, as follows:

> *Translation Generation* can be achieved by selecting the optimal equivalents from a translation memory database. In other words, translators do not

102   *Functions in computer-aided translation systems*

have to produce their own translations. They can simply draw from and make use of an array of equivalents stored in a bilingual database to form their translation of the source text. This has great significance to the profession and pedagogy of translation.

Consistency in Terminology and Style can be achieved by translation teams through the use of a network computer-aided translation system.

Accuracy is increased by computer-aided translation systems, as there is more control over the output.

Translation Quality Assurance is performed quickly. The criteria of translation quality are the same as human translation.

Translation Profitability is increased by computer-aided translation tools, as they generate more income and the number of translation orders is larger.

Shorter Turnaround can be achieved with the use of computer-aided translation systems, as translation can be produced within a shorter period of time. It is generally agreed that computer-aided translation is four or five times faster than human translation.

Higher Translation Volume is achieved by computer-aided translation tools. It is estimated that a human translator can translate 250 words per hour, completing around 2,000 words per day. In computer-aided translation, around 1,250 words can be translated per hour, resulting in 10,000 words in a day. The translation volume is, therefore, about five times higher than in human translation.

Translation Cost is reduced, as what has been translated does not need to be translated again. This leads to better planning of budgets and reduces the relative translation costs.

Effort-saving is a direct consequence of the provision of centralized translation data, which is created by and distributed among translators.

Translation Management is more efficient with the use of computer-aided translation systems. It goes from project planning to analysis and preparation, translation, review, delivery, translation memory refinement, and project evaluation. The entire progress of a translation project is under the control of a project manager. Long texts, for example, can be divided up among several translators, and the project is completed with terminological and stylistic consistency through computer-aided translation.

With all these advantages, computer-aided translation is becoming increasingly popular. It is generally agreed that a human translator who uses a computer-aided translation system is able to produce a large quantity of quality translation in a speedy manner.

(C)   TYPES OF COMPUTER-AIDED TRANSLATION SYSTEMS

Before computer-aided translation systems are introduced, it should be noted that, first, competition in the translation system market is fierce, as new computer-aided translation systems are produced every three or four months. Second, the

Functions in computer-aided translation systems 103

number of systems is relatively large. There are fourteen types of computer-aided translation systems. Third, several changes have taken place in the industry. Computer-aided translation systems are moving from sentence-based to text-based, standalone to network, and from manual to automatic. In the following, all computer-aided translation systems have been divided into fourteen types, including some sub-types.

Corporate computer-aided translation systems are a type of computer-aided translation tools targeted at corporate users. With their corporate translation management system, they can help manage translation projects. Corporate computer-aided translation systems can be further divided into the following sub-types:

(1) Bilingual corporate computer-aided translation systems Across, produced by Soget in Milan, Italy, is an example of a bilingual corporate computer-aided translation system. It is a Corporate Translation Management system with all the management functions for translation projects. It creates and manages translation memories and terminology databases, as well as translations to and into virtually any language.

(2) Multilingual corporate computer-aided translation systems MultiTrans can be cited as an example of such systems. It has the following features: (1) it is compatible with conventional translation memory tools; (2) the TextBase TM and its Alignment Agent capture and organize all the past translations; (3) the TermBase provides a terminology bank of pre-approved, standardized terms in multiple languages; (4) the Translation Agent help to edit the output; and (5) the Analysis Agent provides comprehensive project analysis and reporting tools to support optimal project workflow decisions.

Custom-specific computer-aided translation systems are tailor-made to meet the specific needs of the user. Increasingly, corporations want to have computer-aided translation systems specially designed for them. These custom-specific systems are provided by major system providers, such as Translation Management System, produced by SDL, and the Custom-Specific Service, provided by Yaxin in China.

Example-based computer-aided translation systems, such as Déjà Vu, combine translation memory technology with example-based machine translation techniques; i.e., they can convert fuzzy matches into exact matches, and the exact matches and examples in this type of system are interchangeable. When an input text enters into the translation memory database and glossary database, it produces a translation if there is an exact match and it can also put together fuzzy matches to form exact matches.

The first method of example-based computer-aided translation is to 'correct the differences' between the input text and the match stored in the translation memory through the use of a terminology database. For example, when the sentence, 'He always tells lies' is stored in the translation memory database, the new sentence, 'He never tells lies' would be translated by substituting 'always'

104   *Functions in computer-aided translation systems*

with 'never', if 'never' was in the terminology database. This means that a fuzzy match is turned into an exact match by 'repairing' it, i.e., substituting one word with another word. The second method involves putting together a combination of terms from the terminology database and translations of the sentences or parts of the sentences in the translation memory database to propose a complete translation (Benis 2007: 28–32).

Intelligence-based computer-aided translation systems are a relatively new type of system that can translate previously unseen segments by making use of pre-translated and similarly structured examples. This kind of system is based on human intelligence. A typical example of this is the Human Intelligence System, which is a second-generation computer-aided translation system that can translate previously unseen segments by making use of pre-translated, similarly structured examples.

Language-pair-specific computer-aided translation systems are for translating a specific language pair, such as translation between French and German. Computer-aided translation systems are generally divided into systems without any dictionaries and systems with bilingual dictionaries for a specific language pair, or multilingual dictionaries for a number of specific language pairs. Language-pair specific systems deal with a specific language pair and have a selected bilingual dictionary that provides a word-for-word translation of the source text, as well as some specialized dictionaries for the translation of writings in some specific domains. They can be further divided into:

(1) Bilingual language-pair-specific computer-aided translation systems This kind of system focuses on the translation of a specific language pair. Yaxin, which was first developed by SJTU Sunway Software Co. Ltd., is an example of a language-specific computer-aided translation system for translation between Chinese and English.

The use of Yaxin as a translation tool is fairly simple. First, the source language and target language must be selected through the language settings in 'System Setting'. Second, the dictionary must be selected from the four system dictionaries for the translation project at hand. Third, in order to retrieve the text file from a source for translation, the cursor must be placed at the beginning of the text, and the icon must be clicked. The translation with the original text will then appear in the uppermost 'Translation Box' in the interface. Finally, the user can edit the translation by modifying the terminology database and building up and updating the translation memory database.

Other bilingual language-pair-specific computer-aided translation systems include 'AnglaHindi', for English into Hindi; 'Sakhr CAT Translator', for translation between English and Arabic; and 'Cevirmen', for Cevirmen and English translation.

(2) Multilingual language-pair-specific computer-aided translation systems This type of system can perform multilingual translation. Functionally, it is similar to its bilingual counterpart but multilingual. Eurolang Optimizer is a typical example. It is

Functions in computer-aided translation systems 105

a multilingual system that handles the major languages of the European community. It combines all functionalities of the pre-translation server and translation workstation on a single personal computer, and is fully compatible with Optimizer's client-server version. It can also produce fuzzy matches, plus technical term assistance.

Memory-based machine translation systems refer to machine translation systems with the function of a translation memory. The first generation, including Transwhiz in Taiwan and MetaTexis, was able to translate a text by machine translation before using the translation memory, improving the quality of translation through customized translation memories and glossaries. The second type consists of a machine translation system with a customized translation memory for the translation of texts in a specific area, combining the advantages of translation memories and transfer-based machine translation.

Open-sourced computer-aided translation systems provide the open-source community with features and concepts that have been used by commercial offerings for years to improve translation efficiency and quality. By changing the source code, a customer-specific system is created.

A typical example of an open-source system is Transolution, an open-source computer-aided translation platform written in Java. It can be used for both software and documentation. It does sentence segmentation and interactive translation memory. It performs tag protection and translates file format based on XLIFF standard.

Prediction-based computer-aided translation systems are illustrated by TransType. These systems observe the way a translator types a text and periodically propose extensions to it, which the translator may accept, modify, or ignore simply by continuing to type. It is automatic translation through the keying-in method.

Publication-oriented computer-aided translation systems are created for translations that need to be printed. In the past, little attention was paid to the need of delivering translation projects in the form of a package, including the publication of the output in hardcopy. Some computer-aided translation systems nowadays, such as Translator's Intuition, have the function of desktop publishing. Translator's Intuition not only does terminology management, word processing, and prepares the translation memory at the word, phrase, sentence, and paragraph levels, but also performs desktop publishing.

Sentence-based computer-aided translation systems are the most common computer-aided translation systems, as normally the basic unit of a text in a translation memory is a sentence. Automatic text segmentation often requires manual verification of alignments, which is labour-intensive and, therefore, relatively slow. The translation units, made up of decontextualized sentences, are usually saved on a file exported to a location, to be imported to a new translation project when it is useful. For this reason, these kinds of systems are also known as 'file-based computer-aided translation systems'.

Two examples of this are Systran and Wordfast. Systran is one of the most popular computer-aided translation systems on the market. It has a revolutionary new user interface, giving greater productivity to meet increasing workloads. In addition, its automated 'project preparation and management' can cut the

106 *Functions in computer-aided translation systems*

set-up and coordination times for multiple-language projects. Its new batch-mode automated quality assurance cuts the user's review time. Wordfast offers a transparent, open format for all its data. It can translate a wide array of tagged documents. It can be connected to MT engines and it is easy to integrate in the workflow of translation agencies. Its data can be shared over the web.

Server-based computer-aided translation systems, such as Elanex Translation Inventory, feature a centralized storage of all clients' translations and offer instant availability to all registered users. Some of the major advantages of this type of system are its instant accessibility from anywhere in the world, the easy management, and a better matching due to the storage of a massive amount of data.

Statistical computer-aided translation systems, such as MemorySphere, scan the source text and compare strings against a database of pre-translated text to reuse previously translated materials. They deliver indexes of complete or segmented sentences, create word and phrase matches using a bilingual morphology analyser, and align on a word-by-word basis. They can be customized to suit the style of the translator or editor. Bilingual translation memories are created by translators, and exact match and partial or block match techniques are implemented. The provision of statistics for all the major components in the system is the chief characteristic of this type of computer-aided translation tool.

Terminology-based computer-aided translation systems provide the translation of terms or set phrases. Linear B Searchable Translation Memories can be cited as an example of this type of system. It is a simple searchable bilingual corpus that provides users with equivalents (exact marches). Actually, since it does not feature a translation memory database, this system is not a computer-aided translation system in the strict sense of the term.

Text-based computer-aided translation systems can align and translate PDF, HTML, XML, and SGML files and use Unicode to manage characters. A typical example of a text-based system is Similis, produced by Lingua et Machina (France) in 2006. Similis is a translation memory system that uses a new three-module architecture, which includes the server, the manager, and the translation tool. It automatically retrieves bilingual terminology to reprocess sentences and word chunks in context.

In contrast to sentence-based systems, this type is operationally simpler, as it does not have sentence alignment, and more context-bound, because the sentences in the text are not decontextualized.

Translation memory-based machine translation systems

This type of computer-aided translation system originates from the idea of machine translation systems with a translation memory function. It has the advantage of maintaining high speed automatic translation with control over the output. There

Functions in computer-aided translation systems 107

are basically two types of memory-based machine translation system, classified according to the order in which translation memory is used:

(1) Automatic translation and translation memory-based machine translation systems These systems translate by automatic translation before using the translation memory. MetaTexis, for instance, combines fast, innovative, and powerful functions with a low price. It is intuitive and user-friendly and can import and export TMX documents. Most important, it offers high security when handling the translation memories and terminology databases.

(2) Translation memory-based and automatic translation machine translation systems In the second case the comparison with the translation memory is performed before processing the input text with an automatic translation engine. In other words, the exact matches stored in the database will be used to translate the source text while the remaining unmatched text will be automatically translated by the machine translation system.

A typical example of this is Multi-Lingual Translation System (MLTS), which provides a rough draft of an understandable and acceptable translation. It translates texts in a specific subject area by using customized dictionaries. It operates on five different levels: (1) translation memory, (2) morphological analysis, (3) syntactic analysis, (4) semantic analysis, and (5) transfer. Moreover, it combines the advantages of a translation memory with the transfer approach.

Translator-based computer-aided translation systems, such as TransAssist, help the translator search the translation memory database for past translations. It allows any number of translation and glossary memory files to be loaded simultaneously and searched automatically. The translation memory of the system is used to compare user-defined selected text to find previous translations stored in the database that are identical or similar to the currently selected text.

Web-based computer-aided translation systems offer an online service delivery bilingual or multilingual platform. Freeway, for example, is free for registered users and provides better collaboration among team members. It also provides better management with a centralized, Internet-enabled language asset management system with translation memory, glossary, and machine translation capabilities. It gives higher web services connectivity and it also has better security for data contained within the software.

This is the newest system, which runs entirely on the web to provide a global workbench for a team of translators to work collectively and for the project manager to run the projects efficiently.

Web-based computer-aided translation systems can be further classified into two groups, as discussed below.

(1) Web-based bilingual computer-aided translation systems Yaxin can be cited as an example of this type of system, as it is an online service delivery platform provided free for registered users.

108 Functions in computer-aided translation systems

(2) Web-based multilingual computer-aided translation systems Yaxin can also be used in a multilingual manner, with all the features and functions working very much like the bilingual system.

(D) REMARKS ON COMPUTER-AIDED TRANSLATION SYSTEMS

The first observation we can make is that Chinese has become an important language in computer-aided translation. According to an article in *SDL Newsletter*, which was released in October 2007, there has been a strong increase in Eastern European language translations as the European Union expands with the entry of more East European countries; moreover, the rise of Chinese translation is most significant as a result of its economic growth and its important position in the global market.

The second observation is that there has been a rapid increase in the number of computer-aided translation systems in the last decade. It should be noted that when Trados was created in 1984, not much progress was made in the first ten years in terms of system production and the number of users. Most of the systems were developed in Europe, where multilingual computer-aided translation was popular. In recent years, however, there has been a revitalization of interest in computer-aided translation.

The third observation is that there has been a closer integration between computer-aided translation and machine translation. It is a matter of having more machine translation and less computer-aided translation, or vice versa.

The last observation is that web-based customer-specific systems have become the major trend in the field, and they have replaced desktop translation memory systems.

Localization

Localization, the second major type of data processing, is an area that is gaining increasing attention in the field of machine translation (Dunne 2006; Pym 2004). Localization, as explained by Esselink (2003: 67), is about customizing things for a 'local' audience, which involves 'taking a product and making it linguistically, technically and culturally appropriate to the target locale where it will be used and sold'. Localization can be defined linguistically as translating a product to suit the target users, technically as adjusting technical specifications to suit the local market, and culturally as following the norms and conventions of the target community (Chan 2004: 134).

(a) Definitions of localization

Though localization can be regarded macroscopically as an umbrella concept, covering basically any activity that serves the interest of the local community, it is conventionally and computationally interpreted to refer to two major types of localization: software localization and web localization.

Software localization concerns the process of adapting and translating a software application into another language to make it linguistically and culturally appropriate for a local market (Corbolante and Irmler 2001: 516–535; Fluixà 2004; Forssell 2001). There are differences between software localization and traditional document translation. Whereas translation is an activity performed on a finalized source text, software localization is the translation and adaptation of a software product and its documentation. Software localization projects are usually undertaken while the source product is still in development so as to have simultaneous shipment of all language versions. Translation, therefore, is only one of the activities in a localization project; further activities include project management, software engineering, testing, and desktop publishing.

Web localization, on the other hand, concerns the translation of the software's user interface or information on a webpage into another language, thus allowing greater worldwide acceptance of the product (Dain, Frumkers, and Sanchez 2003; MacDermott 2004). The main purpose of localization is, therefore, to maximize the understandability and usability of a product so that it can be used in different parts of the world with optimum effectiveness. Figures by Internet World Statistics in 2009 revealed that there was an estimated 1.8 billion Internet users globally, of which Asia accounted for 42.4 per cent, or a total of 764,435,900 Internet users (http://www.internetworldstats.com/stats.htm). Localizing a product into an Asian language means that a product becomes accessible to the huge non-English speaking market in Asia. Web localization, in short, is the translation of a website into a specific language, which is an efficient and cost-effective means to expand market share and increase product sales.

Web localization is actually much the same as software localization. As aptly put by Pym (2010: 1), 'The localization of a website differs from non-hypertext translation with respect to the identification of translatable elements, the tools needed to render them, their non-linearity, the way in which the translation process is prepared and coordinated, and the extent of the changes that may be introduced'. Since websites are regularly or frequently modified and updated, web localization is also characterized by the translation of new and changed content with the use of translation memories (Zetzsche 2003).

The rapid growth of the software and web localization industry is indicative of the increasing popularity of localization tools in the world of translation and e-commerce.

(b) Localization, internationalization, and globalization

Localization is closely related to internationalization and globalization. Internationalization is the first step of localization and, in turn, localization involves the globalization of a software product. Therefore, both internationalization and localization are key parts in the globalization process (Elrich 2006; Luong, Lok, Taylor, and Driscoll 1995; O'Donnell 1994; Uren, Howard, and Perinotti 1993). Internationalization covers all the activities in the development process which can

110   *Functions in computer-aided translation systems*

adapt a product or programme to different countries and cultures or locales, thus enabling a product at a technical level for localization (Kumhyr, Merrill, and Spalink 1994: 142–148). In practice, this means that, in order to make it neutral and functional, no language-dependent or -specific information, such as currencies, dates, times, etc., should be included in the programme codes. Software internationalization is the first task before adapting the software to a particular country.

Procedurally speaking, a software product that is to be localized has to be internationalized at its earliest development stage. It will then be localized in the target languages, resulting in its globalization for English, German, or French application.

(c)   *History of the localization industry*

The localization industry as we know it today has its beginnings in the late 1970s, when translators began to form companies that could offer professional language services. Besides translation, these language service providers (LSPs) began to engage in project management. In the early 1980s, many software developers, whose systems were mainly published in the language they spoke, realized that they had to localize their products in order to sell them overseas (cf. Esselink 2000). Simultaneously, LSPs also began to embrace technology to improve their services. At that time, the work of localization was performed either by single-language vendors (SLVs) of small companies or multi-language vendors (MLVs) of international corporations, which worked on large-volume translation projects into multiple languages. This period can be considered the beginning of localization.

An important trend began to take shape in the 1990s. Many localization vendors either merged with others or were acquired so that a broader range of services could be offered to more customers and a larger market share could be gained. Examples of major consolidations in the late 1990s were the acquisitions of Alpnet, Sykes and Trados by SDL, Mendez by Lernout & Hauspie, and Mendez, Berlitz, Planet Leap, and Bowne by Lionbridge.

By 2000, the most popular localization languages were French, Italian, German, Spanish, Brazilian Portuguese, and Japanese. Around 80 per cent of the localization work was outsourced by clients, and the major source language was English. Due to taxation and the availability of skilled engineers, Ireland has been the world centre of localization. Most major software firms have a significant presence in this country, whereas the largest markets for localized products have been France, Germany, and Japan. Medium-sized markets are Italy, Spain, Sweden, Norway, and the Netherlands. Software developers often want their products localized into French, Italian, German, Spanish, and Japanese first. These languages were usually followed by Swedish, Norwegian, Danish, Dutch, or Brazilian Portuguese.

At present, the localization industry grows at a yearly average of 30 per cent, and the need for localization specialists is more obvious than ever. Translators need more computer knowledge, while engineers need more language skills. As a result of this development, many translation institutions and universities have begun to offer localization courses (Camrass 2006; Francois 2003; Guzmán 2005; Kosaka and Itagaki 2003: 229–249; Larsen 2004).

Functions in computer-aided translation systems 111

(d) Aspects of localization

Software and web localization can be studied from five aspects: (1) computational; (2) linguistic; (3) cultural; (4) economic; and (5) legal.

(1) COMPUTATIONAL ASPECTS

Most programmers design software that addresses, generally, local requirements. Software localization will certainly enlarge the pool of software users. The field of software localization is growing fast. There are a large number of software developers who look for companies to assist them with the globalization of their systems. Failing to localize software severely limits its sales potential. It is very important that the localized software retains the functionality of the original while making changes in the following areas:

(i) Programming guidelines There are some parts of the internationalized programme that should remain unchanged. For instance, the programming language keywords, such as 'if' and 'char', and the variable names for data type, such as 'string' and 'integer', cannot be changed. Command names, such as 'sort', and environment variables, such as 'path' and 'display', should also remain unvaried regardless of the locale.

(ii) Programming languages Not all programming languages are equally suitable for developing international applications. Centura, for instance, is not suitable, while Delphi and Borland Builder, as they are not Unicode-based, only offer limited support. C or C++ and Windows resources, on the other hand, can process resources directly by using Unicode and separating the code and the localizable information. Lastly, Java and .NET, such as C# and Visual Basic 7, are perfectly suitable for localization.

(iii) Graphic User Interface (GUI) The GUI defines how the various elements look and function. An effective user interface is the key to a successful programme. Localization of the user interface is easier provided that context information is available. It should also be noted that most translations get longer when translated from English to other European languages. The final internationalization step is to change the user interface in such a way that it can accommodate long translations. One of the solutions for this is to set every user interface item as wide as possible.

(iv) Dialogue box resizing The dialogue box is a type of window used to enable reciprocal communication or 'dialogues' between a computer and its user. Most of the operating systems on the market support the use of tabbed dialogue boxes. It is worth mentioning that default messages may have to be resized to fit the box size, as the length of a message may be truncated if the message exceeds the storage of a buffer, which is a storage item to compensate the difference in data flow when transferring from one device to another. It is therefore necessary to change the size of the user interface component to allow the expansion of the text.

112 *Functions in computer-aided translation systems*

(v) Double-byte enabling Codes can also pose problems in localization. Characters in Indo-European languages are encoded by one byte; however, in order to encode a single Chinese, Japanese, or Korean character, at least two bytes are required. Chinese, for example, is double-byte, while Japanese can be single-, double-, or even triple-byte for Kana and Kanji. As a result, when English software is localized into Japanese, the translation may be truncated as a result of buffer storage. This is due to the fact that, in software localization, the buffer may not be able to accommodate more bytes than those for which it was originally set, causing technical problems when localizing software that was originally based on a one-byte language into a two-/three-byte language.

(vi) Menu bar A menu bar displays a list of machine functions for selection by the operator. What is displayed varies from programme to programme. In the case of Microsoft Word, we have 'File' 檔案, 'Edit' 編輯, 'View' 檢視, 'Insert' 插入, 'Format' 格式, 'Tools' 工具, 'Table' 表格, 'Window' 視窗, and 'Help' 說明. In the case of Visual Basic, other functions such as 'Project', 'Debug', and 'Run' are added.

(vii) Command buttons Command buttons, or simply buttons, can be clicked to initiate a series of actions by the computer according to what is put down in the algorithm. Buttons labelled with 'Print' and 'Exit' are commonplace. For a software product such as a machine translation system, we have buttons like 'Translate' or more specific labels such as 'CE' 漢英 and 'EC' 英漢.

(viii) Packaging elements Packaging elements refer to functions which are included in the programme's package, such as 'Spell Check', for a word processor, and 'Slide Show', for PowerPoint. In the case of localizing a software product for Chinese users, 'Spell Check' may not be needed.

(ix) Online help For some programmes, such as Visual Basic, pressing the 'Help' button (說明) opens the online assistance. Software products that provide online help are, for example, RoboHelp, WebWorks Help, and Doc-to-Help. Efforts should be made to ensure that the same terminology is used for both the programme and the documentation, which can be achieved with the use of computer-aided translation systems.

(x) Readme file A Readme file provides important information about the software. It usually contains file contents, ways to open files, and interpretation of data in the files.

(xi) User guide A user guide includes detailed information on the components and operation of the software. Localization of the User Guide is basically document translation, which can be done by a machine translation engine or a computer-aided translation system.

Functions in computer-aided translation systems   113

(xii) Graphics   Graphics are symbols produced by a process, such as handwriting, drawing, or printing. In the process of software localization, embedded graphics are a frequent source of problems, and special consideration must be given to the number and type of graphics. What is more, text should not be used alongside graphics, such as the use of the word 'help' when a question mark on the button serves the same purpose.

(xiii) Icon   An icon is a graphic presentation of an object on a computer screen. Translating icons in HTML format is not an easy task for some localization software.

(xiv) Hot-keys and short-cut keys   Adjustments may be required, as the names of the keys are localized.

(xv) Audio   Some software may include audio, such as songs. When such software is localized, the original sounds, dialogue, or songs might need to be substituted for a version in the target language, or, in the case of music, into a genre or piece that is more suitable for the target users.

(xvi) Video subtitles   The need to translate subtitles into the target language goes without saying. This is a technically difficult area which requires subtitling software to insert the subtitles.

(2) LINGUISTIC ASPECTS

'Localization', say Ashworth and O'Hagan (2002: 66), 'can be defined as a process to facilitate globalization by addressing linguistic and cultural barriers specific to the Receiver who does not share the same linguistic and cultural background of the Sender'. Several aspects of linguistic localization are worth noting.

(i) Language of the locale   Translating a text from one language into another gives it a new life by overcoming linguistic barriers, revitalizing it on a different soil. Localization is to give a product a life beyond a locality. In doing so, it is important to identify the locales in which languages are used, such as the French and Italian of the Western European scripts, Greek and Russian of the Eastern European scripts, and Chinese and Japanese of the Asian scripts.

(ii) Language varieties   In software localization, varieties within a single language also need to be addressed, for example, American and British English, and simplified and standard Chinese characters.

(iii) Directionality of language   Languages are written in different directions, such as horizontally from left to right, or right to left, or vertically from right to left, or left to right. Some languages, such as Chinese, can be written horizontally

114 Functions in computer-aided translation systems

from left to right and right to left, and vertically from left to right or right to left. When a text contains strings written from left to right, such as numbers or English, it has to put them from left to right. The directionality of languages thus causes typographical problems, which have to be resolved before the text can be localized.

(iv) Linguistic adjustments Linguistic adjustments may be necessary due to the limited screen space when localizing software. Some localization software, such as Visual Localize, can allow the user to remove limits on a character set to facilitate linguistic adjustments. The issue of screen space can be compared to the addition of subtitles to a movie shown on a small screen.

(v) Typographical changes Typographical or logographical changes may be necessary when localizing from one language into another. The use of abbreviations for different command buttons is illustrative of such changes.

(vi) Terminological consistency Terminological consistency is required when localization is applied to more than one product. When terminological variations are necessary, localization software is functionally capable of performing multiple translations of the same term as determined by the context. Consider the terminological issues when localizing a product for both Mainland China and Taiwanese users.

(vii) Fragment translation Apart from document translation, such as the User Guide, most of the work of software and web localization translation is decontextualized fragment translation of terms and phrases, which relies heavily on pre-established terminology and translation memory databases.

(viii) Punctuation marks There are differences in punctuation marks in different languages. For example, English places a period at the end of a sentence, whereas Chinese uses a small circle; book titles are italicized in some Indo-European languages, whereas Chinese put them in guillemots 《》.

(ix) Diacritics Some languages have special characters which cannot be displayed correctly on some computers, such as Ÿ, ÿ, Ð, ð, ß, and þ. They might cause problems in localization.

(x) Time and date formats A variety of conventions and formats for time and date have been used or adopted by the same language and different languages. In other words, the elements of time and dates have been put in different orders in different languages. Basically, there are three methods of expressing written dates: (1) year-month-day, as in Chinese, such as 2010年12月10日; (2) month-day-year, as in American English, such as 11/12/10, which would refer to November 12, 2010; and (3) day-month-year, as in French and German, such as jeudi 10 décembre 2010 (French) and Donnerstag, 10. Dezember 2010 (German). These differences should be noted when localizing a software product.

Functions in computer-aided translation systems   115

(xi) Phone numbers   Phone numbers are different all around the world. For web localization, it may be necessary to indicate the country code of the phone numbers on the webpage. For example, the phone number of a company in San Jose, California, the United States, should include the country code +1, the area code 408, and the number.

(xii) Units of measure   Basically, two major measure systems are in use: the imperial British system and the metric measurement system. Software produced in the United Kingdom with the system of pounds, miles, and gallons would have to be changed to kilogrammes, centimetres, and litres when they are used in Australia or Japan.

(xiii) Number formats   The number format varies from language to language. For instance, in English and Japanese, a comma is used to indicate thousands, whereas a dot separates the decimals, as in '12,345.56'. In other countries such as Italy, Germany, or Spain, it is the opposite, as in '12.345,56'.

In addition, there are some variations in nomenclature. The American billion (1,000,000,000), for example, is equivalent to the British thousand million; whereas the American trillion would be equal to the British billion.

(xiv) Currency formats   Different ways are also used for different currencies, such as symbols (£ , $), alphabetic characters (SFrs), or combinations (Cz$). Renminbi or RMB may have to be inserted in localizing foreign-language software into a simplified Chinese system. For example, for a sum of 112233, it is 112 233€ in French Francs, $112,233 in American Dollars, 112.233€ in German Deutsch Marks, and ¥112,233 in Japanese Yen.

(xv) Address formats   There are various means of formatting addresses, postal codes, provinces, and states.

CULTURAL ASPECTS

Cultural localization is about the creation of locally acceptable images and traditionally practiced conventions, involving the modification of graphic elements to meet local cultural norms (Schäler 2002: 21–23). This is possible as a result of the reduction of cultural elements in the internationalization process. Culturalization of software or a website is therefore a very important part of a localization project. What is culturally unsuitable might have to be removed in the process of localization.

(i) Intercultural communication   Translation is the transmission of culture; it is a type of intercultural communication. Translation in the context of software localization means the enlargement of the users for that product across cultural boundaries.

(ii) Cultural correctness   The factor of cultural correctness, which involves cultural perceptions, as well as religious and political influences, has to be assessed in software localization.

116 *Functions in computer-aided translation systems*

(iii) Ideological acceptability Translation is the translation of ideology, involving the transfer of thoughts and ideas from one language (the source language) to another (the target language) by means of the written word. Some ideologically unacceptable messages might have to be screened out in the process of localization.

(iv) Colour conventions The cultural associations of colour must be considered. As colour is culture-bound, different colours have different associations. Red, for example, means danger in European cultures, but festivity in the Chinese culture.

(v) Cultural symbols It should be noted that graphics with a specific cultural symbol, such as a sign of a landmark in a specific place, should be avoided in order not to cause any confusion.

Economic aspects

Economies move at breath-taking speed on a global scale. Telecommunications technology has globalized economies and opened enormous markets. The power of the Internet allows a small company to have an international presence, while localization promotes products globally so that they are easily understood by target users, regardless of their language or culture (Allied Business Intelligence 2002).

It is clear that localization increases the sale of products. If the sales of a certain product decline in a particular market, localization can make that product profitable in other places. Localization has thus become a thriving business (DePalma 2006). It is estimated that over 70 per cent of software suppliers localize new releases. Models of mobile phones that are out of fashion in a certain location, for instance, might have a huge market in underdeveloped regions. As quoted by Lynne Bowker (2002b: 12), 'Allied Business Intelligence estimated the worldwide market for localization and web-site translation to be about US$11 billion in 1999, and they predict that it will grow to US$20 billion by 2004'. That explains why so many international companies have created multiple-language websites to promote the sale of their products, such as Kodak and Benz.

It is obvious that in an increasingly global economy, there is also an increased pressure to produce high-quality multilingual content on time and on budget. Localization project teams must be as productive as possible to meet tight deadlines. Multiple translation projects have to be managed at the same time to ensure simultaneous shipment of the product. Terminology databases and translation memory databases must be created to reuse previously translated content to maximize efficiency. The economic aspects of a localization procedure should not be neglected.

Legal aspects

Localization has to meet all the legal requirements that are enforced in the user's region. Special attention must be paid to avoid infringement of intellectual

Functions in computer-aided translation systems 117

property. Copyright and personal data protection regulations, for example, differ from country to country.

Localization project management

When a software product is to be localized, a localization project will be created either by an in-house localization group or an outsourced team, which usually involves the software developer with its in-house translation staff, the software developer's subsidiary in the target language country, the distributor(s) of the software in the target language country, and the localization vendor (Esselink 1998: 5). For the actual management of a typical localization project, a localization team usually consists of a project manager, translator, localization specialist or senior translator, proofreader/QA specialist, localization engineer, testing engineer, and desktop publisher (Dunne 2006). The project manager schedules the project, assigns resources, reports to the client, and monitors the project workflow. The translator is responsible for translating software and linguistic quality assurance. Localization specialists review the work that translators do and manage terminology. Localization engineers are responsible for internationalization, localization engineering, technical quality assurance, and all technical aspects of software localization projects. Testing engineers perform the testing of a translated product to ensure that the localized product is fully functional, linguistically accurate, and that no issues have been introduced during the localization process. They often perform tests on a product to ensure that it functions correctly and satisfactorily. It is very important to test the software application before releasing it to the market, as the cost of correcting a problem increases over time. Desktop publishers take care of the layout of the printed or online material and sometimes do preparation for pre-press production.

(1) PRE-LOCALIZATION STAGE

The pre-localization stage involves extensive consultation to solicit expectations about the localization process and what must be achieved. The availability of human resources to execute localization must be checked, and the solution of possible problems prior to starting with the localization process, worked out.

(2) LOCALIZATION STAGE

(i) Project planning The project manager should find out the needs of clients, work out costs, and provide quotations. The project manager, with the input from the localization team, creates a project strategy and plan based on file types, project scope, and turn-around time, and provides a timeframe for product delivery.

(ii) Project execution The project execution concerns, strictly speaking, the translation stage, in which translation technology, and in particular computer-aided

118   *Functions in computer-aided translation systems*

translation tools, such as translation memory and terminology management tools, plays an essential role. This is due to the fact that both recurrence and repeatability are common in localization, which involves the translation of user interfaces, manuals, specifications, and others.

(iii) Quality management The project manager works closely with their client counterparts throughout the project to ensure effective communication. This is a type of quality control procedure to make sure that issues are quickly identified and promptly resolved.

(iv) Quality delivery At this stage, timely and quality delivery must be observed. In-country reviewers may also be asked to assess the quality of the final product.

(3) POST-LOCALIZATION STAGE

After the delivery of the product, follow-up work and maintenance service have to be provided. Adjustment may also be required, based on feedback on the product.

Localization procedure

There is hardly a standard procedure for localization (Cañestro 2005; DiFranco and Irmler 2003). It depends on a number of variables, such as the purpose of localization, the type of content, the target user, the release cycle, and the size of the product. There are, nevertheless, some tasks and phases common in the localization workflow. A localization project usually goes through four phases, as detailed in the following.

(I) PREPARATION OR CREATION OF A NEW LOCALIZATION PROJECT
      BY LOCALIZATION MANAGER

The major tasks to be performed in this phase are: (1) the creation of a project plan, outlining the schedule and financial details of the project as a form of pre-production planning; (2) the setup of the project team, consisting of project managers, engineers, and linguists; (3) the analysis of the product with a localizability test, in order to ensure that the product is suitable for localization; and (4) the study of the terminology of the product for terminology development (Stoeller 2003).

(II) TRANSLATION OF THE PROJECT BY TRANSLATORS

Translators working on localization projects have to be able to use translation technology in their work, such as terminology management systems, machine translation systems, and computer-aided translation systems. The use of computer-aided translation systems, especially terminology management and translation

Functions in computer-aided translation systems 119

memory tools, are of particular importance in the localization procedure, as it involves some major advantages, such as:

> *Reusing translations for repetitive texts.* Software documentation tends to be repetitive. For documentary translation, two types of repetitions can be distinguished: internal and external. Internal repetitions refer to textual repetitions within the document itself, whereas external repetition refers to textual repetitions inherent to a family of documents.
>
> *Reusing translations for updated information:* Software applications are regularly updated. Existing translations can be reused in new versions of help files or manuals.
>
> *Terminological consistency by termbase and translation memory database:* Consistency in terminology in team translation is maintained with the use of both the terminological and translation memory databases in a computer-aided translation system. The translator can also export and import translation memory exchange (TMX) files to and from translation memory tools.

(III) ENGINEERING THE LOCALIZATION PROJECT BY ENGINEERS

Localization engineers extract text strings from the software to localize them. Their tasks include adjustment of documentation layout and dialogue box resizing due to text swell; adaptation of accelerator keys, tooltips, tab order, menu options, and buttons; sorting of the orders in list boxes; compilation of help files; localization of multimedia files and embedded graphics containing text; and re-creation of sound effects containing text.

(IV) TESTING OF THE LOCALIZED APPLICATION BY THE
QUALITY ASSURANCE TEAM

After the work of translation and engineering is done, the localized application is run and the localization system can check the application for consistency against the localized software, as well as conduct user interface testing, functional testing, and cosmetic testing. Regular reviews will be conducted to prevent errors found in testing from recurring in future projects.

The future of the localization industry

In view of the rapid changes in various areas in the present digital age, it is hard to predict how the localization industry will develop over the next decade (O'Hagan 2003). The size of the industry, moreover, is extremely hard to know and the revenue that can be generated from localization is uncertain. Looking into the future, there are a number of areas which deserve our examination.

120 *Functions in computer-aided translation systems*

The first concerns the change in the languages for localization. Up to the present, localization has been made predominantly from English into other major languages, such as French, German, and Spanish. The trend of 'reverse localization', or localization into English, though starting to emerge, is not yet obvious (Schäler 2005). It is worth noting the emergence of 'strategic languages', which represent new market areas with a potential for new revenue streams, as opposed to the keeping of a number of 'maintenance languages', such as French, Italian, German, and Spanish (FIGS), whose market has to be maintained and served but has little potential for market growth. As far as the growth of localization languages is concerned, Chinese seems to be becoming the number one language at present, followed by Japanese and Spanish.

The second area that we should examine regards the needs or degrees of localization that software developers and producers deem necessary. According to Singh and Pereira (2005), there are five degrees of web localization: 'standardized', 'semi-localized', 'localized', 'highly localized', and 'culturally customized'. The differentiations among these lie in the necessity of translation, which is essential for the 'localized' and 'highly localized' options.

The third is related to the way localization is performed. Localization can be carried out in-house, within localization companies by language-service vendors through outsourcing, by online translation systems such as Google Translate or Google Translator Toolkit, or by non-professional translators through 'crowdsourcing'. It can be predicted that more words will be translated in a shorter period of time at a lower total cost through the use of global information management systems on the market or tailor-made for companies (DiFranco 2006).

Data editing stage

Data editing in the context of computer-aided translation consists of performing interactive editing through an interface provided by the system with a number of functions. The amount of editing depends on how much of the contents are totally reusable, as in the case of exact matching; partially reusable, as in the case of fuzzy matching; or totally non-reusable, as in the case of no matching. It also depends on how much of the contents are totally acceptable, partially modifiable with the application of translation methods, or entirely rejectable, which requires considerable rewriting.

Interactive editing for computer-aided translation systems

Editing in the case of computer-aided translation is interactive. Interactive editing is a process involving human intervention. It begins with the building of a terminology database and a translation memory database. When a source is put into a machine translation system for processing, it makes use of the databases to produce a draft translation, which is better than one which is made without human input.

Editing environments

The workbench on which editing is carried out is the editing platform of a system. According to Hutchins, 'a workbench provides facilities for computer-aided translation system operators to prepare input text, post-edit output and produce quality translations or publications' (Hutchins 1998: 288; Kugler, Ahmad, and Thurmair 1995; Lewalle 1998). The way a workbench is designed is closely related to the functions that a system offers.

Types of editing environments

There are two types of editing environments: platform-dependent environments and platform-independent environments (Lagoudaki 2009).

Table 3.4 Editing Environments of Nine CAT Systems

Name of the System	Name of the Editing Environment	Project File Extension
Across	CrossDesk	No system file extension
Déjà Vu X2	Editing Interface	*.dvprj* (project)
		.dvsat (satellite file)
		.dvpng (package)
Fluency Translation Suite (2013)	Fluency Workspace	(1) *.ftfx*
		(2) same as source format
MemoQ 6.2	Translation Editor	*.mprx*
OmegaT	Main window	*.project*
SDL-Trados Studio 2011	Editor	*.sdlxliff*
Snowman	SL-TL	*.stp*
	(project name)	
Translation Workspace	(1) Microsoft Word Plug-in	(1) *.rtf*
	(2) XLIFF Editor	(2) *.xlz*
Wordfast Classic (6.03t)	Workfast Workspace	Word format extension
XTM	XTM Workbench XTM Editor	No system file extension
Yaxin CAT 4.0	Yaxin CAT Platform 雅信輔助翻譯 平台	Word format extension

122 *Functions in computer-aided translation systems*

(A) PLATFORM-DEPENDENT ENVIRONMENTS

Platform-dependent environments are plug-in environments that, in turn, can be classified into two different types: text plug-in environment, such as Microsoft Word; and website plug-in environment, such as Google Translate.

Text plug-in environments

In order to work on a computer-aided translation system with a platform-dependent environment, a toolbar of the software must be installed in the 'Add-ins' ribbon of the text processor (e.g., Wordfast Classic for Microsoft Office). The buttons are usually assigned for commonly used functions for translation, such as 'Start Translation', 'Next Segment', 'Previous Segment', 'Get Translation' (from translation memory), 'Look Up a Term', 'Add a New Term', 'Finish Translation', and 'Clean Up the Current Document'. Usually, the software also provides users with shortcuts of the respective functions, which are usually customizable.

Some systems install the toolbars in a new ribbon so that the functions of the software can be separated from others. The new ribbon is usually named after the software, as shown in Figure 3.1.

When users click the 'Start Translation' button, the first source segment next to the pointer will be open in an inline text box. Another box is open below for translators to enter or edit translation. If a match is found in the translation memory, it is displayed in the box and a number indicates the match rate.

Translation should be entered strictly in the translation box. Some markers (tags) are also added to protect the text information at the beginning of a segment, at the separation of the source and translation text, and at the end of the translated segment. The translator must be careful not to damage the segmentation markers.

The colours of the inline box are useful indicators of the status of the translation. For example, after a document is pre-translated, the colour of the translation box can help to distinguish between source text and different types of target text (100% match, fuzzy match, or machine translation match).

In order to display the translation memory match and terms in the same window, some computer-aided translation systems offer a separate workbench.

When users click the 'start translation' button, a separate window will pop up. Many developers and researchers call this kind of window 'Workbench'. It can provide more functions than the toolbar, such as 'Analysis', 'Translation Memory Import', 'Translation Memory Export', 'Concordance Search', and 'Generate Target File'. Many translators like to move the workbench above the text editor and resize it to one third or one fourth of the screen, for easier consultation.

The translation memory match and the recognized term from terminology databases are displayed in the workbench. The match rate of the translation match is also often shown in this workbench, typically in the bottom bar. The workbench usually also provides a pane for displaying the terms found in the termbase(s).

Website plug-in environment

Some software, such as LogoVisa, PROMT, Memsource Cloud, and Translation Workspace, offer two interfaces.

This is a useful and practical categorization. Even the editor of the web browser-based computer-aided translation systems can fall into the two categories. For example, the translation editors of Translation Workspace and WebWordSystem are installed in Microsoft Word as text editor add-ins. The resources from the translation memories and termbases are still retrieved from online databases, but the translation editing environment can work as an offline application.

Other translation editors of web-based computer-aided translation systems run on a web browser, which can also be seen as an independent workstation. Wordfast Anywhere, shown in Figure 3.1, illustrates this.

Examples of computer-aided translation systems with platform-dependent environments include Anaphraseus, Anymem, Dr. Eye, Felix, Fusion, GE-CCT, Huajian IAT, LogiTerm LogoVista, LongRay, Memsource Editor, MetaTexis, MultiTrans, Similis, Snowball, TCloud, Translation Workspace, Visual Transmate, WebWordSystem, and Wordfast Classic.

(B) PLATFORM-INDEPENDENT ENVIRONMENTS

Platform-independent environments refer to editing environments that do not depend on a separate platform, a common type of which is the parallel translation

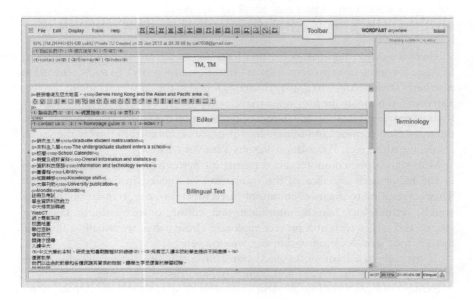

Figure 3.1 Editing Interface of Wordfast Anywhere

124   *Functions in computer-aided translation systems*

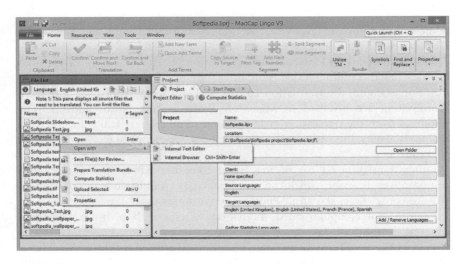

Figure 3.2 MadCap Lingo V9

editor. The user interfaces of standalone computer-aided translation systems have parallel translation editors. In most cases, the source text and translation text are displayed side-by-side or in a two-column table. The left column contains the segments of the source document, while the right one contains empty places where users enter translations. Users may scroll up and down to browse the source and target text in the editor. A typical user interface of the parallel translation editor is shown in Figure 3.2.

There are different panes in the user interface to display useful information to facilitate the translation process, such as 'Translation Memory', to show translation matches; 'Terminology', to display the terms found in the current segment; 'Project Explorer', to navigate the files in the translation project; and 'Concordance Search', to show the concordancing search results in translation memories. In some instances, the translation memory and terminology panes are combined to display the search results together, e.g., 'Translation Results Pane' in MemoQ.

Most standalone computer-aided translation systems have three or four panes in the major user interface of the translation editing environment by default. They correspond to the most commonly used functions, e.g., translation memory search, terminology search, interlinear text editor, or two-column table for source and target text, and project explorer. These panes are usually adjustable in size, font size, location within the window, etc.

As for web-based computer-aided translation systems, further possible panes include project management and comments and discussion panes.

Examples of platform-independent environment systems include Across, Araya XLIFF Editor, Atlas, Autshumato, CafeTrans, Crowdin, EsperantiloTM, Fluency, Fortis, GlobalSight, Google Translator Toolkit, Heartsome TMX Editor, Isometry,

Functions in computer-aided translation systems 125

Lingotek Collaborative Translation Platform, LogoVista, Madcap Lingo, Memsource Web Editor, MLTS An-Nakel Al Arabi, OmegaT, OmegaT+, Open Language Tools, OpenTM2, PC-Transer, ProMemoria, PROMT, SDL-Trados Studio, SDLX, Swordfish, Systran, TM-database, Transit, Transoo Editor, Transwhiz, TraTools, Wordbee, Wordfast Anywhere, and Wordfast Pro.

Features of the interactive editing environments

(A) SIMULTANEOUS HANDLING OF MULTIPLE FILES

Fortis Revolution Editor, for example, allows the translator to load multiple files in a single window so that several files can be simultaneously handled. This makes it easier to do searching in global tasks.

(B) AUTOMATIC SYNCHRONIZATION OF THE SOURCE TEXT
AND THE TARGET TEXT

A translator's workbench, such as Fortis Revolution Editor and Workbench of SDL-Trados, automatically recognizes translation units and records the translated segments dynamically. It automatically synchronizes the source language and the target language, providing the translator with easy access to information. In other words, a translator's workbench provides the previous translation to translators if it finds the translating sentence similar to or completely the same as the stored sentence. Then, the translator can refer to the previous translation and decide to accept, reject, or edit the suggested translation. A translator's workbench therefore combines translation memory database and termbases to provide useful translation suggestions.

(C) HIGHLIGHTING DIFFERENT TYPES OF INFORMATION

For easy reference, some systems, such as Fortis Revolution Editor, use different colours in the workbench to indicate the status of the text. These include 'Not Translated', 'Pre-translated', 'Manually Translated', and 'Validated'.

Concluding remarks on interactive editing

The work of data editing is multi-fold; therefore, there are a number of points that deserve our attention.

> *Completeness of Translation:* Fortis Revolution Editor, for example, has a function which can verify whether or not the translation is complete.
> *Consistency in Style:* Fortis Revolution Editor identifies errors in the use of consistent phrases and terminology.
> *Consistency in Form:* Fortis Revolution Editor verifies whether the formal aspects are correct.

126 *Functions in computer-aided translation systems*

Correctness in numbers and units

> *Correctness in Spelling:* Atlas, for example, has the function of Assistance to find typos in the original text (spell check) (http://www.fujitsu.com/global/services/software/translation/atlas).

Post-editing for machine translation systems

Post-editing is defined as 'an activity undertaken for the purpose of rendering a machine output text suitable for use' (Chan 2004: 175).

Methods to edit machine translation output are necessary, as recent developments in the field of computational linguistics have shown that fully automatic high-quality translation (FAHQT) is a dream rather than a reality. It is thus more realistic to take into account various possible interactions between a human translator and a machine translation system.

Purposes of editing

Post-editing has several purposes, the most important of which are: (1) making sure that the source text has been translated accurately (accuracy); (2) removing what is not faithful to the original text (faithfulness); (3) making the output conform to the grammatical conventions of the target language (grammaticality); (4) checking that the translation is idiomatic (idiomaticity); and (5) ensuring that the information transmitted is adequate (informativeness). Editing also involves the correction of different types of errors.

As connection to machine translation is fast becoming the norm of the industry, methods to post-edit machine output are important to quality assurance of the target text.

Standards of the target text

Editing, as mentioned above, ensures that the five standards of translation are maintained in the target text.

Accuracy, as mentioned above, involves the correct comprehension of the source message, a proper transfer of the meaning of that message, and the generation of that message as exactly as possible into the target language. Accuracy affects the degree of syntactical modification required for post-translation revision, as we have sentences that need revision of major errors, sentences that need revision of minor errors, sentences that need retranslation, and sentences that have not been translated at all.

The second standard, faithfulness, can be divided, in the context of machine translation, into different levels based on the following situations:

(1) The entire contents of the original text have been very faithfully translated.
(2) The entire contents of the original text have been faithfully reproduced.

Functions in computer-aided translation systems 127

(3) The translation is generally faithful to the original.
(4) The translation is generally faithful to the original text, but there are linguistic errors.
(5) The structure and contents of the original work are not well preserved in the translation.
(6) The structure and contents of the original are poorly translated.
(7) The translation reflects neither the structure nor the contents of the original text.

Grammaticality, on the other hand, is about conforming to the standard grammatical usage of the target language. This is relatively easy for a human translator, but extremely difficult for an automatic translation system.

Idiomaticity is also important, because an idiomatic translation reproduces the meaning of the source language in the natural form of the receptor language. Clearly, an idiomatic translation by a machine translation system is still a goal to be achieved.

Finally, informativeness concerns the transmission of information from the source text to the target text. The treatment of figures, the translation of proper names, and the rendition of jargon all constitute an informational translation. Often, machine translation users only need a 'rough translation' of the original focusing on a summary of the original. In the present age of information explosion, it is impossible and obviously unnecessary to translate everything in the text. Gist translation, which is to have a rough translation of what is contained in the text, may save a lot of time and energy.

Correction of errors

To make sure that the target text is accurate, faithful, grammatical, idiomatic, and informative, a number of errors in the target text need to be corrected. They include linguistic, terminological, syntactical, referential, stylistic, and typological errors.

Linguistic errors produced by an MT system may include: (1) the inversion of meaning; (2) the omission of words; (3) the addition of words originally nonexistent; (4) the deviation of meaning from the original; and (5) the emergence of modifications which are not called for.

Terminological errors, on the other hand, are errors in translating the most important terms in a text. These keywords are certainly more important than the general vocabulary.

Syntactical errors refer to errors occurring at the sentence level. These errors are in general less serious than terminological errors as far as comprehensibility is concerned.

Referential errors are about facts in the real world and concern propositions such as 'water is solid'. Referential errors might not be produced by the author of the text, but by the erroneous matching of source-text lexemes with target-text lexemes, which makes the meaning of the translation rather 'out of this world'.

128 *Functions in computer-aided translation systems*

Stylistic errors involve using language that is inappropriate to the content and intention of the text. Machine translation outputs are often stylistically inappropriate.

Typological errors refer to the errors in translating the typological conventions of specific text types. They serve as a test of the quality of a machine translation system when using it to translate samples of different text types, such as journalistic, technical, and literary writings, to see if the outputs are intelligible and accurate.

Stages of editing

Editing in the context of machine translation refers to pre-editing a source text before it is mechanically processed, revising the generated text during machine processing, and post-editing the machine output before the target text is finalized.

Post-editing factors

Post-editing refers to an activity undertaken for the purpose of rendering the machine translation output suitable for use. Post-editing is important in evaluating the accuracy, cost, and acceptability of machine translation systems. Post-editing is required when MT output has failed to capture ideas in the original, reproduce the style of writing, transfer different senses of expressions, remove cultural differences, and produce a fluent target text. The density of post-editing serves to indicate the accuracy of the raw translation, and the time required for post-editing directly affects the cost of machine translation, while acceptability of the output depends largely on the amount of post-editing required.

The quality of post-editing is closely related to the language and computing skills of the reviser, including translation and bilingual competence, and the knowledge of machine translation. Post-editing is about applying the methods of human translation to edit a machine output, which is usually produced by a dictionary-based machine translation approach or a literal approach in human translation. Post-editing is also about knowing the references for consultation and editing.

There are a number of factors affecting post-editing, as described below.

> *Target Users* can be classified according to age, such as children and adults; education, such as secondary school students/university graduates; language, such as major and minor language speakers; profession, such as lawyers; and organization, such as government departments.
>
> *Text Length* and *Text Quantity* also affect editing. Lengthy texts are time-consuming to edit, whereas short texts take less time to edit. However, there are exceptions, such as poems, slogans, and end-clippers.

The *Expected Quality* of the translation varies with the end-user. When the translation is for reference, internal consumption, or concerns basic information, minimal editing is required. On the other hand, when the target text is for formal occasions, publicity, or legal and serious purposes, heavy editing is required.

Turn-around Time refers to the time between the placement of a translation assignment and its delivery. The time required to complete a translation assignment is usually decided by the type of service requested, the type of text to be translated, the degree of editing required, and the availability of staff to complete the assignment or project.

Life Expectancy of the Translation concerns how long the translation is to be used and also affects the degree of editing. Translations may be used instantly, such as subtitles; for a short term, such as announcements; for a medium term, such as roadwork notices; and for a long term, such as legislative documents.

The *Purposes of a Translation* are varied. Translations may be used for information purposes. For instance, machine translation has been used as a tool to collect information on certain areas or regions for political or intelligence purposes. They may also be used for internal or external distribution, which require minimal post-editing. However, if the purpose of translation is to publish it, then the quality of translation has to be high, the time of production is relatively long, and the revision work tends to be enormous.

Edit Distance refers to the amount of editing that is required to close up the distance between a machine translation output and a correct translation example. There are two types of edit distance: single and multiple. Single edit distance refers to the amount of editing that is required to close up the distance between a machine translation output and a single correct translation example, whereas multiple edit distance refers to the amount of editing that is required to close up the distance between a machine translation output and a number of correct translation examples.

There are several types of post-editing, namely full post-editing, maximum post-editing, minimal post-editing, and rapid post-editing.

Full post-editing involves editing the output in full so as to produce a text which is of the same quality as a professional human translation. Maximum post-editing is to make the greatest possible revisions on machine-translated texts so that they can be published and read by a large number of people. Minimal post-editing refers to machine-translated texts that do not need much editing before dissemination. This is described by Jeffrey Allen as 'a fuzzy, wide-ranging category'. In a minimal post-editing, a text is edited with a specific readership in mind. The amount of editing may be quite extensive if the text is required to be of fairly high quality, or quite limited if the text's usefulness is likely to be short-lived or if the information is more important than the style

130 *Functions in computer-aided translation systems*

of delivery. Rapid post-editing, as defined by Alan Melby, is a 'strictly minimal editing on texts in order to remove blatant and significant errors . . . stylistic issues should not be considered'.

Post-editing issues

There are several lexical issues relating to post-editing.

Mistranslated words

Mistranslated words are words which are translated wrongly by a machine translation system. Mistranslation is caused by the coverage of the database and the approach that the system adopts. Inference can be applied to the output of a dictionary-based machine translation system.

Words can be wholly mistranslated or partially mistranslated. In the case of Chinese-English translation, a partially wrong translation may end up being wholly mistranslated. For instance, *Shi chang* 市場, which means 'market', may be translated as 'city' 場, and *li ding* 釐定, meaning 'gauge', may be rendered as 'decide' 釐. In both cases, the translations are incorrect.

Not Translated Words

Abbreviated as NTWs, these are words present in a source text that cannot be translated by a machine translation system, which leaves them untranslated in the output. There are all sorts of NTWs, depending on the information contained in the database of the system. Local expressions, journalistic jargon, and chatroom abbreviations, for example, are usually not translated.

Do-not-translate words

Computationally, it is possible to create a list of words, such as personal names and place names, that will be left untranslated by a machine translation system. For instance, proper names in kindred languages, such as 'John' and 'Mary' in English-French translation, are considered 'do-not-translate' words. Proper names in non-kindred languages are normally translated.

Though the creation of 'do-not-translate' words is usually done at the pre-editing stage, post-editors need to translate proper names at the output stage for those names which are left untranslated and translated wrongly.

Omitted words

When translating long and complicated sentences, some systems simply leave them untranslated and omit them altogether.

Functions in computer-aided translation systems   131

Unfound words

Local terms, which may not be stored in a system produced in a different country, are considered unfound words and are usually poorly translated.

Unknown proper nouns

Proper-noun translation is extremely difficult for machine translation systems. Proper names include personal names, object names, place names, group names, art names, trademark names, and names of historical events. In Chinese, for instance, a proper noun 專有名詞 may refer to the name of a person, place, or object, such as London 倫敦, Beijing 北京, John 約翰, Chen Qiang 陳強, or Coke 可樂.

The regional variations in proper noun translation are problematic. Transliteration systems for mainland China (Hanyu pinyin) and for Taiwan (Wade-Giles) are inconsistent. Similarly, transliteration for proper names in Hong Kong and Macau is less systematic.

In Chinese, there are several ways to translate proper nouns: (1) following the original pronunciation of the proper noun (*ming sui zhu ren* 名隨主人), such as Tokyo as 東京 and Kim Il Sung as 金日成; (2) using the most popular translation of the proper noun (*yue ding su cheng* 約定俗成), such as Churchill as 邱吉爾, Roosevelt as 羅斯福, and 孫中山 as Sun Yat-sen; or (3) following the standard transliteration of the proper noun. In English-Chinese translation, this means transliterating the proper noun according to its standard pronunciations, such as putting Belgrade into *bei er ge lai de* 貝爾格萊德.

Unknown acronyms

An acronym is an abbreviation formed by using the first letters, or initials, of a series of words, and each constituent letter is pronounced separately BBC (pronounced as b-b-c), IBM (pronounced as i-b-m), FBI: Federal Bureau of Investigation (f-b-i), UFO: Unidentified flying object (u-f-o), VIP: Very important person (v-i-p). Acronyms are difficult to translate by a machine translation system.

Unknown Net language

Net language, otherwise known as 'Netlish', 'Weblish', or 'Cyberspeak', is a sublanguage, or a kind of ICQ language, that is used in Internet-based communication. Net language is not merely about abbreviated set expressions, slang, or jargon, but also the use of emoticons.

132 *Functions in computer-aided translation systems*

Translation methods used in editing

There are a large number of translation methods for pre-editing, interactive editing, and post-editing. This section discusses both the general methods used by human translators and the methods used in computer-aided translation.

Methods for human translation

Editing requires the use of human translation methods to produce a high quality translation. The following are some of the common methods translators use in translation.

Addition is a common method in translation. It involves the provision of some essential information for a better comprehension of the translated passage. According to Eugene Nida, the method of addition is used for the following purposes: (1) filling out elliptical expressions; (2) obligatory specification; (3) grammatical restructuring; (4) amplification from implicit to explicit status; (5) answers to rhetorical questions; (6) classifiers, which is to add a classifier to a noun when translating from Chinese to English or a measure word in English-Chinese translation, such as *a chair* 一張椅子 where *Zhang* 張 is added to the translation to conform to the Chinese usage of measure words; (7) connectives, such as the translation of '春 *chun* 夏 *xia* 秋 *qiu* 冬 *dong*' into 'spring, summer, autumn, *and* winter'. The addition of 'and' is grammatically necessary; (8) categories of the receptor languages that do not exist in the source language; and (9) doublets.

Interpolation, explanation, and annotation are all methods of addition, which can help bring out the semantic and contextual meaning of the original (Barik 1971: 199–210; Newmark 1988; Nida 1964).

Amplification is used to add some words in the target text to produce an accurate translation in keeping with the usage of the language to be translated into (Shen R. 1984: 144–157). Amplification is a translation method similar to addition, expansion, explicitation, and, sometimes, paraphrasing. Amplification also involves bringing out in full what has been ellipted in the sentence.

Block-out Method is, according to Hilaire Belloc (1931: 26–27), a method that can be used in the translation of prose. He says in *On Translation*:

> The translator should, I think, not plod on, sentence by sentence, still less word by word, but always 'block out' his work. When I say 'block out' I mean that he should read over his material at large to grasp it as a whole in the original before he undertakes the translation, and after that, when the translation is under way, he should take it at least section by section, paragraph by paragraph, and ask himself before each what the whole sense is which he has to render, what the effect of the unit as a whole may be, before reproducing it in another tongue.

Borrowing is a translation technique that takes a word or phrase from the source language and uses it in the target language. The specific item borrowed

Functions in computer-aided translation systems 133

is called a loan word or phrase. It is fairly common to pronounce the loan word according to the sound system of the target language (Ching 1966: 107–116; Gonzalex 1991: 179–188; Hervey, Higgins, and Loughridge 1995; Vinay and Darbelnet 1958/1995).

Bottom-up Translation is a translation method that begins with the smallest translation unit continuing up to the largest. This method is generally considered unable to yield acceptable results (Chan 2004: 26).

Compensation is defined by Sándor Hervey, Ian Higgins, and Michael Loughridge (1995: 27) as 'techniques of making up for the loss of important ST [Source Text] features through replicating ST effects approximately in the TT [Target Text] by means other than those used in the ST'. Four aspects of compensation can be distinguished (1995: 27–32): 'compensation in kind', which refers to 'making up for one type of textual effect in the ST by another type in the TT'; 'compensation in place', which consists in 'making up for the loss of a particular effect found at a given place in the ST by creating a corresponding effect at an earlier or later place in the TT'; 'compensation by merging', which is to 'condense ST features carried over a relatively long stretch of text . . . into a relatively short stretch of the TT'; and 'compensation by splitting', which is used 'where there is no single TL word that covers the same range of meaning as a given ST word'.

Conversion involves converting one system into another, such as converting the Chinese traditional measurement system into either the metric system or the British imperial system.

Copywriting concerns the writing of advertising or publicity copy. Due to cultural differences, it is impossible to translate an advertisement in the source culture satisfactorily into the advertising cultures of other countries and regions. Adverts for foreign countries should, therefore, always be produced in those countries through copywriting (Séguinot 1994: 247–265; Smith and Klein-Braley 1997: 173–184; Weller 1992: 145–154).

Cultural Adaptation involves adapting a translation to the cultural environment of the target language (Nord 1994: 59–67).

Cultural Equivalence concerns an approximate translation where a source language cultural word is translated by a target language cultural word. If the concept has its origin in the source language, knowledge of its culture is necessary. In other words, cultural equivalence refers to the matching of a source language culture-specific term with a corresponding target language term which can fully and effectively convey the original meaning and image. Cultural equivalents replace the source language with target language equivalents and, therefore, are inaccurate per se. They are used on the ground that, in the case of cultural differences, they constitute a procedure for securing the equivalent pragmatic effect, which means producing the nearest possible effect on the target language readership to the one obtained on the source language readership.

Translation theorists suggest that the connotations of an English summer day may not be understood by other people as beautiful and hot. Where the source

134　*Functions in computer-aided translation systems*

language culture is important, it has to be preserved; where it is not, there is a choice between a culture-free universal component as well as a target cultural equivalent.

The more effective use of cultural equivalents in translation is explanatory rather than emotional, and particularly for uninformed and not much interested readerships. Cultural equivalents are to give a general impression; they are inaccurate in many details, since cultural terms are per se peculiar to one language community (Briere 1988: 34–39; Loehlin 1962: 140–141; Reyburn 1969: 158–167; Reyburn 1970: 26–35; Sarcevic 1985: 127–133).

Cultural Substitution is a translation method that, according to Mona Baker, can be explained as 'replacing a culture-specific item or expression with a target-language item which does not have the same propositional meaning but is likely to have a similar impact on the target reader' (Baker 1992: 31; Beekman and Callow 1974).

Cultural Transplantation is close to adaptation and represents a systematic attempt to convert the source culture setting into a receptor culture one. Transplanting a culture to another is not like simply moving an object from one place to another. Rather, the transplantation should be conditional and selective, as the source culture and language are living entities, which cannot and indeed should not be removed mechanically (Li T. 1988: 28–30; Tu G. 1996: 9–12).

Definitional Translation involves defining a source term in the translation. Two things have to be kept in mind: (1) no definition can give all the information; and (2) the information provided must be relevant.

Denominalization is a translation method by which a nominal structure of the source text is put into a verbal structure in the target text.

Descriptive Equivalent means to provide an explanation or give an account of the source language expression in the target language text. Descriptive equivalents are normally used as footnotes, as they are too long to fit the target text. Functional equivalents would fare better.

Diagrammatic Translation concerns the transfer of the content of the source text into a diagram rather than a text (Gouadec 1990).

Direct Equivalence provides a one-to-one equivalent to the source term, such as translating *bei* 杯 as 'cup' and *cha chi* as 'teaspoon' (Chan 2002: 17).

Direct Transfer refers to a translation procedure which reproduces certain elements of information in the source text, such as numbers, dates, or proper names, directly into the target text without any changes.

Double Translation is a translation procedure where the translator makes two separate attempts to cover the meaning of a word, e.g., 'autonomy – the activities of a self-administered body'.

Ethnographic Translation aims to pay full attention to the cultural background of both the authors and the recipients and takes into account differences between source and target language. An example of this is the 'translation' of the Christian religious traditions based in the Middle East into the cultural norms of modern-day America (Casagrande 1954: 335–340; Nida 1945: 194–208).

Explanation clarifies what the source term means in the translation.

Extratextual Gloss is a translation method used when the translator considers it necessary to offer some explanation of the meaning or the implications of a cultural term in the form of a gloss external to the main text, such as footnotes, endnotes, glossaries, commentaries in brackets, translations in brackets, translations in italics, etc. (Aixelb 1995: 115).

Facsimile Approach reproduces the source text like the operation of a copying machine. In 1963, Georges Moumin proposed the idea of a transparent translator, whose presence in the translation would be totally unnoticed. It is as if the reader of the translation looks at a work of art through a pane of glass; there is absolutely no obstruction between the author and the reader (Xu 1988: 49–53).

Footnotes are used by translators to provide information that will help the reader understand the translated text more fully (Osborn 1982: 414). According to Robert G. Bratcher, they can be classified into nine categories plus an additional note: (1) Textual Notes, to show textual variants or alternative readings on which the translation is based; (2) Translational Notes, which provide other possible translations of the same text, also known as alternative renderings; (3) Linguistic Notes, which explain plays on words, popular derivations of meaning, or professional jargon; (4) Cultural Notes, which explain the cultural elements in the text; (5) People, notes that identify important personalities and explain their significance as far as the immediate text is concerned; (6) Historical Events, notes that identify important events and explain their significance in the context of the immediate text; (7) Places, to identify important geographical locations and explain their significance; (8) Dates, notes that identify the dates of events and people as accurately as possible; (9) References, which refer to other sources relevant to the text; and, finally, (10) Source Text, notes that refer to the source of the text being translated.

It should be emphasized that too many footnotes are inappropriate and unnecessary. Moreover, the types of footnotes to be used and their frequency depend on the kind of translation being prepared and the audience for whom it is intended. Footnotes are meant to be functional.

Formulation Translation is defined by Omar Sheikh Al-Shabab (1996: 52) as 'a kind of translation in which the translator bypasses pre-dictionary translation and resorts to conventions and ready modes of (pre-dictionary) translations which have been accepted'. Most daily activities of professional translation can be regarded as formulation translation (Al-Shabab 1996).

Free Translation reproduces the content without the form of the original. In other words, the linguistic structure of the source text is ignored and the emphasis has been shifted to the reproduction of the meaning the original text intends to convey to the reader. Free translation ranges from paraphrasing and adaptation to rewriting. It reproduces the matter without the manner, or the content without the form of the original. It is a kind of target-language-biased translation in which there is a global correspondence between the textual

136   *Functions in computer-aided translation systems*

units of the source text and those of the target text, such as sentence-to-sentence correspondence or paragraph-to-paragraph translation (Dan H. 1994: 95–102; Daniels 1973: 12–20; Gao Z. 1988: 2–5; Li Q. 1990: 18–22; Wen J. 1989: 653–654).

Generalization concerns the translation of what is specific in the source text into the general in the translation.

Generic Translation is a translation technique that pays special attention to the grammatical, lexical, and stylistic markers characteristic of a special type of text. This means that a translator has to be sensitized to the textual similarities of the two languages he or she is working in. When a translator is translating a text, he or she is influenced by previous translations of similar texts, and has to consider the same problems (Neubert 1995: 1016–1028).

Gist Translation refers to a type of translation in which the target text expresses only a condensed version of the source text message (Hervey, Higgins, and Loughridge 1995: 9). Gisting is, therefore, the production of a rough or outline translation of a text to provide an insight into the subject and overall content of the source text. It is often done before a 'proper' or 'custom' translation is produced so as to determine whether a text contains useful information before a custom translation is commissioned. The term 'gisting' is sometimes used in connection with machine translation, which is used by some translation providers for that purpose.

Gloss Translation is, according to Eugene A. Nida, a type of translation that aims at reproducing 'as literally and meaningfully as possible the form and content of the original' (1964: 159).

Grammatical Equivalence, as its own name indicates, is equivalence on the grammatical level (Baker 1992: 82–118).

Grammatical Translation, as defined by J. C. Catford (1965: 71), is a restricted translation in which the source language grammar of a text is replaced by equivalent target language grammar, but with no replacement of lexis.

Grammatical Transposition is defined by Hervey, Higgins, Cragie, and Gambarotta (2000: 215) as: 'translating an ST expression having a given grammatical structure by a TT expression having a different grammatical structure containing different parts of speech in a different arrangement'.

Graphological Translation is a restricted translation in which the source language graphology (writing system) of a text is replaced by equivalent target language graphology (Catford 1965; Ju and Zhu 1959: 40–43).

Illustration refers to the method of using an illustration to translate a word involving a physical entity which does not have an equivalent in the target language (Baker 1992: 42).

Image-conversion Method involves converting the cultural image(s) in the source text into comprehensible expressions in the target language.

Imitation is a partial translation method. According to John Dryden, there are three forms of translation: metaphrase, paraphrase, and imitation. In his preface to *Ovid's Epistles* (1680), he gives a detailed explanation of 'imitation':

Functions in computer-aided translation systems 137

The third way (of translation) is that of imitation, where the translator (if now he has not lost that name) assumes the liberty, not only to vary from the words and sense, but to forsake them both as he sees occasion; and taking only some general hints from the original, to run division on the groundwork, as he pleases. . . . I take imitation of an author . . . to be an endeavour of a later poet to write like one who has written before him, on the same subject; that is, not to translate his words, or to be confined to his sense, but only to set him as a pattern, and to write, as he supposes that author would have done, had he lived in our age, and in our country.

Indicative Translation concerns a type of translation that is not intended for publication or wide dissemination but simply for a user to get an indication of the content of a document (Melby 1995: 37).

Indirect Translation refers to a translation process in which the translator does not translate directly from the language of the original, but indirectly from a translated version of the original work. To translate through an intermediary language is, in theory, not a satisfactory method, as the quality of the translation will be seriously affected by the first translation of the original. This method has been frequently employed either to overcome the serious language barrier that exists between the source text and the target text, say between Chinese and German, or to facilitate an easy rendition of the source text by working between kindred languages, say between Chinese and Japanese. In Bible translating, for example, most Chinese versions are produced through English rather than the original Hebrew or Greek texts. Indirect translation is the same as 'intermediate translation' or 'second-hand translation' (Gutt 1991; Rado 1975: 51–59).

Information Translation concerns the transmission of information of the original text to the reader. This means to convey only the referential contexts, but neither the style nor the form. The standard of presentation required may vary considerably, and may range from paraphrasing to summary. The transmission of correct information in a speedy manner is considered to be one of the most important functions of machine translation. The treatment of figures, the translation of proper names, the rendition of jargon, all constitute an informational translation. Machine translation users only need a 'rough translation' of the original, focusing on a summary of the original.

Interlinear Translation refers to a word-for-word translation that takes no account of the context but respects the details of the source language grammar by matching part of speech in the source text by the same part of speech in the target text. The primary senses of all words in the original are translated as though out of context, and the word-order of the original is retained. Strictly interlineal translation is rare and is done only for some very specific purposes, such as language teaching and descriptive linguistics. It is a kind of source-text-biased translation and an extreme form of literal translation (Gutt 1991; Steiner 1975: 296–413).

138   *Functions in computer-aided translation systems*

Interpolation explains a source expression in the translation.

Interpretation is a method in poetry translation. Translators may consciously or unconsciously employ expressions already existent in the target language to translate a foreign poem. As a result, the target readers may associate the translation to another poem in their culture which is essentially different from the original poem.

Intersemiotic Translation is mentioned by Roman Jakobson (1959: 233), who states that 'intersemiotic translation or transmutation is an interpretation of verbal signs by means of signs of nonverbal sign systems'. This means translating from one semiotic code to another (Jakobson 1959: 232–239).

Intracultural Translation is a term used by Susan Bassnett and André Lefevere as a synonym of 'rewriting'. They hold the view that 'certain texts originally translated from another culture (the Bible, Lenin, Shakespeare) can become naturalized to such an extent that they are given the same 'intracultural' treatment as texts which have originally been generated within the culture in question' (Lefevere and Bassnett 1990: 9).

Intralingual Translation is mentioned by Roman Jakobson (1959: 233), who says: 'Intralingual translation or rewording is an interpretation of verbal signs by means of other signs of the same language'. Putting classical Chinese into modern Chinese is one example.

Intratextual Gloss is a translation method used when the translators feel that, for the sake of transparency and smoothness, they can or should integrate the gloss into the text (Aixelb 1995: 115). This term is interchangeable with 'interpolation', which is a general term covering various methods that translators use to explain the meaning of an expression in the translation text.

Inversion is a translation technique used in rendering a series of long sentences. The translation begins from the last sentence and goes all the way back to the first (Lin J. 1983: 17–19).

Lexical Equivalence refers to the matching of a term in the target language with a certain term in the source language by the use of a dictionary. Dictionaries and glossaries for language pairs have been developed to provide lexical equivalents (Balasubramanian 1988: 13–20).

Lexical Translation concerns a restricted translation in which the source language lexis of a text is replaced by an equivalent target language lexis, but with no replacement of grammar.

Linguistic Equivalence refers to the linguistic correspondence between the isolated elements of two or more language systems. This is defined by Anton Popovic as 'linguistic equivalence, where there is homogeneity on the linguistic level of both source language and target language texts, i.e. word for word translation' (Abernathy 1961: 95–98; Balasubramanian 1988: 13–20; Bassnett 1980: 25; Popović 1976).

Literal Translation is a translation method that renders the primary meaning of each individual word while retaining all the syntactic features of the source-language text. In a literal translation, the linguistic structure of the source text is followed, but is normalized according to the rules of the target

Functions in computer-aided translation systems 139

language. Literal translation ranges from morpheme-for-morpheme, word-for-word, phrase-for-phrase, and clause-for-clause translation. The smaller the unit is, the greater the literalness. Literal translation adheres to the form and syntactic structure of the original. Thus, this strategy is frequently used in poetry translation.

All the words of the source language are translated into the target language, taking, however, no account of the context. It is grammatically possible but stylistically awkward. Peter Newmark, when explicating his ideas of semantic and communicative translation, says that 'in communicative and semantic translation, provided that equivalent-effect is secured, the literal word-for-word translation is not only the best, it is the only valid method of translation' (Newmark 1981: 51).

Literal translation is a proper procedure to fill the cultural gaps in translation and a transparent method to spread the influence of the source culture on the target culture. But literalism should be used with care. For instance, it should not be used when a literal translation clashes with an existing expression in the target language that infers a meaning different from that of the original text. On top of that, it should definitely not be used when the literal translation result is ungrammatical in the target language (Beekman 1966: 178–189; Chan, S. 1998: 66–73; Lefevere 1975; Newmark 1988: 68–80; Shen D. 1989: 261–278, 1995: 568–579).

Loan Translation is a translation method in which words in one language are borrowed and used in another language. The borrowed words are known as 'loan words' (Carstensen 1988: 85–91; Hervey, Higgins, and Loughridge 1995; Vinay and Darbelnet 1958/1995).

Modification Method refers to the changing of some elements in the source text in the translation to conform to the target language usage.

Modified Transliteration is a type of name transliteration that does not follow the Romanization rules fully, but carefully selects words so that translated names appear to be of the target language and thus easily accessible to the target readers or audience. This method is particularly suitable for drama translation, as syllable-by-syllable transliterations often sound awkward in performance.

Naturalization concerns a translation procedure that first adapts the source-language word to the normal pronunciation, and then, to the normal morphology of the target language. For example, the word *exit* comes from *exitus* (Latin), and *music* from *musica* (Latin).

Nil Equivalence occurs, according to Otto Kade, when no target language expression exists for an expression in the source language (Hatim 2001: 29).

Oblique Translation deals with structural or metalinguistic differences between the source and target texts by adaptation, equivalence, modulation, and transposition (Vinay and Darbelnet 1958/1995: 31–40).

Omission is a translation method which leaves some words in the original untranslated to achieve grammatical accuracy and idiomaticity in the translation (Zhuang Y. 1980: 52–57).

140　*Functions in computer-aided translation systems*

There are two types of omission: general and grammatical. General omissions are made to conform to usage, achieve better diction, remove connectives, produce a context-bound translation, and remove elements in the source language text that might offend the new readership, e.g., sex, death, cruelty, or vulgarisms. Grammatical omissions, on the other hand, involve the omission of adverbs; personal pronouns, such as the subject; pronouns, such as the object; the word 'it'; conjunctions; articles; and prepositions.

Optimal Equivalence concerns the choice of one or several equivalences out of a number of potential equivalents. It can be the result of a trade-off between linguistic/stylistic options, subject preferences, and transfer alternatives. According to Jiri Levy (1967: 1171–1182), a translator begins with a set of possible choices. Each successive choice narrows the field of possible choices until the translator arrives at the single, optimal target language equivalent.

Over-translation refers to a translation that gives more detail than its corresponding source language unit (Duff 1995: 716–730).

Parallel Translation is a term used by the American linguist Joseph B. Casagrande to refer to the comparison of several translations of the same source text to reveal how systematic differences are dealt with at the grammatical and semantic levels (Casagrande 1954: 335–440).

Paragraphing, or more accurately re-paragraphing, is considered by some scholars a useful means to enhance understanding, as it is a kind of 'convenience to the reader' and a 'division composition setting off a unit of thought and making the divisions of the writer's thought visible' (El-Shiyab 1994: 73).

Paraphrasing is an extension or free rendering of the meaning of a sentence. It also means replacing a word in the source by a group of words or phrases in the target text. Paraphrasing is the most common translation technique when there are no formal equivalents. Paraphrases are proper translations (Cromer 1913: 102–114; Gordon 1989: 102–104; Ke P. 1993: 23–27).

Parenthetical Translation is used to include information that might help the target language reader to comprehend the text better.

Partial Translation, according to J.C. Catford, is where 'some part or parts of the source language text are left untranslated: they are simply transferred to and incorporated in the target language text' (Catford 1965: 21).

Phonological Translation refers to the replacement of the source language phonology (sound systems) by equivalent target language phonology.

Place-name Translation involves the translation of a term in the source text by a place-name in the target language text to highlight or add local or regional flavor to the target language equivalent.

Pragmatic Equivalence refers to the equivalence between the pragmatic meaning of the source text and the target text (Baker 1992: 217–260). The production of the pragmatic force of the source text in the target text is pragmatic equivalence.

Pragmatic Translation means that the main concern for the translator is to bring out the intended meaning of a given message that fits the social and cultural context (Hickey 1998; Newmark 1991: 115–128; Reiss 1987: 47–59). To achieve this, it is, as a general principle, always safe to render the expression literally if it is possible to recognize in context the same intended meaning or force of the message in the source language. An example of this is the translation of *yi ru fan zhang* 易如反掌 into English as 'as easy as turning over one's hand'. Nonetheless, when dealing with culture-specific terms, it is crucial to consider very carefully the pragmatic equivalent effect of a translation, such as *qi lu zao ma* 騎驢找馬 'hold on to one job, while seeking a better one' or 'carry coal to Newcastle' *duo ci yi qu* 多此一舉. For the purpose, once more, of better effects, we sometimes put in brief explanations to reveal the intended meaning of the original in the translation, such as *jing shui bu fan he shui* 井水不犯河水, 'well water and river water leave each other – stay out of things that don't concern you'.

Proper-name Rendition involves translating a source-text expression that does not have any proper nouns with a target-text expression that has proper nouns.

Recasting refers to the translation method which modifies the order of the units in the source text to conform to the linguistic conventions of the target text (Dembowski 1989: 185–212).

Recategorization refers to a translation method which changes the word class or part of speech in the source text in the process of producing the target text. This method is similar to 'shifts in parts of speech'.

Reordering involves putting the words of the source text in a different order when translating them into the target text.

Repetition refers to (1) a translation method when some parts of the sentences need to be repeated in the translation; and (2) a rhetorical term to refer to the repeating of some words for forceful expression (Shan Q. 1991: 292–306). Repetition as a translation method is practiced at several grammatical categories, including pronouns, appositives, verbs, nouns, and mood.

Rephrasing is a type of translation process that adds nothing to and omits nothing from the message content of the source text, while expressing the message in terms that are radically different from those of the source text (Hervey, Higgins and Loughridge 1995).

Restricted Translation is, according to J.C. Catford, the 'replacement of source language textual material by equivalent target language textual material, at only one level' (Catford 1965: 22).

Restructuring concerns the process of writing the meaning in an idiomatic style, suitable to the audience for which it is intended. Problems in restructuring will send translators back to analysis and transfer.

Revision is a procedure by which the translation is examined and reviewed by a member or members of the translation team in order to ensure that it is an accurate and faithful rendering of the meaning of the original text into the language of the translation, in a style equivalent to that of the original (Graham 1987: 99–105; Hosington and Horguelin 1980; Keeley 1989: 54–69; Newmark 1991: 101–114; Nida 1951: 18–24; Payne 1987: 43–51; Rosenstreich 1985: 7–8; Vasconcellos 1987: 409–416).

142 *Functions in computer-aided translation systems*

According to Peter Newmark, there are two basic procedures in revision: (1) a reading of the translation without looking at the original, as an independent piece of writing, and (2) a thorough comparison of the version with its original (Newmark 1991: 105). Several purposes of revision can be identified: (1) control of the accuracy of translation equivalents, including control of the completeness of a translation, e.g., omissions; (2) quality control of the style, e.g., for eliminating Anglicism, Gallicisms, and other forms of source language interference that can creep into a text; and (3) restoring written language characteristics in texts which were dictated.

Revision is decisive in the production of a satisfactory translation. Seamus Heaney recalls his experience in translating *Buile Suibhne* with the following words: 'It was only after the translation had been completed for the second time and I had earned that familiarity which I had originally arrogated – it was only then that the work truly yielded over' (Heaney 1989: 20).

Rewriting could be defined as a manipulation in the true sense of the word. Through rewriting, new things and concepts can be introduced to the target community. However, rewriting can also repress innovation and contain manipulation of all kinds. Translation is 'the most obviously recognizable type of rewriting', which is 'potentially the most influential', as it is 'able to project the image of an author and/or a (series) of works beyond the boundaries of their culture of origin' (Lefevere 1992: 9).

Sentence Translation, as its own name indicates, concerns the sentence, which is generally regarded as an operational unit in routine types of translation (Katoh and Aizawa 1994: 28–33).

Sentence-splitting Translation is a method of translating long sentences from English into Chinese by translating the main clause first and putting into it antecedents in the relative clauses.

Shifts in Parts of Speech in translation between Chinese and English are necessary, due largely to the frequency of using nouns and prepositions in English writings (Catford 1965: 73–82).

Source-equivalent Translation refers to the translation technique that involves the retrieval of the original source for use in the translation. It is a form of back translation requiring research abilities rather than language competence.

Source-oriented Translation is a type of translation which closely reproduces the original structure and form of the source text (McAlester 1999: 169–175; Ssu K. 1982: 40–55; van Kesteren 1978: 44–68).

Stylistic Equivalence concerns the recreation of the style of the source text and the author in the translation. It is also defined by Anton Popovic as: 'where there is functional equivalence of elements in both original and translation aiming at an expressive identity with an invariant of identical meaning' (Bassnett 1980/1991: 25). Style generally refers to the levels of language that authors use to express their ideas (Popovic 1976).

Stylistic Translation refers to the rendering of the original which involves working at a high level of elegance in the target language (Chang N. 1984: 366–371; Menacere 1992: 28–37; Xiao L. 1992: 121–133).

Substitution involves using a substitute word to replace a word or phrase that has been used before to avoid repetition.

Summary Translation refers to a type of partial translation in which the gist of the document is translated (Sofer 1995).

Transference (loan, transcription) is the process of transferring a source-language word, or a lexical unit, to a target language text as a translation procedure (Duff 1981: 85–109). Normally, proper nouns are transferred.

In the process of translation, a source language expression may be transferred to a target language text without altering its form and meaning. This method is used when (1) no ready target language equivalent covering all shades of meaning of the source language expression can be found; (2) there is a creation of stylistic exoticism; (3) it is necessary to avoid lengthy explanations of the SL expression; (4) frequency of contact minimizes the need for translation; and (5) the source text presumes cultural superiority over the target community.

Translation Couplet is defined by Peter Newmark (1981: 32) as a 'literal translation or translation label plus transcription'.

Translation Label is a provisional equivalent marked with inverted commas, which can later be discreetly withdrawn or accepted (Newmark 1981). This involves providing a provisional designation for the source-language term in the target text but later settling on something more faithful to its meaning in the original.

Translation Triplet consists in rendering the source language expression three times in the target language text. It can be a mixture of different methods (Newmark 1981, 1988: 76).

Transliteration is transference by Romanization when translating proper names, geographical names, names of institutions, names of mass media, and national customs and clothes.

Transliteration and Explanation is a translation method that partially transliterates and partly explains a word or phrase in the target text.

Transmutation refers to the interpretation of verbal signs by non-verbal signs. Turning out a poem from a painting or an opera out of a play are examples of transmutation. It is equivalent to 'intersemiotic translation' (Birch 1970).

Transposition replaces one grammatical unit with another. The rendering of a source language element by a target language element which is semantically but not formally equivalent is also an example of transposition (Carne-Ross 1964: 3–21; Chesterman 1997: 95).

Under-translation refers to the situation where the translation gives less detail and is more general than the original (Duff 1995: 1108–1117).

Word Translation is a kind of literal translation in which each word (or morpheme) in the source language is replaced by a word (or morpheme) in the target language (Kastovsky 1990: 45–49; Miremadi 1992: 137–143; Newmark 1991: 87–100; Steiner 1975/1992: 110–235).

Word-for-word Translation is often demonstrated as an interlinear translation, with the target language translations immediately below the source language

144 *Functions in computer-aided translation systems*

words (Feng S. 1981: 7–10). The source language word-order is preserved and the words translated singly by their most common meanings, out of context. One-to-one correspondence between orthographic words and elements of meaning within and across languages do not exist (Korovina 1982: 282–283).

Methods for computer-aided translation

The translation methods of computer-aided translation are also vastly different from those of machine translation and human translation. Basically, they are based on the concept of reusability.

Method of reusing translations

One of the main advantages in computer-aided translation is that one does not have to translate the sentences that one has translated before. This means that the more one translates, the less one has to translate.

This is the method of reusing translations, which can be divided into two types: reusing translations by oneself and reusing translations by others. Both can be taken as a kind of translation recycling (Merkel 1993: 139–149).

Method of selection

The centralized translation memory database of a computer-aided translation system stores translations made by translators of a translation team. Each translator in the team can select translations from the database for text generation.

In the case of a work that has been translated by different hands, permission has to be sought from the copyright holders of individual translations before they can be stored in the database for reuse with acknowledgement. This can be illustrated by the translation of a sentence in *Lun yu* 《論語》 (*The Analects of Confucius*): 有朋自遠方來, 不亦樂乎, which comes from the opening passage of the book: 子曰 : 學而時習之, 不亦悅乎？有朋自遠方來, 不亦樂乎？人不知而不慍, 不亦君子乎. Five translations by different hands were put on the translation memory database, as follows:

> 有朋自遠方來, 不亦樂乎？
> Is it not delightful to have friends coming from distant quarters?
>
> (Legge 1861: 1)

> Is it not a job to have friends from afar?
>
> (Lau 1979: 3)

> To have friends coming from afar: is this not a delight?
>
> (Leys 1997: 1)

Isn't it also great when friends visit from distant places?

(Muller 2007)

And to have a friend visit from somewhere far away – isn't that still a great joy?

(Hinton 1998: 3)

The translator of this sentence, after comparing the different translations, can select Muller's translation as the translation to be used in the target text, which is: 'Isn't it also great when friends visit from distant places?'

Method of modification

This technique involves modifying the translations stored in the database as the basis to generate a translation. Using again the example given above, a new translation can be generated through modification, as follows: 'Is it not a pleasure to have friends from afar to see you?'

The finalizing stage

When methods of human and computer-aided translation have been used to ensure that the source text has been properly translated, a translator can use tools for quality assurance in the translation system, which runs automatic checks to ensure that the final output is the correct translation of the source.

Checking

There are a number of aspects and areas where checking is essential. Due to differences in languages, checking varies from language to language. The following covers, in alphabetical order, the various types of checking for quality assurance.

Grammar Check is used to check the grammatical accuracy of the target text. Grammar checkers are not used for some languages, such as Chinese.

Number Check determines whether the numbers in the source text are missing in the target text and whether the numbers in words have been properly dealt with.

Punctuation Check ensures that there are no multiple punctuations, that the number of opening brackets equals the number of closing brackets, and that the punctuation mark is used at the end of a phrase or sentence.

Space Check checks whether there are multiple spaces, any missing spaces at the end of a sentence, or spaces before punctuation marks.

Spelling Check helps to identify and correct spelling mistakes. If a spelling mistake is detected during the check, the word will be highlighted in colour. When the user clicks on the word, the system displays a number of suggested spellings for the word for the user to choose from.

146 *Functions in computer-aided translation systems*

Spell checking has to make use of online dictionaries, such as openoffice dictionaries, to check spellings. XTM, for example, covers 90 languages. Some languages, such as Chinese and Japanese, are not spelt, and cannot have spell check.

Style Check makes sure that the same or similar style has been reproduced in the target text.

Syntax Check checks the syntactical well-formedness of the translation.

Text Check checks whether the source and target texts are identical.

Translatability Check is a tool for users to decide whether machine translation is needed for text generation, while 'TransCheck' is an aid for automatic validation of human and machine translation.

Translation Check is a tool to check the quality of machine translation against human translation. An example of a translation checker is TransCheck, which is an aid for automatic validation of human and machine translations.

Typography Check is a function present in Wordfast. When a project is completed, the project manager has to deliver the completed work to the client. This is normally facilitated by a tab or function, such as 'Finalize Translations' in the Wordbee Translator.

Updating

The translation memory database is automatically updated when the user modifies the target and leaves a segment. All subsequent modifications to the translation are automatically updated in the translation memory with their time stamps.

References

Abernathy, Robert (1961) 'The Problem of Linguistic Equivalence', Roman Jakobson (ed.) *Proceedings of the 12th Symposium on Applied Mathematics: On Structure of Language and Its Mathematical Aspects*, Providence, RI: American Mathematical Society, 95–98.

Aha, David W. and Kalyan Moy Gupta (2004) 'Heuristic Acronym Extraction Using Linguistic Features', *Proceedings of the International Conference on Natural Language Processing (ICON-2004)*, International Institute of Information Technology, Hyderabad, India.

Ahmad, Khurshid (1995) 'Pragmatics of Specialist Terms: The Acquisition and Representation of Terminology', Petra Steffens (ed.) *Machine Translation and the Lexicon*, Berlin: Springer Verlag, 51–76.

Aixelb, Javier Franco (1995) 'Specific Cultural Items and Their Translation', Peter Jansen (ed.) *Translation and the Manipulation of Discourse*, Leuven: CETRA, The Leuven Research Center for Translation, Communication and Cultures, 109–223.

Allied Business Intelligence (2002) *Language Translation, Localization, and Globalization: World Market Forecasts, Industry Drivers, and eSolutions*, New Jersey: Allied Business Intelligence.

Functions in computer-aided translation systems   147

Al-Shabab, Omar Sheikh (1996) *Interpretation and the Language of Translation: Creativity and Convention in Translation*, London: Janus Publishing Company.

Aráujo, Luzia A. (2000) 'Translation, Terminology, Computers, and Translation Training', *Proceedings of the 7th Conference of the International Society for the Study of European Ideas (ISSEI-2000), Workshop 501: Teaching Translation in the Information Age*, Bergen, Norway.

Arranz, Victoria, Elisabet Comelles, and David L. Farwell (2005) 'The FAME Speech-to-Speech Translation System for Catalan, English and Spanish', *Proceedings of MT Summit X*, Phuket, Thailand.

Arranz, Victoria, Elisabet Comelles, David L. Farwell, Climent Nadeu, Jaume Padrell, Albert Febrer, Dorcas Alexander, and Kay Peterson (2004) 'A Speech-to-speech Translation System for Catalan, Spanish, and English', Robert E. Frederking and Kathryn B. Taylors (eds.) *Machine Translation: From Real Users to Research*, Berlin: Springer Verlag, 7–16.

Ashworth, David and Minako O'Hagan (2002) *Translation-mediated Communication in a Digital World: Facing the Challenges of Globalization and Localization*, Clevedon: Multilingual Matters.

Atserias, Jordi, Irene Castellón, Montse Civit, and German Rigau (2000) 'Semantic Analysis Based on Verbal Subcategorization', *Proceedings of the 1st International Conference on Intelligent Text Processing and Computational Linguistics (CICLing-2000)*, Mexico City, Mexico.

Austermühl, Frank (2001) 'Computer-assisted Terminology Management', *Electronic Tools for Translators*, Manchester: St. Jerome Publishing Company, 102–123.

Ayan, Necip Fazil and Bonnie J. Dorr (2006) 'Going Beyond AER: An Extensive Analysis of Word Alignments and Their Impact on MT', *Proceedings of the Joint Conference of the International Committee on Computational Linguistics and the Association for Computational Linguistics (COLING/ACL-2006)*, Sydney, Australia.

Baker, Mona (1992) *In Other Words: A Coursebook on Translation*, London and New York: Routledge.

Balasubramanian, K. (1988) 'Problems of Lexical Equivalence in Translation', K. Karunakaran and M. Jayakumar (eds.) *Translation as Synthesis: A Search for a New Gestalt*, New Delhi: Bahri Publications Private Limited, 13–20.

Ball, Sylvia (2003) 'Joined-up Terminology—The IATE System Enters Production', *Translating and the Computer 25*, London: The Association for Information Management.

Bangalore, Srinivas and Giuseppe Riccardi (2000) 'Stochastic Finite-state Models for Spoken Language Machine Translation', Carol J. van Ess-Dykema, Clare R. Voss, and Florence Reeder (eds.) *Proceedings of the Workshop of Embedded Machine Translation Systems (ANLP/NAACL-2000)*, Association for Computational Linguistics, Seattle, Washington, DC, the United States of America, 52–59.

Bannock, Graham, Ron Baxter, and Evan Davis (1998) *The Penguin Dictionary of Economics*, 6th edition, London: Penguin.

Barik, Henri C. (1971) 'A Description of Various Types of Omissions, Additions, and Errors of Translation Encountered in Simultaneous Interpretation', *Meta* 16(4): 199–210.

Barlett (2003) *Barlett's Roget's Thesaurus*, Boston: Little, Brown and Company.

Barlow, Michael (1992) 'Using Concordance Software in Language Teaching and Research', *Proceedings of the 2nd International Conference on Foreign Language Education and Technology*, Nagoya, Japan.

148 Functions in computer-aided translation systems

Barlow, Michael (1996) 'Analysing Parallel Texts with ParaConc', *Proceedings of the Joint International Conference of the Association for Literary and Linguistic Computing and the Association for Computing and the Humanities (ALLC-ACH-96)*, University of Bergen, Bergen, Norway.

Barlow, Michael (2004) 'Parallel Concordancing and Translation', *Translating and the Computer 26*, London: The Association for Information Management.

Barnett, Jim, A. Corrada, G. Gao, Larry Gillik, Yoshiko Ito, S. Lowe, L. Manganaro, and Barbara Peskin (1996) 'Multilingual Speech Recognition at Dragon System', *Proceedings of the 4th International Conference on Spoken Language Processing (ICSLP-96)*, Philadelphia, PA, the United States of America, 2191–2194.

Barzilay, Regina and Noemie Elhadad (2003) 'Sentence Alignment for Monolingual Comparable Corpora', *Proceedings of the 41st Annual Meeting of the Association for Computational Linguistics (ACL-2003)*, Sapporo, Japan.

Bassnett, Susan (1980/1991) *Translation Studies*, London and New York: Routledge.

Bédard, Claude (1991) 'Machine PreTranslation: A Further Step in Terminology Management', *The ATA Chronicle* 19–20.

Beekman, John (1966) 'Literalism: A Hinderance to Understanding', *The Bible Translator* 17(4): 178–189.

Beekman, John and John Callow (1974) *Translating the Word of God*, Grand Rapids, MI: Zondervan.

Belloc, Hilaire (1931) *On Translation: The Taylorian Lecture 1931*, Oxford: The Clarendon Press.

Benis, Michael (2007) 'Déjà Vu: Taking a Second Look at CAT in a Mature Market', *ITI Bulletin* Issue Nov–Dec, 28–32.

Bernardi, Ulrike, András Bocsák, and Jörg Porsiel (2005) 'Are We Making Ourselves Clear? Terminology Management and Machine Translation at Volkswagen', *Proceedings of the 10th Workshop of the European Association for Machine Translation: Practical Applications of Machine Translation*, Budapest, Hungary, 41–49.

Bernth, Arendse (2003) 'Controlled Generation for Speech-to-speech MT Systems', *The Joint Conference of the 8th International Workshop of the European Association for Machine Translation and the 4th Controlled Language Applications Workshop (EAMT/CLAW-2003)*, Dublin City University, Dublin, Ireland, the United Kingdom, 1–7.

Bernth, Arendse and Michael C. McCord (2000) 'The Effect of Source Analysis on Translation Confidence', John S. White (ed.) *Envisioning Machine Translation in the Information Future*, Berlin: Springer Verlag, 89–99.

Bestgen, Yves (2006) 'Improving Text Segmentation Using Latent Semantic Analysis', *Computational Linguistics* 32(1): 5–12.

Birch, Cyril (1970) 'Translating and Transmuting Yuan and Ming Plays: Problems and Possibilities', *Literature East and West* 14(4): 491–509.

Blanchon, Herve, Christian Boitet, and Laurent Besacier (2004) 'Spoken Dialogue Translation Systems Evaluation: Results, New Trends, Problems and Proposals', *Proceedings of the International Workshop on Spoken Language Translation (IWSLT-2004)*, Kyoto, Japan.

Block, Hans Ulrich, Stefanie Schachtl, and Manfred Gehrke (2000) 'Adapting a Large Scale MT System for Spoken Language', Wolfgang Wahlster (ed.) *Verbmobil: Foundations of Speech-to-speech Translation*, Berlin: Springer Verlag, 394–410.

Functions in computer-aided translation systems 149

Boitet, Christian (1995) 'Machine-aided Human Translation', *Survey of the State of the Art in Human Language Technology*, Grenoble.

Boitet, Christian (1996) 'Machine-aided Human Translation', Ronald Cole, Joseph Mariani, Hans Uszkoreit, Annie Zaenen, and Victor Zue (eds.) *Survey of the State of the Art in Human Language Technology*, Available from http://www.cse.ogi.edu/CSLU/HLTsurvey/, Section 8.4.

Bolshakova, Elena I. (2001) 'Recognition of Author's Scientific and Technical Terms', *Proceedings of the 2nd International Conference on Intelligent Text Processing and Computational Linguistics (CICLing-2001)*, Mexico City, Mexico.

Bowker, Lynne (2002a) 'Terminology-management Systems', *Computer-aided Translation Technology: A Practical Introduction*, Ottawa: University of Ottawa Press, 77–91.

Bowker, Lynne (2002b) *Computer-aided Translation Technology: A Practical Introduction*, Ottawa: University of Ottawa Press.

Bowker, Lynne (2003) 'Terminology Tools for Translators', Harold Somers (ed.) *Computers and Translation: A Translator's Guide*, Amsterdam and Philadelphia: John Benjamins Publishing Company, 49–65.

Bowker, Lynne (ed.) (2006a) *Lexicography, Terminology, and Translation: Text-based Studies in Honour of Ingrid Meyer*, Ottawa: University of Ottawa Press.

Bowker, Lynne (2006b) 'Terminography in the Age of Translation Memory Tools: Reflections on Past Developments and Suggestions for the Future', *Programme of an International Conference on Computer-aided Translation: Theory and Practice*, Department of Translation, The Chinese University of Hong Kong, Hong Kong, China.

Briere, Eloise (1988) 'In Search of Cultural Equivalencies: Translations of Camara Laye's L'Enfant Noir', *Translation Review* 27: 34–39.

Briscoe, Philip (2004) 'Getting to Grips with Global Terminology Management', *Programme of the Annual Conference of the Association of Translation Companies: Getting in Shape for the Future—Working towards a New Environment for the Translation Profession*, School of Oriental and African Studies, University of London, London, the United Kingdom.

Cabré Castellvi, M. Teresa (2006) 'From Terminological Data Banks to Knowledge Databases: The Text as the Starting Point', Lynne Bowker (ed.) *Lexicography, Terminology, and Translation: Text-based Studies in Honour of Ingrid Meyer*, Ottawa: University of Ottawa Press, 93–106.

Camrass, Roger (2006) 'Atomization of the Localization Industry', *Proceedings of the Localization World Conference*, Barcelona, Spain.

Cañestro, Andrés Pérez (2005) 'Localisation: Searching for the Origins of the Terms and Its Meaning: An Introduction to the Localisation Process as Opposed to Traditional Translation', *Translating Today* 2.

Carne-Ross, D.S. (1964) 'Translation and Transposition', William Arrowsmith and Roger Shattuck (eds.) *The Craft and Context of Translation: A Critical Symposium*, New York: Doubleday and Co., 3–21.

Carstensen, B. (1988) 'Loan Translation: Theoretical and Practical Issues', *FoL* 22: 85–91.

Casagrande, Joseph B. (1954) 'The Ends of Translation', *International Journal of Applied Linguistics* 20(4): 335–440.

Catford, J.C. (1965) *A Linguistic Theory of Translation: An Essay in Applied Linguistics*, London: Oxford University Press.

150 *Functions in computer-aided translation systems*

Ćavar, Damir, Uwe Küssner, and Dan Tidhar (2000) 'From Off-line Evaluation to On-line Selection', Wolfgang Wahlster (ed.) *Verbmobil: Foundations of Speech-to-speech Translation*, Berlin: Springer Verlag, 597–610.

Champollion, Yves (2006) 'Very Large Translation Memories: Is the Free Model Viable?' *Translating and the Computer 28*, London: The Association for Information Management.

Chan, Sin-wai (1991) 'Problems in Philosophical Translation: Translating the Major Concepts in *An Exposition of Benevolence*', Roger Ames, Chan Sin-wai, and Ng Mau-sang (eds.) *Interpreting Culture through Translation*, Hong Kong: The Chinese University Press, 79–85.

Chan, Sin-wai (1998) 'In Defence of Literalism: My Experience in Translating *Stories by Gao Yang*', *The Humanities Bulletin* 5: 66–73.

Chan, Sin-wai (2002) 'The Making of *TransRecipe*: A Translational Approach to the Machine Translation of Chinese Cookbooks', Chan Sin-wai (ed.) *Translation and Information Technology*, Hong Kong: The Chinese University Press, 3–22.

Chan, Sin-wai (2004) *A Dictionary of Translation Technology*, Hong Kong: The Chinese University Press.

Chan, Sin-wai (ed.) (2004) *Translation and Bilingual Dictionaries*, Tubingen: Max Niemeyer.

Chang, Naihui 常乃慰 (1984) 〈譯文的風格〉 ('Style of the Translated Text'), Editorial Division, *Translators' Notes* 《翻譯通訊》編輯部 (ed.) 《翻譯研究論文集》 (*Essays on Translation Studies*), Beijing: Foreign Language Teaching and Research Press, 366–371.Chantrier, Cyril (2005) 'EXTER: A Breakthrough Solution for Efficient Terminology Extraction', *Translating and the Computer 27*, London: The Association for Information Management.

Chen, Guanghuo 陳光火 (2000) 〈語言分析〉 ('Linguistic Analysis'), 《電子翻譯》 (*Electronic Translation*), Tianjin: Tianjin University Press, 63–71.

Chen, Zheng and Lee Kai-Fu (2000) 'A New Statistical Approach to Chinese Pinyin Input', *Proceedings of the 38th Annual Meeting of the Association for Computational Linguistics (ACL-2000)*, Hong Kong, China.

Cherry, Colin and Dekang Lin (2003) 'A Probability Model to Improve Word Alignment', *Proceedings of the 41st Annual Meeting of the Association for Computational Linguistics (ACL-2003)*, Sapporo, Japan, 88–95.

Chesterman, Andrew (1997) *Memes of Translation: The Spread of Ideas in Translation Theory*, Amsterdam and Philadelphia: John Benjamins Publishing Company.

Ching, Eugene (1966) 'Translation or Transliteration: A Case in Cultural Borrowing', *Chinese Culture* 7(2): 107–116.

Chiu, Aman and Björn Jernudd (2002) 'Chinese IT Terminology Management in Hong Kong', Chan Sin-wai (ed.) *Translation and Information Technology*, Hong Kong: The Chinese University Press, 95–114.

Choi, Freddy Y.Y., Peter Wiemer-Hastings, and Johanna D. Moore (2001) 'Latent Semantic Analysis for Text Segmentation', *Proceedings of the 2001 Conference on Empirical Methods in Natural Language Processing (EMNLP-2001)*, Carnegie Mellon University, Pittsburgh, PA, the United States of America.

Chow, Yen-Lu, M. Dunham, Owen Kimball, M. Krasner, Francis G. Kubala, John Makhoul, S. Roucos, and Richard Schwartz (1987) 'BYBLOS: The BBN Continuous Speech Recognition System', *Proceedings of the IEEE International Conference*

Functions in computer-aided translation systems 151

on Acoustics, Speech and Signal Processing (ICASSP-87), Dallas, the United States of America, 89–92.

Chuang, Thomas C., G.N. You, and Jason S. Chang (2002) 'Adaptive Bilingual Sentence Alignment', Stephen D. Richardson (ed.) *Machine Translation: From Research to Real Users*, Berlin and New York: Springer Verlag, 11–30.

Compiling Group of *A Classified and Illustrated Chinese-English Dictionary*, Guangzhou Institute of Foreign Languages 廣州外國語學院《漢英分類插圖詞典》編寫組 (ed.) (1981) 《漢英分類插圖詞典》(*A Classified and Illustrated Chinese-English Dictionary*), Guangzhou: Guangdong People's Publishing House.

Corbeil, Jean-Claude and Ariane Archambault (eds.) (2006) *Merriam-Webster's Visual Dictionary*, Springfield, MA: Merriam-Webster, Inc.

Corbolante, Licia and Ulrike Irmler (2001) 'Software Terminology and Localization', Sue Ellen Wright and Gerhard Budin (eds.) *Handbook of Terminology Management*, Amsterdam and Philadelphia: John Benjamins Publishing Company, Vol. 2, 516–535.

Corness, Patrick (2002) 'Multiconcord: A Computer Tool for Cross-linguistic Research', Bengt Altenberg and Sylvian Granger (eds.) *Lexis in Contrast: Corpus-based Approaches*, Amsterdam and Philadelphia: John Benjamins Publishing Company, 307–326.

Coughlin, Josette M. (1990) 'MT or CAT: Criteria for the Independant Translator to Select a Computerized System', *Meta* 35(2): 455–457.

Cromer, E.B. (1913) 'Translation and Paraphrase', *Edinburgh Review* 218: 102–114.

Dain, Len, Lisa Frumkes, and Ivo Sanchez (2003) 'In Lieu of Content Management Systems: Internal Management of Medium-sized Web Site Localization', *Proceedings of the Localization World Conference 2003*, Seattle, Washington, DC, the United States of America.

Dan, Hanyuan 但漢源 (1994) 〈直譯意譯的別論與共識〉('Literal and Free Translation: Differences and Similarities in Point of View'), 《語言與翻譯》(*Language and Translation*) 1: 95–102.

Daniels, Guy (1973) 'The Tyranny of Free Translation', *Translation* 73(1): 12–20.

de Gispert, Adria, Jose B. Marino, and Josep Maria Crego (2004) 'Phrase-based Alignment Combining Corpus Cooccurrences and Linguistic Knowledge', *Proceedings of the International Workshop on Spoken Language Translation (IWSLT-2004)*, Kyoto, Japan.

Dembowski, Peter F. (1989) 'Two Old French Recastings/Translations of Andreas Capellanus's *De Amore*', Jeanette Beer (ed.) *Medieval Translators and Their Craft*, Michigan: Western Michigan University, 185–212.

Deng, Yonggang and William Byrne (2005) 'HMM Word and Phrase Alignment for Statistical Machine Translation', *Proceedings of Human Language Technology Conference and Conference on Empirical Methods in Natural Language Processing (HLT/EMNLP-2005)*, Vancouver, BC, Canada.

Deng, Yonggang and William Byrne (2006) 'MTTK: An Alignment Toolkit for Statistical Machine Translation', *Proceedings of the Human Language Technology Conference – Annual Meeting of the North American Chapter of the Association for Computational Linguistics (HLT-NAACL-2006)*, New York, the United States of America.

152 *Functions in computer-aided translation systems*

DePalma, Donald A. (2006) 'Quantifying the Return on Localization Investment', Keiran Dunne (ed.) *Perspectives on Localization*, Amsterdam and Philadelphia: John Benjamins Publishing Company.

DiFranco, Carla (2006) 'Localization Cost', Keiran Dunne (ed.) *Perspectives on Localization*, Amsterdam and Philadelphia: John Benjamins Publishing Company.

DiFranco, Carla and Ulrike Irmler (2003) 'Localization Process Standardization in the Windows Localization Group', *Proceedings of the Localization World Conference 2003*, Seattle, Washington, DC, the United States of America.

Duff, Alan (1981) *The Third Language: Recurrent Problems of Translation into English*, Oxford: Pergamon Press.

Duff, Alan (1995) 'Overtranslation', Chan Sin-wai and David E. Pollard (eds.) *An Encyclopaedia of Translation: Chinese-English. English-Chinese*, Hong Kong: The Chinese University Press, 716–730.

Dunne, Keiran (ed.) (2006) *Perspectives on Localization*, Amsterdam and Philadelphia: John Benjamins Publishing Company.

Dunne, Keiran (2006) 'Putting the Cart Behind the Horse: Rethinking Localization Quality Management', Keiran Dunne (ed.) *Perspectives on Localization*, Amsterdam and Philadelphia: John Benjamins Publishing Company.EAGLES (1996) *EAGLES Evaluation of Natural Language Processing Systems*, Copenhagen: Center for Sprogteknologi.

Editorial Committee, *Xiandai Hanyu cihai* (2003) 《現代漢語辭海》 (*A Dictionary of Contempoary Chinese*), Beijing: China Book Press.

Elliston, John S.G. (1979) 'Computer Aided Translation: A Business Viewpoint', Barbara M. Snell (ed.) *Translating and the Computer*, Amsterdam: North-Holland Publishing Company, 149–158.

Elrich, Manya (2006) 'Virtual Hermes or Globalisation by Localisation', *Proceedings of the 6th Portsmouth Translation Conference: Translation Technologies and Culture*, School of Languages and Area Studies, University of Portsmouth, Portsmouth, the United Kingdom.

El-Shiyab, Said M. (1994) 'The Rhetoric of Paragraphing across Cultures: Some Effects on Translation', Robert de Beaugrande, Abdulla Shunnaq, and Mohamed H. Heliel (eds.) *Language, Discourse and Translation in the West and Middle East*, Amsterdam and Philadelphia: John Benjamins Publishing Company, 73–77.

Esselink, Bert (1998) *A Practical Guide to Software Localization*, Amsterdam and Philadelphia: John Benjamins Publishing Company.

Esselink Bert (2000) *A Practical Guide to Localization*, rev. ed., Amsterdam and Philadelphia: John Benjamins Publishing Company.

Esselink, Bert (2003) 'Localisation and Translation', Harold L. Somers (ed.) *Computers and Translation: A Translator's Guide*, Amsterdam and Philadelphia: John Benjamins Publishing Company, 67–86.

Fabricz, Karoly (2005) 'Developing Translation Memories', *Translation Today* 3: 34–36.

Fang, Gaolin, Hao Yu, and Fumihito Nishino (2006) 'Chinese-English Term Translation Mining Based on Semantic Prediction', *Proceedings of the Joint Conference of the International Committee on Computational Linguistics and the Association for Computational Linguistics (COLING/ACL-2006)*, Sydney, Australia.

Feng, Shize 馮世則 (1981) 〈意譯、直譯、逐字譯〉 ('Free Translation, Literal Translation and Word-for-word Translation'), 《翻譯通訊》 (*Translators' Notes*) 2: 7–10.

Functions in computer-aided translation systems 153

Feng, Zhiwei 馮志偉 (1994) 〈語言的自動分析和生成技術〉('Automatic Analysis and Generation Technology of Languages'), 《自然語言機器翻譯新論》 (*New Essays on Machine Translation of Natural Languages*), Beijing: Language Press, 79–121.

Feng, Zhiwei 馮志偉 (2004) 〈語義自動分析〉 ('Automatic Semantic Analysis'), 《機器翻譯研究》 (*Studies on Machine Translation*), Beijing: China Translation and Publishing Corporation, 467–565.

Fletcher, Roger (1997) 'First Impressions of ViaVoice: Continuous Dictation Software from IBM', *Translation Journal* 1(2).

Fluixà, Noemi (2004) 'Software Localisation: Outsourcing Or In-house?' *Localisation Reader 2004–2005*.

Forssell, Dag (2001) 'One Translator's Thoughts on Software Localization', *Translation Journal* 5(3).

Francois, Monica (2003) 'Training Localization: Success for Global Audiences', *Proceedings of the Localization World Conference 2003*, Seattle, Washington, DC, the United States of America.

Gao, Yuqing, Hakan Erdogan, Yongxin Li, Vaibhava Goel, and Michael Picheny (2001) 'Recent Advances in Speech Recognition System for IBM DARPA Communicator', *Proceedings of the 7th European Conference on Speech Communication and Technology (EuroSpeech 2001– Scandinavia)*, Aalborg, Denmark, 503–506.

Gao, Zhiqing 高枝青 (1988) 〈翻譯一只能是意譯〉 ('Free Translation – The Only Way to Translate'), 《中國翻譯》 (*Chinese Translators Journal*) 5: 2–5.

Gelbukh, Alexander F., Grigori Sidorov, Sang-Yong Han, and Erika Hernández-Rubio (2004) 'Automatic Syntactic Analysis for Detection of Word Combinations', *Proceedings of the 5th International Conference on Intelligent Text Processing and Computational Linguistics (CICLing-2004)*, Chung-Ang University, Soeul, Korea, 240–244.

Gillam, Lee, Khurshid Ahmad, David Dalby, and Christopher Coz (2002) 'Knowledge Exchange and Terminology Interchange: The Role of Standards', *Translating and the Computer 24*, London: The Association for Information Management.

Gliozzo, Alfio and Carlo Strapparava (2006) 'Exploiting Comparable Corpora and Bilingual Dictionaries for Cross-language Text Categorization', *Proceedings of the Joint Conference of the International Committee on Computational Linguistics and the Association for Computational Linguistics (COLING/ACL-2006)*, Sydney, Australia.

Goldwater, Sharon and David McClosky (2005) 'Improving Statistical MT through Morphological Analysis', *Proceedings of Human Language Technology Conference and Conference on Empirical Methods in Natural Language Processing (HLT/EMNLP-2005)*, Vancouver, BC, Canada.

Gonzalex, Felex Rodriguez (1991) 'Translation and Borrowing of Acronyms: Main Trends', *International Review of Applied Linguistics* 29(2): 179–188.

Gordon, W. Terrence (1989) 'Parody and Paraphrase: Translation and C.K. Ogden's Basic English', *Meta* 34(1): 102–104.

Gouadec, Daniel (1990) 'Traduction Signalétique', *Meta* 35(2): 332–341.

Goutte, Cyril, Kenji Yamada, and Eric Gaussier (2004) 'Aligning Words Using Matrix Factorisation', *Proceedings of the 42nd Annual Meeting of the Association for Computational Linguistics (ACL-2004)*, Barcelona, Spain, 502–509.

Gove, Philip Babcock (1971) *Webster's Third New International Dictionary of the English Language Unabridged*, Springfield, MA: G. & C. Merriam Company.

Graham, John D. (1987) 'Checking, Revision and Editing', Catriona Picken (ed.) *Translating and the Computer 8: A Profession on the Move*, London: Aslib, 99–105.

154 *Functions in computer-aided translation systems*

Guo, Chen 郭晨 (2002) 〈漢語語音技術〉 ('Technology on Chinese Speech') 《第一屆學生計算語言學研討會論文集》 (*SWCL-2002: First Students' Workshop on Computational Linguistics: Proceedings*), Institute of Computational Linguistics, Peking University, Beijing, China, 337.

Gutt, Ernst-August (1991) *Translation and Relevance: Cognition and Context*, Oxford: Basil Blackwell.

Guzmán, Rafael (2005) 'Learning for Localisation Tools Training: Importance of E-learning for Translators', *Translating Today* 2.

Hatim, Basil (2001) *Teaching and Researching Translation*, Essex: Pearson Education Limited.

Hawker, Sara (ed.) (2008) *Pocket Oxford Dictionary and Thesaurus*, New York: Oxford University Press.

Heaney, Seamus (1989) 'Earning a Rhyme: Notes on Translating *Buile Suibhne*', Rosanna Warren (ed.) *The Art of Translation: Voices from the Field*, Boston: Northeastern University Press, 13–20.

Hervey, Sandor, Ian Higgins, and Michael Loughridge (1995) *Thinking German Translation: A Course in Translation Method: German to English*, London and New York: Routledge.

Hervey, Sandor, Ian Higgins, Stella Cragie, and Patrizia Gambarotta (2000) *Thinking Italian Translation*, London and New York: Routledge.

Hickey, Leo (1998) *The Pragmatics of Translation*, Clevedon: Multilingual Matters.

Hinton, David (tr.) (1998) *The Analects*, Washington, DC: Counterpoint.

Hornby, Albert Sydney (2013) *Oxford Advanced Learner's English-Chinese Dictionary*, 8th edition, Hong Kong: Oxford University Press.

Hosington, Brenda M. and Paul A. Horguelin (1980) *A Practical Guide to Bilingual Revision*, Montreal: Linguatech.

Hou, Min 侯敏 (2001) 〈漢語自動分析中的若干問題與對策〉 ('Some Problems and Countermeasures in Automatic Chinese Analysis'), Huang Changning 黃昌寧 and Zhang Pu 張普 (eds.) 《自然語言理解與機器翻譯》 (*Natural Language Understanding and Machine Translation*), Beijing: Tsinghua University Press, 204–210.

Hou, Min 侯敏 and Sun Jianjun 孫建軍 (1996) 〈漢語自動分詞中的歧義問題〉 ('Disambiguation in the Automatic Segmentation of the Chinese Language'), 《語言文字應用》 (*Applied Linguistics*) 1: 68–72.

http://dictionary.reference.com.

http://oxforddictionaries.com.

http://www.across.net/documentation/UserManual.

http://www.fujitsu.com/global/services/software/translation/atlas.trans.

http://www.internetworldstats.com/stats.htm.

http://www.merriam-webster.com.

http://www.onelook.com.

http://www.xtm-intl.com.

http://www.yourdictionary.com.

Huang, Changning 黃昌寧 (1997) 〈中文信息處理中的分詞問題〉 ('The Issue of Segmentation in Chinese Information Processing'), 《語言文字應用》 (*Applied Linguistics*) 1: 72–78.

Hutchins, John (1998) 'The Origins of the Translator's Workstation', *Machine Translation* 13: 287–307.

IBM Speech Recognition Group (1985) 'A Real-time, Isolated-word, Speech-recognition System for Dictation Transcription', *Proceedings of IEEE International Conference on*

Acoustics, Speech and Signal Processing (ICASSP-85), Tampa, FL, the United States of America.

Ion, Radu, Alexandru Ceauşu, and Dan Tufiş (2006) 'Dependency-based Phrase Alignment', *Proceedings of the 5th International Conference on Language Resources and Evaluation (LREC-2006)*, Genoa, Italy.

Isabelle, Pierre, Marc Dymetman, George Foster, Jean-Marc Jutras, Elliott Macklovitch, François Perrault, Ren Xiaobo, and Michel Simard (1993) 'Translation Analysis and Translation Automation', *Proceedings of the 5th International Conference on Theoretical and Methodological Issues in Machine Translation of Natural Languages: MT in the Next Generation (TMI-93)*, Kyoto, Japan, 201–217.

Ishikawa, Masahiko and Ryoichi Sugimura (1992) 'Natural Language Analysis Using a Network Model – Modification Deciding Network', *Proceedings of the 4th International Conference on Theoretical and Methodological Issues in Machine Translation of Natural Languages: Empiricist vs Rationalist Methods in MT (TMI-92)*, Montreal, Quebec, Canada, 55–66.

Ittycheriah, Abraham and Salim Roukos (2005) 'A Maximum Entropy Word Aligner for Arabic-English Machine Translation', *Proceedings of Human Language Technology Conference and Conference on Empirical Methods in Natural Language Processing (HLT/EMNLP-2005)*, Vancouver, BC, Canada.

Jaekel, Gary (2000) 'Terminology Management at Ericsson', Robert C. Sprung (ed.) *Translating into Success: Cutting-edge Strategies for Going Multilingual in a Global Age*, Amsterdam and Philadelphia: John Benjamins Publishing Company, 159–171.

Jakobson, Roman (1959) 'On Linguistic Aspects of Translation', Reuben A. Brower (ed.) *On Translation*, Cambridge, MA: Harvard University Press, 232–239.

Jones, Daniel (2011) *Cambridge English Pronouncing Dictionary*, 18th edition, Cambridge: Cambridge University Press.

Jones, Ian (1999) 'Terminology Management in NATO', *Translating and the Computer 21*, London: The Association for Information Management.

Ju, Ying 菊英 and Zhu Lin 竹林 (1959) 〈名詞的象譯〉 ('Graphic Translation of Common Nouns'), 《外語教學與翻譯》 (*Foreign Language Teaching and Translation*) 10: 40–43.

Kashioka, Hideki (2005) 'Word Alignment Viewer for Long Sentences', Proceedings of *MT Summit X*, Phuket, Thailand.

Kastovsky, Dieter (1990) 'Word-formation and Translation', *Meta* 35(1): 45–49.

Katoh, N. and T. Aizawa (1994) 'Machine Translation of Sentences with Fixed Expressions', *Proceedings of the 4th Conference on Applied Natural Langauge Processing*, Stuttgart, Germany, 28–33.

Keeley, Edmund (1989) 'Collaboration, Revision, and Other Less Forgivable Sins in Translation', John Biguenet and Rainer Schulte (eds.) *The Craft of Translation*, Chicago: The University of Chicago Press, 54–69.

Ke, Ping 柯平 (1992) 〈視點轉換、具體化和概略化— 再談變通和補償手段〉 ('More on the Metyhods of Change and Compensation – Shifts of Perspective, Specification and Generalization'), 《中國翻譯》 (*Chinese Translators Journal*) 1: 24–26.

Ke, Ping 柯平 (1993) 〈釋義、歸化和回譯—三談變通和補償手段〉 ('On Means in Translation: Paraphrase, Adapation, and Back Translation, Part 3'), 《中國翻譯》 (*Chinese Translators Journal*) 1: 23–27.Kim, Seonho, Juntae Yoon, and Dong-Yul Ra (2004) 'Two-level Alignment by Words and Phrases Based on Syntactic Information', *Proceedings of the 5th International Conference on Intelligent*

156   *Functions in computer-aided translation systems*

Text Processing and Computational Linguistics (CICLing-2004), Chung-Ang University, Soeul, Korea, 306–317.

King, Philip and David Woolls (1996) 'Creating and Using a Multilingual Parallel Concordancer', Marcel Thelen and Barbara Lewandowska-Tomasczyk (eds.) *Proceedings of the Conference on Translation and Meaning: Part 4*, Maastricht: Euroterm, 459–466.

Klein, Ernest (1971) *Klein's Comprehensive Etymological Dictionary of the English Language*, Philadelphia, PA: Elsevier Publishing Company.

Koehn, Philipp, Amittai Axelrod, Alexandra Birch Mayne, Chris Callison-Burch, Miles Osborne, and David Talbot (2005) 'Edinburgh System Description for the 2005 IWSLT Speech Translation Evaluation', *Proceedings of the International Workshop on Spoken Language Translation (IWSLT-2005)*, Pittsburgh, PA, the United States of America.

Kolak, Okan and Philip Resnik (2005) 'OCR Post-processing for Low Density Languages', *Proceedings of Human Language Technology Conference and Conference on Empirical Methods in Natural Language Processing (HLT/EMNLP-2005)*, Vancouver, BC, Canada.

Koller, Werner (1995) 'The Concept of Equivalence and the Object of Translation Studied', *Target* 7(2): 191–222.

Korovina, T.I. (1982) 'Multilingual Word-for-word Translation Using a Display', *Cybernetics* 14(2): 282–283.

Kosaka, Takashi and Masaki Itagaki (2003) 'Building a Curriculum for Japanese Localization Translators: Revisiting Translation Issues in the Era of New Technologies', Brian James Baer and Geoffrey S. Koby (eds.) *Beyond the Ivory Tower: Rethinking Translation Pedagogy*, Amsterdam and Philadelphia: John Benjamins Publishing Company, 229–249.

Kugler, Marianne (1995) 'Proof-reading Documentation—Introduction', Marianne Kugler, Khurshid Ahmad, and Gregor Thurmair (eds.) *Translator's Workbench*, Berlin: Springer Verlag, 109.

Kugler, Marianne, Khurshid Ahmad, and Gregor Thurmair (eds.) (1995) *Translator's Workbench*, Berlin: Springer Verlag.

Kumar, R. Sathish and R.S.D. Wahida Banu (2004) 'Selectional Preferences Acquisition Using Tree Cut Model and Semantic Similarity', *Proceedings of the International Conference on Natural Language Processing (ICON-2004)*, International Institute of Information Technology, Hyderabad, India.

Kumhyr, David, Carla Merrill, and Karin Spalink (1994) 'Internationalization and Translatability', *Proceedings of the 1st Conference of the Association for Machine Translation in the Americas: Technology Partnerships for Crossing the Language Barrier (AMTA-1)*, Columbia, MD, the United States of America, 142–148.

Lagoudaki, Elina (2009) 'Translation Editing Environments', *MT Summit XII Workshop: Beyond Translation Memories New Tools for Translators MT*, 29 August 2009, Ottawa, Canada.

Langlais, Philippe, George Foster, and Guy Lapalme (2000) 'Unit Completion for a Computer-aided Translation Typing System', *The 6th Applied Natural Language Processing Conference and 1st Meeting of the North Amercian Chapter of the Association for Computational Linguistics: Proceedings of the Conferences, and Proceedings of the ANLP-NAACL-2000, Student Research Workshop*, Seattle, Washington, DC, the United States of America, 135–141.

Functions in computer-aided translation systems 157

Langlois, Lucie (1996) 'Bilingual Concordancers: A New Tool for Bilingual Lexicographers', *Proceedings of the 2nd Conference of the Association for Machine Translation in the Americas: Expanding MT Horizons (AMTA-2)*, Montreal, Quebec, Canada, 34–42.

Larsen, Inger (2004) 'Training Tomorrow's Localisers', *The Linguist* 43(5).

Lau, D.C. (tr.) (1979) *Confucius: The Analects*, Hong Kong: The Chinese University Press.

Lazzari, Gianni (2000) 'Spoken Translation: Challenges and Opportunities', *Proceedings of the 6th International Conference on Spoken Language Processing (ICSLP-2000)*, Beijing, China.

Lee, Kai-Fu, Hsiao-Wuen Hon, and Raj D. Reddy (1990) 'An Overview of the SPHINX Speech Recognition system', *IEEE Transactions on Acoustics, Speech, and Signal Processing* 38: 35–45.

Lee, Tan, Wai Kit Lo, and Pak Chung Ching (2002) 'Towards Highly Usable and Robust Spoken Language Technologies for Chinese', Yu Shiwen (ed.) *Proceedings of the 2nd China-Japan Natural Language Processing Joint Research Promotion Conference (CJNLP-2002)*, Beijing: Institute of Computational Linguistics, Peking University, 259–265.

Lee, Young-Suk and Salim Roukos (2004) 'IBM Spoken Language Translation System Evaluation', *Proceedings of the International Workshop on Spoken Language Translation (IWSLT-2004)*, Kyoto, Japan.

Lefevere, André (1975) 'The Translation of Poetry: Some Observations and a Model', *Comparative Literature Studies* 7(4): 384–392.

Lefevere, André (1992) *Translation: Rewriting and the Manipulation of Literary Fame*, London and New York: Routledge.

Lefevere, André and Susan Bassnett (eds.) (1990) *Translation, History and Culture*, London and New York: Pinter Publishers.

Legge, James (1861) *The Chinese Classics with a Translation, Critical and Exegetical Notes, Prolegomena, and Copious Indexes: Volume 1, Confucian Analects, the Great Learning, and the Doctrine of the Mean*, Published at the author's, 1.

Levy, Jiri (ed.) (1967) *To Honor Roman Jakobson: Essays on the Occasion of His Seventieth Birthday*, The Hague: Mouton.

Lewalle, Pierre (1998) 'The Translator's Workbench and Beyond: Off-line Add-ons to On-line Tools', *Proceedings of the 3rd Workshop of the European Association for Machine Translation: Translation Technology: Integration in the Workflow Environment*, Geneva, Switzerland, 71–72.

Leys, Simon (tr.) (1997) *The Analects of Confucius*, New York: WW Norton.

Lin, Dekang and Colin Cherry (2003) 'Word Alignment with Cohesion Constraint', *Proceedings of the Human Language Technology and North American Chapter of Association of Computational Linguistics 2003 (HLT/NAACL-2003)*, Edmonton, Alberta, Canada.

Lin, Jihai 林基海 (1983) 〈英譯漢『反譯法』探討〉 ('The Method of "Reverse Translation" in English-Chinese Translation'), 《翻譯通訊》 (*Translators' Notes*) 5: 17–19.

Lin, Mao-sung 林茂松 and Chen Pin-chi 陳蘋琪 (2006) 〈電腦輔助翻譯軟體中模糊比對功能之效益評估：以目前台灣翻譯市場專業英中技術文件翻譯者為例〉 ('An Analysis of Fuzzy Match Function in CAT Software – A Case Study on Three Professional Technical Translators in Taiwan'), 《第十屆台灣國際口筆譯教學研討會：如何將口筆譯過程模型化》 (*Proceedings of the 10th Taiwan Symposium on*

158 *Functions in computer-aided translation systems*

Translator and Interpreter Training: Modelling the Processes of Translation and Interpretation), Fu Jen University, Taiwan. Li, Quan'an 李全安 (1990) 〈直譯與意譯之爭是一場什麼樣的爭論?〉 ('Literal Translation Versus Free Translation: What Kind of Dispute Is This?'), 《中國翻譯》 (*Chinese Translators Journal*) 5: 18–22.

Li, Tairan 李泰然 (1988) 〈翻譯—文化的移植〉 ('Translation: The Transplantation of Culture'), 《中國翻譯》 (*Chinese Translators Journal*) 2: 28–30.

Li, Xiaoming 李小明, Yi Lifu 易立夫, Yang Jing 楊靜, and Sun Jincheng 孫金城 (2002) 〈一種新的針對漢語 TTS 的韻律詞自動切分方法〉 ('A New Automatic Segmentation Method of Prosodic Word for Chinese TTS'), 《第一屆學生計算語言學研討會論文集》 (*SWCL-2002: First Students' Workshop on Computational Linguistics: Proceedings*), Institute of Computational Linguistics, Peking University, Beijing, China, 329–333.

Loehlin, C.H. (1962) 'Cultural Equivalents', *The Bible Translator* 13(2): 140–141.

Longman (2003) *Longman Dictionary of English Language & Culture*, London: Longman.

Lowerre, Bruce T. and Raj D. Reddy (1980) 'The HARPY Speech Recognition System', Wayne A. Lea (ed.) *Trends in Speech Recognition*, Englewood Cliffs, NJ: Prentice-Hall, 340–360.

Luong, Tuoc V., James S.H. Lok, David J. Taylor, and Kevin Driscoll (1995) *Internationalization: Developing Software for Global Markets*, New York: John Wiley.

Lü, Yajuan 呂雅娟, Zhao Tiejun 趙鐵君, Li Sheng 李生, and Yang Muyun 楊沐昀 (2001) 〈統計和詞典方法相結合的雙語語料庫詞對齊〉 ('Word Alignment Based on Statistics and Lexicon'), Huang Changning 黃昌寧 and Zhang Pu 張普 (eds.) 《自然語言理解與機器翻譯》 (*Natural Language Understanding and Machine Translation*), Beijing: Tsinghua University Press, 108–115.

Ma, Xiaoyi (2006) 'Champollion: A Robust Parallel Text Sentence Aligner', *Proceedings of the 5th International Conference on Language Resources and Evaluation* (*LREC-2006*), Genoa, Italy.

MacDermott, Lynda (2004) 'Localising the Web', *The Linguist* 43(1).

Maia, Belinda (2003) ' "Some Languages Are More Equal Than Others": Training Translators in Terminology and Information Retrieval Using Comparable and Parallel Corpora', Federico Zanettin, Silvia Bernardini, and Dominic Stewart (eds.) *Corpora in Translator Education*, Manchester: St. Jerome Publishing, 43–53.

Mayhew, Anthony Lawson and Walter W. Skeat (2004) *A Concise Dictionary of Middle English*, Oxford: Clarendon Press.

McAlester, Gerard (1999) 'The Source Text in Translation Assessment', Gunilla Anderman and Margaret Rogers (eds.) *Word, Text, Translation: Liber Amicorum for Peter Newmark*, Clevedon: Multilingual Matters Ltd., 169–175.

McDonald, Scott and Chris Brew (2004) 'A Distributional Model of Semantic Context Effects in Lexical Processing', *Proceedings of the 42nd Annual Meeting of the Association for Computational Linguistics* (*ACL-2004*), Barcelona, Spain, 17–24.

Melby, Alan K. (1995) *The Possibility of Language: A Discussion of the Nature of Language, with Implications for Human and Machine Translation*, Amsterdam and Philadelphia: John Benjamins Publishing Company.

Menacere, Mohamed (1992) 'Arabic Discourse: Overcoming Stylistic Difficulties in Translation', *Babel* 1: 28–37.

Merkel, Magnus (1993) 'When and Why Should Translations Be Reused', *Papers from the XIII AAKKI Symposium*, Vaasa, Finland, 139–149.

Functions in computer-aided translation systems 159

Miller, David, Sean Boisen, Richard Schwartz, Rebecca Stone, and Ralph Weischedel (2000) 'Named Entity Extraction from Noisy Input: Speech and OCR', *Proceedings of the 6th Applied Natural Language Processing Conference*, Seattle, Washington, DC, the United States of America, 316–324.

Miremadi, Seyed-Ali (1992) 'Language Users' Linguistic Creativity: Word-formation for Translation', Cay Dollerup and Anne Loddegaard (eds.) *Teaching Translation and Interpreting: Training, Talent, and Experience*, Amsterdam and Philadelphia: John Benjamins Publishing Company, 137–143.

Mitamura, Teruko, Kathryn Baker, David Svoboda, and Eric H. Nyberg (2003) 'Source Language Diagnostics for MT', *Proceedings of MT Summit IX*, New Orleans, LA, the United States of America.

Mohit, Behrang and Srini Narayanan (2003) 'Semantic Extraction with Wide-coverage Lexical Resources', *Proceedings of the Human Language Technology and North American Chapter of Association of Computational Linguistics 2003 (HLT/NAACL -2003)*, Edmonton, Alberta, Canada.

Moldovan, Dan I., Marius Pasca, Sanda M. Harabagiu, and Mihai Surdeanu (2002) 'Performance Issues and Error Analysis in an Open-domain Question Answering System', *Proceedings of the 40th Annual Meeting of the Association for Computational Linguistics (ACL-2002)*, Philadelphia, PA, the United States of America, 33–40.

Moore, Robert C. (2002) 'Fast and Accurate Sentence Alignment of Bilingual Corpora', Stephen D. Richardson (ed.) *Machine Translation: From Research to Real Users*, Berlin and New York: Springer Verlag, 135–144.

Morii, Shuji, Katsuyuki Niyada, Satoru Fujii, and Masakatsu Hoshimi (1985) 'Large Vocabulary Speaker-independent Japanese Speech Recognition System, *Proceedings of the IEEE International Conference on Acoustics, Speech and Signal Processing (ICASSP-85)*, Tampa, FL, the United States of America, 866–869.

Muller, Charles (tr.) (2007) *The Analects of Confucius*, Available from http://www.acmuller.net/con-dao/analects.html.

Nagata, Masaaki (2000) 'Synchronous Morphological Analysis of Grapheme and Phoneme for Japanese OCR', *Proceedings of the 38th Annual Meeting of the Association for Computational Linguistics (ACL-2000)*, Hong Kong, China.

Nakagawa, Hiroshi (2004) 'Term Extraction from Small Text', *AAMT Journal* 36.

Nakamura, Satoshi, Konstantin Markov, Takatoshi Jitsuhiro, Zhang Jin-Song, Hirofumi Yamamoto, and Genichiro Kikui (2004) 'Multi-lingual Speech Recognition System for Speech-to-speech Translation', *Proceedings of the International Workshop on Spoken Language Translation (IWSLT-2004)*, Kyoto, Japan.

Nastase, Vivi and Stan Szpakowicz (2005) 'Customisable Semantic Analysis of Texts', *Proceedings of the 6th International Conference on Intelligent Text Processing and Computational Linguistics (CICLing-2005)*, Mexico City, Mexico, 303–314.

Nelken, Rani and Stuart M. Shieber (2006) 'Towards Robust Context-sensitive Sentence Alignment for Monolingual Corpora', *Proceedings of the 11th Conference of the European Chapter of the Association for Computational Linguistics (EACL-2006)*, Trento, Italy.

Neubert, Albrecht (1995) 'Textlinguistics', Chan Sin-wai and David E. Pollard (eds.) *An Encyclopaedia of Translation: Chinese-English. English-Chinese*, Hong Kong: The Chinese University Press, 1016–1028.

Newmark, Peter (1981) *Approaches to Translation*, Oxford: Pergamon Press.

Newmark, Peter (1988) *A Textbook of Translation*, Hertfordshire: Prentice-Hall.

Newmark, Peter (1991) *About Translation*, Clevedon: Multilingual Matters Ltd.

160 *Functions in computer-aided translation systems*

Nida, Eugene (1945) 'Linguistics and Ethnology in Translation Problems', *Word* 1: 194–208.

Nida, Eugene (1951) 'Problems of Revision', *The Bible Translator* 2: 18–24.

Nida, Eugene (1964) *Towards a Science of Translating*, Leiden: E.J. Brill.

Nida, Eugene A. (1985) 'Translating Means Translating Meaning', *Publication of FIT*, Unesco.

Nida, Eugene A. and Charles R. Taber (1969) *The Theory and Practice of Translation*, Leiden: E.J. Brill.

Nkwenti-Azeh, Blaise (1998) 'Term Banks', Mona Baker (ed.) *Routledge Encyclopedia of Translation Studies*, London and New York: Routledge, 249–251.

Nord, Christiane (1994) 'Translation as a Process of Linguistic and Cultural Adaptation', Cay Dollerup and Annette Lindegaard (eds.) *Teaching Translation and Interpreting 2: Insights, Aims, Visions*, Amsterdam and Philadelphia: John Benjamins Publishing Company, 59–67.

Nyberg, Eric H., Teruko Mitamura, David Svoboda, Jeongwoo Ko, Kathryn Baker, and Jeffrey Micher (2003) 'An Integrated System for Source Language Checking, Analysis and Term Management', *Proceedings of MT Summit IX*, New Orleans, LA, the United States of America.

Oakes, Michael and Tony McEnery (2000) 'Bilingual Text Alignment—An Overview', Simon Philip Botley, Anthony Mark McEnery, and Andrew Wilson (eds.) *Multilingual Corpora in Teaching and Research*, Amsterdam and Atlanta: Rodopi, 1–37.

O'Donnell, Sandra Martin (1994) *Programming for the World: A Guide to Internationalization*, Engelwood Cliffs: Prentice Hall Inc.

O'Hagan, Minako (2004) 'Conceptualising the Future of Translation with Localization', *International Journal of Localisation*: 15–22.

Oh, Jong-Hoon, Kyung Soon Lee, and Key-Sun Choi (2000) 'Term Recognition Using Technical Dictionary Hierarchy', *Proceedings of the 38th Annual Meeting of the Association for Computational Linguistics (ACL-2000)*, Hong Kong, China.

Okazaki, Naoaki and Sophia Ananiadou (2006) 'A Term Recognition Approach to Acronym Recognition', *Proceedings of the Joint Conference of the International Committee on Computational Linguistics and the Association for Computational Linguistics (COLING/ACL-2006)*, Sydney, Australia.

Osborn, Noel (1982) 'Basic Types of Footnotes for Old Testament Translations', *The Bible Translator* 33(4): 414–418.

Pang, Bo, Kevin Knight, and Daniel Marcu (2003) 'Syntax-based Alighment of Multiple Translations: Extracting Paraphrases and Generating New Sentences', *Proceedings of the Human Language Technology and North American Chapter of Association of Computational Linguistics 2003 (HLT/NAACL-2003)*, Edmonton, Alberta, Canada, 102–109.

Paolillo, John (2004) 'Latent Structure Analysis: Semantic or Syntactic?' *Proceedings of the International Conference on Natural Language Processing (ICON-2004)*, International Institute of Information Technology, Hyderabad, India.

Payne, Jerry (1987) 'Revision as a Teaching Method on Translation Courses', Hugh A. Keith and Ian Mason (eds.) *Translation in the Modern Languages Degree*, London: Centre for Information on Language Teaching and Research, 43–51.

Pearson, Jennifer (1996) 'Electronic Text and Concordances in the Translation Classroom', *Teanga* 16: 85–95.

Functions in computer-aided translation systems 161

Pearson, Jennifer (2000) 'Teaching Terminology Using Electronic Resources', Simon Philip Botley, Anthony Mark McEnery, and Andrew Wilson (eds.) *Multilingual Corpora in Teaching and Research*, Amsterdam: Rodopi, 92–105.

Piao, Scott S. L., Guangfan Sun, Paul Rayson, and Qi Yuan (2006) 'Automatic Extraction of Chinese Multiword Expressions with a Statistical Tool', *Proceedings of the 11th Conference of the European Chapter of the Association for Computational Linguistics (EACL-2006)*, Trento, Italy.

Popovič, Anton (1976) *Dictionary for the Analysis of Literary Translation*, Edmonton: Department of Comparative Literature, the University of Alberta.

Pux, Simone (2003) 'Implementing a Client/Server Based Terminology Management System', *Proceedings of the Localization World Conference 2003*, Seattle, Washington, DC, the United States of America.

Pym, Anthony (2004) *The Moving Text: Localization, Translation, and Distribution*, Amsterdam and Philadelphia: John Benjamins Publishing Company.

Pym, Anthony (2010) 'Web Localization', Available from www.tinet.cat/~apym/ on-line/translation/2009_website_localization_feb.pdf.

Quirion, Jean and Jacynthe Lanthier (2006) 'Intrinsic Qualities Favouring Term Implantation: Verifying the Axioms', Lynne Bowker (ed.) *Lexicography, Terminology, and Translation: Text-based Studies in Honour of Ingrid Meyer*, Ottawa: University of Ottawa Press, 107–118.

Radó, György (1975) 'Indirect Translation', *Babel* 21(2): 51–59.

Reeder, Florence M. (2006) 'Measuring MT Adequacy Using Latent Semantic Analysis', *Proceedings of the 7th Biennial Conference of the Association for Machine Translation in the Americas (AMTA-2006): Visions for the Future of Machine Translation*, Boston Marriott, Cambridge, MA, the United States of America.

Reiss, Katharina (1987) 'Pragmatic Aspects of Translation', Gideon Toury (ed.) *Translation across Cultures*, New Delhi: Bahri Publications Pvt. Ltd., 47–59.

Reyburn, William D. (1969) 'Cultural Equivalences and Non-equivalences in Transaltion I', *The Bible Translator* 20(4): 158–167.

Reyburn, William D. (1970) 'Cultural Equivalences and Non-equivalences in Translation II', *The Bible Translator* 21(1): 26–35.

Ribeiro, António, José Gabriel Pereira Lopes, and João Mexia (2000) 'A Self-learning Method of Parallel Texts Alignment', *Proceedings of the Conference of the Association for Machine Translation in the Americas: Envisioning Machine Translation in the Information Future (AMTA-2000)*, Cuernavaca, Mexico City, Mexico, 30–39.

Rosenstreich, Susan L. (1985) 'Revision: Present and Future Tenses', Patricia E. Newman (ed.) *American Translators Association Conference— 1985*, Medford, NJ: Learned Information, Inc., 7–8.

Sager, Juan C. (1998a) 'Terminology: Standardization', Mona Baker (ed.) *Routledge Encyclopedia of Translation Studies*, London and New York: Routledge, 255–258.

Sager, Juan C. (1998b) 'Terminology: Theory', Mona Baker (ed.) *Routledge Encyclopedia of Translation Studies*, London and New York: Routledge, 258–262.

Sarcevic, Susan (1985) 'Translation of Culture-bound Terms in Laws', *Multilingua* 3: 127–133.

Schäler, Reinhard (2002) 'The Cultural Dimension in Software Localication', *Localisation Focus: The International Journal of Localisation* 1(2): 21–23.

Schäler, Reinhard (2005) 'Reverse Localisation', *Translating and the Computer 27*, London: The Association for Information Management.

162 *Functions in computer-aided translation systems*

Schogt, Henry G. (1988) *Linguistics, Literary Analysis, and Literary Translation*, Toronto: University of Toronto Press.

Séguinot, Candace (1994) 'Translating and Advertising: Going Global', *Current Issues in Language and Society* 1(3): 247–265.

Sestier, C. (2001) 'eTermino Q & A – Multilingual Terminology Assistant', *Translating and the Computer 23*, London: The Association for Information Management.

Shan, Qichang 單其昌 (1991) 〈重復的譯法〉 ('Methods of Translating Repetitions'), 《漢英翻譯入門》 (*The ABC of Chinese-English Translation*), Hebei: Hebei Education Press, 292–306.

Shen, Dan (1989) 'Literalism: NON-"Formal-equivalence"', *Babel* 4: 261–278.

Shen, Dan (1995) 'Literalism', Chan Sin-wai and David E. Pollard (eds.) *An Encyclopaedia of Translation: Chinese-English. English-Chinese*, Hong Kong: The Chinese University Press, 568–579.

Shen, Ruoyun 沈若芸 (1964) 〈漢譯英的增詞與減詞問題〉 ('Addition and Omission of Words in Chinese-English Translation'), 《外語教學與研究》 (Foreign Language Teaching and Research), 2: 39–44.

Simard, Michel, George Foster, Marie-Louise Hannan, Elliott Macklovitch, and Pierre Plamondon (2000) 'Bilingual Text Alignment – Where Do We Draw the Line?' Simon Philip Botley, Anthony Mark McEnery, and Andrew Wilson (eds.) *Multilingual Corpora in Teaching and Research*, Amsterdam: Rodopi, 38–64.

Singh, Nitish and Arun Pereira (2005) *The Culturally Customized Web Site: Customizing the Web Sites for the Global Market*, Oxford: Elsevier Butterworth.

Smith, Andrew E. (2003) 'Automatic Extraction of Semantic Networks from Text using Leximancer', *Proceedings of the Human Language Technology and North American Chapter of Association of Computational Linguistics 2003 (HLT/NAACL-2003)*, Edmonton, Alberta, Canada.

Smith, V. and C. Klein-Braley (1997) 'Advertising – A Five-stage Strategy for Translation', Mary Snell-Hornby, Z. Jettmarova, and K. Kaindl (eds.) *Translation as Intercultural Communication: Selected Papers from the EST Congress – Prague 1995*, Amsterdam and Philadelphia: John Benjamins Publishing Company, 173–184.

Sofer, Morry (1995) *Guide for Translators*, Rockville, Maryland: Schreiber Publishing.

Somers, Harold L. and Yuri Sugita (2003) 'Evaluating Commercial Spoken Language Translation Software', *Proceedings of MT Summit IX*, New Orleans, LA, the United States of America.

Ssu, Kuo 思果 (1982) 〈亦步亦趨 － 照原文詞序的譯法〉 ('Follow Closely － The Method of Following the Word-order of the Source Text'), 《翻譯新研》 (*More Studies in Translation*), Taipei: Great Earth Press, 40–55.

Steiner, George (1975) *After Babel: Aspects of Language and Translation*, New York: Oxford University Press.

Stevenson, Angus (2007) *The Shorter Oxford English Dictionary*, 6th edition, Oxford: Oxford University Press.

Stevenson, Angus (2010) *Oxford Dictionary of English*, London: Oxford University Press.

Stoeller, Willem (2003) 'Risky Business: Risk Management for Localization Project Managers', *Proceedings of the Localization World Conference 2003*, Seattle, Washington, DC, the United States of America.

Sui, Zhifang 穗志方 (2002) 〈信息科學技術領域術語自動識別策略〉 ('The Strategies on the Automatic Term Recognition in the Domain of Information Science

Functions in computer-aided translation systems 163

and Technology'), Yu Shiwen (ed.) *Proceedings of the 2nd China-Japan Natural Language Processing Joint Research Promotion Conference (CJNLP-2002)*, Beijing: Institute of Computational Linguistics, Peking University, 318–322.

Sun, Le, Youbing Jin, Lin Du, and Yufang Sun (2000) 'Word Alignment of English-Chinese Bilingual Corpus Based on Chunks', *Proceedings of the Joint Sigdat Conference on Empirical Methods in Natural Language Processing and Very Large Corpora (EMNLP/VLC-2000)*, Hong Kong University of Science and Technology, Hong Kong, China, 110–116.

Sun, Maosong 孫茂松 (2001) 〈漢語自動分詞研究的若干最新進展〉 ('New Advances in the Study of Automatic Segmentation of the Chinese Language'), 《輝煌二十年—中國中文信息學會二十周年學術會議》 (*Proceedings of Conference of the 20th Anniversary of CIPSC*), Tsinghua University Press, Beijing, 20–40.

Sun, Maosong 孫茂松 and Benjamin K.Y. T'sou 鄒嘉彥 (1995) 〈漢語自動分詞研究中的若干理論問題〉 ('Several Theoretical Issues Relating to Automatic Segmentation of the Chinese Language'), 《語言文字應用》 (*Applied Linguistics*) 4: 40–46.

Tang, Li, Donghong Ji, Yu Nie, and Lingpeng Yang (2004) 'An Application of a Semantic Framework for the Analysis of Chinese Sentences', *Proceedings of the 5th International Conference on Intelligent Text Processing and Computational Linguistics (CICLing-2004)*, Chung-Ang University, Soeul, Korea, 41–44.

Taskar, Ben, Lacoste-Julien Simon, and Klein Dan (2005) 'A Discriminative Matching Approach to Word Alignment', *Proceedings of Human Language Technology Conference and Conference on Empirical Methods in Natural Language Processing (HLT/EMNLP-2005)*, Vancouver, BC, Canada.

Tatsuo, Yamashita and Yuji Matsumoto (2000) 'Language Independent Morphological Analysis', *Proceedings of the 6th Applied Natural Language Processing Conference*, Seattle, Washington, DC, the United States of America, 232–238.

Taylor, Chris and Anthony Baldry (2001) 'Computer Assisted Text Analysis and Translation: A Functional Approach in the Analysis and Translation of Advertising Texts', Erich H. Steiner and Colin Yallop (eds.) *Exploring Translation and Multilingual Text Production: Beyond Content*, Berlin and New York: Mouton de Gruyter, 277–305.

Thurmair, Gregor (2003) 'Making Term Extraction Tools Usable', *Proceedings of the Joint Conference Combining the 8th International Workshop of the European Association for Machine Translation and the 4th Controlled Language Applications Workshop: Controlled Language Translation (EAMT-CLAW-2003)*, Dublin City University, Dublin, Ireland, the United Kingdom.

Tsai, Jia-Lin (2006) 'Using Word Support Model to Improve Chinese Input System', *Proceedings of the Joint Conference of the International Committee on Computational Linguistics and the Association for Computational Linguistics (COLING/ACL-2006)*, Sydney, Australia.

Tu, Guoyuan 屠國元 (1996) 〈翻譯中的文化移植—妥協和補償〉 ('Cultural Transplantation in Translating'), 《中國翻譯》 (*Chinese Translators Journal*) 2: 9–12.

Ulrych, Margherita (1997) 'The Impact of Multilingual Parallel Concordancing on Translation', Barbara Lewandowska-Tomaszczyk and Patrick James Melia (eds.) *Proceedings of the Conference on Practical Applications in Language Corpora (PALC-97)*, Łódź, Poland, 421–435.

Uren, Emmanuel, Robert Howard, and Tiziana Perinotti (1993) *Software International and Localization*, New York: Van Nostrand Reinhold.

164 Functions in computer-aided translation systems

van Kesteren, Aloysius (1978) 'Equivalence Relationships between Source Text and Target Text', James S. Holmes, Jose Lambert, and Raymond van den Broeck (eds.) *Literature and Translation: New Perspectives in Literary Studies*, Leuven: ACCO, 44–68.

Varantola, Krista (1998) 'Translators and Their Use of Dictionaries', B.T. Sue Atkins (ed.) *Using Dictionaries*, Tübingen: Max Niemeyer Verlag, 179–192.

Vasconcellos, Muriel (1987) 'A Comparison of MT Postediting and Traditional Revision', Karl Kummer (ed.) *Across the Language Gap: Proceedings of the 28th Annual Conference of the American Translators Association*, Medford, NJ: Learned Information, Inc., 409–416.

Vinay, Jean-Paul and Jean Darbelnet (1958/1995) *Comparative Stylistics of French and English: A Methodology for Translation*, translated and edited by Juan C. Sager and M.-J. Hamel, Amsterdam and Philadelphia: John Benjamins Publishing Company.

Vintar, Spela (2001) 'Using Parallel Corpora for Translation-oriented Term Extraction', *Babel* 47(2): 121–132.

Vollnhals, Otto (1999) *Multilingual Dictionary of IT Security: English-German-French-Spanish-Italian*, Belin: De Gruyter Mouton.

Wacholder, Nina, Judith L. Klavans, and David K. Evans (2000) 'Evaluation of Automatically Identified Index Terms for Browsing Electronic Documents', *Proceedings of the 6th Applied Natural Language Processing Conference*, Seattle, Washington, DC, the United States of America, 302–309.

Wang, Fu Lee, Xiaotie Deng, and Feng Zou (2006) 'Towards Unified Chinese Segmentation Algorithm', *Proceedings of the 5th International Conference on Language Resources and Evaluation (LREC-2006)*, Genoa, Italy.

Watanabe, Taro, Kenji Imamura, and Eiichiro Sumita (2002) 'Statistical Machine Translation Based on Hierarchical Phrase Alignment', *Proceedings of the 9th International Conference on Theoretical and Methodological Issues in Machine Translation (TMI-2002)*, Keihanna, Japan, 188–198.

Weller, Georganne (1992) 'Advertising: A True Challenge for Cross-cultural Translation', Cornelia N. Moore and Lucy Lower (eds.) *Translation East and West: A Cross-cultural Approach*, Honolulu, Hawaii: University of Hawaii Press, 145–154.

Wen, Jiasi 聞家駟 (1989) 〈是直譯還是意譯?〉 ('Is It Literal or Free Translation'), Wang Shoulan 王壽蘭 (ed.) 《當代文學翻譯百家談》 (*Views on Translation by One Hundred Contemporary Literary Translators*), Beijing: Beijing University Press, 653–654.

Wonsever, Dina and Jean-Luc Minel (2001) 'Contextual Rules for Text Analysis', *Proceedings of the 2nd International Conference on Intelligent Text Processing and Computational Linguistics (CICLing-2001)*, Mexico City, Mexico.

Woolls, David (1997) *Multiconcord: Software for Multilingual Parallel Concordancing*, Birmingham: CFL Software Development.

Woolls, David (2000) 'From Purity to Pragmatism: User-driven Development of a Multilingual Parallel Concordancer', Simon Philip Botley, Anthony Mark McEnery, and Andrew Wilson (eds.) *Multilingual Corpora in Teaching and Research*, Amsterdam: Rodopi, 116–133.

Wright, Sue Ellen and Gerhard Budin (1997) *Handbook of Terminology Management*, Amsterdam and Philadelphia: John Benjamins Publishing Company.

Wu, Hua and Haifeng Wang (2004) 'Improving Domain-specific Word Alignment with a General Bilingual Corpus', Robert E. Frederking and Kathryn B. Taylors (eds.) *Machine Translation: From Real Users to Research*, Berlin: Springer Verlag, 262–271.

Xiao, Liming 蕭立明 (1992) 〈語言變體與文學翻譯〉 ('Variations in Style and Literary Translation'), 《翻譯新探》 (*New Explorations into Translation Studies*), Taipei: Bookman Publishing Co. Ltd., 121–133.

Xu, Jun 許均 (1988) 〈簡論喬治. 穆南的翻譯觀〉 ('On Georges Mounin's Views on Translation'), 《語言與翻譯》 (*Language and Translation*) 1: 49–53.

Xu, Jia, Richard Zens, and Hermann Ney (2005) 'Sentence Segmentation Using IBM Word Alignment Model 1.' *Proceedings of the 10th Workshop of the European Association for Machine Translation: Practical Applications of Machine Translation*, Budapest, Hungary, 280–287.

Yamamoto, Kaoru, Yuji Matsumoto, and Mihoko Kitamura (2001) 'A Comparative Study on Translation Units for Bilingual Lexicon Extraction', *Proceedings of the Association for Computational Linguistics 39th Annual Meeting and 10th Conference of the European Chapter: Data-driven Machine Translation (ACL-EACL-2001)*, Toulouse, France, 87–94.

Yarowsky, David, Grace Ngai, and Richard Wicentowski (2001) 'Introducing Multilingual Text Analysis Tools via Robust Projection across Aligned Corpora', *Proceedings of the Human Language Technology Conference (HLT-2001)*, San Diego, California, the United States of America, 109–116.

Yarowsky, David and Richard Wicentowski (2000) 'Minimally Supervised Morphological Analysis by Multimodal Alignment', *Proceedings of the 38th Annual Meeting of the Association for Computational Linguistics (ACL-2000)*, Hong Kong, China.

Yu, Jiangsheng, Zan Hongying, Liu Yang, and Wen Zhenshan (2002) 'Building WordNet-like Term Bank', Yu Shiwen (ed.) *Proceedings of the 2nd China-Japan Natural Language Processing Joint Research Promotion Conference (CJNLP-2002)*, Beijing: Institute of Computational Linguistics, Peking University, 45–51.

Yu, Shiwen 俞士汶, Zhu Xuefeng 朱學鋒, and Duan Huiming 段慧明 (2000) 〈大規模現代漢語標注語料庫的加工規範〉 ('Guidelines for Segmentation and Part-of-speech Tagging on Very Large Scale Corpus of Contemporary Chinese'), Yu Shiwen 俞士汶 and Zhu Xuefeng 朱學鋒 (eds.) 《計算語言學文集》 (*Papers on Computational Linguistics*), Beijing: Department of Computer Science and Technology 北京大學計算機科學技術系 and Institute of Computational Linguistics 北京大學計算語言學研究所, Peking University, Vol. 4, 125–132.

Yu, Yunxia 余雲霞 et al. (1986) 《漢英逆引詞典》 (*A Reverse Chinese-English Dictionary*), Beijing: The Commercial Press.

Zaky, Magdy M. (2000) 'Translation and Meaning', *Translation Journal* 4(4).

Zauberga, Ieva (2005) 'Handling Terminology in Translation', Krisztina Károly and Ágota Fóris (eds.) *New Trends in Translation Studies: In Honour of Kinga Klaudy*, Budapest: Akadémiai Kiadó, 107–116.

Zetzsche, Jost (2003) *Translation Databases for Web Site Localization*, London: Multilingual Press.

Zhang, Boran 張柏然 (ed.) (2004) 《新時代英漢大詞典》 (*New Age English-Chinese Dictionary*), Beijing: The Commercial Press.

Zhang, Ying and Stephan Vogel (2005) 'An Efficient Phrase-to-phrase Alignment Model for Arbitrarily Long Phrase and Large Corpora', *Proceedings of the 10th Workshop of the European Association for Machine Translation: Practical Applications of Machine Translation*, Budapest, Hungary, 294–301.

166 *Functions in computer-aided translation systems*

Zhang, Yujie, Ma Qing, and Hitoshi Isahara (2005) 'A Multi-aligner for Japanese-Chinese Parallel Corpora', Proceedings of MT Summit X, Phuket, Thailand.

Zhao, Bing, Klaus Zechner, Stephen Vogel, and Alex H. Waibel (2003) 'Efficient Optimization for Bilingual Sentence Alignment Based on Linear Regression', *Proceedings of the Human Language Technology and North American Chapter of Association of Computational Linguistics 2003 (HLT/NAACL-2003)*, Edmonton, Alberta, Canada.

Zhuang, Yichuan 莊繹傳 (1980) 〈哪些詞可以不譯〉 ('Which Words Can Be Left Untranslated'), 《漢英翻譯 500 例》 (*500 Examples of Chinese-English Translation*), Beijing: Foreign Language Teaching and Research Press, 52–57.

Zielinski, Daniel (2005) 'Research Meets Practice: T-survey 2005: An Online Survey on Terminology Extraction and Terminology Management', *Translating and the Computer 27*, London: The Association for Information Management.

4 Computer-aided translation
Free and paid systems

Introduction

Computer-aided translation can be defined as the use of computer-based tools to assist human translators during the translation process. As remarked by Bowker (2002: 60), a wide range of tools is encompassed by this definition. However, the term 'computer-aided translation' is limited to software that is specifically intended for translation tasks, excluding other general applications.

Computer-aided translation tools can be classified in several different ways. One of the earliest and most extended classifications is based on the extent to which the translation process is automated (Hutchins and Somers 1992: 147; Lehrberger and Bourbeau 1988: 5–7). Within the framework of this classification, a distinction is made between Machine-Aided Human Translation (MAHT), as a human activity assisted by computer tools, and Human-Aided Machine Translation (HAMT), in which the translation is essentially carried out by computer software but human input is required in order to resolve some translation-related problems. As there are different degrees of cooperation between computers and human translators, it is sometimes difficult to classify computer-aided translation tools into the aforementioned categories. Further criteria for the classification of computer-aided translation tools include the languages involved, for instance, language-specific systems (e.g., Transwhiz and Snowman) versus Unicode-compliant systems (e.g., SDL-Trados), and the operating systems computer-aided translation software functions on, such as cross-platform systems versus software that is compatible exclusively with Mac OS, Linux, or MS Windows.

Nonetheless, in this chapter we have selected a classification method that is as simple as it is effective: free and paid computer-aided translation tools. Free computer-aided translation tools, on the one hand, are mostly standalone systems, some of which include project-management functions. Paid or commercial systems, on the other hand, can be divided into three main groups: (i) standalone systems, which can be used either offline or online, depending on the needs of the user; (ii) network-based systems, which in turn can be divided into server-based or Internet-based tools; and (iii) hybrid systems, in the forms of computer-aided translation systems including online machine translation engines, or machine translation systems with the function of a translation memory.

168 *Computer-aided translation*

Free and open-source systems

According to Bowker, McBride, and Marshman (2008: 27), in relatively recent years, two tendencies have been developing in parallel. Firstly, an ever-growing number of translators are making use of computer-aided translation systems, especially of translation memory (TM) tools. Simultaneously, computer users are increasingly opting for different types of free and open-source software (OSS). Therefore, the question of incorporating free or low-cost computer-aided translation tools into the translation process has come to the fore.

There are many reasons for making computer-aided translation tools freely available to users, yet one of the most obvious is to entice potential customers into purchasing an advanced version of the software in question. These potential buyers, who are mostly non-frequent users, are given the opportunity to gain some hands-on experience during a trial period, usually ranging from one to three months, before deciding whether to purchase the product or not. Systems such as MemoQ, Déjà Vu, and SDL-Trados follow this practice. Most free systems, however, are easily accessible online, including Google Translator Toolkit and Wordfast Anywhere. Finally, there are also some free computer-aided translation tools, such as Across Personal Edition, Tr-AID, Anaphraseus, and OmegaT, which can only be downloaded upon registration.

Another purpose of translators being offered free editions of computer-aided translation tools is so that they can use that version to work for their employers, who in turn use server or cloud editions. This is the case of Memsource Personal, which is freely downloadable in order to allow the user to connect to Memsource Cloud or Memsource Server.

According to our study, there are currently 25 free computer-aided translation systems which are either accessible online or downloadable from the Internet. These computer-aided translation tools are known for their accessibility as well as their easy installation process. It normally takes only a few steps to install computer-aided translation online systems into a computer (OmegaT being a clear example). Besides, free systems generally have very intuitive user interfaces, panels, and toolbars. In some instances, they are amateur projects, often produced in a public and collaborative manner by freelance translators or programmers, who voluntarily devote their time to system development.

Given the above, free computer-aided translation software may come across as an attractive option, yet the usability or reliability of these systems is highly questionable. Their versions, source codes, and the operating systems they work on should be of concern to users. For instance, some of these free computer-aided translation tools are old versions of existing software, such as Across Personal Edition, Similis, and WordFisher. In addition, although several free systems have already been upgraded to a more functional version, there are still some that have remained unchanged for quite a long period of time (e.g., the latest version of ForeignDesk was released in 2002). Regarding the source code, it is found that, out of the 25 free systems that were studied, thirteen are open-source software, which means that their source codes are accessible, permitting users to

Computer-aided translation 169

study, change, improve, or distribute them. Finally, users should consider the possible limitations regarding the operating systems on which free computer-aided translation tools work. Although an interesting number of free computer-aided translation tools are now cross-platform systems, most of them are still intended for the dominant Microsoft Windows (MS Windows). There are other free computer-aided translation systems, nonetheless, that are designed exclusively for other operating systems, such as Mac OS (e.g., AppleTrans). Most surprising is the case of Gtranslator, an application for the GNOME desktop environment.[1]

In addition to the above issues, there exist further disadvantages that should be considered before opting for free computer-aided translation tools. To begin with, these systems usually have fewer functions compared to paid software. Occasionally, these tools have no functions for alignment or project management, and translation memory search engines often lack filtering, customization, and other advanced features. Besides, there are further restrictions set on free computer-aided translation tools, such as limitations on data storage (e.g., Wordfast Classic puts a limit on the number of translation units for an unlicensed copy, and Google Translator Toolkit can only store a few thousand terms and translation units), restrictions on file formats, and limitations on the languages supported (e.g., MT2007 supports only 12 European languages).

Despite the above, it should be pointed out that our research reveals that some free computer-aided translation systems are fully functional and can adequately meet the needs of ad hoc users.

Paid systems

Standalone systems

The origin of standalone computer-aided translation systems can be traced back to the idea of a translator's workbench, proposed in 1980 by Martin Kay in his article entitled 'The Proper Place of Men and Machine in Language Translation' (Kay 1980; Kay 1997a: 3–23; Kay 1997b: 35–38). According to Kay, a translator's workbench consists of a platform on which electronic translation tools are available to the translator, who can use them in translation practice.

At present, there are 53 commercially available standalone computer-aided translation systems. These programmes can work either online or offline; in other words, they do not require a network connection to function, yet some of them can be linked to server-based or networked systems through licensing and with the use of a password.

Standalone systems are usually available in two editions: standard and professional. Standard editions, on the one hand, are mainly targeted at entry-level translators, student learners, or occasional translators, given their restrictions on the capacity of translation memory databases and their limited functions. They are usually less expensive and, therefore, more affordable. Professional editions, on the other hand, are aimed at advanced users and professionals, for most of them are fully functional.

170 Computer-aided translation

The majority of these programmes are compatible with popular operating systems, such as Microsoft Windows and Mac OS, but some of them are cross-platform systems, which can be used in different hardware and software. Araya, CafeTran, Heartsome Translation Suite, PROMT, Swordfish, and Wordfast, to give but a few examples, belong to the group of cross-platform standalone computer-aided translation systems. It should also be noted that some standalone editions are customizable, such as Fusion, SDL-Trados, and Yaxin CAT. Furthermore, most standalone editions, being Unicode-compliant, are not language-specific; thus, they can be used for most languages in the world. Nonetheless, a number of them have been developed particularly for specific language pairs, such as MLTS and Sakhr, for Arabic-English translation; Snowman, Dr. Eye, GE-CCT, and TransWhiz, for Chinese-English translation; Snowman, Dr Eye, and TransWhiz, for Chinese-Japanese translation; ProMemoria, PROMT, and Systran, for French-English translation; and Atlas, Crossroad, LogoVista, and Honyaku, for Japanese-English translation.

Network-based systems

Networked systems are operated on database servers in a network environment (Chan 2004: 205). An obvious advantage of these systems, but an advantage nonetheless, is that they are instantly available anywhere in the world (needless to say, anywhere where the Internet can be accessed). In addition, all team members of a project can share centralized translation memories and terminology, enabling project collaboration and management. There are two types of network-based systems: server-based and Internet-based systems.

Server-based computer-aided translation tools provide centralized storage of all clients' translation material as well as instant availability to all registered users. In this way, all the members of a translation team can easily look up and update a centralized translation memory database, which can be accessed from any location, to increase translation reuse, consistency, and quality. Moreover, a centralized terminology database is provided, allowing users to maintain brand and industry terms consistently throughout multiple documents and languages and to share termbases with colleagues. The advantages of this type of software include easier management and better matching, due to the enormous size of data storage. Server-based systems also support project collaboration, for they enable project managers to easily access and distribute projects, and to monitor progress with no trouble.

The second type of networked systems, Internet-based computer-aided translation tools, allow information to be translated from one language into another through the Internet. Nowadays, as up-to-the-minute information is constantly found on the Internet, the translation of websites and webpages is growing increasingly popular and important. More and more, web translation is becoming the major trend in the trade. Internet-based computer-aided translation systems usually serve three functions: (1) as an assimilation tool to transmit information to the user; (2) as a dissemination tool to make messages comprehensible; and

Computer-aided translation 171

(3) as a communication tool to enable communication between people with different language backgrounds. There are a number of Internet-based computer-aided translation products on the market, eleven of which will be introduced later in this chapter. What deserves our special attention is that cloud-based platforms are fast becoming the major form of Internet-based computer-aided translation systems.

Review of available free and paid systems

Across

Across Systems GmbH is a company based in Karlsbad (Germany) and Glendale (California, USA) that offers translation products tailored to the demands of freelance translators, enterprises, and language service providers.

Across Personal Edition is a free-of-charge full-featured computer-aided translation system aimed at freelance translators and designed to work either as a standalone application or via the Standby Remote Client, which allows users to access the customer's Across Language Server. Its latest version, Across v5.7, was released in March 2013, and it is compatible with Windows 7 and Windows 8 operating systems.[2]

Out of all the free systems, Across Personal Edition is probably one of the most functional, including a series of professional features, such as:

(i) Translation memory (crossTank), which, in addition to other frequent methods, can be filled up by alignment, an extremely useful feature that is absent in most free translation memory tools.
(ii) Terminology system (crossTerm), where terms can be stored along with synonyms, definitions, images, etc. Moreover, Across Personal Edition allows the storage of 'do-not-use words', preventing the use of some restricted words (e.g., some companies may restrict some word usage for marketing reasons).
(iii) Multiple-format translation editor (crossDesk), which supports a great number of document formats, overcoming one of the most recurrent problems in free computer-aided translation systems. On top of that, it is also compatible with three open standard file formats, namely XLIFF, TMX, and TBX.
(iv) Integrated project and workflow management (crossProject).
(v) Quality assurance checker (crossCheck).

Scholars, such as Muegge (Chereshnovska 2013: 21), consider it a very powerful tool and recommend it to be used not only by freelance translators but also by institutions that provide translation training programmes.

Across Language Server is a server-based solution that constitutes the fifth generation of its central software platform, with Across Language Server v.5, released in October 2009, being the first platform of this generation.

172   *Computer-aided translation*

In his review for the magazine *Multilingual*, Sikes (2009: 16) describes Across Language Server v.5 as a 'client-server system that consolidates translation memory (crossTank) and terminology management (crossTerm) on a central database server platform'. This version includes other elements with the purpose of assisting the translation process: crossProject and crossCheck, which are also present in Across Personal Edition; and two source authoring assistance tools, namely, crossAuthor and crossAuthor Linguistic. Rösener explains the importance of the incorporation of these authoring tools into the system. He claims that by integrating authoring tools with a translation memory system using a single environment, users may benefit, not only from the use of common authoring aids (e.g., spell, grammar, etc.), but also from the terminology database, which can be used by the authoring tool to control terminology in the source and target text (Rösener 2010: 4–5).

Across Language Server v.5 went through several versions before the release of Across Language Server v5.7 in May 2013. As stated on the official website,[3] new features of this version include change tracking, logistics and supply chain management, terminology management with web-based workflows, text display maintaining the original format, and XLIFF-file support.

Anaphraseus

Anaphraseus is a free and open-source computer-aided translation tool written in OpenOffice.org Basic by freelance translators Oleg Tsygany, Dmitri Gabinski, and Sergei Medvedev.

As Tsygany recalls, the idea started in 2007, when he was working with Wordfast Classic and realized that, since Wordfast worked exclusively with MS Word, it could not be run on any operating system other than Windows (Tsygany 2009: 59). He aimed then to create a cross-platform, free, open-source translation memory tool as an alternative to Wordfast. Tsygany initially called the newly created software OpenWordfast, a name that was later changed to Anaphraseus. Analogously to the way Wordfast Classic works with MS Word, Anaphraseus works with OpenOffice.org Writer. It thus supports every format OpenOffice.org Writer can handle and can be used in most existing operating systems, e.g., in Linux/Unix, Mac OS, and MS Windows (Tsygany 2009: 58).

Anaphraseus offers a number of basic functions, such as terminology recognition; Wordfast-compatible text segmentation; translation memory, which can contain up to 500,000 units either in plain-text or Unicode; and fuzzy search, compatible both with Wordfast and OmegaT translation-memory formats. In addition, although a machine translation system is not included in the programme, Anaphraseus can be linked to online machine translation tools, such as Google Translate, Microsoft Bing, and Apertium.

Anaphraseus is still in the 'beta' stage, as clearly remarked by its creator (Tsygany 2009: 59), and still has some weaknesses. One of the major drawbacks is related to the fact that, as an OpenOffice.org extension, it is slower than MS Word-based computer-aided translation tools, in particular when handling large

Computer-aided translation 173

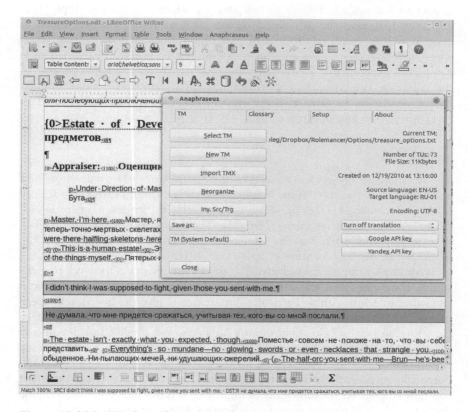

Figure 4.1 Main Window of Anaphraseus

files. On top of that, it currently works only with unformatted text, skipping formulas and images.

Despite its current disadvantages, Anaphraseus is a promising tool with the potential of becoming more powerful and functional.

AppleTrans

Developed by Apple Computer Inc., AppleTrans is a standalone, light-weight text editor designed to run on Mac OS. It is freeware, which means that it is available to users free of charge, yet the source code is withheld by the developers.

AppleTrans is aimed at professional translators. It features an online multilingual corpus, which represents the translation memory. However, in order to extend corpus features, it is necessary to install some additional plug-in modules.

AppleTrans is a limited computer-aided translation tool. As reported by users,[4] despite its 'Mac-like' appearance, part of the interface is unlabelled and many

174 Computer-aided translation

important features are difficult to find and use. More importantly, AppleTrans has proved to have compatibility problems with some file formats, which in many occasions result in the loss of part of the document formatting (even when such documents have a frequent extension such as *.docx* or *.xlsx*). This is considered unacceptable for most professional translators. Perhaps, because of the inability to overcome these shortcomings, AppleTrans has been discontinued by the developer. In fact, its latest version, AppleTrans 1.2, was released in September 2006 and operates on Mac OS 10.3 or later versions.

Autshumato

The Autshumato Project was funded by the South African Department of Arts and Culture and counts with the support of other institutions such as the Centre for Text Technology (CTexT), which is responsible for its development in collaboration with the University of Pretoria. The project was named by a Khoi-khoi leader who worked as an interpreter between the Europeans and the Khoi-khoi in the 17th century (Groenewald 2010: 27).

According to the official website,[5] the aim of the project is to develop open-source computer-aided translation tools and resources for the eleven official languages in South Africa. Particular importance is given to the development of machine translation systems for three of the South African language pairs (i.e., English into isiZulu, English into Afrikaans, and English into Sesotho sa Leboa). According to Groenewald (2010: 27), these systems would provide translators, especially those working for the government, with a tool that could potentially increase their efficiency, consistency, and productivity. On the other hand, he emphasizes the difficulties of improving this machine translation engine due to the lack of parallel corpora for South African languages.

Autshumato Integrated Translation Environment (ITE) is a free computer-aided translation application based on a popular open-source computer-aided translation system, OmegaT, and developed within the framework of the Autshumato Project. It provides a single translation environment that includes a translation memory tool, the abovementioned machine translation system, and a glossary to assist the translation process.

Autshumato ITE has two major advantages. First, although it was specifically developed for the eleven official languages in South Africa, this tool is, in essence, language independent and can be adapted for translating between any language pair. Second, it is a cross-platform application, being able to run on Windows XP, Windows Vista, and Windows 7, as well as Linux and Mac OS.

Crowdin

Crowdin is an Internet-based collaborative translation platform developed by Crowdin.net in Ukraine. The company started to develop the system in 2006, but it was not publicly released until January 2009. By the first year after its launch, it already counted the support of more than 1,000 companies registered as users.

Computer-aided translation 175

Crowdin was born from the concept of crowdsourcing translation. Anastasious and Gupta (2011: 637–638) describes the phenomenon of crowdsourcing as a 'large group of people who are available and willing to perform a task that an outsourcer(s) had asked for'. In line with this definition, crowdsourcing translation consists of a group of people who are eager to translate content submitted online, usually for low or no payment, and a platform, such as Crowdin, where the 'crowd' can work.

According to its website,[6] Crowdin has a series of useful characteristics. First of all, it supports all the popular localization file formats and is able to handle both documents and software projects. It is optimal for webpage translation and its design suits the demands of multilingual translation projects. Another interesting feature is that it provides users with reports and information concerning translation activities, translation quotations, analyses of translation memory databases, and even biographical information of translators. Moreover, it allows the members of a translation project to disseminate information, conduct online communication, and send messages to each other. Last but not least, it supports up to 109 languages.

A typical workflow in Crowdin is described by Morera, Lamine, and Collins (2012: 197) as follows. To begin with, the project must be configured either as 'managed', whereby members of the crowd have to be accepted by a project manager, or 'open', whereby any person can participate. Once the project has been configured, the crowd gains access to the source text. At this point, the matches retrieved from Crowdin's translation memory as well as the translations generated by machine translation engines, provided by Google and Microsoft, are made available to users who can suggest alternative translations or vote for or against already translated segments until they are approved. Finally, an authorized user can decide to close the project at any time of the process.

It is not surprising that systems such as Crowdin are rapidly increasing in popularity, for not only do they produce exceedingly short turnaround times but they are also extremely cost-effective.

Déjà Vu

Déjà Vu is a full-featured and customizable paid computer-aided translation system that combines translation memory technology with Example-Based Machine Translation (EBMT) techniques. It was developed by Atril Language Engineering SL, a France-based family company founded by Emilio Benito and his son Daniel in 1993.

Déjà Vu's intuitive single user interface set up an entirely new concept, contrasting with the set of separate applications that were being offered by other computer-aided translation systems at that time. One of the main strengths of Déjà Vu was indisputably its outstanding customer care service. All of Déjà Vu's early users, and competitors for that matter, remember how Emilio Benito himself responded promptly to all the questions posed by his ever-increasing clientele (Nogueira 2004: online; Reynolds 2014: online). Not only did he

176 *Computer-aided translation*

solve technical problems but, as García and Stevenson highlight, many of the suggestions and wishes of the users were taken into consideration and incorporated into the young computer-aided translation system. On top of that, after purchasing the initial license, users could benefit from these upgrades without any additional costs (García and Stevenson 2010: 16). Based on the above, it is not surprising that Déjà Vu became one of the most popular computer-aided translation tools during the 1990s, especially among freelance translators. Emilio Benito worked as the president and founder of Atril until his retirement in early 2003.

Déjà Vu differs from other translation memory systems in terms of the match retrieval technique. As aptly explained by Lagoudaki (2006: 4), there are different match retrieval techniques, some of which are (i) character-string-based matching, and (ii) linguistically enhanced matching. Déjà Vu uses the former method and extends it by implementing EBMT techniques, which improve its fuzzy matching.

The latest versions of Déjà Vu are Déjà Vu X3 Professional, Déjà Vu X3 Workgroup, and Déjà Vu TEAMserver, which include new features such as AutoWrite, SmartView, Intelligent Quality, and DeepMiner. According to the official website, TEAMserver enables teams and translators to share their work in real time, increasing the productivity, consistency, and quality of the translations. Translators can work directly on Déjà Vu, while linking their project to the TEAMserver database, thus benefitting automatically from the translations performed by other members of the team.

Atril claims that Déjà Vu is 'the most powerful and customizable computer-aided translation system on the market'.[7] Its clients include over 3,000 translation companies and private firms and over 8,500 freelance translators throughout the world. In fact, according to Wassmer (2003: 17), many important companies and institutions, such as IBM, Siemens, Adobe, and the Canadian Parliament, are on the list of Atril's customers. Indeed, Déjà Vu is still one of the most popular and dear translation memory systems. According to the Translation Memory Survey conducted by Lagoudaki in 2006, Déjà Vu was found to be not only known and used by a great number of translation professionals, but also the best rated by users. The participants of the TM Survey 2006 can be divided into different groups. The first group includes those who are not users of translation memory systems but would be willing to try or purchase one. Déjà Vu placed second in the list of most popular tools according to non-TM-users, with 61 per cent of the respondents knowing of its existence, only surpassed by Trados (Lagoudaki 2006: 15). A second group encompassed the translation-memory users. To the question of which translation memories did they actually use, 23 per cent of respondents admitted using Déjà Vu, becoming the fourth most used translation memory tool (Lagoudaki 2006: 19). Finally, when translation-memory users were asked to rate the four most used translation memory systems, Déjà Vu obtained the higher satisfaction index, with an average rating of 4 (1 being 'Not satisfied at all' and 5 being 'Excellent'). It is therefore concluded that, from a general perspective, Déjà Vu seems to be more

Computer-aided translation 177

satisfactory compared to Wordfast (3.9), SDL-Trados 2006 (3.4), and Trados (3.3) (Lagoudaki 2006: 24).

EsperantiloTM

EsperantiloTM is a free and open-source translation memory tool that works as a standalone system. According to its developer, Artur Trzewik, EsperantiloTM is part of the more extensive programme Esperantilo, which focuses exclusively on Esperanto language (http://www.esperantilo.org). This broader programme contains some additional functions, such as grammar checker for Esperanto language, a simple text editor, multilingual user dictionaries, compatibility with TMX, and an integrated machine translation for the following language pairs: Esperanto into English, Polish, German, Russian, and Swedish; and English and Polish into Esperanto.

Esperantilo's latest updated version, Esperantilo 0.993, was released in December 2011 and runs on MS Windows and Linux.

This software is not as complete and functional as other free computer-aided translation tools, yet it could be of help when translating into or from Esperanto.

ESTeam Translator

ESTeam Translator is a multilingual system that combines interactive translation with fully automatic translation, enables an unlimited number of translators to be connected in a globally networked environment, and leverages administrative tasks. It was first released in 1995 by the Swedish company ESTeam AB.

As explained by Kranias and Samiotou (2004: 331), ESTeam implements an innovative system for integrating translation memory and machine translation. This method, which can be classified as EBMT, a matching retrieval technique used by other systems such as Déjà Vu, aims to post-edit fuzzy matches automatically by using a machine translation engine in context. As noted above, this technique enhances the fuzzy matches' retrieval and, simultaneously, enables low-score fuzzy matches to be used. Therefore, translation costs are substantially reduced at the same time that the process efficiency is increased.

Out of all the features offered by ESTeam Translator, two are particularly worth mentioning. Firstly, data is stored in a single translation memory with a hierarchical domain structure defined by the translator (e.g., Science/Chemistry/ Chemical Compounds). Thus, when users are translating a certain segment, the system gives preference to translation memory data under the same domain as the source text. Secondly, the system is not pair-based. Therefore, when a certain language is added to the system, it is automatically linked to all supported languages. For instance, by translating from English into French and English into Portuguese, resources between French and Portuguese are automatically built (http://www.esteam.se).

ESTeam Translator runs on MS Windows operating system and supports 23 European languages, i.e., Czech, Danish, Dutch, English, Estonian, Finnish, French,

178 *Computer-aided translation*

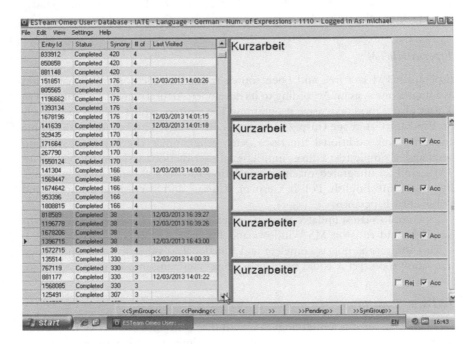

Figure 4.2 User Data of ESTeam

German, Greek, Hungarian, Icelandic, Italian, Latvian, Lithuanian, Maltese, Norwegian, Polish, Portuguese, Slovak, Slovenian, Spanish, Swedish, and Turkish.

According to ESTeam's website,[8] this system is targeted at large governmental and corporate organizations with extensive translation needs. In actual fact, ESTeam's users include the Translation Department Organizing Committee for the Olympic Games, ATHENS 2004; Translation Center for the bodies of the European Union; and CompuMark, Thomson Corporation.

Fluency

Fluency is a computer-aided translation tool developed by Western Standard Corporate, a company from Utah, United States. Western Standard was founded in 1997 and, originally, was solely a publishing company. In 2006, it was awarded a government contract that involved language technology development, so they began to offer translation services for the government sector. Ever since 2010, the translation division has been focused exclusively on translation technology and no longer offers translation services.

According to Western Standard,[9] Fluency was initially designed as an in-house translation tool between 2006 and 2009, based on design specifications proposed by translators, and became commercially available only since 2010.

Fluency Translation Suite 2011 and Fluency Enterprise Solutions were the first server-based editions. The latest server-based version of the software is Fluency Translation Suite 2013, which provides access to online machine translation systems, including Google Translate, Microsoft Bing, and APIs for other machine translation engines. It is remarkable that it implements a terminology management module with large bilingual dictionaries in 35 different languages. In addition, it has a WYSIWYG interface, displaying the created document in a very similar way to the end result. Finally, it supports a wide variety of file formats and all ISO-639–1 languages, Unicode, and double-byte characters.

ForeignDesk

ForeignDesk was open-sourced in 2001 by International Communications Inc. and Lionbridge Technologies Inc. It was established as the first free, open-source software targeted at professional translators. Even though the initiative was not successful, it opened the way to all the open-source computer-aided translation tools that followed.

ForeignDesk works as a standalone programme, and its features include translation memory and terminology management tools, as well as a project assistant option, which allows users to streamline the translation process. It is TMX-compliant and contains interesting fuzzy matching applications.

ForeignDesk's most popular user was Choice Hotels International, one of the largest hotel companies in the world. Dierk Seeburg, Web Content Administrator at Choice Hotels International, explained in an interview for Open Source Update[10] (McKay 2005: online) that one of the main features that lead to the use of ForeignDesk was its customizability for XML files, which allowed them to create custom filters for all their XML-based files. Besides, Seeburg claims that they particularly appreciated the fact that, while working on a particular translation segment, the best fuzzy match was always displayed in the fuzzy match window, making it easier to browse through the list of fuzzy matches with lower matching percentages.

Despite it being used by large corporations, it should be noted that ForeignDesk has not been improved in a long period of time. In fact, the newest version, ForeignDesk 5.7.3, was released in May 2002, more than a decade ago.

GE-CCT

GE-CCT, *Wei ge xie tong fan yi xi tong* 格微協同翻譯系統, or Global Envoy Collaborative Computer Translation, was developed by Global Envoy Software Co. Ltd. 沈陽格微軟件有限責任公司, which was founded in Shenyang, China, in 1999. GE-CCT was released in 2009, after 20 years of prior experimentation.

GE-CCT has four main editions: Personal Edition, Corporate Edition, Graduate Edition, and University Teaching Edition. Features of this software include millions of specialized terms, automatic term extraction, pre-translation, and quality

180 *Computer-aided translation*

assurance checking. In 2013, GE-CCT provided English-Chinese and Chinese-English translation, Russian-Chinese and Chinese-Russian translation, and Japanese-Chinese computer-aided translation.[11]

GlobalSight

GlobalSight TMS is an open-source server-based Translation Management System (TMS), which is written in Java, based on the code of Ambassador TMS. GlobalSight's predecessor, Ambassador TMS, was originally developed by GlobalSight Corporation, a company based in Maryland (USA). The company was later acquired by Transware and, finally, by Welocalize. According to Welocalize's official website (http://www.welocalize.com), Derek Coffey, now Senior Vice President of Technology and Development at Welocalize, had a key role in the process of open-sourcing Ambassador as GlobalSight TMS in 2009, and has led the development of the product ever since.

GlobalSight TMS offers multi-functional features, such as alignment, machine translation, project management, terminology management, and user administration (http://www.globalsight.com).

Moran and Lewis (2011) used GlobalSight with the purpose of evaluating machine translation in a low-cost manual way. The explanation they offer about the reasons for their choice can provide an insight into the benefits of using this particular computer-aided translation tool. As quoted from their research article (Moran and Lewis 2011: 13):

'A number of factors combine to make GlobalSight our TMS of choice.

(i)   It is free and open-source.
(ii) It is an active project which is undergoing continual improvements.
(iii) It has a sophisticated web services application programming interface (API).
(iv) It is functionally similar to existing proprietary solutions like SDL's WorldServer.
(v)   It is owned by Welocalize, who are a CNGL industrial partner'.[12]

> Merely one year after open-sourcing GlobalSight, in 2010, Derek Coffey announced a new paid utility based on the concept of Software as a Service (SaaS). According to Coffey, this service was driven by the needs of an increasing number of companies, who wanted to use large-scale software, such as GlobalSight, but lacked the infrastructure or support teams necessary in order to deploy the system in-house. GlobalSight SaaS was initially provided by Yan Yu, CEO of Spartan Consulting, who claimed that, in only a few months, more than 20 companies from different countries had signed up for the 60-day free trial and were actually pleased with the software.
>
> (Coffey 2010: online)

Currently, GlobalSight SaaS is provided by LocalizationSmart, a service unit that operates under Globalme Language & Technology. In the official website,[13]

Computer-aided translation 181

they emphasize that GlobalSight SaaS is extremely easy to use. Basically, the client needs to inform the provider of the particularities of the translation process as well as of the number of users that will be working on the project, and LocalizationSmart will subsequently set up the workflow profiles, translation memories, and user accounts in a private GlobalSight instance. Furthermore, in-depth training is offered to administrators, project managers, and translators, together with a faultless customer support service.

Google Translator Toolkit

Google Translator Toolkit, a free online SaaS product of California-based Google Inc., was launched in June 2009 and received with great expectation. In an early review, García and Stevenson (2009: 16) described Google Translator Toolkit as a user-friendly tool, intuitive, and with a small number of basic options. In fact, this is one of its main strengths, as it can be easily used by both professional translators and amateurs.

One of the most characteristic features of Google Translator Toolkit is that it promotes collaboration among individual translators or teams, allowing them to create translation memories and term databases that can eventually be shared with others. This can pose potential privacy and confidentiality issues, as the option that is set by default involves sharing the information with Google and, thus, everyone in the world (García and Stevenson 2009: 16). Moreover, as Pym points out (2011: 5), when using Google Translator Toolkit, users are required to upload documents in a Google-owned 'cloud', where the confidentiality of the material can be compromised. It seems therefore obvious that the use of this tool is restricted to translators with no professional secrets, such as volunteer translators.

An additional feature of Google Translator Toolkit, which is not present in many other free computer-aided translation tools, is the possibility of post-editing a pre-translation of the source text provided by Google's machine translation engine, Google Translate. Google Translator Toolkit not only offers the possibility to generate machine translation matches when no matches are found in the translation memory, but also to practically impose that option, activating it by default and advising against disabling it (García 2011: 219). The effects that post-editing may have in the translation's quality and productivity are a major topic of discussion. García (2011) conducted an experiment to evaluate both the productivity and quality provided by translation students translating from English into Chinese and vice versa when using this option in Google Translator Toolkit. García concluded that higher quality was achieved, if not greater productivity, especially by less-skilled students. Ramos (2010), in turn, conducted a similar experiment but focused on three different language pairs: English into Spanish, English into Portuguese, and Portuguese into Spanish. The results of the study were positive, and she is now a strong supporter of post-editing machine translation.

Google Translator Toolkit supports about 300 languages but imposes size limits for source texts (1MB), translation memories (50MB), and glossaries

182   *Computer-aided translation*

(1MB). On top of that, some important computer-aided translation tool functions, such as quality checkers and project management, are not present in this system.

In conclusion, Google Translator Toolkit is more a document-based rather than a project-based tool. Most experts agree that the aim of this software is not to contribute directly to the translation industry, but to acquire free-of-cost bilingual information from its users in order to optimize its machine translation system (García 2011: 219; García and Stevenson 2009: 18). It is, therefore, more recommended for volunteers and amateurs rather than professional translators.

GTranslator

GTranslator was created by Fatih Demir in 2000 and later developed by Juan José Sánchez Penas, Pablo Sanxiao, and collegues. This computer-aided translation tool is an enhanced gettext (*.po* files) editor designed for GNOME, an open-source desktop environment that is particularly intended for Linux and Unix-based operating systems. According to Sourceforge, from which the software can be freely downloaded (http://sourceforge.net/projects/gtranslator/), the latest updated version, GTranslator 1.9.7, was released in April 2013.

As claimed on the official website,[14] GTranslator is able to handle all forms of gettext files. The most useful features that the software includes are: find and replace tools, different translator profiles, and easy navigation. It also includes a so-called 'message table', which offers an overview of the translations and allows users to add messages in the *.po* file. In addition, GTranslator offers a plug-in system that enables many interesting plug-ins (e.g., Alternate Language, Insert Tags, Open Tran, Integration with Subversion, and Source Code Viewer) to be installed.

Notwithstanding the aforementioned features, GTranslator is still a relatively small project and should be further developed in order to equal some of its competitors.

Heartsome

Araya is a server-based computer-aided translation system developed by Heartsome Europe GmbH, a company founded in 2002 that focuses on two different fields: translation technology and tourism. The founder and director of the company, Klemens Waldhör, has extensive experience in the area of translation technology and computer-aided translation tools. Back in 1996, he contributed to the development of Euramis, a series of email-based applications which provided access to a variety of services (e.g., translation memory, aligner, etc.) with the purpose of supporting the translation service at the European Commission (Directorate-General for Translation of the European Commission 2005: 13). Euramis was among the first translation support systems that consistently implemented client-server architecture, a concept that was later reused by Sun

Computer-aided translation 183

Microsystem as SunTrans. Some years later, Waldhör built on this experience to create Heartsome, which in 2004 split into two independent companies, one in Germany and another in Singapore. They continued developing the software separately, and Araya was then created by the European branch from the earlier versions of Heartsome's computer-aided translation tool.

In addition to most common functionalities present in other professional systems (e.g., TMX Editor, XLIFF Converter, Monolingual Terminology Extractor, Bilingual Terminology Extractor, Server, and Web Server), Araya has two features which are of particular importance: (i) it supports all languages, including double-byte languages and bi-directional languages, without any restrictions in combination or in the direction of translation; and (ii) it is compatible with OASIS XLIFF (i.e., XML Localization Interchange File Format), supporting a full process of localization. In fact, the editing interface of Araya is called Araya XLIFF Editor.

As aforementioned, Araya includes most translation-memory professional functionalities, including a TMX editor, a highly sophisticated tool for the construction and maintenance of translation memory databases and files based on the TMX standard. Furthermore, it can be integrated through XML-RPC support without heavy efforts into existing processes. In the information brochure provided by the company,[15] it is claimed that, with the use of XML, XLIFF, and TMX, Araya's server is optimally prepared to integrate and co-operate with any other systems.

Last but not least, Araya is a cross-platform programme, being able to run in most existing operating systems, including Linux, Solaris, Unix, and MS Windows.

Isometry

Isometry emerged as an amateur work developed by Finite Field, a Japanese company represented by Toshiya Kazuyoshi (一好俊也). When it was first released, back in 2006, Isometry was an elementary MS Windows application aimed at freelance translators. It offered relatively basic functions like concordance search, automatic term recognition, and dictionary. Moreover, it was only able to support translation memories in TXT or TSV formats (http://www.finite-field.com/home).

In 2011, Finite Field announced on a ProZ.com forum[16] that Isometry 2.0 had been released as a drastically different new version that worked as a web application. The new web-based version of Isometry was promising, but there was a problem: it was only compatible with Google Chrome. Developers explained, in the same forum thread, that this was due to two major technical issues. First, Isometry 2.0 gave its users the option of storing the translation data either in a local computer or on a 'cloud' server. The problem lies with the fact that web browsers limit local storage for each website. In the case of Chrome, for instance, the limit is five MB, yet this restriction can be overcome by installing the web application through Chrome Web Store. Second, in order

184   *Computer-aided translation*

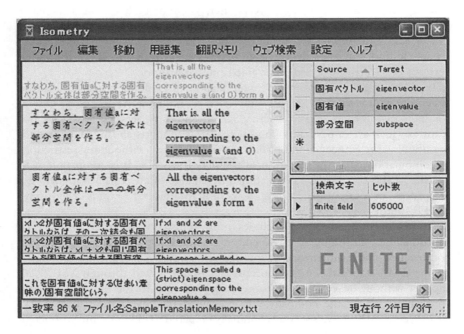

Figure 4.3 Translation Editor of Isometry

to store a large amount of data, Isometry 2.0 used Web SQL Database, which is only supported by Google Chrome and Safari.

Very recently, the latest version of Isometry, Isometry 3, has been launched by RimageArts Inc., and, according to its new official website (http://www.isometry-trans.com/en/), it is accompanied by a rich new set of features, the most interesting of which are listed below:

(i) Partial match results can be instantly retrieved by hovering the mouse pointer over the text. Moreover, Isometry plays with variants of words in seventeen different languages, e.g., 'house' and 'houses' are considered variants of the same word, so, given that 'house' is stored in the translation memory, results could be retrieved for 'houses'.

(ii) Character-based fuzzy search has been introduced.

(iii) Isometry 3 allows several translators to work on a single project by giving the option of sharing translation documents, translation memories, and glossaries.

(iv) The quality assurance tool has been improved. In the case where a single term can be translated in multiple different ways, the quality checker can detect the absence of all these equivalents in the translated paragraph and subsequently create a warning. Furthermore, it is possible to create individual check rules that later can be shared with others.

Computer-aided translation 185

(v) It is possible to synchronize data with another computer so that they can be used as a pseudo multi-screen. Thus, some information, such as translation-memory results and glossaries, can be visualized in a second computer or tablet.
(vi) Machine translation can be used by integrating Google Translate.
(vii) Right-to-left languages are supported.
(viii) Isometry 3 includes an auto-alignment tool. Alignment tools are lacking in most free computer-aided translation systems. Its implementation in this version is, therefore, highly appreciated.
(ix) In Isometry 3, the source text is segmented in paragraphs, reflecting the preference of the developers, who consider this feature ideal for ID-based translations, such as localization. There is, however, the possibility of sentence-based segmentation.
(x) Isometry 3 is still constrained to operate on the Google Chrome browser. On the other hand, this fact enables it to run on most platforms, such as Windows, Mac OS, Linux, and Android.

It is undeniable that Isometry has evolved greatly ever since its creation. However, it still appears to carry a very important problem: very limited file format support. At present, Isometry 3 can handle only plain text (*.txt*), HTML (*.html*), Microsoft Word 2007/2010 (*.docx*), Microsoft Excel 2007/2010 (*.xlsx*), and Isometry files (*isom*). In addition, plain text and HTML files must be encoded in UTF-8.[17] It should also be pointed out that Isometry 3 is no longer an unconditionally free computer-aided translation tool and, in order to push users into purchasing a subscription, some restrictions have been introduced into the free version. For instance, the size of Microsoft Word and Excel files is restricted to 200 KB, and the number of translation documents is limited to 20.

Lingotek Collaborative Translation Platform/Translation Management System

Lingotek Collaborative Translation Platform, now called the Translation Management System, is a cloud-based product of the Utah-based company Lingotek Inc., founded in 2005. The first version of Lingotek was launched in 2006 as a browser-based translation memory tool. Three years later, in October 2009, Lingotek Collaborative Translation Platform was released in the form of SaaS.

Like Crowdin, this system is a translation tool intended to support crowdsourcing translation or, in the words of Robert Vandenberg, CEO of Lingotek, 'to replace any piece of the translation workflow with multiple people, volunteer or otherwise' (Vandenberg 2009: 4). In his presentation, Vandenberg also gives an estimate of the costs of translations performed by a 'crowd' compared to those performed by professional translators, as shown in Table 4.1.

186 *Computer-aided translation*

Table 4.1 Comparison between the Costs of Translations Performed by Lingotek Community Translation and Industry Standards

	Industry Standards	*Lingotek Community Translation*
Professional translator daily output	2500 words/day	125,000 words/day
Cost	$525/day	$100/day
Average cost per word	$0.21/word	$0.0008/word

Adapted from Vandenberg 2009: 21

According to the official website,[18] Lingotek Collaborative Translation Platform has several remarkable characteristics: (i) the translation project management mode is updated, making the design of the translation workflow more flexible; (ii) the system supports online chats, enhancing communication among the members of a translation team; (iii) it can be integrated with API systems, such as Sharepoint, Drupal, Salesforce, Jive Social CRM, and Oracle UCM; (iv) it is integrated with two machine translation systems, namely Microsoft Bing and Google Translate, and allows users to plug-in other engines if necessary; (v) it supports *.xliff* file format, translation memory database file formats, such as *.tmx*, and terminology file formats, such as *.csv*, *.tbx*, and *.xls*; and (vi) it supports 245 languages and sublanguages.

LogiTerm

LogiTerm is a product of Terminotix Inc., a Canadian company based in Quebec and specialized in computer-aided translation. The latest version, LogiTerm 5.2, released in September 2012, is available in three different versions: LogiTerm Pro, LogiTerm Web, and LogiTerm Web Extension Module.

Logiterm Pro is targeted at general users or students, whereas LogiTerm Web and Web Extension Module are aimed at corporate users. According to Terminotix's website,[19] LogiTerm Web has four accessible databases, which are named Terminology, Bitexts, Full Text, and Reference. Terminology database is where terms are stored; Bitexts database displays previous translations that have been aligned with their respective originals; Full Text database allows users to search unilingual archives; and Reference database stores information that is relevant to the project. In addition to a comprehensive set of features, common to most computer-aided translation systems, LogiTerm Web supports more than 100 file types and all languages covered by Latin-1 or Unicode.

LongRay CAT

Beijing Zhongke Langrui Software Technology Ltd (北京中科朗瑞軟件技術有限公司) launched LongRay CAT in December 2006. The latest version of the software, LongRay CAT V.3, was released in September 2009 in four different

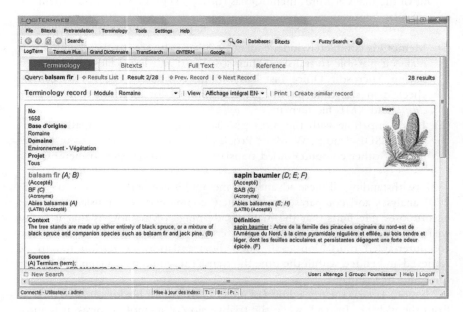

Figure 4.4 User Interface of LogiTerm Web

editions, namely Personal Edition, Enterprise Edition, Educational Edition, and Translation Management Platform Edition.[20]

The main features of the Translation Management Platform Edition include project management, real-time project progression monitoring, simultaneous communication, and support of about 60 languages. Moreover, the system can handle a number of file formats, yet it is most compatible with MS Word, MS Excel, and MS PowerPoint file formats.

MemoQ

MemoQ is a computer-aided translation tool developed by Kilgray Translation Technologies, an independent translation technology provider from Hungary. Kilgray was established in 2004 by three Hungarian language technologists. In actual fact, the name of the company originated from the founders' names: Kis Balázs (KI), Lengyel István (L), and Ugray Gábor (GRAY). According to the official website,[21] Kilgray worked on the technology for four years before its large-scale debut in 2009. By the end of 2010, Kilgray had established six offices in five different countries, i.e., Hungary, the United States, Germany, France, and Poland.

Within recent years, this powerful computer-aided translation system has become increasingly popular, especially after winning the Best Translation Software Award granted by the Institution of Translation and Interpretation in 2011 (ITI 2011: online).

188 *Computer-aided translation*

Out of the many features memoQ has (http://kilgray.com), two of them are of particular importance:

(i) MemoQ is completely independent of other software, to the extent that it makes it possible to translate Microsoft Word and Excel files even without having Microsoft Office installed on the computer. The results can be checked in real time on the preview window for *.doc*, *.docx*, *.ppt*, *.pptx*, *.html*, and XML file formats.
(ii) It is compatible with the most popular computer-aided translation tools, such as SDL-Trados, Wordfast Pro, and STAR Transit, facilitating former users of other computer-aided translation tools to transfer to memoQ.

Notwithstanding all these advantages, memoQ is not perfect. Jaworski (2013: 270) analyses and compares it with a new computer-aided translation system he proposes. He finds that the main disadvantage of memoQ is that it is not well optimized for search speed. This is crucial to determine the usability of a computer-aided translation tool, since the translation suggestion has to be retrieved and edited within the time the translator would have taken to translate the segment manually.

MemoQ 4free is the free edition of memoQ. It cannot be downloaded directly from the website. Instead, when the trial version of memoQ expires, it is automatically downgraded to the free version, which has only basic translation memory features and limited functionality. According to the comparison chart provided by Kilgray (kilgray.com/memoq/memoQcomparisonChart.pdf), memoQ 4free does not include important features such as proofreading options, automatic text aligner, and translation memory and terminology editor. Moreover, it imposes further limitations on the resources, being unable to import translation memories, termbases, and translation projects.

We can conclude that memoQ 4free is aimed at translators who are merely getting acquainted with translation technology or who have not decided, by the end of the trial period, whether to purchase the advanced version of the software.

MemoQ Server is one of the paid computer-aided translation solutions provided by Kilgray Translation Technologies. It allows a number of translators to work on a single project while sharing translation memories, terminology, and translation documents in real time.[22] In addition, collaboration among the members of a team, including the project manager, is supported by specific functions of project management and communication. As mentioned above, memoQ products are compatible with the majority of computer-aided translation tools. As a result, translators are given the option of working on a project with users of competing tools, as well as processing translation projects from a variety of different systems.

MemoQ Server is available in two editions: ServerFive and Enterprise edition. ServerFive, on the one hand, consists of one memoQ server and five mobile licenses. The Enterprise edition, on the other hand, includes memoQ's software development kit (Web Service API) along with ServerFive.

Computer-aided translation 189

The latest version of memoQ Server, memoQ Server 2014, was released in June 2014 and, according to Kilgray, it includes the following new features:[23]

(i) Project templates and workflow automation: In this new version, the management of recurring project types is completely automated, focusing the attention on the details of the projects. This feature is available for both local and online projects.
(ii) Simplification of online projects: In memoQ Server 2014, there is merely one type of online project. Synchronization has been greatly improved, as well as the functionality for resolving inconsistencies between the project on the server and a desktop.
(iii) Image Localization: This functionality enables the translator to manage image localization within a standard localization process.

MEMOrg

MEMOrg is an online computer-aided translation system developed in 2008 by Serious Business, a private company in Romania. According to its website,[24] MEMOrg offers three online resources for translators:

(i) Free online dictionary, which includes extensive terminology from a number of domains and, currently, contains equivalents for four language pairs, namely English-French, English-Polish, English-Romanian, and English-Spanish.
(ii) Translator directory, which offers translators, translation companies, and translation customers the possibility of creating an account and, thus, gaining access to other online tools, such as the translation memory and project management system.
(iii) Online MEMOrg Translation Memory (MEMOrgTM), which runs on an online platform, allowing translators to work directly from a browser in most operating systems.

The latest version of this system, MEMOrg 2.0, can only be accessed via invitation from existing members or by signing up with a new account. Features of MEMOrg 2.0 include the aforementioned translation memory and free online dictionary as well as shared field-structured databases and a user-friendly interface.

Perhaps the biggest benefit of using MEMOrg is that source segments, translated segments, and glossary and spelling entries are all stored in a single database. Therefore, the same translation memory can be used regardless of the language combination. Furthermore, according to Serious Business,[25] more than ten million valid equivalences have been incorporated into MEMOrg in advance. A minor remark, but one worth mentioning nonetheless, is that, although the system is Unicode-compliant, it works best with European languages and left-to-right orthography, such as Albanian, Bulgarian, Danish, English, Finnish, French, German,

190 *Computer-aided translation*

Greek, Hungarian, Italian, Polish, Romanian, Russian Spanish, and Swedish. The file formats that the system can handle, on the other hand, are very limited, supporting only Microsoft Word and Excel, RTF, HTML, XHTML, and XML files.

Memsource

Memsource was developed by Memsource Technologies, a company founded in Prague, Czech Republic, in 2010.

Memsource Cloud was launched in private beta in early 2011 and was released to the public later that year. The latest version, Memsource Cloud 4.3, was released on 18 May 2014 and is currently available in different subscription packages: Personal and +1 Freelancers Edition, both of which are aimed at translators; Team Start, Team, and Ultimate Edition, aimed at translation agencies; and Biz Start, Biz Team, and Biz Ultimate Edition, aimed at translation buyers. In addition, Memsource offers two special purpose packages, namely Academic and Developers Edition.

On its official website,[26] Memsource provides a list of reasons given by its customers as to why they chose Memsource Cloud. Some of these reasons are summarized below so as to enlighten some of the advantages in deploying this system.

(i)   Translators do not necessarily have to purchase a license in order to use Memsource. Therefore, a translation company that is subscribed to any Memsource editions can ask any translator to translate for them.
(ii) Unlike most cloud-based translation systems, Memsource can support offline translation using Memsource Editor.
(iii) Data in Memsource is encrypted, preventing any kind of privacy and confidentiality issues.
(iv) Memsource Cloud is a multiplatform system and, therefore, can be installed on Windows, Macintosh, and Linux operating systems, amongst others.
(v)   All data, including translation memories and glossaries, is centralized; thus, all project members can use and update it.

In addition to the foregoing features, Memsource Cloud includes termbase maintenance; a free web-based translator's workbench, i.e., Memsource Web Editor; project management functions; and integrated machine translation, which can be controlled by the project manager. Last but not least, it supports 20 common file formats and all languages in Unicode.

MetaTexis

MetaTexis is a computer-aided translation system developed by MetaTexis Software and Services in Germany. This company was founded by Hermann Bruns, who began to programme the software in the summer of 2000. He presented his new computer-aided translation tool in public for the first time at the ProZ. com conference in Porto Santo Stefano, Italy. The first version, MetaTexis 1.0.0,

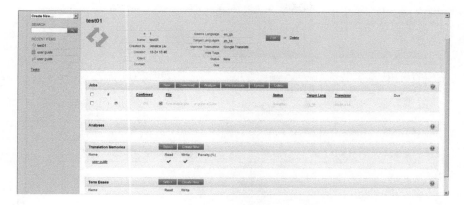

Figure 4.5 Project Management Page of Memsource Cloud

was officially released in Germany in April 2002, whereas the latest version, 3.17, was released a decade later, in 2012.[27]

MetaTexis products are available in two different editions: MetaTexis for Word and MetaTexis Server. The former is a Microsoft Word plug-in computer-aided translation system, whereas the latter is a server-based system that enables users' programmes, which are operated on computers connected to the server via LAN or Internet, to access centrally stored translation memories and terminology databases. MetaTexis Server is further divided into three editions based on the maximum number of active users allowed: Team Edition, which allows three users; Office Edition, which allows five users; and Enterprise Edition, which allows an unlimited number of users. All these server-based editions have the database access function of MetaTexis for Word; support professional database formats such as Microsoft Access, Microsoft SQL Server 2005, and MySQL; and what is most important, can be linked to the popular Trados Workbench.

The system is easy to install and run; it takes only a few minutes to install and configure the server. However, MS Windows is required for the MetaTexis Server to operate.

MT2007

MT2007 was created by Andrew Manson, who aimed to develop a free tool that was easy to use, to the extent that it would allow translators to start working with it immediately, without the need for previous training. In actual fact, not only the training can be dispensed with, but also the installation process; in order to use MT2007, the only requirement is to decompress the RAR file.

MT2007 is certainly easy to use. On the other hand, it lacks numerous features that leading systems have, and it is subject to several limitations. To begin with, it is written in C#. Consequently, it requires Microsoft NET Framework 2.0, which

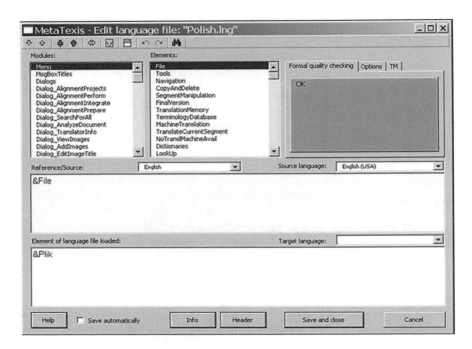

Figure 4.6 Editing Interface of MetaTexis

in turn can only work on MS Windows. Therefore, MT2007 cannot be used in any operating system other than MS Windows. As for now, each project can have only one source file, which must have one of the following supported formats: MS Word 2007 (i.e., *.docx*, *.doc*), MS Excel 2007 (i.e., *.xlsx*, *.xlsm*), MS PowerPoint 2007 (i.e., *.pptx*, *.pptm*), OpenDocument Text (i.e., *.odt*), OpenDocument Spread Sheet (i.e., *.ods*), XML, TMX, XLIFF, and Simple XML formats. Finally, it only supports twelve European languages (i.e., English, Russian, Danish, Dutch, Finnish, French, German, Italian, Norwegian, Portuguese, Spanish, and Swedish).

The current usability of MT2007 is questionable. Nonetheless, Manson claims on MT2007's official website (http://mt2007-cat.ru/) that a new version, Catnip, includes new features with the purpose of increasing the speed of the translation process and the functionality of the software. In addition, a future networking system, which might not be free, will be introduced in order to allow several translators to work on a single project, with a single terminology database, and communicate with the other members of the team via an inbuilt messaging system.

MultiTrans

MultiTrans, developed by MultiCorpora R&D Inc. in Canada, is a type of multilingual computer-aided translation system targeted at corporate users with

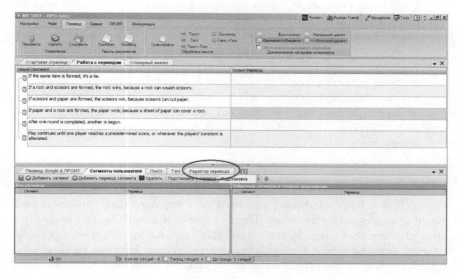

Figure 4.7 Translation Editor of MT2007

management as its core element. The scope of MultiCorpora lies within the idea of improving the efficiency of translators. Gerry Gervais, founder of the company, was serving as manager of a Canadian government translation department when, in 2006, he proposed the idea of a corpus-based TextBase tool with an innovative leveraging functionality. The new concept was baptized 'Advanced Leveraging Translation Memory' (ALTM). ALTM is better than the traditional translation memory tools, which are based on a database of isolated whole sentences, in that it freely aligns documents and performs deep matching in a contextualized previous translation. In fact, Gervais himself defines MultiTrans as 'a translation support and language management solution that is based on a multilingual full-text repository of previously translated content' (Gervais 2003: 1). He puts emphasis on the fact that this software has provided support to a great number of global organizations and professionals in the language industry, leading to an improvement in translation productivity and quality for all types of content, including pharmaceutical, banking, and other sectors worldwide.

The latest version, MultiTrans Prism version 5.6, was released in June 2013 at the Localization World conference in London. According to the official website,[28] MultiTrans Prism offers a range of flexible server solutions to meet the needs of its users. There are four server-based MultiTrans Prism tools:

(i) MultiTrans Prism Enterprise Server, which includes business/project/ workflow management, ALTM, and terminology management tools, combined into one single package;

194 *Computer-aided translation*

(ii) MultiTrans Prism Blue, which is targeted at those organizations who do not want to deploy the full translation management system in-house or already have translation memory and terminology tools installed but need to automate only their project management functions;

(iii) MultiTrans Prism Yellow, which includes translation memory, ALTM, and terminology management tools, as well as a powerful server configuration, and is aimed at organizations who have existing project and workflow management tools but are interested in the benefits of ALTM;

(iv) and MultiTrans Prism Red, which is mainly focused on terminology management.

OmegaT

OmegaT is a free, standalone, open-source computer-aided translation tool aimed at professional translators. The fact that it is written in Java makes it a cross-platform tool, running on Linux, Mac OS, and MS Windows operating systems, amongst others. OmegaT has an intuitive user interface and is easy to use. According to the official website,[29] it includes traditional computer-aided translation features, such as fuzzy matching, match propagation, and simultaneous use of multiple translation memories.

A major advantage of OmegaT is that, although it is an independent application, it can be combined with other software, such as:

(i)   OpenOffice.org, a fully functional text editor, which is also free and open source;

(ii) Okapi Framework, which enables a number of file formats that cannot be processed directly by OmegaT to be translated; and

(iii) LF Aligner, an automatic alignment tool for creating translation memory files by aligning texts with their respective translations.

OmegaT is used not only by professional translators, but also by scholars, who benefit from its advantages in their research. Alegría et al. (2013) remarked that one of the reasons that led to the decision of using OmegaT was that it permits users to access external machine translation systems. The machine translation services that can be selected are typically Google Translate, Apertium, or Belazar; however, this is relatively easy to customize by adding more services. Since the focus of Alegría's research was on the Basque Language, he integrated a Spanish-Basque machine translation engine. Moreover, thanks to OmegaT's flexibility regarding third-party applications, they were also able to integrate a Basque spell-checker to assist translators during the translation process (Alegría et al. 2013: 108). For their part, Zaremba, Laukaitis, and Vasilecas (2009: 251) studied the possible application of OmegaT in translations involving the Lithuanian language. One of the most useful features for their work was that it supports Unicode UTF-8, enabling non-latin alphabets to be used. Furthermore, they were allowed to use the same translation memory for translating from English into Lithuanian and vice versa.

Computer-aided translation 195

OmegaT has the support of a great number of translators. In 2006, a survey conducted by the Imperial College London's scholar Elina Lagoudaki revealed that OmegaT is the most popular of the open-source computer-aided translation tools. The results of the survey are divided into several groups. The first group regards those professionals that Lagoudaki calls non-TM-users, i.e., those who do not use a translation memory system but will be willing to try or buy one. To the question of which computer-aided translation tools had they heard about, OmegaT was mentioned by ten per cent, becoming the ninth most popular translation memory tool and, more remarkably, being the only open-source computer-aided translation tool in the list.

Table 4.2 Most Popular TM tools with Non-TM-users

TM tool	Percentage
Trados	76%
Déjà Vu	61%
Wordfast	51%
SDL-Trados 2006	49%
SDLX	36%
STAR Transit	25%
MultiTrans	18%
Passolo	11%
OmegaT	10%

Adapted from Table 3 in Lagoudaki 2006: 15

Table 4.3 Top 10 Most Widely Used TM Tools

TM tool	Percentage
Trados	51%
Wordfast	29%
SDL-Trados 2006	24%
Déjà Vu	23%
SDLX	19%
STAR Transit	14%
Alchemy Catalyst	8%
OmegaT	7%
Logoport	6%
Passolo	5%

Adapted from Table 7 in Lagoudaki 2006: 20

196 *Computer-aided translation*

Table 4.4 Top 10 Most Widely Used TM Tools by other than Windows OS Users

TM tool	Percentage
Wordfast	27%
OmegaT	15%
Trados	13%
Déjà Vu	13%
SDL-Trados 2006	9%
Heartsome	7%
AppleTrans	5%
Alchemy Catalyst	2%
Loc Factory	2%
OmegaT+	2%

Adapted from Figure 24 in Lagoudaki 2006: 21

A second group of respondents comprises the translation-memory users. When participants in this group were asked about which translation memory tool they used, OmegaT was found to be used by seven per cent, placing eighth in the list (including paid computer-aided translation tools).

Finally, among the users of operating systems other than MS Windows, OmegaT was found to be the second most widely used translation memory tool, surpassed only by Wordfast.

In the above results, percentage totals may be more that 100 per cent because respondents were allowed to select more than one tool.

More recently, an unofficial survey in 2010[30] revealed that, amongst 458 professional translators, OmegaT was used around a third as much as popular paid systems such as Wordfast, Déja Vu, and MemoQ.

OmegaT+

OmegaT+, first launched in 2005, is a free server-based computer-aided translation system developed by Rhythmous Systems in Quebec, Canada. It is written in Java, which makes it a cross-platform computer-aided translation tool. The newest version, OmegaT+ 1.0.M3.1., was released on 23 October 2012. It should be noted that OmegaT+ and OmegaT are two completely different systems and were developed separately by different teams.

According to the official website,[31] OmegaT+ supports all languages in ISO 639 Language Codes and can handle the following document formats: OpenXML formats (*.docx*, *.xlsx*, *.ppt*), ODF formats (OpenDocument), and plain text (*.txt*). OmegaT+ can be particularly useful for localization projects due to the fact that it supports most localization files, such as Help and Manual

Computer-aided translation 197

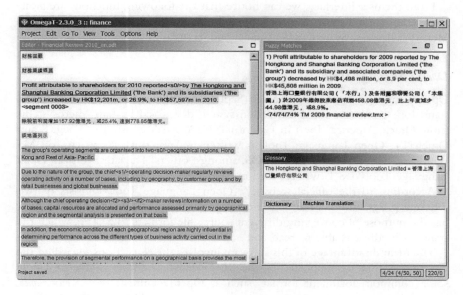

Figure 4.8 Editor of OmegaT

(*.hmx*, *.hmxp*, *.xml*), HHC/HHK (HtmlHelp), HTML/XHTML, INI, Java properties (*.properties*), Mozilla DTD (*.dtdPO*), SRT (SubRip), Typo3 (*.xml*), XLIFF, XML, XTag, and Windows Resources (*.rc*).

Although it is not a very powerful tool per se, OmegaT+ is most useful when used together with a series of applications:

(i) bitext2tmx: a free application which creates translation memories in TMX format by aligning an original and its translation in text format (*.txt*). The corresponding TMX document can be imported by OmegaT+ in order to be used as a translation memory. This application was originally developed by Susana Santos Antón, in collaboration with Sergio Ortiz-Rojas and Mikel L. Forcada within the framework of the project 'Finite-state translators based on bitexts harvested from the net' (2004–2006). The current software developer is Raymond Martin, OmegaT+'s developer (bitext2tmx. sourceforge.net).

(ii) LanguageTool: an open-source spell-checker tool created by Daniel Naber for his thesis (Naber 2003). It currently supports 29 languages to a different degree, yet the most accurate, according to the number of XML rules, are French, German (with Austria, Germany, and Switzerland variations), Catalan, Polish, and English (with all its variations).

(iii) Validator: an application to validate TMX and fix invalid characters in TMX that can cause problems when used.

198   *Computer-aided translation*

From the user interface, we can notice that the following functions are available: Translation Editor, Matches, Machine Translation, Message, Document, Metrics, Glossary, Search, and Original and Translation.

Open Language Tools

Open Language Tools, launched in September 2006, is a free, open-source, standalone computer-aided translation system developed by Sun Microsystems (now Oracle America, Inc.) in California, USA. Analogously to OmegaT and OmegaT+, Open Language Tools is written in Java; thus, it can run on MS Windows, Linux, Solaris, and Mac OS, amongst others. The latest version, Open Language Tools 1.3.1, was released in March 2010.

According to the official website,[32] Open Language Tools consists of two different programmes: a translation editor and a XLIFF Filter. The XLIFF filter has the purpose of converting different source file formats to XLIFF, which the translation editor is able to read and edit.

The main disadvantage of this software involves the restrictions regarding the file formats that are supported by the XLIFF filter. The filter is able to handle some common document formats such as OpenDocument (e.g., *.odw*, *.odc*, *.odi*) and plain text (*.txt*). However, it does not support Microsoft Word format, which is probably the most widely used format by professional translators. This limitation significantly restricts the usability of the programme.

OpenTM2

OpenTM2, launched in June 2010, is a project that IBM jointly developed with LISA, Welocalize, Cisco, and Linux Solution Group eV (LiSoG) in the United States. IBM contributed to OpenTM2 with several modules of the outdated IBM Translation Manager/2. In fact, TM2 stands for Translation Manager/2.

According to the official website,[33] features of OpenTM2 include: (i) an easy-to-use user interface; (ii) built-in dictionaries for European languages; (iii) a terminology management system with dictionary structure; (iv) dictionary filters, which contribute to the improvement of terminology management; (v) history reports for reference; and (vi) support of 47 different languages.

It should be noted, however, that OpenTM2 is still under development and, hitherto, advanced features and functions, which are present in commercial computer-aided translation systems, are not available. For instance, developers remark on the official website that OpenTM2 is not a terminology management tool, but a translation memory workbench; therefore, the management of terminological resources is limited. One of the developers' main goals involves enabling OpenTM2 to interact with third-party terminology management tools, which may well enhance the functionality of the software. In addition, developers aim to improve the support for open standards in the translation and localization industry.

Further significant drawbacks of OpenTM2 are the fact that it is restricted to the MS Windows operating system and, as of July 2010, the only supported project file formats were: HTML (UTF-8 and ASCII), JAVA properties file, OpenOffice files, XHTML, XLIFF, and generic XML. Fortunately, it supports the import and export of TMX-format translation memory databases.

The latest version of OpenTM2, v 0.9.5, includes a new scripting engine that enables tasks to be automated, thus allowing translators to quickly create automatic tasks by writing a simple script file.

OpenTMS

Open*TMS* is an acronym for 'Open Source Translation Management System', which is a cross-platform web-based system developed by Klemens Waldhör and Rainer Kemmler in Germany. OpenTMS is implemented in Java and requires Java 1.5 or later editions to operate. It has some basic translation memory functions, such as pre-translation, concordance search, and configuration of matching rates. The processes of OpenTMS involve (i) converting the source file; (ii) translating the file in the 'Translation Editor' while consulting terminology and translation memory databases; and (iii) back-converting the file to its original format.

OpenTMS has been discontinued and is now part of the project OpenTM2. Developers are investigating whether OpenTMS could be another translation memory component plug-in for OpenTM2 or, alternatively, whether OpenTMS could become the server-based component for OpenTM2 (http://www.opentm2.org).

PROMT

PROMT is a well-known machine translation system developed in Russia by PROMT Ltd., a company established in 1991 by Svetlana Sokolova, the incumbent CEO, and Alexander Serebryakov, the incumbent CTO, both of whom earned doctorates in computational linguistics. The interest of the company was, initially, confined to the development of rule-based machine translation (RBMT) software, yet in April 2005 they incorporated the translation memory engine of Trados into their product at that time, PROMT v.7.8. Since then, all subsequent professional versions of the system have been integrated with a translation memory module, which has proved to function appropriately.

One of the features that have always characterized PROMT is the possibility of using and editing a number of available dictionaries. In 2004, PROMT offered three different types of dictionaries (Guerra 2004: 122–123):

(i) Single large general-purpose dictionary for each language pair, which was provided by PROMT Ltd. and could be used as a terminological reference during the translation process. This type of dictionary was locked, which prevented its entries from being modified or deleted.

200 *Computer-aided translation*

(ii) Domain-specific dictionaries, which could be purchased separately.
(iii) User or customized dictionaries, the most interesting of the three types. They could be created and modified by using the Dictionary Editor tool. Customized dictionaries enable users to adapt the software to their specific needs, thus gaining control and speed over both the translation and the post-editing process.

New versions of the software keep offering these applications, allowing translators to create their own electronic dictionaries, for manual or automatic use.

In May 2014, the company announced the release of the latest version of the software, PROMT 10, which is offered in desktop series and corporate series.[34] The corporate series encompasses server-based systems, which in turn are available in several editions: PROMT Translation Server 10, PROMT Translation Server 10 DE, PROMT Cloud, and Industry Products. Industry Products refers to server solutions designed specifically for key industries of the Russian economy.

The computer-aided translation functions of PROMT 10 include all the utilities that were present in the previous version, PROMT 9.5, such as automatic term and translation memory concordance, term extraction, spelling check, dictionaries, and terminology management, as well as some new features, such as a new cross-platform web interface, a corporate mobile application, and individual customization. Regarding file format support, users can import terminology documents with *.txt*, *.xls*, *.tbx*, *.xml*, and *.olif* formats, and translation memory documents with *.tmx* and *.tmw* formats.

PROMT Ltd. claims that along with millions of home users, they count the support of 15,000 corporate customers of all sizes in a broad range of fields, including some prominent companies, such as Norilsk Nickel, TripAdvisor, Gazprom, Cisco, Lukoil, and PayPal. The contribution by Beregovaya and Yanishevsky, both members of the staff at PROMT Ltd., describes PROMT system deployment at PayPal (Beregovaya and Yanishevsky 2010). PayPal is an exemplary company in terms of localization efforts. Consequently, prior to deploying machine translation technology in the localization process, the company required a number of essential factors, the most important of which were: (i) high-quality machine translation to help serve their localized markets in a a cheaper and faster way; (ii) interaction with SDL Idiom WorldServer; (iii) flexibility in handling metadata; (iv) independent engine management by client linguists and engineers; and (v) support for a wide range of content types and languages (including local variations). In order to address the client challenges, PROMT Translation Server Developer Edition was used. In addition, both linguistic customization (e.g., identification and repair of inconsistencies between the translation memory and the glossary, conversion of existing product glossaries into PROMT customized dictionaries, and coding of client glossary terms in PROMT Dictionary Editor) and engineering customization (e.g., advanced metadata handling using PROMT-Idiom XLIFF Connector and pre- and post-processing rules) were performed by the PROMT team for PayPal. According to Beregovaya and Yanishevsky (2010: 4), with the preceding customization, PayPal increased productivity by nearly 30 per cent.

SDL

SDL is a British localization and translation technology company founded in 1992 by Mark Lancaster. It has now grown into a listed company with numerous offices in various countries in the world and a huge impact on the translation industry. In 1995, the company acquired its first translation memory technology, and since 2001, it has been growing exponentially, mainly through acquisitions of other software: Alpnet (in 2001), Trados (in 2005), Tridion (in 2007), Idiom (in 2008), and Language Weaver (in 2010). After integrating these systems into their own products, SDL has launched several translation programmes. The first computer-aided translation system developed by SDL was called SDLX, but it was discontinued around 2009, making way for the dominant SDL-Trados, one of the most popular computer-aided translation tools on the market, with its latest version, SDL-Trados Studio 2014, being probably the leader in the industry. The integration of acquired software into SDL products resulted also in the creation of a number of server-based systems, such as SDL Studio GroupShare, SDL TMS, and SDL WorldServer.

SDL Studio GroupShare is a collaborative translation system specifically designed for small to medium-sized localization teams that use SDL-Trados Studio and SDL MultiTerm. SDL Studio GroupShare provides users with a single platform to allow them to collaborate in centralized translation memory databases, terminology databases, and translation projects. The latest version, SDL Studio GroupShare 2014 SP1, was released in April 2014.

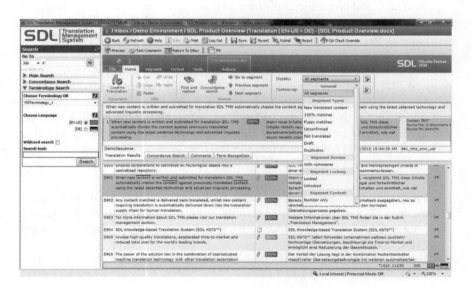

Figure 4.9 SDL TMS 2013

202 *Computer-aided translation*

SDL TMS, on the other hand, is a translation management system that is specifically designed to handle large and complex localization projects with a set of application processing procedures that governs the entire translation workflow. The features of SDL TMS include translation vendor selection, work distribution, project management, and file production, publishing, delivery, and closure. The latest version, SDL TMS 2011 SP4, was released in May 2013.

SDL WorldServer is a translation management system that attempts to simplify and expedite localization processes. It was originally developed by Idiom Technologies Inc., who commercialized the software as Idiom WorldServer. Idiom WorldServer soon became the most popular localization tool at the time, counting important customers such as Adobe, Autodesk, Continental Airlines, eBay, Mattel, and Travelocity. Bill Trippe, Senior Analyst at Gilbane Group, explains the reasons for the implementation of Idiom WorldServer in the localization workflow at Autodesk:

> Autodesk can point to a number of efficiencies from its use of Idiom WorldServer. As noted above, many of these efficiencies come from the use of a central repository and centralized workflow system that give users continuous visibility into project status.
>
> Another set of efficiencies comes from the capabilities of the WorldServer system itself. Autodesk gains efficiency from production tools such as the one that segments the XML assets into individual sentences for the translation memory (a step they used to perform by running a script). A system such as WorldServer has a number of features like this that automate common tasks and provide a large group of users (as at Autodesk) with significant efficiencies.
>
> (Trippe 2007: 9)

In 2008, Idiom Technologies was acquired by SDL International, who released SDL WorldServer in February 2011. SDL WorldServer 2011 has a number of functions, including document alignment, translation memory, and a machine translation system, as well as content, project, and business management. The latest update of this system, 10.4, was released in October 2013 and includes some enhancements over previous versions, the most important of which are:

(i) Project management enhancements: A Project Dashboard has been implemented in SDL WorldServer Home Page in order to provide updated information about active open projects and overall system usage upon login (SDL 2013: 2).
(ii) Improvements in the SDL WorldServer–SDL-Trados Studio Integration (SDL 2013: 7).

Computer-aided translation 203

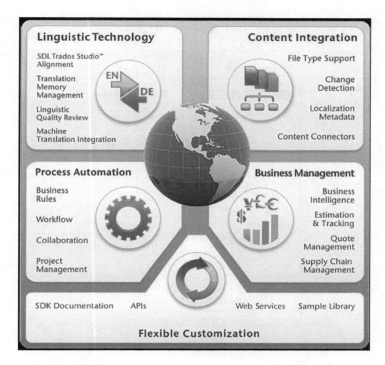

Figure 4.10 SDL WorldServer

Similis

Similis (Freelance) is a free translation memory system developed by Emmanuel Planas at Lingua et Machina, which he founded in 2002 in France.

Based on the corporate website,[35] Similis is targeted for professional translators, translation agencies, and translators working for companies. Its interface is user-friendly and intuitive, to the extent that a professional translator should be able to master it after just one day of training.

Similis was the first computer-aided translation software to use sub-segment aligned units, which Planas defined as a second-generation translation memory system (Planas 2005). Planas explains that the first-generation translation memory tools (which encompass the popular Trados and Wordfast, amongst many others) treat the text as a code, being incapable of identifying syntactical groups. Similis, on the other hand, combines two types of programmes, which enables it to work at a morphological, lexical, and syntactic level. These programmes consist of a linguistic analysis engine and a phrase-chunking tool. Typically, chunks are noun phrases, which consist of determiners, adjectives, nouns, and pronouns; or verb phrases, which in turn consist of a single verb or an auxiliary verb plus an

204 Computer-aided translation

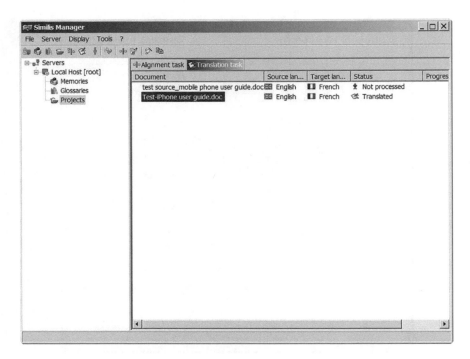

Figure 4.11 Similis Manager

infinitive. According to Planas (2005: 6), when a first-generation translation memory is imported, Similis not only preserves the corresponding segments, but also analyses each source and target segment for each translation unit, extracting translations of the chunks and producing the associated bilingual terminology.

In Similis, translation projects can be created via 'Similis Manager', whose most important features are: (i) import, enrich, and export translation memories; (ii) fully automatic alignment; and (iii) automatic terminology extraction from the alignment. The translation can be utterly edited by using the 'Similis Translation Tool'.

As aforementioned, Similis can automatically align files, extract terms from them, and update previous glossaries with new terminology data. However, the only file formats that the alignment tool can handle are MS Word formats (*.doc*, *.docx*), MS Excel formats (*.xls*, *.xlsx*), and HTML.

The user can also pre-translate or analyse the source text before the translation in order to check the statistics report, as shown in Figure 4.12.

Similis is old and the company stopped its development in 2008. It is very limiting in terms of the document formats and languages that it can support and the operating system it can work on. Hitherto, Similis can only run on MS Windows operating systems and support the following document formats: MS Word formats, PDF, RTF, TXT, and HTML/SGML/XML. Besides, the system

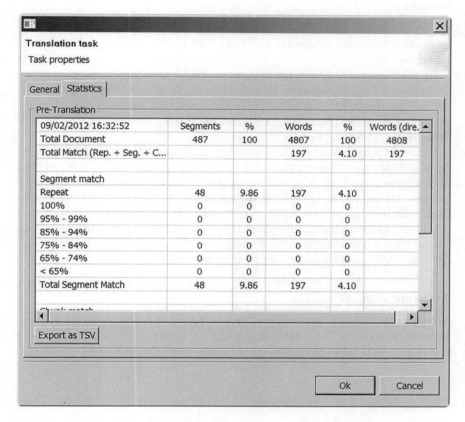

Figure 4.12 Similis: Statistics of Translation Tasks

supports only European languages (e.g., Dutch, English, French, German, Italian, Spanish, and Portuguese).

Similis can be used either as a standalone version or as a server edition. In addition to Similis Freelance, which is now made free, the other versions include: Similis LSP, Similis Server, and Libellex.

Similis LSP allows users to centralize translation memories and glossaries on a computer and to share the projects with translators who have Similis Freelance installed on their computers. Similis Server, in turn, enables a group of translators to work on a network using the centralized translation memories and glossaries. Libellex, to which the company's efforts are now dedicated, consists of an online work platform for all the employees of a company that can be accessed through a browser. Based on the corporate website, Libellex's value rests on the following features: (i) it has its own internal machine translation engine, which is periodically re-trained from its translation memories; and (ii) it has two modes of access, i.e., a simple interface for general users and the professional interfaces for language experts.

Snowman

Snowman (Free) is a free standalone computer-aided translation system developed by Foshan Snowman Computer Co. Ltd., China. The system was launched in November 2009.

As of August 2013, the latest version, V1.33, provides translations from Chinese into English, Japanese, French, Spanish, Russian, Korean, and German. It runs on the latest Windows operating system and supports the following document formats: plain text (*.txt*) and Microsoft Word/Excel/PowerPoint 2003 (http://www.gcys.cn).

Snowman (Free) is very restricted regarding the supported formats and languages, yet it includes some features that could be of help, particularly when translating from Chinese into English or vice versa. One of the most interesting features of Snowman (Free) is that it offers a dictionary of 300,000 Chinese and English pairs (which can be extended to 600,000 by purchasing the standard version). Moreover, it is linked to the online machine translation system Google Translate, providing a word-for-word machine translation when a match cannot be found in the translation memory. Snowman is also accessible to other online dictionaries.

Synthema WebCAT

Synthema WebCat was developed by SyNTHEMA, an Italian company that was founded in Pisa in 1994 and has engaged in language intelligence, machine translation, data mining, and speech solutions from the time of its founding.

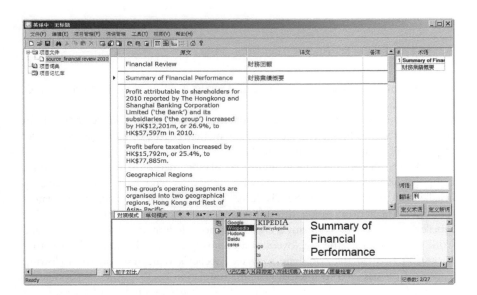

Figure 4.13 User Interface of Snowman

Back in 1995, SyNTHEMA started developing a machine translation system called PeTra (name that originated from Personal Translator), which has been in constant development and upgrading ever since. According to SyNTHEMA's website,[36] PeTra implements an advanced RBMT technology developed by SyNTHEMA. The latest version, PeTra 3.0, includes some computer-aided translation tool utilities, such as a translation memory database and a terminology database. PeTra products have been integrated with other advanced software, namely Terminology Wizard and WebCat.

Terminology Wizard, on the one hand, is a professional Terminology Analysis tool for creating electronic dictionaries, which can be imported into machine translation systems and computer-aided translation tools, enabling them to be used during the translation process. Synthema WebCat, on the other hand, is a recently developed Internet-based system that is offered on the basis of SaaS. This system intends to minimize the purchase cost and maintenance fees of computer-aided translation systems for the higher education sector. WebCat includes a number of functions, such as machine translation and automatic terminology concordance, to name but a few.

TinyTM

TinyTM was initially developed by Frank Bergmann, from Germany, who released TinyTM 0.1 in April 2008.

According to the official website (http://tinytm.sourceforge.net), where the software can be downloaded free of charge, TinyTM consists of three parts: 'Translation Client', 'TM-Server', and 'Protocol', which connects the translation environment with the TM-server. TinyTM 0.1 version is intended for software developers only, with the purpose of showing the viability of the project. Thus, it is not yet suitable for end-users.

The developers of this software compare TinyTM to the most popular of free computer-aided translation tools, OmegaT. They remark that, whereas OmegaT is written in Java, TinyTM is designed for MS Word, which is used by the majority of translation professionals around the world. Another noteworthy difference is that OmegaT is a single-user desktop application, while TinyTM is server-based, making it possible for several translators to work on the same text. Despite the dissimilarities, they claim that OmegaT and TinyTM could be combined so translators can benefit from the best features of both systems, for instance, by using advanced features that are offered by OmegaT in the server-based environment provided by TinyTM.

TM-database

TM-database is a standalone freeware computer-aided translation tool. It was developed in 2007 by a Russian translator, Sasha P., from the ASUATek Computer Inc. (TDD), China, yet currently it is maintained by a team of translators at ASUS. The latest version, TM-database v1.82, was released in 2012. TM-database is written in C++ and uses pure Win32 API and STL, which, according

208   Computer-aided translation

to the official website (http://yehongmei.narod.ru), ensures a higher execution speed and a smaller programme size. Since Win32 API is a Windows application programming interface, TM-database is constrained to operate either on MS Windows NT/2000/XP/Vista/7 or on Linux (by using Wine, which enables MS Windows applications to run on Unix-like operating systems).

This free computer-aided translation system supports merely twelve languages, namely Bulgarian, English, French, German, Hungarian, Italian, Russian, Spanish, Turkish, Chinese, Japanese, and Korean. Although twelve may seem a limited number of supported languages, it is noteworthy that it includes some character-based languages, which are generally not supported in most free computer-aided translation systems. In addition, TM-database can handle a number of common document formats, including Microsoft office (*.xml*, *.htm*, *.xls*), InDesign (*.inx*), Unicode text (*.uni*), Plain Text (*.txt*), Qt sources (*.ts*), PHP sources (*.txt*), Android resources (*.xml*), Microsoft resources (*.res/resx*), Java resources (*.properties*), and XLIFF files (*.xlf*) formats.

TM-database is a tool aimed at professional translators and, as such, it offers some interesting features, for instance: (i) customizable segmentation; (ii) translation memory tool, including fuzzy matching and match propagation; (iii) glossary and dictionary matching; (iv) translation memory and reference material searching; and (v) spell-checker.

As aforementioned, TM-database has a terminology tool for searching and managing terms; however, this tool has not been integrated with the translation editor. On top of that, this system lacks both terminology management and project management functions.

Tr-AID

Tr-AID, a product of the Institute for Language and Speech Processing (ILSP) in Greece, was launched in 1995 as the first translation memory tool developed by a Greek organization. As quoted from the official website (http://www.ilsp. gr/traid_eng.html), the aim of this project was 'to give the Greek and foreign markets access to innovative language technologies'.

Tr-AID was fully embedded in Microsoft Word environment for Windows 95 and 98 and had all the common functions of translation memory tools, making it easy to learn how to use the system and convenient to translate, edit, post-edit, and proofread any translation work.

This computer-aided translation tool was very innovative when it was launched, having uncountable benefits for translation professionals. However, the last version, Tr-AID 2.0, was released in December 2002, and the project was later discontinued by the developers.

Translation Workspace

Translation Workspace is a cloud-based translation productivity platform developed by Lionbridge Technologies Inc., which was founded in the United States in 1996.[37]

Translation Workspace is a spin-off of a former computer-aided translation system called Logoport, which consisted of a real-time translation memory platform. Logoport started to operate in early 2005, and by 2009 it had handled more than two billion words and serviced more than 19,000 users and 700 customers.

Translation Workspace is available in two editions: server-based and Internet-based editions. On the official website,[38] an array of Translation Workspace's functions are highlighted, including real-time project management and project collaboration, licensing management, import and export of materials, online vetting, quality assurance tools, real-time terminology and translation memory search and management, translation fee analysis and report, project status enquiry, usage analysis and report of translation memory databases, and material security management.

Transit

Transit is a workstation for translation and localization developed by STAR Group, headquartered in Switzerland. Transit products are unique in that, unlike other computer-aided translation tools, they are not exclusively sentence-based translation memory tools but instead the whole texts are available so that the translator can benefit from the context.

According to the official website,[39] Transit's latest version, Transit[NXT], is intuitive and easy to use thanks to the use of colours for title-bars, straightforward icons, and an improved synchronization between different windows. Moreover, given that mark-ups can be handled separately from the translation process and are dealt with mostly by the system, the translator can concentrate entirely on the text.

In addition to the foregoing, Transit[NXT] has introduced two significant features concerning fuzzy matches: 'bubble windows' and dual fuzzy matches. Now, when translating a certain segment, fuzzy matches are displayed in 'bubble windows', allowing the translator to make a more efficient use of the editor. These windows are only displayed when there are translation suggestions and disappear from the interface once the suggestion has been accepted. Besides, as noted above, a 'Dual Fuzzy' function is available for target-language matches. This means that, when the translator enters a new translation, a target fuzzy window is also displayed, containing relevant matches from the target-language reference files. STAR claims that this feature automatically improves consistency between texts.[40] Furthermore, access to machine translation engines is provided, yet only if the user considers it appropriate.

Given the above, one can say that Transit[NXT] is a powerful computer-aided translation system. Furthermore, it is not limited by format and language support, being able to handle a broad range of desktop publishing formats and file types and up to 33 languages, including Afrikaans, Basque, Belarussian, Bulgarian, Catalan, Croatian, Czech, Danish, Dutch, English, Estonian, Finnish, French, German, Greek, Hungarian, Icelandic, Italian, Latvian, Lithuanian, Norwegian,

210 *Computer-aided translation*

Polish, Portuguese, Romanian, Russian, Serbian, Slovak, Slovenian, Spanish, Swedish, Turkish, and Ukrainian. Special versions also include Arabic, Chinese, Indonesian, Japanese, Korean, Thai, and Vietnamese.

Licenses for STAR products are generally time-limited, available for three months, six months, or a year. However, a perpetual server license with full functionality is available for purchase from the STAR Group Webshop.[41]

Transolution

According to the official website,[42] Transolution is an open-source computer-aided translation suite supporting the XLIFF standard. The suite is divided into modules with the purpose of making it more flexible. It consists of an XLIFF Editor, a translation memory engine, and filters to convert different formats to and from XLIFF. The use of XLIFF means that almost any content can be localized as long as there is a filter for it (XML, SGML, PO, RTF, StarOffice/ OpenOffice, etc.).

The development of this computer-aided translation tool has been on hold since 2006. However in 2013, the developer Fredrik Corneliusson announced on the new official website that Transolution had been moved to the free code hosting site Butbucket, and had been improved with a new Windows build that would enable it to run in current versions of MS Windows. The latest version of this software, Transolution 0.4b8, was released in August 2013, and some new improvements can be expected in the future.

WebWordSystem

WebWordSystem is an Internet-based computer-aided translation system developed by WebWordSystem ApS, a company that was originally founded in Denmark in 2005 and currently has another branch in California, USA. The main developers of the system were Diane and Erik Rohde, who came up with the idea due to the lack of inexpensive and user-friendly software on the market at that time.[43]

WebWordSystem shares many features with other popular systems for translation support. Like other web-based computer-aided translation tools, it allows the translators to access the system from wherever they are and benefit instantly from the translations performed by other colleagues; thus the translators experience no constraints concerning the location. Nonetheless, it should be noted that this system is relatively limited in terms of supported file formats, being able to handle only those formats that can be opened by Microsoft Word.

According to its website,[44] WebWordSystem offers different editions for large corporations, small translation teams, and freelancers. The editions that are targeted at companies include: Corporate solution, aimed at groups of 7–12 translators working in the same company; Enterprise solution, aimed at groups of 3–6 translators working in the same company; and Biz solution, for 2 translators working in the same company. These three solutions provide translators

Computer-aided translation 211

with a translation memory and a termbase as well as access to a very interesting resource: the WebWordSystem Public Area. The Public Area consists of a marketplace where translators can purchase and sell previously translated sentences and terms, which are obviously quality controlled.

Wordbee Translator

Wordbee, a company based in Luxemburg and Portland, USA, launched the Internet-based computer-aided translation system Wordbee Translator[45] in 2008.

Wordbee Translator is a cloud-based computer-aided translation tool and translation project management system that is focused on collaborative translation. As a computer-aided translation tool, it includes translation memory and a terminology database, and it is seamlessly connected to machine translation engines, such as Microsoft Translator, Softissimo/Reverso, and Google Translate. Wordbee is offered as SaaS and can be accessed via any browser, and is, therefore, a cross-platform system. Currently, the most recent versions of all popular browsers are indeed supported. Moreover, it can manage all languages and a variety of file formats, including electronic document formats such as those of Microsoft Office and OpenDocument; desktop publishing formats, such as Adobe InDesign and Adobe Framemaker; flowchart formats, such as Microsoft Visio; software localization formats, such as XLIFF, Java properties, and ResX; PDF format; and computer-aided translation software document format, such as SDL-TradosTag (*.ttx*) and Transit (*.ppf*). Finally, like most Internet-based computer-aided translation systems, Wordbee also provides personalized solutions for large corporations, small translation teams, and freelancers.

Wordfast

Wordfast LLC, a company founded by Yves Champollion in 1999, is probably the world's second largest provider of Translation Memory software solutions, after SDL-Trados. It offers four editions of tools: Wordfast Classic and Wordfast Pro (under the Wordfast Translation Studio), Wordfast Anywhere, and Wordfast Server (Condak 2004: 87–108; Gerasimov 2001, 2002; Miller 2002).

Wordfast Anywhere is a browser-based computer-aided translation system that allows translators to work on projects from anywhere where they have access to an Internet connection. It can be used in any platform that supports Internet browsing, from a desktop computer to a mobile device. Unlike other browser-based computer-aided translation tools, such as Isometry, which only supported Google Chrome, Wordfast Anywhere can work in most existing browsers.

One of the major advantages of Wordfast Anywhere is that it is extremely easy to use. It is based on the popular Wordfast Classic, which according to Wordfast's website (www.wordfast.com) is considered the easiest computer-aided translation tool on the market to learn and use. In fact, according to the TM Survey 2006, conducted by Lagoudaki (2006: 25), Wordfast was preferred by

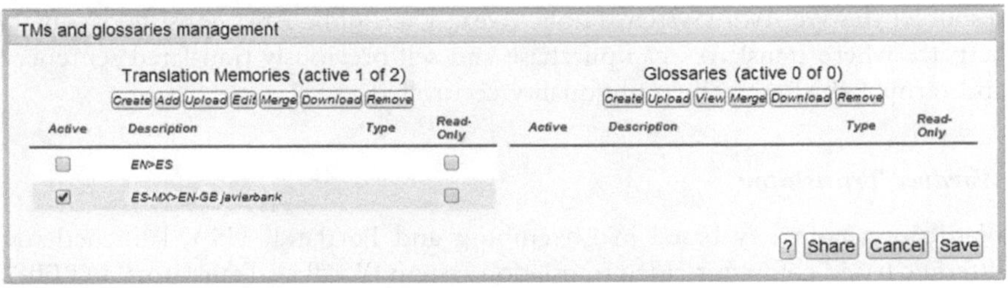

212 Computer-aided translation

Figure 4.14 Screenshot of TMs and Glossaries Management in Wordfast Anywhere

users who considered themselves to have 'adequate' computer skills, and it was ranked high in usability.

Wordfast Anywhere enables translation memories[46] and glossaries to be uploaded, as shown in Figure 4.14.

An online aligner allows users to upload previously translated source files and their corresponding translations in order to create a translation memory. In addition to accessing the translation memories that have been created or uploaded by the user, Wordfast Anywhere offers the option to retrieve machine translations from four different providers, namely WorldLingo (which is free and unlimited), Google, iTranslate4, and Microsoft; or, alternatively, to access the so-called 'Very Large Translation Memory' (VLTM), which, according to the official website, consists of a large set of translation memories created from public-domain data.

The most important fact that makes this computer-aided translation tool usable by professional translators is that, unlike Google Translator Toolkit, Wordfast Anywhere offers complete confidentiality. Wordfast claims that all data that is uploaded and stored in the translator's private workspace remains strictly confidential and is never shared (unless the user decides so), disclosed, or recycled in any way.

Wordfast Anywhere supports common file formats, such as plain text (*.txt*), Microsoft Word (*.doc*, *.docx*), Microsoft Excel (*.xls*, *.xlsx*), Microsoft PowerPoint (*.ppt*, *pptx*), RTF, PDF (including scanned PDF documents), Acrobat InDesign (*.inx*), Acrobat FrameMaker (*.mif*), TTX, and TXML.

Finally, installation is not required; this system can be used immediately by accessing the website www.freetm.com. The only details required to register are an email address and a password.

Wordfast Anywhere is probably the most functional of all the free computer-aided translation tools. It includes all the advanced features of commercial systems without restrictions. Nonetheless, many translators are still reluctant to depend on a browser-based application.

Computer-aided translation 213

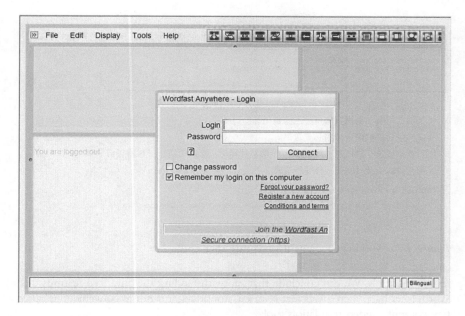

Figure 4.15 Screenshot of the Login Window in Wordfast Anywhere

WordFisher

WordFisher is a free system developed by a translator named Tibor Környei from Hungary, for translators who work in the MS Word environment. The programme is written in the WordBasic language and it depends entirely on MS Word, which becomes its main disadvantage. The drawback is not solely due to MS Word dependence, which has proved not to be a disadvantage for other popular computer-aided translation tools such as Wordfast Classic. The problem lies with the fact that WordFisher requires MS Word 6.0 or above to work, but is not compatible with MS Word 2007 and any other later versions, thus limiting its usage nowadays.

WordFisher had some interesting features. For instance, it included an alignment option, which many other computer-aided translation tools lack; it allowed context check within the project; and it was able to automatically build a bilingual corpus. Corpora could be later uploaded to any translation memory system, avoiding time-consuming preparatory work. However, Környei (2000: online) remarks that, although they can be searched directly by WordFisher, it is recommendable to handle larger corpora by using external programmes.

WordFisher had numerous supporters, but in recent years, the usage of this computer-aided translation system has decreased compared to other computer-aided

214 *Computer-aided translation*

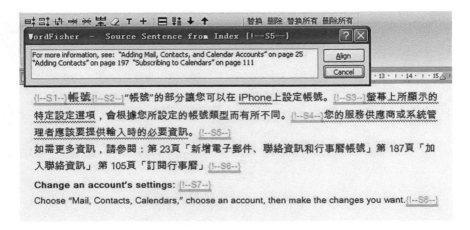

Figure 4.16 Working Document of WordFisher

translation tools. We can conclude that, notwithstanding the advanced features that WordFisher had when it was first released, nowadays, it is not as convenient as other free computer-aided translation tools.

XTM

XTM International,[47] a company headquartered in the United Kingdom, was founded in 2002 by Andrzej Zydron and Robert Willans to promote their innovative approach to the translation of XML files: XML:tm (Zydron 2003: online; Zydron 2004: online). Soon after, in 2004, XML:tm developed into the first version of XTM, an XML-based content management and translation system. In 2005, Lingo24 teamed up with XTM International, investing in the development of this computer-aided translation tool and integrating it with Lingo24's internal systems. Hazel Mollison, Communications Executive at Lingo24, published an article listing the advantages that had led to the implementation of this particular system (Mollison 2007: online). According to Mollison, the system has a number of key features designed to support the translator's work, such as an intuitive Java user interface, which displays and facilitates the processing of different translation memory matches and supports spellchecking by using customized dictionaries and quality assurance functions. Mollison also emphasizes XTM's extreme scalability for supporting professional translation services. Based on the foregoing, she concludes that XTM's results are indeed cost-saving at the same time that the overall quality is increased.

On top of the features mentioned by Mollison, XTM includes a wide range of functions, such as management of automated workflow; collaborative projects, users, and clients; translation memory database and terminology management;

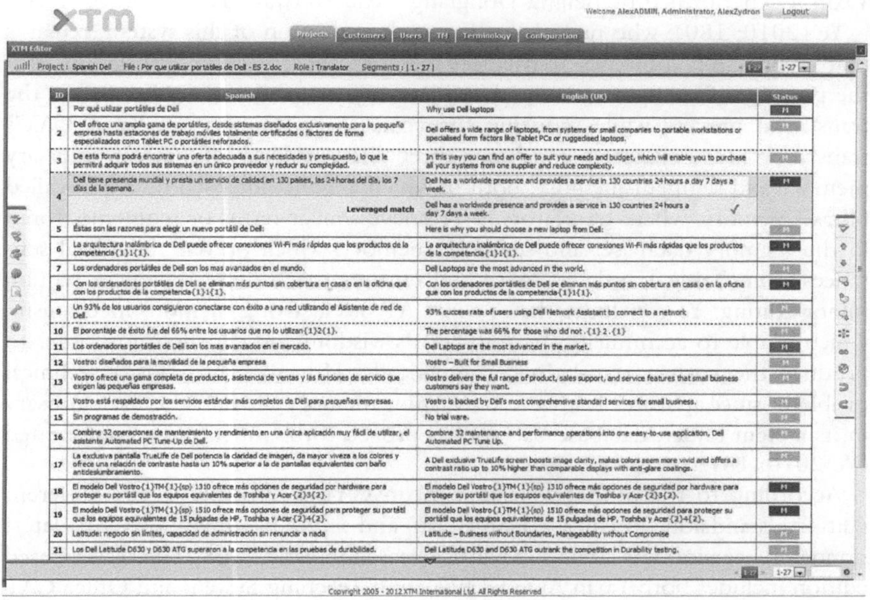

Figure 4.17 XTM Cloud

reports of translation memory analysis and translation fees; integration with machine translation engines (Google Translate and Asia Online); online editing mode and quality checking tools; real-time project progress status enquiry; and plug-in content management systems application programming interface (API). Furthermore, the system is not limited in terms of file formats, since it is capable of handling Microsoft Office, OpenOffice, FrameMaker, InDesign (*.inx* and *.idml*), HTML, XML (generic), PDF, RTF, Microsoft Visio (*.vdx*), Java properties, DITA, RESX, and TTX formats.

XTM is available in two editions: server-based XTM Suite and XTM Cloud. XTM Cloud, in turn, has editions for freelancers, small translation teams, and language service providers. XTM Cloud was first released in September 2010 and has continued to be upgraded ever since.

Little wonder then that XTM has secured a growing list of clients, including numerous Language Service Providers, such as Cuttingedge, Language Scientific, Omnilingua, and Prisma.

Yaxin CAT

Yaxin CAT is a server-based computer-aided translation system developed by Beijing Orient Yaxin Software Technology Co., Ltd. 北京東方雅信軟件技術有限公司. Since 1994, this company has developed a series of translation systems

216 *Computer-aided translation*

with the participation of some other companies. In 2005, the development of Yaxin was performed by Beijing Dongfang Yaxin Software Technology Co. Ltd.

Ye (2010: 180), who provides a thorough evaluation of this system, remarks that Yaxin CAT combines translation memory with machine translation with the purpose of aiding translators to achieve higher quality and efficiency in the translation process while reducing the costs. According to Ye, Yaxin CAT's translation memory system consists of three different kinds of memory: glossary memory and segment memory, both of which are encompassed in the so-called phrase memory, where translators can retrieve similar terms or segments stored in the memory database; and sentence memory, which prevents identical sentences from being translated twice and ensures that similar sentences require minor editing. Ye concludes that Yaxin CAT has a strong memory mechanism, which is able to accumulate the translator's wisdom and experience in order to produce the correct translation automatically. However, he finds a technical problem: since it stores both the translation memory file and the user glossary in its system folder, database backup has proved to be much more complicated (Ye 2010: 181).

According to the official website,[48] Yaxin CAT is available in two different editions: standalone (Yaxin CAT Software) and server-based editions. The latest standalone version was Yaxin CAT 4.0, released in early 2008. The server-based edition includes both Yaxin Aided Translation Teaching System and Office CAT System, targeted at two different groups of users.

YOOmanage

YOOmanage is a product of CrossLang,[49] a company based in Ghent, Belgium. The company was founded in 2002 with the aim of specializing in translation technology solutions. Heidi Depraetere, founder of the company, has been engaged in language technology for more than 20 years.

YOOmanage is a hosted infrastructure based on translation management technology, including Translation Management Systems, to control linguistic resources and streamline translation processes; a Terminology Management tool, to increase translation quality and performance; Translation Memory tools, to reuse previously translated materials and reduce translation costs; a Machine Translation engine and Workflow Technology, to automate the process; and Linguistic Technology, to aid the translator in building the target text. Besides, it incorporates a server-based centralized translation memory, which implements advanced matching and search functions, and a terminology database, where terms are stored in order to ensure accuracy and consistency in all the translations within a company.

YOOmanage is especially targeted at companies with large-scale translation initiatives. However, CrossLang also offer solutions adapted to different kinds of users. For instance, CrossLang has developed YOOsource, a simple and user-friendly translation and editing platform especially intended for crowdsourcing translation of webpages.

Machine translation

Machine translation systems are typically divided into two types: commercial systems, which are available on the market, and experimental systems, which are still under development or accessible solely to restricted groups of users. The demand for commercial systems depends on the need for information dissemination, assimilation, and interchange with applications in the areas of organizational intranets, professional translation, translator workstations, machine translation tools, occasional user systems, web translation, and Internet translation services.

There are a large number of commercial translation systems on the market, ranging from unidirectional to multidirectional systems, from one-to-many to many-to-one renderings, from major languages to minority languages, from automatic translation to interactive operations, from installed translation software to networked systems, from offline to online translation, from single options to multiple choices, from simple functions to sophisticated functions, and from high-end products to low-end outputs. With this much choice, the best course to take is to settle on the system that best suits one's needs and budget. Moreover, it is also important to know the approaches that have been used in the design of the machine translation system that one intends to use.

Approaches to machine translation

A major indicator of the phenomenal development of machine translation is the dramatic increase in the number of approaches to machine translation that attempt to deal with issues of text types and contexts in translation. Within the short span of 65 years, from 1947 to 2012, a total of 22 approaches have been developed for machine translation, fourteen of which, due to their particular importance, will be further discussed in alphabetical order in the following.

Case-based machine translation

This approach to machine translation was proposed by Wang Jiande, Chen Zhaoxiong, and Huang Heyan of the Computing Institute of Technology of the Chinese Academy of Science (Wang, Chen, and Huang 2001). It is somehow an Interactive Hybrid Strategies Machine Translation (IHSMT) system that combines rule-based reasoning and case-based reasoning to improve the quality of machine translation through human-machine interaction and a learning model of human-machine tracking and memorizing (HMTM).

Concept-based machine translation

According to Ripplinger (1994: 1), concept-based machine translation can be described as follows: 'the integration of world knowledge in the parsing process is used to constrain possible PP_attachments, to facilitate reference disambiguation and thus to minimize overgeneration. This requires careful specification of the

218 *Computer-aided translation*

knowledge base that describes the concepts and their relationship inherent in the application domain. The complexity should be deep enough to allow for all interpretations possible but narrow enough to rule out irrelevant interpretations'. Concept-based machine translation can also be applied to the field of interpreting. Further details about this machine translation approach can be found in contributions by a great number of scholars (Gu and Gao 2004; Horiguchi, Tsuchiya, Kojima, Watabe, and Kawaoka 2002; Zhou and Liu 2000).

Context-based machine translation

Context-based machine translation (CBMT) is a corpus-based approach that is not based on parallel texts but, instead, on a translation model with a bilingual dictionary and a decoder using a context through long n-grams and cascaded overlapping. The translation process of this approach has been greatly improved by in-language substitution of tokens and phrases in both the source and target texts (Carbonell, Klein, Miller, Steinbaum, Grassiany, and Frey 2006; Galley, Graehl, Knight, Marcu, DeNeefe, Wang, and Thayer 2006; Hovy, King, and Popescu-Belis 2002: 43–75; Kjærsgaard 1987: 109–112).

Corpus-based machine translation

Corpus-based machine translation refers to the use of a large pre-existing corpus of translated texts to build a machine translation system. There are three types of corpus-based machine translation, namely memory-based machine translation, example-based machine translation, and statistics-based machine translation (Carl 2000; Dash 2004: 57–79; Wantanabe, Kurohashi, and Aramak 2000).

Data-driven machine translation

Data-driven machine translation refers to an approach that develops algorithms and programmes to exploit data in the development of machine translation engines, both by using large bilingual corpora created by human translators, analogously to statistical machine translation and example-based machine translation, and by applying these data in machine learning in translation (Hearne and Way 2003: 165–172; Hearne and Way 2006; Richardson, Dolan, Menezes, and Pinkham 2001).

Example-based machine translation

The example-based machine translation approach is essentially based on examples. The idea was first suggested by Makoto Nagao in 1984 in his article 'A Framework of a Mechanical Translation between Japanese and English by Analogy Principle' (Nagao 1984). Also known as 'translating through analogy', it was based on the idea that advances in computer technology have made it possible to gain access to the huge corpora of previously translated analogous examples to allow matching of bilingual expressions. A typical example of EBMT is the *Pangloss Mark III* Machine Translation System. More details about EBMT have been collected by

Computer-aided translation 219

numerous scholars (Aramaki, Kurohashi, Kashioka, and Kato 2005; Auerswald 2000: 418–427; Carl and Way 2003; Somers 1999: 113–157).

Interlingua-based machine translation

This is an approach in machine translation whereby translation proceeds in two different stages: input sentences are first analysed into some abstract and ideally language-independent meaning representation, from which, subsequently, translations in several different languages can be potentially produced (Cavalli-Sforza, Czuba, Mitamura, and Nyberg 2000: 169–178; Dave, Parikh, and Bhattacharyya 2001: 251–304; Lee 2001).

Knowledge-based machine translation

Knowledge-based machine translation attempts to apply knowledge engineering techniques to simulate the various kinds of knowledge that human translators have for use in the computer. Indeed, it is assumed that with the knowledge-based approach, the computer should be able to disambiguate, process illogical expressions, and find implicit meaning from insufficient information (Asaduzzaman and Ali 2003: 77–97).

Memory-based machine translation

Memory-based machine translation refers essentially to a type of machine translation system that contains the technology of a translation memory (Hodász 2006).

N-gram-based machine translation

N-gram-based machine translation is an approach in machine translation that combines a translation model based on n-grams of bilingual units (known as tuples) with four feature functions: (i) a target-language model that provides information about the structure and fluency of the target language; (ii) a word-bonus model that depends on the partial translation hypothesis length; (iii) a source-to-target lexicon model that provides a translation probability estimate for a given tuple between its source and target sides in the source-to-target direction; and (iv) a target-to-source lexicon model that provides a translation probability estimate for a given tuple between its source and target sides in the target-to-source direction (Crego, Gispert, and Marino 2005; Marino, Banchs, Crego, Gispert, Lambert, Fonollosa, and Costa-jussà 2006: 527–549).

Rule-based machine translation

Rule-based machine translation is a relatively traditional machine translation method which depends on the preparation and maintenance of a large number of rules and lexical information in the form of dictionaries, both general and

220   *Computer-aided translation*

specialized. Further research in this machine translation approach has been carried out by Charoenpornsawat, Sornlertlamvanich, and Charoenporn (2002), Elming (2006), Proszeky (2005: 207–218), as well as Zhu and Wang (2005).

Shake-and-Bake machine translation

The Shake-and-Bake approach is divided into two stages. The first stage involves analysing the source language sentences with the source language grammar, which produces highly constrained lexical and phrasal signs. The second stage consists of obtaining a tile set translation of the lexical entries by the use of the bilingual lexicon to produce their target language equivalents, with the tile relative word ordering being instantiated by the target language grammar. The Shake-and-Bake machine translation approach has been widely studied since the early 1990s (Beaven 1992: 603–609; Brew 1992: 610–616; Carl, Rascu, and Schmidt 2005: 66–72; Whitelock 1992: 784–791, Whitelock 1994: 339–359).

Statistical machine translation

Statistical machine translation refers to an approach in machine translation which uses statistically or probability based techniques to perform part of the tasks of machine translation, such as word disambiguation (Al-Onaizan and Papineni 2006; Knight 2003: 17–19; Koehn, Och, and Marcu 2003). At present, statistical machine translation is probably the most extended machine translation approach, being used by the leaders of the industry (Google and Microsoft).

Transfer-based machine translation

This is an approach in machine translation whereby the translation proceeds in three stages. Firstly, the machine analyses the input sentences into an abstract internal representation, which still retains the characteristics of the source language text. Secondly, the representation is entered to a transfer component, which produces a representation which has the characteristics of the target language. Finally, the representation generates a target sentence. More information about transfer-based machine translation can be found in the contributions by Gdaniec (1998: 408–420) and Nagao and Tsujii (1986: 97–103).

Hybrid systems: Translation Memory (Computer-aided Translation) with Machine Translation

The hybrid translation model Translation Memory (Computer-aided Translation) + Machine Translation goes back to 1994, when IBM Translation Manager/2 started using logic-based machine translation to handle the segments for which no matches could be found in the translation memory. The major distinction of the IBM hybrid approach compared to present-day systems lies with the way in which the machine translation system is integrated. In the case of IBM, the

Computer-aided translation 221

machine translation engine was a built-in system. Current hybrid systems, on the other hand, are integrated with online machine translation engines. Eighteen years after the introduction of hybridity by IBM, this model has become the norm in translation products. A list of hybrid computer-aided translation tools with their respective integrated online machine translation systems is provided in Table 4.5.

Table 4.5 CAT Systems and their MT Links

Computer-aided Translation Systems	Online Machine Translation Systems Linked
Across	Google, Moses, Lucy LT, Microsoft
Alchemy Publisher	Google, PROMT
Autshumato	Google, Apertium, Belazar
CafeTran	Google
Déjà Vu	Google
Fluency	Google, Microsoft, and APIs for other engines (such as Systran)
GlobalSight	Google, PROMT
Google Translator Toolkit	Google
Heartsome Translation Suite	Google
Lingotek Collaborative Translation Platform	Google, Microsoft
LongRay CAT	Google, Yahoo, Microsoft
MemoQ	Google, iTranslate4.eu MT
MemorySphere	AppTek's TranSphere Machine Translation
Memsource	Google, Microsoft
MetaTexis	Google, Babel Fish, Free Translation, LEC, Microsoft
MultiTrans	Google, Systran
OmegaT	Google, Apertium, Belazar
ProMemoria	Systran
SDL-Trados	Google, Systran, SDL Automated Translation
SDLX	SDLX AutoTrans
Snowman	Google, Microsoft, Yahoo
Swordfish	Google
TM-database	Google
Transit	Systran, Logos, Reverso
Trans Suite 2000	Systran
Wordbee Translator	Google, Reverso
Wordfast Anywhere	Google, Microsoft, WorldLingo
XTM	Google

222 Computer-aided translation

Machine translation systems used by computer-aided translation systems

Table 4.6 provides a list of fifteen online translation systems that are linked to computer-aided translation systems.

The preceding machine translation systems will be discussed in alphabetic order below.

Apertium

The origin of the Apertium Project can be traced back to April 2004, when Mikel L. Forcada, one of Apertium's developers, started contacting human language technology research groups in Spain about the possibility of obtaining funding to build a free and open-source machine translation system for the four official languages in Spain. Merely three months later, in July 2004, the Spanish Ministry of Industry, Tourism, and Commerce agreed to fund the development of two different machine translation systems: Matxin, for Spanish to Basque; and Apertium, to translate between Spanish and Catalan, as well as Spanish and Galician (Forcada, Tyers, and Ramírez-Sánchez 2009: 3).

Although the platform was initially designed for closely related language pairs, it was later expanded to handle more divergent pairs. Currently, Apertium

Table 4.6 Online Systems Linked to CAT Systems

Name of Online Translation System	Number of Computer-aided Translation Systems Linked
Google Translate	23
Microsoft (Bing)	8
Systran	5
Belazar	2
PROMT	2
Reverso	2
Yahoo! Babel Fish	2
Apertium	1
iTranslate4.eu	1
LEC Translate	1
Lucy LT	1
Moses	1
SDL Automated Translation	1
AppTek's TranSphere Machine Translation	1
WorldLingo	1

supports the translation of 35 languages, including some minority languages, such as as Asturian, Breton, Bulgarian, Catalan, Esperanto, Icelandic, Macedonian, Occitan, and Welch. However, not all the possible language pairs between these languages are available.[50]

As aforementioned, Apertium was created as free open-source software. According to Forcada, this was due to the following reasons:

- 'To give everyone free access to the best possible machine-translation technologies.
- To establish a modular, documented, open platform for shallow-transfer MT and other human language processing tasks.
- To favour the sharing and reuse of existing linguistic data and to make integration with other FOS technologies easier.
- To benefit from collaborative development of both the engine and language-pair data for existing or new language pairs, from industry, academia and independent developers.
- To help shift MT business from the obsolescent and vulnerable licence-centred model to a service-centred model.
- To radically guarantee the reproducibility of experimental research on MT.
- Because the results of publically funded research must be made available to the public.'

(Forcada 2009: 5)

Apertium can be accessed online at the website http://www.apertium.org/index.eng.html#translation.

Figure 4.18 Apertium Translation Interface

224 *Computer-aided translation*

AppTek's TranSphere® Machine Translation

AppTek's TranSphere® Machine Translation is a hybrid system that combines Rule-based Machine Translation (RBMT) with Statistical Machine Translation (SMT). It provides portability across various platforms and operating systems, being able to run on standalone workstations, servers, and browsers. One unique feature is that TranSphere can be integrated with AppTek's automatic speech recognition product, namely Plain Speech.

According to the leaflet provided at the Ninth Conference of the Association for Machine Translation in the Americas (AMTA) in 2010,[51] AppTek's TranSphere® MT supports the language pairs listed in Tables 4.7 and 4.8.

AppTek's TranSphere® Machine Translation cannot be accessed online. Therefore, in order to purchase the software, it is necessary to contact the developers via email.[52]

Table 4.7 Bi-directional Language Pairs Supported in AppTek's TranSphere® MT

Bi-directional Translation	
English-Arabic	English-Polish
English-Farsi	English-Portuguese
English-Spanish	English-Russian
English-Dari	English-Italian
English-Chinese	English-Turkish
English-Korean	English-Ukrainian
English-Japanese	French-Italian
English-Hebrew	German-French
English-German	German-Italian
English-French	Spanish-French
English-Dutch	Spanish-Italian

Table 4.8 Language Pairs for which Uni-directional Translation is Supported in AppTek's TranSphere® MT

Uni-directional Translation
Tagalog > English
Urdu > English
Indonesian > English
Pashto > English
Persian > Arabic
Greek > English

Computer-aided translation 225

Babel Fish/Yahoo! Babel Fish

Babel Fish was a web translation service based on Systran's technology and created, originally, by AltaVista. The system was named after a fictitious creature in Douglas Adams' work *The Hitchhiker's Guide to the Galaxy*. As quoted from the book:

> The Babel fish is small, yellow, leech-like, and probably the oddest thing in the universe. It feeds on brain wave energy, absorbing all unconscious frequencies and then excreting telepathically a matrix formed from the conscious frequencies and nerve signals picked up from the speech centres of the brain, the practical upshot of which is that if you stick one in your ear, you can instantly understand anything said to you in any form of language: the speech you hear decodes the brain wave matrix.
>
> (Adams 1979: 49)

AltaVista was later acquired by Yahoo, who changed the name of the system to Yahoo! Babel Fish. It must be pointed out that Yahoo! Babel Fish should not be confused with The Babel Fish Corporation, which also offers free machine translation services at www.babelfish.com.

In 2012, Microsoft announced the acquisition of Yahoo! Babel Fish, merging it with the Microsoft Machine Translation system Bing Translator,[53] which will be discussed later in this section.

Belazar

Belazar is a product developed by Belarusian Linguistic Technologies. It is a free machine translation system focused on the translation from Belarusian to Russian and vice versa. Although it is a very limited system, regarding the language pairs that it is able to deal with, it has been integrated into one of the most popular open-source computer-aided translation systems: OmegaT.

Google Translate

Google Translate is a statistical machine translation (SMT) service provided by Google Inc. to translate a section of text, document, or webpage into another language.

In its origins, Google's machine translation system used the rule-based technology of Systran. However, over the course of the years, intensive research was already being carried out in the model of SMT. In April 2006, Franz Joseph Och, Research Scientist and Head of Google Translate, finally announced the birth of Google Translate as a statistical online system for the translation of Arabic to and from English. Nonetheless, it was not until 2007 that Google gave up using Systran for the translation between languages other than Arabic, Chinese, and Russian, to focus exclusively on their newly developed system.

By 2008, Google Translate could already translate between 34 languages (without any kind of language pair restrictions), including Catalan, Filipino, Hebrew,

226 *Computer-aided translation*

Indonesian, Latvian, Lithuanian, Serbian, Slovak, Slovenian, Ukrainian, and Vietnamese (Och 2008: online). Merely one year later, in September 2009, the number of supported languages had increased to 51, and translation was offered for the outstanding number of 2,550 language pairs. Furthermore, and more important, Google Translate could be used within other Google products. For instance, to name but a few services, users could translate emails within GMail, webpages using Google Toolbar, RSS news feeds in Google Reader, and documents in Google Docs (Och 2009: online).

In June 2011, Google released a paid version of Google Translate, which was due, according to the developers,[54] 'to the substantial economic burden caused by extensive abuse'.

Google is linked to 23 computer-aided translation systems (refer to Table 4.6), accounting for 82.14 per cent of all the hybrid computer-aided translation – machine translation systems.

iTranslate4

iTranslate4 is a project supported by the EU Competitiveness and Innovation Framework Programme. The purpose of this initiative, which started in March 2010, was to create the first European website providing free online translation from any European language to any other. In fact, the name iTranslate4 comes from 'Internet Translators for all European Languages'.[55]

It should be noted that, in addition to the Research Institute for Linguistics of the Hungarian Academy of Sciences, coordinator of the project, iTranslate4's consortium is constituted by some of the biggest European brands of machine translation systems, i.e., MorphoLogic (Hungary), Systran (France), Linguatec (Germany), pwn.pl (Poland), SKYCODE (Bulgaria), Amebis (Slovenia), Sunda Systems (Finland), PROMT (Germany), and Trident MT (Latvia). Besides, other machine translation providers are welcome with open arms to join the initiative and make access to their services available through the itranslate4.eu website. In fact, at present, iTranslate4's users can also benefit from the services of four new partners, namely GrammarSoft (Denmark), Lingenio (Germany), Apertium (Spain), and ParsTranslator (Iran).

In practice, the system displays translations performed by several machine translation engines. The number of translations displayed and the preferred translation service providers can be modified through the user settings. Once the different translation options are displayed, users can choose and mark the best translation.

Although the system can be freely accessed online (at http://itranslate4.eu/en/), translation quotas must be purchased in order to be able to use the Firefox, Chat, MemoQ, Trados Studio, and Wordfast plug-in applications.

LEC Translate

Language Engineering Company[56] (LEC) has been developing machine translation systems since the foundation of the company in 1985. LEC is primarily an

Computer-aided translation 227

Original Equipment Manufacturer provider, supplying the core technology to some of the leading firms in the translation software industry. Some of the companies that use LEC's technology in their products are LogoVista, Cross Language, Panasonic, Babylon, Avanquest, and Softissimo.

LEC Translate is an automatic translation system that can be used to translate emails, webpages, documents, and instant messages. It can deal with Asian, European, Eastern European, and Middle Eastern languages, more specifically Arabic, Brazilian, Chinese, Dutch, English, Farsi, French, German, Hebrew, Indonesian, Italian, Japanese, Korean, Pashto, Persian, Polish, Portuguese, Russian, Spanish, Tagalog, Turkish, Ukrainian, and Urdu. However, it must be borne in mind that not all the language pairs between the above languages are available.

LEC can be purchased either for a specific language or for a group of languages, and is available in three editions: Personal, Business, and Pro. In addition, it offers free quick text machine translations generated by LEC's engine as a demo. An LEC Translation Demo can be accessed online at https://www. lec.com/translate-demos.asp.

Lucy LT

Lucy LT is a product of Lucy Software, a company founded in 2006. Although the company is relatively recent, the system has been around for quite a few years. Before, however, it was known as Comprendium (Comprendium 2004), a transfer-based machine translation system that was acquired in 2009, changing its name to Lucy LT.

Lucy LT offers translation for emails, websites, help desk content, and documentation. In order to do so, the system supports a full range of document formats, from plain text (ASCII) to Microsoft Office formats (*.docx*, *.xlsx*, *.pptx*), XML, HTML, and HTML5.

Currently, 29 translation directions are supported, yet the output quality depends in large measure on the language pair. Alonso stated that Catalan-Spanish was, by far, the language pair that yielded the best translation quality out of the 23 translation directions offered in 2005 by Lucy LT's predecessor Comprendium (Alonso 2005: 24). According to Translation Quality Evaluations made within the company, it produced an outstanding 93 per cent of good and understandable sentences. On the other hand, Jenny Lu, Senior Director of Localization at CA Technologies, explains how the company performed some trials on four machine translation engines, including the system in question (Lu 2010: 1). They used Lucy LT for four languages, namely French, German, Spanish, and Italian. In the case of Italian, the quality obtained by Lucy LT was significantly lower than expected; and, consequently, they had to implement another machine translation system, Moses. Currently, they use both Lucy LT and Moses for translations involving Italian. For the other languages, however, Lucy fulfilled the expectations. Lu claims that, by implementing these systems, CA Technologies dramatically increased the translation output, even to 100 per

Free Translation - Lucy LT KWIK Translator

Figure 4.19 Lucy LT KWIK Translator

cent for some languages, while reducing the post-editing costs considerably (Lu 2010: 3).

Lucy Software also offers a free online machine translation tool: Lucy LT KWIK Translator, which can be accessed at http://www.lucysoftware.com/english/machine-translation/kwik-translator.

Microsoft Translator (Bing Translator)

As stated by Wendt, responsible for Bing Translator and Microsoft Translator services, Microsoft had deployed its own SMT system for internal use since 2002. However, they used to integrate third-party machine translation engines with their products, and it was not until 2007 that the system became available to the general public at the Microsoft website (Wendt 2010: unpaged).

Computer-aided translation 229

Microsoft Translator offers different solutions adapted to the users:

(i) Collaborative Translation Framework, which started being available in March 2010.[57]
(ii) Translator Hub, a translation portal and web service that enables to build, train, and deploy customized automatic translations systems between virtually any pair of languages.
(iii) Translator App for Windows Phone, which is capable of translating printed text by simply pointing the camera at it.
(iv) Microsoft Translator in Office, as a substitute of WorldLingo, a third-party machine translation engine that used to be integrated with Microsoft Office.
(v) Multilingual App Toolkit, which can be used to localize Windows Store and Windows Phone applications inside Visual Studio.
(vi) Translations in Internet Explorer.
(vii) Bing Translator (previously Live Search Translator and Windows Live Translator).

Microsoft unveiled Bing in June 2009, with Bing Translator being only one in its entire range of services. Bing Translator is based on the statistical machine translation model and is able to detect automatically the language of a given text. As aforementioned, in 2012, Microsoft acquired Yahoo! Babel Fish, incorporating all the languages of that system into Bing Translator.

According to its website,[58] Microsoft Translator works closely with a number of translation memory tools, which are divided into three groups according to the extent to which they integrate Microsoft products:

(i) Gold Partners, who integrate Microsoft Translator Hub and Collaborative Translations together with Microsoft Translator. Lionbridge Translation Workspace, SDL-Trados Studio, Memsource, Fluency, and XTM Cloud are Microsoft's Gold Partners.
(ii) Silver Partners, who integrate Microsoft Translator Hub together with Microsoft Translator. Lingotek, Déjà Vu, Multicorpora, and Wordbee are Microsoft's Silver Partners.
(iii) Bronze Partners, who integrate only Microsoft Translator. Microsoft's Bronze Partners include MemoQ, GlobalSight, Wordfast, and OmegaT, amongst others.

Moses

Moses is an SMT system that can be trained to translate virtually between any language pair. It was created in 2005 at the University of Edinburgh by Hieu Hoang, a student of Philipp Koehn, and in 2006 the European Union project Euromatrix contributed to the funding of its development. At present, Moses

230 Computer-aided translation

is an open-source project, which incorporates contributions from many sources and is mainly used at academic institutions as the basic infrastructure for SMT research (Koehn et al. 2007).

As mentioned above, Moses is an implementation of the statistical approach to machine translation. In SMT, translation systems are trained on two different sets of data: (i) large quantities of parallel data, from which the system learns how to translate segments; and (ii) large quantities of monolingual data, from which the system learns the structure of the target language. In addition, Moses follows a phrase-based SMT approach, in which the input sentences are divided into text chunks and subsequently matched to target phrases (Koehn 2007: 224).

On the official website,[59] online demos can be used for translating text segments and webpages between the following language pairs: Czech into and from English; English into and from German, Spanish, and French; English into Russian; Finnish into and from Swedish and English; and Haitian Creole into English.

Moses has been successfully combined with RBMT engines (such as Lucy LT) to create a hybrid system in order to reduce the errors produced by both models (Eisele et al. 2008; Federman et al. 2010).

PROMT Translator

As aforementioned, PROMT is a renowned machine translation system developed in Russia by Svetlana Sokolova and Alexander Serebryakov. In its origins, the PROMT engine had been developed as an RBMT system, yet since 2011 PROMT has also offered solutions based on SMT as well as a PROMT Deep-Hybrid translation engine, which combines both RBMT and SMT.

Currently, PROMT covers over 100 specialized domains and provides machine translation for sixteen languages, i.e., English, Russian, German, French, Spanish, Italian, Portuguese, Ukrainian, Kazakh, Turkish, Bulgarian, Latvian, Japanese, Polish, and two variants of Chinese, resulting in a total of 64 translation directions.

Furthermore, PROMT offers free machine translation services with PROMT Translator, which have interesting features for a free online translator, such as virtual keyboard to help the user type special characters. However, only eight languages can be selected and not all the language pairs between those languages are supported. PROMT Translator can be accessed at http://www.online-translator.com.

Reverso

Reverso is an online translation system marketed by Reverso-Softissimo, a company that works with a team of experts based in France, Russia, China, Germany, the United Kingdom, and the United States.

Computer-aided translation 231

In 2002, PROMT[60] announced that, together with Softissimo, they had released the new versions Reverso Pro 5 and Reverso Expert, which provided translation for the following directions: English-French-English, English-German-English, and French-Spanish. Reverso 5 products are based on the advanced PROMT automatic translation technology and provide translation of documents, emails, and websites. It is worth noting, nonetheless, that the system has not been updated since.

Reverso also provides free machine translation services of English into and from French, Spanish, Italian, German, Hebrew, Portuguese, Russian, Arabic, and Chinese. Like PROMT, it offers a virtual keyboard and a spell-check function. Reverso's free translation service can be accessed online at http://www.reverso.net/text_translation.aspx?lang=EN.

SDL Automated Translation

SDL offers a series of SMT solutions (as shown in Figure 4.20), which have been integrated both with other SDL products and third party applications. Recently, the SDL Automated Translation system has been integrated with SDL-Trados Studio tools, enabling translators to introduce machine translation in the translation workflow.

The new machine translation system offered by SDL,[61] SDL BeGlobal, is a cloud platform that offers automated translation for business. According to SDL, this leads to a number of benefits: (i) companies can publish content in a wide range of languages, improving the satisfaction of their customers, who can find up-to-date information in their own language; (ii) all the employees of a company

SDL BeGlobal	With SDL BeGlobal, a secure, cloud platform, companies can deliver multilingual communication across all content types, including digital & internet content. Additional productivity gains can be achieved by integrating with translation memory and translation management solutions.
SDL GlobalConnect	SDL GlobalConnect extends the power of SDL BeGlobal into other applications through pre-integrated solutions, such as chat, email and knowledge bases. With these integrations, content managers can have on demand, one click translation within an existing application.
SDL LW Enterprise Translation Server	Designed for government entities that need secure access to translation solutions, this language translation server offers scalable, on-premise deployment with straight-forward integration into existing applications and workflows.
SDL EasyTranslator	Created for students and consumers, this all-in-one desktop companion enables users to translate text instantly from any document and to chat in real-time with anyone using popular chat services – all in over 35 languages.

Figure 4.20 SDL Automated Translation Solutions

232 *Computer-aided translation*

can communicate in other languages in an immediate and inexpensive way; and (iii) the greater the amount of content that is available in multiple languages, the easier it is for customers to serve themselves through a company's website, reducing the costs associated to sales and customer service.

SDL also offers instant text machine translation with SDL EasyTranslator, mainly aimed at students and consumers. SDL EasyTranslator is offered both as a free version, which can be downloaded from SDL's website,[62] and as a paid premium version with extended features.

Systran

Systran dates to 1968, being among the oldest firms in the machine translation industry. Historically, Systran systems used RBMT technology, yet in 2009 the company introduced the first hybrid machine translation engine, which implemented both RBMT and SMT technology. Systran's technology has been widely used by other machine translation providers (e.g., Google, WorldLingo, Yahoo! Babel Fish) and has contributed to a number of projects (e.g., iTranslate4).

Systran 7 is the latest version of desktop products. This version provides options for users to create user dictionaries, translation memories, and normalization dictionaries. Users can also set up translation options that include dictionaries and domains, filters, and linguistic resources. Linguistic resources are stored in named profiles in order to improve the translation quality with functions such as Do-Not-Translate terms, acronym detection, automatic spellcheck, Not-Found-Word transliteration, and writing style parameters.

During the translation process, once the translator has specified the file to translate and selected the correspondent user dictionaries and translation memories (up to ten respective databases can be selected for each project), Systran will automatically populate the translation with either 100 per cent translation memory matches or with machine translations (when 100 per cent matches are not found in the translation memory). However, it should be noted that the system does not provide any fuzzy matches.

Systran 7 Premium Translator also integrates a Document Aligner function, which aligns files in a variety of formats to build translation memories. It can translate between 52 language pairs, and includes five specialized dictionaries. In addition, it supports multiple file formats, including Microsoft Word, PDF, OpenOffice documents (ODT, ODS, ODP), Microsoft Excel, Microsoft Power-Point, TXT, RTF, and HTML.

Systran has recently released a version 8 for the server products. This new product includes innovations such as fuzzy matches, an online translation editor or professional post-editor, and a new generation of hybrid engines that cover around 50 different languages.

Systran developed Version 8 for desktop in 2015.

Computer-aided translation 233

In order to experience Systran machine translation engine, a complete online translator can be used for free at http://www.systranet.com/translate.

WorldLingo

WorldLingo was founded in 1998 by the Australian businessman Phil Scanlan. Scanlan purchased a Systran Enterprise Server 5 system and started selling machine translation solutions for websites, as well as providing free website translation widgets that redirected users to WorldLingo's website. In addition, he closed a deal with Microsoft to integrate WorldLingo into all Microsoft Office products. However, in recent years Microsoft has substituted WorldLingo for its own SMT system, and Systran 5 technology is far updated, which leads to a drastic decrease in WorldLingo's popularity. Surprisingly, in 2011, the language service provider TransPerfect announced that they had acquired World-Lingo,[63] so an improvement of the system may be expected.

Currently, WorldLingo is integrated into the popular web-based computer-aided translation tool Wordfast Anywhere and, in addition, it continues to offer free website translation services at http://www.worldlingo.com/en/products_services/worldlingo_translator.html.

Remarks

The linkage between online translation systems with computer-aided translation systems is fast becoming a norm in the industry to synergize the speed of machine translation with the quality of computer-aided translation. Nevertheless, there are a number of issues to be addressed.

(i) Use of data in a hybrid system: It is generally noted that the data processed by a computer-aided translation system is not the same as the data used in the online machine translation system to which it is linked. The output is therefore inconsistent in the use of terms and expressions, as it is based on two different sets of data. Efforts have to be made to enable the use of the same data when generating the target text.

(ii) Origin of the hybrid system: It is true that the combination of MT-TM can be traced back to 1994, when IBM built a logic-based machine translation system into its IBM Translation Manager. This feature, however, was not given great publicity, as the output of the machine translation engine was still far from satisfactory and it was not an online system that was readily available to users.

(iii) Price: As IBM Translation Manager was targeted at corporate users, its price may not be affordable to average users. This is another reason why the forerunner of a hybrid system did not enjoy the popularity it deserved.

(iv) Maturity of hybrid systems: The integration of machine translation into a computer-aided translation system may not be procedurally convenient.

234 *Computer-aided translation*

Integration of MT with TM Systems

The integration of translation memory into machine translation systems is about the use of translation units and terminology database in automatic translation. There are sixteen machine translation systems which have a translation memory component, namely Atlas, Crossroad, Dr. Eye, EsperantiloTM, Hongyaku, Huajian IAT, LogoVista, MLTS, PC-Transer, PeTra, PROMT, Systran, Transwhiz, Xpro7, MT2007, and 翻訳ブレイン (Translation Brain), some of which have been previously discussed in this chapter. The incorporation of a translation memory in a machine translation system is not as effective as the use of machine translation in computer-aided translation systems. Nonetheless, it is indeed clear that we need to know more about machine translation, as hybrid systems grow in popularity each year.

Notes

1 GNOME is not an operating system itself, but an open-source desktop environment designed for Linux and Unix-based operating systems (www.gnome.org: 2010).
2 With the latest patches and service packs (http://www.across.net).
3 http://www.across.net.
4 Opinions retrieved from the blog http://howtoappletrans.blogspot.hk/, by Chris Moore.
5 http://autshumato.sourceforge.net.
6 http://crowdin.net.
7 www.atril.com.
8 http://www.esteam.se.
9 http://www.westernstandard.com.
10 Open Source Update was an e-newsletter for language professionals interested in free and open-source software, edited by Corinne McKay. Although the newsletter is no longer being published, the articles can be retrieved from McKay's website: http://translatewrite.com.
11 http://www.ge-soft.com.
12 CNGL is the Centre for Global Intelligence Content, a collaborative academia-industry research center. Both John Moran and David Lewis are part of this project (http://www.cngl.ie/).
13 http://localizationsmart.com.
14 http://projects.gnome.org/gtranslator.
15 www.heartsome.de/en/heartsome_en.pdf.
16 The forum thread is called 'Web-based free CAT tool Isometry 2.0 published' and can be visited at: http://www.proz.com/forum/cat_tools_technical_help/189572-web_based_free_cat_tool_isometry_20_is_published.html.
17 UTF-8 is an encoding form for Unicode characters that uses 8-bit (Unicode Consortium, 2010:24).
18 http://www.lingotek.com.
19 http://www.terminotix.com.
20 http://www.zklr.com.
21 http://kilgray.com/company.
22 http://kilgray.com/products/memoq-server.
23 http://kilgray.com/products/memoq-server/whatsnew.
24 http://www.memorg.ro.
25 http://www.serious.ro/translation-memory-romanian.php.

Computer-aided translation 235

26 http://blog.memsource.com/why-memsource-cloud.
27 http://www.metatexis.com/news.htm.
28 http://multicorpora.com/products-services/server-solutions.
29 http://omegat.org.
30 The survey was conducted by the blogger Kevin Lossner and can be viewed in his blog at: (http://www.translationtribulations.com/2010/07/results-of-june-translation-tools.html).
31 http://omegatplus.sourceforge.net.
32 http://java.net/projects/open-language-tools.
33 http://www.opentm2.org.
34 http://www.promt.com/media/news/50268.
35 http://www.lingua-et-machina.com.
36 http://www.synthema.it.
37 http://www.lionbridge.com.
38 https://geoworkz.com.
39 http://www.star-group.net.
40 www.star-ts.com/download/pdf/star/brochures/transit-nxt.pdf.
41 https://shop.star-group.net.
42 https://bitbucket.org/fredrik_corneliusson/transolution.
43 http://www.webwordsystem.com/en/about-the-company.aspx.
44 http://www.webwordsystem.com.
45 http://www.wordbee-translator.com.
46 A translation memory may have a maximum of 500,000 translation units in order to be uploaded in a single file. However, a single translation memory in Wordfast Anywhere can store up to 1,000,000 translation units.
47 http://www.xtm-intl.com.
48 http://www.yxcat.com.
49 http://www.crosslang.com.
50 http://www.apertium.org.
51 http://amta2010.amtaweb.org/AMTA/papers/8–00–00-TechShowCase.pdf.
52 info@apptek.com.
53 http://blogs.msdn.com/b/translation/archive/2012/05/30/welcoming-yahoo-babel-fish-users.aspx.
54 https://developers.google.com/translate/v2/faq#pricing.
55 http://itranslate4.eu/project.
56 https://www.lec.com/about.asp.
57 http://blogs.msdn.com/b/translation/archive/2010/03/15/collaborative-translations-announcing-the-next-version-of-microsoft-translator-technology-v2-apis-and-widget.aspx.
58 http://www.microsoft.com/en-us/translator/for-translators.aspx.
59 http://www.statmt.org/moses/?n=Public.Demos.
60 http://www.promt.com/media/news/9687.
61 http://www.sdl.com/products/sdl-beglobal/index-tab2.html.
62 http://www.sdl.com/products/easytranslator.
63 http://www.businesswire.com/news/home/20111114005202/en/TransPerfect-Merges-With% C2%A0WorldLingo#.U7pDVpSSxLI.

References

Alegria, Iñaki, Unai Cabezon, Unai Fernandez de Betono, Gorka Labaka, Aingeru Mayor, Kepa Sarasola, and Arkaitz Zubiaga (2013) 'Reciprocal Enrichment between Basque Wikipedia and Machine Translation', in Iryna Gurevych and Jungi Kim (eds), *The People's Web Meets NLP*, Berlin: Springer Berlin Heidelberg, 101–118.

236 Computer-aided translation

Al-Onaizan, Yaser and Kishore Papineni (2006) 'Distortion Models for Statistical Machine Translation', *Proceedings of the Joint Conference of the International Committee on Computational Linguistics and the Association for Computational Linguistics (COLING/ACL-2006)*, Sydney, Australia.

Alonso, Juan Alberto and András Bocsák (2005) 'Machine Translation for Catalan-Spanish: The Real Case for Productive MT', *Proceedings of the Tenth Conference on European Association of Machine Translation (EAMT 2005).*

Anastasiou, Dimitra and Rajat Gupta (2011) 'Comparison of Crowdsourcing Translation with Machine Translation', *Journal of Information Science* 37(6): 637–659.

Aramaki, Eiji, Sadao Kurohashi, Hideki Kashioka, and Naoto Kato (2005) 'Probabilistic Model for Example-based Machine Translation', Proceedings of *MT Summit X*, Phuket, Thailand.

Asaduzzaman, Mostafa M. and Muhammad Masroor Ali (2003) 'A Knowledge Based Approach to Bangla-English Machine Translation for Simple Assertive Sentences', *International Journal of Translation* 15(2): 77–97.

Auerswald, Marko (2000) 'Example-based Machine Translation with Templates', Wolfgang Wahlster (ed.) *Verbmobil: Foundations of Speech-to-speech Translation*, Berlin: Springer Verlag, 418–427.

Beaven, John (1992) 'Shake and Bake Machine Translation', *Proceedings of the 14th International Conference on Computational Linguistics (COLING-92)*, Nantes, France, 603–609.

Bellnter.Net.

Beregovaya, Olga and Alex Yanishevsky (2010) 'PROMT at PayPal: Enterprise-scale MT Deployment for Financial Industry Content', *Proceedings of the Ninth Biennial Conference of the Association for Machine Translation in the Americas.*

Bowker, Lynne (2002) *Computer-aided Translation Technology: A Practical Introduction*, Ottawa: University of Ottawa Press.

Bowker, Lynne, Cheryl McBride, and Elizabeth Marshman (2008) 'Getting More Than You Paid for? Considerations in Integrating Free and Low-cost Technologies into Translator Training Programs', *Redit* 1: 26–47.

Brew, Chris (1992) 'Letting the Cat out of the Bag: Generation for Shake-and-bake MT', *Proceedings of the 14th International Conference on Computational Linguistics (COLING-92)*, Nantes, France, 610–616.

Carbonell, Jaime G., Steve Klein, David Miller, Mike Steinbaum, Tomer Grassiany, and Jochen Frey (2006) 'Context-based Machine Translation', *Proceedings of the 7th Biennial Conference of the Association for Machine Translation in the Americas (AMTA-2006)*: Visions for the Future of Machine Translation, Boston Marriott, Cambridge, MA, the United States of America.

Carl, Michael (2000) 'A Model of Competence for Corpus-based Machine Translation', *Proceedings of the 18th International Conference on Computational Linguistics (COLING-2000)*, Saarbrucken, Germany.

Carl, Michael and Andy Way (2003) *Recent Advances in Example-based Machine Translation*, Dordrecht: Kluwer Academic Publishers.

Carl, Michael, Ecaterina Rascu, and Paul Schmidt (2005) 'Using Template Grammars for Shake and Bake Paraphrasing', *Proceedings of the 10th Workshop of the European Association for Machine Translation: Practical Applications of Machine Translation*, Budapest, Hungary, 66–72.

Cavalli-Sforza, Violetta, Krzysztof Czuba, Teruko Mitamura, and Eric H. Nyberg (2000) 'Challenges in Adapting an Interlingua for Bidirectional English-Italian

Translation', John S. White (ed.) *Envisioning Machine Translation in the Information Future*, Berlin: Springer Verlag, 169–178.

Chan, Sin-wai (2004) *A Dictionary of Translation Technology*, Hong Kong: The Chinese University Press.

Charoenpornsawat, Paisarn, Virach Sornlertlamvanich, and Thatsanee Charoenporn (2002) 'Improving Translation Quality of Rule-based Machine Translation', *Proceedings of the Workshop on Machine Translation in Asia (COLING-2002)*, Taipei, Taiwan.

Chereshnovska, Marta (2013) 'Training for Technical Translators: An Interview with Uwe Muegge', Available from http://works.bepress.com/uwe_muegge/82.

Coffey, Derek (2010) 'What's Happening with GlobalSight?' Online Posting. 19th March 2010. GlobalSight Community, Available from http://www.globalsight.com/index.php?option=com_idoblog&task=userblog&userid=305&Itemid=68.

Comprendium (2004) 'Comprendium Translator System Overview', Available from http://www.mt-archive.info/Comprendium-2004.pdf.

Condak, Milan (2004) 'Workflow in Wordfast and Invisible Machine Translator', *International Journal of Translation* 16(1): 87–108.

Crego, Josep Maria, Adria de Gispert, and Jose B. Marino (2005) 'The TALP Ngram-based SMT System for IWSLT '05', *Proceedings of the International Workshop on Spoken Language Translation (IWSLT-2005)*, Pittsburgh, PA, the United States of America.

Dash, Niladri Sekhar (2004) 'Issues Involved in the Development of a Corpus-based Machine Translation System', *International Journal of Translation* 16(2): 57–79.

Dave, Shachi, Jignashu Parikh, and Pushpak Bhattacharyya (2001) 'Interlingua-based English–Hindi Machine Translation and Language Divergence', *Machine Translation* 16(4): 251–304.

Directorate-General for Translation of the European Commission (2005) 'Translation Tools and Workflow', Available from http://www.nbu.bg/PUBLIC/IMAGES/File/departments/foreign%20languages%20and%20literatures/research/TOOLS%20EN%20booklet_2.pdf.

Eisele, Andreas, et al. (2008) 'Using Moses to Integrate Multiple Rule-based Machine Translation Engines into a Hybrid System', *Proceedings of the Third Workshop on Statistical Machine Translation*, Association for Computational Linguistics.

Elming, Jakob (2006) 'Transformation-based Correction of Rule-based MT', *Proceedings of the 11th Workshop of the European Association for Machine Translation: Machine Translation/Translation Aids— Tools to Increase Quality and to Save Money*, Oslo, Norway, the University of Oslo.

Federmann, Christian, et al. (2010) 'Further Experiments with Shallow Hybrid MT Systems', *Proceedings of the Joint Fifth Workshop on Statistical Machine Translation and Metrics MATR*, Association for Computational Linguistics.

Finite Field (2011) 'Web-based Free CAT Tool Isometry 2.0 Is Published', Online Posting, 14 January 2011, ProZ.com., Available from http://www.proz.com/forum/cat_tools_technical_help/189572-web_based_free_cat_tool_isometry_20_is_published.html#1663151.

Forcada, Mikel L., Francis M. Tyers, and Gema Ramírez-Sánchez (2009) 'The Apertium Machine Translation Platform: Five Years On', *Proceedings of the First International Workshop on Free/Open-Source Rule-Based Machine Translation*.

Galley, Michel, Jonathan Graehl, Kevin Knight, Daniel Marcu, Steve DeNeefe, Wei Wang, and Ignacio Thayer (2006) 'Scalable Inference and Training of Context-rich

238 Computer-aided translation

Syntactic Translation Models', *Proceedings of the Joint Conference of the International Committee on Computational Linguistics and the Association for Computational Linguistics (COLING/ACL-2006)*, Sydney, Australia.

García, Ignacio (2011) 'Translating by Post-editing: Is It the Way Forward?' *Machine Translation* 25(3): 217–237.

Garcia, Ignacio and Vivian Stevenson (2009) 'Google Translator Toolkit: Free Web-based Translation Memory for the Masses', *Multilingual* (Sept) 16–19.

Garcia, Ignacio and Vivian Stevenson (2010) 'Déjà Vu X', *MultiLingual* 21(1): 16–19.

Gdaniec, Caludia (1998) 'Lexical Choice and Syntactic Generation in a Translation System: Transformations in the New LMT English-German System', David L. Farwell, Laurie Gerber, and Eduard Hovy (eds.) *Machine Translation and the Information Soup*, Berlin: Springer Verlag, 408–420.

Gerasimov, Andrei (2001) 'An Effective and Inexpensive Translation Memory Tool', *Translation Journal* 5(3).

Gerasimov, Andrei (2002) 'Review of Wordfast (Windows Version)', *Multilingual Computing and Technology* 13(1).

Gervais, Dan (2003) 'MultiTrans™ System Presentation: Translation Support and Language Management Solutions', *MT Summit IX*.

Groenewald, Hendrik and Liza du Plooy (2010) 'Processing Parallel Text Corpora for Three South African Language Pairs in the Autshumato Project', Guy de Pauw, Handré Groenwald, and Gilles-Maurice de Schyrer (eds.) *Proceedings of the Second Workshop on African Language Technology AfLaT 2010*, 27–30.

Guerra Martinez, Lorena (2004) 'PROMT Professional and the Importance of Building and Updating Machine Translation Dictionaries', *International Journal of Translation* 16(1): 121–139.

Gu, Liang and Gao Yuqing (2004) 'On Feature Selection in Maximum Entropy Approach to Statistical Concept-based Speech-to-speech Translation', *Proceedings of the International Workshop on Spoken Language Translation (IWSLT 2004)*, Kyoto, Japan.Hearne, Mary and Andy Way (2003) 'Seeing the Wood for the Trees: Data-oriented Translation', *Proceedings of MT Summit IX*, New Orleans, LA, the United States of America, 165–172.

Hearne, Mary and Andy Way (2006) 'Disambiguation Strategies for Data-oriented Translation', *Proceedings of the 11th Workshop of the European Association for Machine Translation: Machine Translation/Translation Aids — Tools to Increase Quality and to Save Money*, Oslo, Norway, the University of Oslo.

Hodász, Gábor (2006) 'Towards a Comprehensive Evaluation Method of Memory-based Translation Systems', *Proceedings of the 11th Workshop of the European Association for Machine Translation: Machine Translation/Translation Aids— Tools to Increase Quality and to Save Money*, Oslo, Norway, the University of Oslo.

Horiguchi, Atsushi, Seiji Tsuchiya, Kazuhide Kojima, Hirokazu Watabe, and Tsukasa Kawaoka (2002) 'Constructing a Sensuous Judgment System Based on Conceptual Processing', *Proceedings of the 3rd International Conference on Intelligent Text Processing and Computational Linguistics (CICLing-2002)*, Mexico City, Mexico.

Hovy, Eduard, Margaret King, and Andrei Popescu-Belis (2002) 'Principles of Context-based Machine Translation Evaluation', *Machine Translation* 17(1): 43–75.

http:// www.WordFisher.com.

http://anaphraseus.sourceforge.net.

Computer-aided translation 239

http://autshumato.sourceforge.net.
http://blog.lingo24.com.
http://code.google.com/apis/language/translate.
http://crowdin.net.
http://freetm.com.
http://geoworkz.com.
http://java.net/projects/open-language-tools.
http://kilgray.com.
http://mt2007-cat.ru.html.
http://multicorpora.com.
http://omegat.org.
http://omegatplus.sourceforge.net.
http://opentms.de.
http://projects.gnome.org/gtranslator.
http://pypi.python.org/pypi/Transolution/0.4b5.
http://similis.org.
http://tinytm.sourceforge.net.
http://translate.google.com.
http://translate.google.com/toolkit.
http://www.across.net.
http://www.apertium.org.
http://www.atril.com.
http://www.crosslang.com.
http://www.esperantilo.org.
http://www.esteam.se.
http://www.finite-field.com/home.
http://www.foreigndesk.net.
http://www.gcys.cn.
http://www.ge-soft.com.
http://www.globalsight.com.
http://www.ilsp.gr/traid.
http://www.lingotek.com.
http://www.lingua-et-machina.com.
http://www.lionbridge.com.
http://www.macupdate.com/app/mac/27128/appletrans.
http://www.memorg.ro.
http://www.memsource.com.
http://www.metatexis.com.
http://www.opentm2.org.
http://www.sdl.com.
http://www.star-group.net.
http://www.synthema.it.
http://www.terminotix.com.
http://www.webwordsystem.com.
http://www.westernstandard.com/Fluency/TranslationSuite.aspx.
http://www.wordbee-translator.com.
http://www.yxcat.com.
http://www.zklr.com.
http://yehongmei.narod.ru.

240   Computer-aided translation

Hutchins, John and Harold Somers (1992) *An Introduction to Machine Translation*, London: Academic Press, Available from www.hutchinsweb.me.uk/IntroMT-TOC.htm.

info@apptek.com.

ITI Home, http://www.iti.org.uk., retrieved in 2011

Jaworski, Rafał (2013) 'Anubis-speeding Up Computer-aided Translation', *Computational Linguistics*, Springer Berlin Heidelberg, 263–280.

Kay, Martin (1980) 'The Proper Place of Men and Machines in Language Translation', *Research Report CSL-80-11*, Xerox Palo Alto Research Center, Palo Alto, CA, the United States of America.

Kay, Martin (1997a) 'The Proper Place of Men and Machines in Language Translation', *Machine Translation* 12(1–2): 3–23.

Kay, Martin (1997b) 'It's Still the Proper Place', *Machine Translation* 12(1–2): 35–38.

Kjærsgaard, Poul Soren (1987) 'REFTEX – A Context-based Translation Aid', *Proceedings of the 3rd Conference of the European Chapter of the Association for Computational Linguistics (EACL-87)*, Copenhagen, Denmark, 109–112.

Knight, Kevin (2003) 'Teaching Statistical Machine Translation', *Proceedings of MT Summit IX*, New Orleans, LA, the United States of America, 17–19.

Koehn, Philipp, et al. (2007) 'Moses: Open Source Toolkit for Statistical Machine Translation', *Proceedings of the 45th Annual Meeting of the ACL on Interactive Poster and Demonstration Sessions*, Association for Computational Linguistics.

Koehn, Philipp, Franz Josef Och, and Daniel Marcu (2003) 'Statistical Phrase-based Translation', *Proceedings of the Human Language Technology and North American Chapter of Association of Computational Linguistics 2003 (HLT/NAACL-2003)*, Edmonton, Alberta, Canada.

Környei, Tibor (2000) 'WordFisher for MS Word: An Alternative to Translation Memory Programs for Freelance Translators?' *Translation Journal* 4(1).

Kranias, Lambros and Anna Samiotou (2004) 'Automatic Translation Memory Fuzzy Match Post-editing: A Step Beyond Traditional TM/MT Integration', *Proceedings of LREC2004*, Lisbon, Portugal.

Lagoudaki, Elina (2006) 'Translation Memories Survey 2006: Users' Perceptions around TM Use', *Proceedings of the ASLIB International Conference Translating & the Computer*, 28.

Lee, Young-Suk (2001) *Interlingua-based Open Domain Machine Translation: A Case Study from Korean-to-English Translation*, MS-15178, MIT Lincoln Laboratory.

Lehrberger, John and Laurent Bourbeau (1988) *Machine Translation: Linguistic Characteristics of MT Systems and General Methodology of Evaluation*, Amsterdam and Philadelphia: John Benjamins Publishing Company.

Lu, Jenny (2010) 'Machine Translation (MT) @ CA Technologies: Where Can MT Be Best Successful and What Are the Best MT Engines for Various Languages', *The Ninth Conference of the Association for Machine Translation in the Americas*.

Mariño, José B., Rafael E. Banchs, Josep Maria Crego, Adrià de Gispert, Patrik Lambert, José A.R. Fonollosa, and Marta R. Costa-jussà (2006) 'N-gram-based Machine Translation', *Computational Linguistics* 32(4): 527–549.

McKay, Corinne (2005) 'Focus on Foreign Desk: Q & A with Dierk Seeburg of Choice Hotels International', Available from www.translationdirectory.com/article605.htm.

Computer-aided translation 241

Miller, François (2002) 'Review of Wordfast (Macintosh Version)', *Multilingual Computing and Technology* 13(1).

Mollison, Hazel (2007) 'Lingo24 and XML-INTL Welcome You to XTM', Online Posting, 9 December 2007, *The Lingo-ist*, Available from http://blog.lingo24.com/the-lingo-ist-april-2006.

Moran, John and David Lewis (2011) 'Unobtrusive Methods for Low-cost Manual Evaluation of Machine Translation', *Tralogy* [Online], Session 5: Quality in Translation, Available from http://lodel.irevues.inist.fr/tralogy/index.php?id=141.

Morera, Aram, Aouad Lamine, and J.J. Collins (2012) 'Assessing Support for Community Workflows in Localisation', *Business Process Management Workshops*, Berlin: Springer.

Naber, Daniel (2003) 'A Rule-based and Grammar Checker', PhD thesis, Universität Bielefeld.

Nagao, Makoto (1984) 'A Framework of a Mechanical Translation between Japanese and English by Analogy Principle', Alick Elithorn and Ranan Banerji (eds.) *Artificial and Human Intelligence*, Amsterdam: North-Holland Publishing Company, 173–180.

Nagao, Makoto and Jun-ichi Tsujii (1986) 'The Transfer Phase of the Mu Machine Translation System', *Proceedings of the 11th International Conference on Computational Linguistics (COLING-86)*, Bonn, Germany, 97–103.

Nogueira, Danilo (2004) 'In Memoriam: Emilio Benito', *Translation Journal* 8(2), Available from: http://www.translationjournal.net/journal/28benito.htm.

Och, Franz (2008) 'Doubling Up', Online Post, 30 September 2008, Google Research Blog, Available from http://googleresearch.blogspot.hk.

Och, Franz (2009) '51 Languages in Google Translate', Online Post, 1 September 2009, Google Research Blog, Available from http://googleresearch.blogspot.hk.

Planas, Emmanuel (2005) 'SIMILIS Second-generation Translation Memory Software', *Translating and the Computer* 27.

Prószéky, Gábor (2005) 'Machine Translation and the Rule-to-rule Hypothesis', Krisztina Károly and Ágota Fóris (eds.) *New Trends in Translation Studies: In Honour of Kinga Klaudy*, Budapest: Akadémiai Kiadó, 207–218.

Pym, Anthony (2011) 'What Technology Does to Translating', *Translation and Interpreting* 3(1): 1–9.

Ramos, Luciana Cecilia (2010) 'Post-editing Free Machine Translation: From a Language Vendor's Perspective', *Proceedings of the Conference of the American Machine Translation Association (AMTA)*, Denver, CO: AMTA.

Reynolds, Peter (2014) 'Emilio Benito – An Appreciation', Online Posting, 9 February 2014, Kilgray Blog, Available from http://kilgray.blogspot.hk/2014/02/emilio-benito-appreciation.html.

Richardson, Stephen D., William B. Dolan, Arul Menezes, and Jessie Pinkham (2001) 'Achieving Commercial-quality Translation with Example-based Methods', Bente Maegaard (ed.) *Proceedings of MT Summit VIII: Machine Translation in the Information Age*, Santiago de Compostela, Spain, 293–298.

Ripplinger, Bärbel (1994) 'Concept-based Machine Translation and Interpretation', *Machine Translation— Ten Years On: Proceedings of the 2nd International Conference Organised by Cranfield University*, England, the United Kingdom.

Rösener, Christoph (2010) 'Computational Linguistics in the Translator's Workflow: Combining Authoring Tools and Translation Memory Systems', *Proceedings of the*

242   Computer-aided translation

NAACL HLT 2010 Workshop on Computational Linguistics and Writing: Writing Processes and Authoring Aids, Association for Computational Linguistics, 1–6.

SDL (2013) 'SDL WorldServer 10.4 Release Notes', Available from http://kb.sdl.com/kb/?ArticleId=4912#tab:homeTab:crumb:7:artId:4912.

Sikes, Richard (2009) 'Across Language Server v5', *MultiLingual* 20(7): 16–21.

Somers, Harold L. (1999) 'Review Article: Example-based Machine Translation', *Machine Translation* 14(2): 113–157.

Trippe, Bill (2007) 'Building an Enterprise-class System for Globalization: Autodesk's Worldwide Initiative', *Gilbane Group*, Available from http://gilbane.com/case_studies_pdf/CTW-Autodesk-final0207.pdf.

Tsygany, Oleg (2009) 'Anapraseus: Translators' Workhorse', *Panace@* X(29): 58–60.

Unicode Consortium (2010) *The Unicode Standard, Version 6.0.0*, Mountain View, CA: The Unicode Consortium, 2011.

Vandenberg, Robert (2009) 'Lingotek Community Translation Platform June 2009 Public', Online Posting, 10 June 2009, Available from http://www.slideshare.net/rvandenberg/lingotek-community-translation-platform-june-2009-public.

Wang, Jiande, Chen Zhaoxiong, and Huang Heyan (2001) 'Intelligent Case Based Machine Translation System', *Proceedings of the 3rd International Conference on Theretical and Methodological Issues in Machine Translation of Natural Languages (TMI-90)*, Linguistics Research Center, University of Texas at Austin, Austin, Texas, the United States of America, 235–254.

Wantanabe, Hideo, Sadao Kurohashi, and Eiji Aramak (2000) 'Finding Structural Correspondences from Bilingual Parsed Corpus for Corpus-based Translation', *Proceedings of the 18th International Conference on Computational Linguistics (COLING-2000)*, Saarbrucken, Germany.

Wassmer, Thomas (2003) 'Comparative Review of Four Localization Tools', *Localization Reader 2004*, 17–22.

Wendt, Chris (2010) 'Better Translations with User Collaboration – Integrated MT at Microsoft', *Proceedings of Ninth Biennial Conference of the Association for Machine Translation in the Americas*.

Whitelock, Peter J. (1992) 'Shake-and-bake Translation', *Proceedings of the 14th International Conference on Computational Linguistics (COLING-92)*, Nantes, France, 784–791.

Whitelock, Peter J. (1994) 'Shake and Bake Translation', Christopher J. Rupp, Michael A. Rosner, and Roderick L. Johnson (eds.) *Constraints, Language and Computation*, London: Academic Press, 339–359.

Ye, Qingfang 葉慶芳 (2010) 〈翻譯記憶庫在科技翻譯中的運用以及雅信軟件中翻譯記憶庫的評估〉 ('The Study of TM in Sci-tech Translation and the Evaluation of TM in Yaxin'), 《海外英語》 (*Overseas English*) 10: 179–181.

Zaremba, Mindaugas, Algirdas Laukaitis, and Olegas Vasilecas (2009) 'Hybrid Translation Memory Systems', *Information Technologies 2009: Proceedings of the 15th International Conference on Information and Software Technologies, IT 2009*, 250–255.

Zhou, Joe and Liu Weiqian (2000) 'A Real-time Integration of Concept-based Search and Summarization of Chinese Websites', *Proceedings of the Joint Sigdat Conference on Empirical Methods in Natural Language Processing and Very Large Corpora (EMNLP/VLC-2000)*, Hong Kong University of Science and Technology, Hong Kong, China.

Zhu, Jiang and Wang Haifeng (2005) 'The Effect of Adding Rules into the Rule-based MT System', *Proceedings of MT Summit X*, Phuket, Thailand.

Zydron, Andrzej (2003) 'Translating XML-Based Documents', Online Posting, 27 August 2003, *Ulitzer*, Available from http://andrzejzydron.ulitzer.com/node/40690.

Zydron, Andrzej (2004) 'Translating XML Documents with xml:tm', Online Posting, 7 January 2004, O'Reilly XML.com, Available from http://www.xml.com/pub/a/2004/01/07/xmltm.html.

5 A theoretical framework for computer-aided translation studies

Introduction

To many, computer-aided translation is simply about clicking buttons and saving data on computer systems for reuse in the future. However, computer-aided translation is not simply operational; actually, it is more than meets the eye. To machine translation scholars and system developers, computer-aided translation has been an area that deserves serious attention and academic examination.

In this chapter, a framework for computer-aided translation studies is proposed for the first time. Before we present details of this framework, theoretical frameworks for translation studies proposed by other scholars will be explained and discussed. This will be followed by justifications on the proposed framework and detailed explanations of its divisions and subdivisions.

Frameworks in the past

Several frameworks for translation studies have been proposed in the past, including those of James Holmes (1972/1987: 9–24, 1988: 93–98), Jeremy Munday (2001: 13), Mary Snell-Hornby (1972/1988), and Gideon Toury (1995). These frameworks are discussed chronologically in the following.

James S. Holmes (1972): Map of translation studies

James Holmes is generally considered the first scholar who coined the term 'translation studies'. In his article entitled 'The Names and Nature of Translation Studies' (Holmes 1972: 9–24, 1988: 67–80), he proposed a map of translation studies, the first of its kind. According to Holmes, translation studies has two main objectives: describing the phenomena of translating and translation(s) as they manifest themselves in the world of our experience, and establishing general principles by means of which these phenomena can be explained and predicted. He divides translation studies into pure and theoretical. Pure translation studies can be further subdivided into descriptive translation studies (or translation description) and theoretical translation studies (or translation theory).

A theoretical framework for computer-aided translation studies   245

There are three types of descriptive translation studies: product-oriented descriptive translation studies, function-oriented descriptive translation studies, and process-oriented descriptive translation studies.

There are two major types of theoretical translation studies: general translation theories and partial translation theories, which can be grouped into six main types: (a) medium-restricted theories; (b) area-restricted theories; (c) rank-restricted theories; (d) text-type restricted theories; (e) time-restricted theories; and (f) problem-restricted theories. Applied translation studies can also be divided into translator training, translation aids, and translation criticism. The growth of translation studies depends partly on the efforts made within the translation circle and partly on the recognition by other disciplines of its importance in their own research and development.

Mary Snell-Hornby (1988): Integrated framework for translation studies

Sixteen years later, a syncretic approach to translation was proposed by Mary Snell-Hornby in her book entitled *Translation Studies: An Integrated Approach*, which stresses the importance of treating translation from a wide range of perspectives. Her theoretical framework has been known as an integrated approach to translation.

According to Snell-Hornby, her study is an attempt to present recently developed concepts and methods both from translation theory and linguistics so that they could be usefully employed in the theory, practice, and analysis of literary translation. However, only those concepts and methods in linguistics relevant for translation have been developed for use in translation studies. In fact, this study can also be seen as an attempt to clear the ground for the growth of translatology by removing some deep-rooted misconceptions.

The integrated approach presented by the author is one which attempts to encompass all text-types and includes relevant aspects from related disciplines, especially linguistics, which shows her intention to make translation studies a discipline in its own right. Her approach is shown through a system of relationships established between basic text-types and the crucial aspects of translation. Horizontally, it represents a cline; vertically, it is a stratification model, proceeding from the most general level A to the most particular level F. Level A refers to the conventional areas of translation in a fluid spectrum; Level B is a proto-typology of the basic text-types; Level C consists of the related non-linguistic disciplines; Level D includes the aspects and criteria governing the translation process; Level E refers to areas of linguistics relevant for translation; while Level F contains the phonological aspects of specific relevance for certain areas of translation.

With this prototypological framework, the foundations have been laid for the conception of translation studies as an integrated and independent discipline that covers all kinds of translation and has its own methods to deal with the complexities of translation. It can thus be concluded that Mary Snell-Hornby

246 *A theoretical framework for computer-aided translation studies*

is a syncretic scholar who believes in the application of the various disciplines to the formulation of a theoretical framework.

Gideon Toury (1995): Descriptive translation studies and beyond

It should be noted that in Toury's work, Translator Training – which covers curriculum design and teaching methods – and Translation Aids – which covers dictionaries and information – have been given emphasis in applied extensions of translation studies. This is possibly the first framework in which translation aids have been included to highlight the importance of using tools in translation practice.

Jeremy Munday (2001): Applied branch of translation studies

Munday, in his book *Introducing Translation Studies: Theories and Applications* (2001: 13), goes a step further by putting IT application, which covers translation software, online databases, and the use of the Internet, under Translation Aids in the area of 'applied' translation studies. It can be assumed that translation software refers to both machine translation and computer-aided translation systems, whereas online databases covers both terminology and translation memory databases. The use of the Internet, in turn, is about the use of browsers to find the information we need and the use of machine translation systems in translating websites and other materials on the Internet.

It can be observed that a new framework has been proposed in every decade since the 1970s. It can also be noted that it is only in Jeremy Munday's framework (2001: 13) that IT is mentioned. In fact, there are justifications for the creation of a theoretical framework for computer-aided translation studies.

Justifications for the creation of a theoretical framework for computer-aided translation studies

Though commercial computer-aided translation has been around for about 20 years, it has been the fastest-growing area in the field only in the last decade. Its rapid growth is attributable to several factors:

(1) In terms of research and development, computer-aided translation has been studied and developed in 30 countries, or 16 per cent of the total number of countries in the world.
(2) In terms of the literature on the subject, 8,363 works have been written either in English or Chinese by 5,404 authors between 1948 and 2006, a period of 58 years (Chan 2008: xxix). In China, 736 articles on computer-aided translation have been written since 2004. Of all the publications on translation, those on translation technology are ranked second, after translation studies.

A theoretical framework for computer-aided translation studies

(3) In terms of the development of computer-aided translation systems, over 100 systems have so far been developed, which can be divided into fourteen different categories (Chan 2012: 361–376).
(4) In terms of the number of conferences, there were 26 conferences on computer-aided translation and its related areas from 1993 to 2003, second only to translation studies in terms of number (Chan 2009: 12–15).
(5) In terms of the number of commercial system users, there are more than 6,000 corporations which use computer-aided translation systems to solve their language problems.
(6) In terms of labour force, there are already more than 200,000 computer-aided translators, and the number has been on the rise, especially in China and other emerging countries in Asia.

All these mean that the time has come for us to take a new look at computer-aided translation and approach most of the issues related to computers and translation in a systematic manner.

A proposed theoretical framework of computer-aided translation studies

Table 5.1 A Framework for Computer-aided Translation Studies

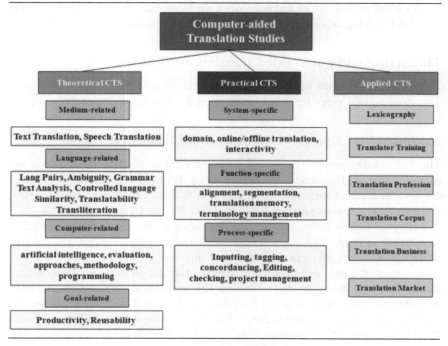

248 *A theoretical framework for computer-aided translation studies*

It should be noted that firstly, this theoretical framework is the first of its kind, establishing computer-aided translation studies as an independent academic area of translation studies. And secondly, it is believed that most if not all of the concepts in computer-aided translation have now been put in their proper places in this framework. To show that these concepts have been discussed and studied in the field, a reference is given to each of these concepts, and each concept in this framework is given a concise explanation.

This framework, as shown above, is made up of three major divisions:

(a) Theoretical Computer-aided Translation Studies, which includes: Medium-related Theoretical Computer-aided Translation Studies, Language-related Theoretical Computer-aided Translation Studies, Computer-related Theoretical Computer-aided Translation Studies, and Goal-related Theoretical Computer-aided Translation Studies.
(b) Practical Computer-aided Translation Studies, which includes: System-specific Practical Computer-aided Translation Studies, Function-specific Practical Computer-aided Translation Studies, and Process-specific Practical Computer-aided Translation Studies.
(c) Applied Computer-aided Translation Studies, which includes: lexicography, translator training, translation profession, translation corpus, translation business, and translation market.

This is the overall theoretical framework for Computer-aided Translation Studies. The following is a detailed description of each division and subdivision.

Theoretical computer-aided translation studies

This refers to the study of the theoretical aspects of computer-aided translation. This division of Computer-aided Translation Studies has four subdivisions.

Medium-related Theoretical Computer-aided Translation Studies

The first subdivision of Theoretical Computer-aided Translation studies is the Medium-related Theoretical Computer-aided Translation Studies. The media are texts and voices, or textual data and speech data. In other words, this subdivision covers text translation and speech translation (Rayner 1995).

Text translation refers to the translation of a text by a computer-aided translation system. The texts to be translated can be existing documents, pasted from other programmes or typed into the programme. Text translation, however, must not be interpreted as the translation of printed documents or documentary translation. It is about the translation of electronic texts in different formats, such as word files, tagged files, and webpages. In the literature of machine translation, texts have been divided into 'Bilingual Text', 'Colloquial Text', 'Comparative Text', 'Parallel Text', and 'Source Text'. Texts have also been studied according to the different ways they are processed,

A *theoretical framework for computer-aided translation studies* 249

such as 'Text Chunking', 'Text Clustering', 'Text Generation', 'Text Abstracting', and 'Text Summarization'.

Speech translation refers to computer-aided translation of a spoken text from one language to another, involving techniques such as speech recognition and production. Speech translation is related to speech recognition, speech process, speech synthesis, and speech generation through the use of speech recognition and speech translation systems (Montgomery, Stalls, Stumberger, Li, Belvin, Arnaiz, and Litenatsky 1995: 101–110).

Language-related Theoretical Computer-aided Translation Studies

The second subdivision of Theoretical Computer-aided Translation Studies is Language-related Theoretical Computer-aided Translation Studies. This subdivision covers language pairs, linguistic ambiguity, grammar, text analysis, controlled language, textual similarity, translatability, and transliteration.

(1) *Language Pairs* refers to the specified input and output languages in a computer-aided translation system. Studies on the translation of around 80 language pairs have been done, mostly with the language pairs of Chinese and English, Japanese and English, and Korean and English (Scannell 2006: 103–108).

(2) *Linguistic Ambiguity* arises when an expression can be interpreted in more than one way. Linguistic ambiguity can be divided into 'lexical ambiguity' and 'syntactical ambiguity'. Disambiguation, i.e., the removal of ambiguities, and word sense disambiguation, are also widely studied (Sammer, Reiter, Soderland, Kirchhoff, and Etzioni 2006).

(3) *Grammar* is the third subdivision. In computer-aided translation, grammatical knowledge is essential in parsing, tagging, and data editing. A number of types of grammar, such as context-free, dependency, functional, head-driven phrase structure, lexical-functional, Montague, phrase structure, stochastic, and universal grammar have been discussed. The idea of translation grammar has been proposed as a grammar for machine translation (Riezler and Maxwell III 2006).

(4) *Text Analysis* is an important step to produce a good translation of the source text (Taylor and Baldry 2001: 277–305). Analysis, which is important in both human and machine translation, is mainly about 'source analysis' and 'translation analysis'. Text analysis is also considered as 'linguistic analysis', which includes, in turn, 'morphological analysis', 'semantic analysis', and 'syntactical analysis'.

(5) *Controlled Language* is a type of natural language developed for specific domains with a clearly defined restriction on controlled lexicons, simplified grammars, and style rules to make it easier to be processed by machine translation systems. It is generally agreed that the use of controlled language helps to produce controlled language translation, which has improved

250 *A theoretical framework for computer-aided translation studies*

consistency, higher reusability, easier processing, greater standardization, and increased translatability (Allen 1999).

(6) *Similarity* refers to the degree of closeness between texts (Patel and Radev 2006). Linguistic similarity is the theoretical foundation for the function of 'Analyse' in computer-aided translation systems. The input text is gauged against the stored translation units and a similarity rate is generated. Similarity in computer-aided translation systems is usually set at 75 per cent, but it varies with the purposes of the translation.

(7) *Translatability* refers to the possibility of translating from one language into another. Machine translatability has a number of issues that are worth studying, such as the techniques for rating translatability, the inter-translatability of natural languages, methods of improving translatability, and the use of a translatability checker to gauge the textual suitability of a translation (O'Brien 2004).

(8) *Transliteration* refers to the act or process of representing or spelling the words, letters, or characters of one language in the words, letters, or characters of another language or alphabet. In the context of computer-aided translation, transliteration covers mainly the issue of using a particular Romanization system to transliterate words and proper names. Also of concern to computer-aided translation are the detection, recognition, extraction, disambiguation, and transliteration of bilingual or multilingual name entities (Knight and Graehl 1997).

Computer-related Theoretical Computer-aided Translation Studies

This part covers the theoretical aspects described below:

(1) *Artificial intelligence*, which refers to the capacity of a machine to replicate the functions and operations of the human brain, such as reasoning and learning (Yang 2006). Artificial intelligence (AI) is closely related to the thinking of a machine translation system. The linguistic aspects of artificial intelligence and the making of AI systems are important issues in this area.

(2) *Evaluation*, which refers to the methods and criteria used in assessing the usability and functionality of a machine translation or computer-aided translation system. Evaluation includes issues of evaluation criteria and methodology for machine translation or computer-aided translation systems (Rico Pérez 2001).

(3) *Approach*, which refers to the tactics used in designing and developing machine translation and computer-aided translation systems. There are 22 approaches to machine translation, and fourteen different types of computer-aided translation systems have been developed based on different approaches. Issues such as the strengths and weaknesses of the different approaches and the use of hybrid approaches are worth examining (Proszéky 2005: 207–218).

A theoretical framework for computer-aided translation studies 251

(4) *Methodology,* which refers to the procedures used in treating the linguistic data in machine translation and computer-aided translation systems. Some methods that are considered particular to machine translation systems are pre-editing and post-editing (Somers 1998: 143–149). Techniques that are particular to computer-aided translation, on the other hand, include translation by reuse, translation by selection, and translation by modification.

(5) *Programming* refers to the use of a set of coded instructions that enables a computer to perform a desired sequence of operations. This area concerns the use of a programming language, such as Java or VBNet, to create a machine translation or computer-aided translation system. The issue of algorithms has been widely discussed (Brown 2000: 125–131).

Goal-related Theoretical Computer-aided Translation Studies

Goal-related Theoretical Computer-aided Translation Studies cover mainly the concepts of productivity and reusability.

(1) *Productivity,* on the one hand, refers to the increase of production in the case of a computer-aided translation system. One of the most important issues in this area is the relationship between productivity and quality, or how to do more with less. The use of tools to enhance productivity is also an issue frequently discussed (Vallianatou 2005).

(2) *Reusability,* on the other hand, concerns the use of stored data in subsequent and next similar translation projects. Reusability is an important function of a computer-aided translation system. The issues of when, why, and how best to reuse translations are important (Merkel 1993: 139–149).

Practical computer-aided translation studies

This refers to the study of the practical aspects of computer-aided translation and can be further divided into four subdivisions.

System-specific Practical Computer-aided Translation Studies

System-specific Practical Computer-aided Translation Studies covers the following topics:

(1) *Domain,* which refers to issues related to the needs of a specific domain or area. It has been known that computer-aided translation has been applied to all types of practical writings. It is expected that computer-aided translation will be applied to more and more domains in practical translation (Filatova, Hatzivassiloglou, and McKeown 2006).

(2) *Online Translation,* which refers to the translation of a text by a computer or computer-aided translation system that is available at all times upon

252 *A theoretical framework for computer-aided translation studies*

users' demand (Zervaki 2002). Online translation is fast becoming a popular topic in computer-aided translation and covers both 'Internet translation' and 'web translation'. Sometimes, 'online translation' is synonymous with 'web translation'.

(3) *Interactivity* refers to the provision of facilities to allow the translator-editor to build up a translation interactively. Interactivity should be understood in the context of human-machine interaction. It covers the topics of interactive machine translation, interactive computer-aided translation, interactive speech translation, interactive translation systems, interactive machine translation systems, interactive computer-aided translation systems, interactive bilingual systems, interactive multilingual systems, interactive speech translation systems, and interactive text-editing systems (Bender, Hasan, Vilar, Zens, and Ney 2005: 33–40).

Function-specific Practical Computer-aided Translation Studies

This part includes alignment, segmentation, translation memory, and terminology management, which are functionally specific to computer-aided translation.

(1) *Alignment* refers to the process of matching up a source text and the target text segment by segment into translation pairs. Technically, we have Automatic Alignment, Fuzzy Alignment, and Statistical Alignment. Linguistically, we have Lexical Alignment, Terminology Alignment, Word Alignment, Phrase Alignment, Clause Alignment, Sentence Alignment, and Text Alignment. A lot of attention has been given to 'word alignment' and 'sentence alignment'. The algorithm, methods, techniques and other practical issues in automatic alignment are also widely examined (Wu 2000: 415–418).

(2) *Segmentation* concerns sentence separation in a computer-aided translation system with the purpose of dividing a text into easily manageable segments. Automatic segmentation is done in computer-aided translation systems. Segmentation can be done at different levels: word segmentation, sentence segmentation, and text segmentation. Some languages are easier to segment; others are not (Wang, Deng, and Zou 2006).

(3) *Translation Memory* (Shih 2006) consists in a database that stores translated sentences along with their respective source segments. The topics often discussed in this area include 'Matching', 'Fuzzy Match', 'Translation Memory System', and 'Translation Memory Exchange (TMX)'.

(4) *Terminology Management* involves the documentation, storage, manipulation, and presentation of specialized vocabulary in a machine translation or computer-aided translation system. This area covers terminology recognition, acquisition, extraction, database, processing, and management systems, all of which are constituent parts of terminology translation (Austermühl 2001: 102–123).

A theoretical framework for computer-aided translation studies   253

Process-specific Practical Cmputer-aided Translation Studies

Process-specific Practical Computer-aided Translation Studies covers the following areas:

(1) *Inputting* refers to the entering of the source text into the computer for machine processing (Zheng and Lee 2000). As there are many writing systems in the world, inputting is not an easy task. A number of inputting methods are discussed, and issues such as optical character recognition and the proofreading of the scanned texts are also covered.

(2) *Tagging* involves providing each word in a sentence with a grammatical label so that its syntactic structure can be shown and properly used. Much has been done on part-of-speech tagging, taggers, and statistical tagging (Leech 1997: 19–33).

(3) *Concordancing* involves using a concordancer to analyse the lexical, grammatical, and textual structure of the source text. It has been generally recognized that 'concordancing' is an effective way of analysing the source text. Concordancing is the first stage of the technology-oriented translation procedure, where statistical and lexical information of the source text are given in a systematic manner (Ulrych 1997).

(4) *Editing* (Rav 1995: 47–57) consists in fine-tuning the text to make it acceptable to the target user. Editing can be further divided into pre-editing, interactive editing, and post-editing. Pre-editing and post-editing are related to machine translation, while interactive editing is for computer-aided translation.

(5) *Checking* avoids errors in the target text. Checking is usually done computationally by checkers, such as 'Controlled Language Checkers' for the proper usage of controlled language text, 'Grammar Checkers' for grammatical accuracy, 'Spelling Checkers' for spelling correctness, 'Style Checkers' for stylistic reproduction, 'Syntax Checkers' for syntactical well-formedness, 'Translatability Checkers' for helping to make decisions on full-text translation, and 'TransCheck' for automatic validation of human and machine translation (Chodorow and Leacock 2000: 140–147).

(6) *Project Management* concerns the tracking and management of the progress of translation projects by a computer-aided translation project management system. Both server-based and web-based systems are used for managing translation projects in the digital age. Management is done in an efficient and effective manner with the use of translation management systems (Rico Pérez 2002).

Applied Computer-aided Translation Studies

This part covers topics which are indirectly related to computer-aided translation, including the following:

(1) *Lexicography,* which is related to the work of compiling, writing, and editing dictionaries. It is related to both machine translation and computer-aided

254 A theoretical framework for computer-aided translation studies

translation, as all systems need bilingual or multilingual glossaries. Lexicography is essential knowledge for anyone interested in machine translation. Topics in this area include computational lexicography, corpus lexicography, lexical acquisition, phrasal lexicon, and translation lexicon (Zhang 2006).

(2) *Translator Training* involves the preparation of translators in the technological competence to work with computer-aided translation systems (Koby and Baer 2003: 211–227). Translator training is no longer by bricks and mortar, but by bricks and clicks. Teaching is both online and offline. The training of translators is based on vocational needs and practical demands rather than on the academic interests of the teachers.

(3) *Translation Profession* refers to a service activity that is performed in a professional setting with computer-aided translation competence to achieve a professional aim (Schäffner 2004). To be able to play a role in a translation team through the use of a server-based computer-aided translation system is professionally essential. Translator competence, the core of which is technological competence, is considered as essential, in addition to translation competence, the core of which is bilingual or multilingual competence.

(4) *Translation Corpus* concerns corpora containing both source language texts and their translations. A translation corpus is based on parallel aligned texts. The use of translation corpora in parallel text processing is a topic which deserves further examination (Véronis 2000).

(5) *Translation Business* involves using machine translation or computer-aided translation systems to run a translation company. Issues such as global collaboration, vendor control, relationship management, profitability enhancement, and task outsourcing are some of the important topics in translation business (Schuh 2006).

(6) *Translation Market* refers to the size of clients who need translation services, human or machine. The market for translation has had a marked growth in recent years. It is getting more and more global, as international cooperation is the norm (Benitatto 2006).

Conclusion

The above is a proposed theoretical framework for computer-aided translation studies. For a framework in a new domain, there is undoubtedly room for improvement. It is hoped that this proposed framework will help to organize concepts and ideas in machine translation and computer-aided translation in a more coherent and logical manner.

References

Allen, Jeffery (1999) 'Adapting the Concept of "Translation Memory" to "Authoring Memory" for a Controlled Language Writing Environment', *Translating and the Computer 20*, London: The Association for Information Management.

A theoretical framework for computer-aided translation studies   255

Austermühl, Frank (2001) 'Computer-assisted Terminology Management', *Electronic Tools for Translators*, Manchester: St. Jerome Publishing Company, 102–123.

Bender, Oliver, Sasa Hasan, David Vilar, Richard Zens, and Hermann Ney (2005) 'Comparison of Generation Strategies for Interactive Machine Translation', *Proceedings of the 10th Workshop of the European Association for Machine Translation: Practical Applications of Machine Translation*, Budapest, Hungary, 33–40.

Benitatto, Renato S. (2006) 'A Global Review of the Translation Market Place', *Programme of the 30th Anniversary Conference of the Association of Translation Companies 2006: Building Strong Markets for Translations – Making Links and Seizing Opportunities*, School of Oriental and African Studies, University of London, the United Kingdom.

Brown, Ralf D. (2000) 'Automated Generalization of Translation Examples', *Proceedings of the 18th International Conference on Computational Linguistics (COLING-2000)*, Saarbrücken, Germany, 125–131.

Chan, Sin-wai (2008) *A Topical Bibliography of Computer (-Aided) Translation*, Hong Kong: The Chinese University Press.

Chan, Sin-wai (2009) *A Chronology of Translation in China and in the West: From the Legendary Period to 2004*, Hong Kong: The Chinese University Press.

Chan, Sin-wai (2012) 'Approaching Localization', Francesca Bartrina and Canne Milan Varela (eds.) *The Routledge Handbook of Translation Studies*, London and New York: Routledge, 361–376.

Chodorow, Martin and Claudia Leacock (2000) 'An Unsupervised Method for Detecting Grammatical Errors', *Proceedings of the 1st Meeting of the North American Chapter of the Association for Computational Linguistics*, Seattle, Washington, DC, the United States of America, 140–147.

Filatova, Elena, Vasileios Hatzivassiloglou, and Kathleen R. McKeown (2006) 'Automatic Creation of Domain Templates', *Proceedings of the Joint Conference or the International Committee on Computational Linguistics and the Association for Computational Lingtuistics (COLING/AL-2006)*, Sydney, Australia.

Holmes, James S. (1972/1987) 'The Name and Nature of Translation Studies', Gideon Toury (ed.) *Translation across Cultures*, New Delhi: Bahri Publications Pvt. Ltd., 9–24.

Holmes, James S. (1988) 'The Name and Nature of Translation Studies', James S. Holmes (ed.) *Translated! Papers on Literary Translation and Translation Studies*, Amsterdam: University of Amsterdam, 93–98.

Knight, Kevin and Jonathan Graehl (1997) 'Machine Transliteration', *Translating and the Computer 26*, London: The Association for Information Management.

Koby, Geoffrey S. and Brian James Baer (2003) 'Task-based Instruction and the New Technology; Training Translators for the Modern Language Industry', Brian James Baer and Geoffrey S. Koby (eds.) *Beyond the Babel Tower: Rethinking Translation Pedagogy*, Amsterdam and Philadelphia: John Benjamins Publishing Company, 211–227.

Leech, Geoffrey (1997) 'Grammatical Tagging', Roger Garside, Geoffrey Leech, and Anthony McEnery (eds.) *Corpus Annotation: Linguistic Information from Computer Text Corpora*, London: Longman, 19–33.

Merkel, Magnus (1993) 'When and Why Should Translations Be Reused', *Papers from the XIII VAAKKI Symposium*, Vaasa, Finland, 139–149.

Montgomery, Christine A., Bonnie Glover Stalls, Robert E. Stumberger, Naicong Li, Robert S. Belvin, Alfredo R. Arnaiz, and Susan Hirsh Litenatsky (1995) 'The

256 *A theoretical framework for computer-aided translation studies*

Machine-aided Voice Translation (MAVT) System', *Proceedings of the 14th Annual International Voice Technologies Application Conference (AVIOS-95)*, San Jose, CA, the United States of America, 101–110.

Munday, Jeremy (2001) *Introducing Translation Studies: Theories and Applications*, London and New York: Routledge.

O'Brien, Sharon (2004) 'Machine Translatability and Post Editing Effort: How Do They Relate?' *Translating and the Computer* 26, London: The Association for Information Management.

Patel, Agam and Dragomir R. Radev (2006) 'Lexical Similarity Can Distinguish between Automatic and Manual Translations', *Proceedings of the International Conference on Language Resources and Evaluation (LREC-2006)*, Genoa, Italy.

Prószéky, Gabor (2005) 'Machine Translation and the Rule-to-rule Hypothesis', Krisztina Károly and Ágota Fóris (eds.) *New Trends in Translation Studies: In Honour of Kinga Klaudy*, Budapest: Akadémiai Kiadó, 207–218.

Rav, Javanta (1995) 'Machine-aided Translation (MAT)-aspects of Editing,' *International Journal of Translation* 7(1–2): 47–57.

Rayner, Manny (1995) 'Speech Translation and Text Translation: Similarities and Differences', *Proceedings of the 6th International Conference on Theoretical and Methodological Issues in Machine Translation (TMI-95)*, The University of Leuven Leuven, Belgium.

Rico Pérez, Celia (2001) 'Reproducible Models for CAT Tools Evaluation: A User-oriented Perspective', *Translating and the Computer 23*, London: The Association for Information Management.

Rico Pérez, Celia (2002) 'Translation and Project Management', *Translation Journal* 6(4).

Riezler, Stefan and John T. Maxwell III (2006) 'Grammatical Machine Translation', *Proceedings of the Human Language Technology Conference – Annual Meeting of the North American Chapter of the Association for Computational Linguistics (HLT-NAACL-2006)*, New York, the United States of America.

Sammer, Marcus, Kobi Reiter, Stephen Soderland Katrin Kirchhoff, and Oren Etzioni (2006) 'Ambiguity Reduction for Machine Translation: Human-computer Collaboration', *Proceedings of the 7th Biennial Conference of the Association for Machine Translation in the Americas (AMTA-2006): Visions for the Future of Machine Translation*, Boston Marriott, Cambridge, MA, the United States of America.

Scannell, Kevin (2006) 'Machine Translation for Closely Related Language Pairs', *Proceedings of the 5th SALTMIL Workshop on Minority Languages and the 5th International Conference on the Language Resources and Evaluation (LREC-2006): Strategies for Developing Machine Translation for Minority Languages*, Genoa, Italy, 103–108.

Schäffner, Christina (2004) 'Squaring: The Circle – The Contribution of Universities to the Needs of the Profession', *Annual Conference of the Association of Translation Companies: Getting in Shape for the Future – Working towards a New Environment for the Translation Profession*, School of Oriental and African Studies, University of London, the United Kingdom.

Schuh, Sarah (2006) 'Technology in Translation Businesses: An Industry Opinion', *Proceedings of the 6th Portsmouth Translation Conference: Translation Technologies and Culture*, School of Languages and Area Studies, University of Portsmouth, the United Kingdom.

A theoretical framework for computer-aided translation studies   257

Shih, Chung-ling (2006) *Helpful Assistance to Translators: MT & TM*, Taipei: Bookman Books Ltd.

Snell-Hornby, Mary (1972/1988) *Translation Studies: An Integrated Approach*, Amsterdam and Philadelphia: John Benjamins Publishing Company.

Somers, Harold L. (1998) 'Machine Translation: Methodology', Mona Baker (ed.) *Routledge Encyclopedia of Translation Studies*, London and New York: Routledge, 143–149.

Taylor, Chris and Anthony Baldry (2001) 'Computer Assisted Text Analysis and Translation: A Functional Approach in the Analysis and Translation of Advertising Texts', Erich H. Steiner and Colin Yallop (eds.) *Exploring Translation and Multilingual Text Production: Beyond Content*, Berlin and New York: Mouton de Gruyter, 277–305.

Toury, Gideon (1995) *Descriptive Translation Studies and Beyond*, Amsterdam and Philadelphia: John Benjamins Publishing Company.

Ulrych, Margherita (1997) 'The Impact of Multilingual Parallel Concordancing on Translation', Barbara Lewandowska-Tomaszczyk and Patrick James Melia (eds.) *Proceedings of the Conference on Practical Applications in Language Corpora* (*PALC-97*), Łódź, Poland.

Vallianatoll, Fotini (2005) 'CAT Tools and Productivity: Tracking Words and Hours', *Translation Journal* 9(4).

Veronis, Jean (2000) *Parallel Text Processing: Alignment and Use of Translation Corpora*, Dordrecht: Kluwer Academic Publishers.

Wang, Fu Lee, Deng Xiaotie, and Zhou Feng (2006) 'Towards Unified Chinese Segmentation Algorithm', *Proceedings of the 5th International Conference on Language Resources and Evaluation* (*LREC-2006*), Genoa, Italy.

Wu, Dekai (2000) 'Alignment', Robert Dale, Hermann Moisl, and Harold L. Somers (eds.) *Handbook of Natural Language Processing*, New York: Marcel Dekker, 415–458.

Yang, Xianze 楊憲澤 (2006) 《人工智能與機器翻譯》 (*Artificial Intelligence and Machine Translation*), Chengdu: Southwest Jiaotong University.

Zervaki, Thei (2002) 'Online Free Translation Services', *Translating and the Computer 24*, London: The Association of Information Management.

Zhang, Yihua (2006) 'Computational Lexicography and Computer-aided Dictionary-making', *International Conference on Computer-aided Translation: Theory and Practice*, Department of Translation, The Chinese University of Hong Kong, Hong Kong, China.

Zheng, Chen and Lee Kai-Fu (2000) 'A New Statistical Approach to Chinese Pinyin Input', *Proceedings of the 38th Annual Meeting of the Association for Computational Linguistics* (*ACL-2000*), Hong Kong, China.

6 The future of translation technology

Introduction

In recent decades, translation technology has become increasingly popular both in Asia and in the West. It is used by professional translators as a core component of a personal workstation, by occasional users as an important means of multilingual information mining, and by international corporations as the foundation of global translation management systems. All the drastic changes resulting from the use of technology in translation practice in past decades have brought a revolution in translation. It would not be improper to describe this great transformation from the traditional to the modern with the words of Zhao Yi 趙翼 (1727–1814), who says in his work *Reading Notes on Twenty-two Histories* (*Er Shi Er Shi Zha Ji*《二十史劄記》), that 'while people are still entrenched in their traditional thinking, a new milieu has been created by the will of Heaven' (人情猶狃於故見, 而天意已另換新局). Whether we like it or not, the technology revolution in translation is now with us.

Nobody knows the beginning of translation, nor its future. What we know is that translation has been with us since time immemorial. Some trace its origin to the legendary Tower of Babel. Others say that translation is as old as mankind; it is one of the oldest professions in the world.

Whatever it is, translation is no longer what it used to be and will continue to change according to the circumstances. In this chapter, we will take a look at its past and its future to see how it will move ahead in the years to come.

Translation: Its main divisions

Translation, as we know, is in part academic and in part vocational. It can be broadly divided into translation theory and translation practice. Translation theory covers the main ideas, concepts, principles, generalizations, or frameworks that explain, account for, or guide the act of translating. From the very old days to the present, both in China and in the West, various concepts or types of theories have been proposed. A study of these theories indicates the future directions for us to follow. Translation practice, on the other hand, covers three areas: text translation (translation), speech translation (interpreting), and machine

Table 6.1 Divisions of Translation

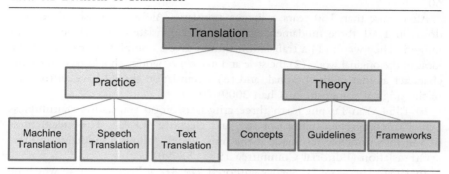

translation, including both machine translation and computer-aided translation. We will trace the major happenings in each area to see what lies ahead.

Translation theory: Past and present

The development of translation theory in the world can be divided into four periods, dominated firstly by the philological approach, secondly, by turns, thirdly, by corpus-based method, and lastly, by technology.

The philological approach (314–1964)

The philological approach, also known as the pre-linguistic approach, was the prevailing theory for a very long time, more specifically, from 314 to 1964. This approach to translation was based on generalizations drawn from translation of religious and literary texts, such as Bible translation and translation of classics in the West, and Buddhist translation and translation of Chinese classics in China.

The earliest discussion of theory may be traced to Dao An 道安 (314–385) in China, who chose to use the method of literal translation in translating Buddhist scriptures. To him, free translation was not usable in religious translation. In a work he wrote in 314, he said that in Buddhist translation, there were five errors to be avoided and three things that were difficult to accomplish (Editorial Committee 1988: 10–11).

Almost three centuries later, in 602, Xuanzang 玄奘, the greatest translator of the Tang dynasty, also shared Dao An's view and said that in rendering Buddhist scriptures, five types of Buddhist terms should be left untranslated, including (1) esoteric terms; (2) terms with many meanings; (3) things nonexistent in China; (4) ancient terms; and (5) terms for generating merits (Editorial Committee 1988: 87).

In the West, it was not until 1680 that John Dryden proposed the Three Categories of Translation, i.e., 'metaphrase', 'paraphrase', and 'imitation', which

260 *The future of translation technology*

were actually three types of translation methods for literary works (Chan 2009: 60).

After more than 160 years, a literary translator, Alexander Fraser Tytler, laid down in 1791 three fundamentals by which a translation should be made or judged. They were: (1) a translation should give a complete transcript of the ideas of the original work; (2) the style and manner of writing should be of the same character as that of the original; and (3) a translation should have all the ease of the original composition (Chan 2009: 70).

In 1854, Yan Fu put forth three criteria of good translation: faithfulness (*xin* 信), comprehensibility (*da* 達), and elegance (*ya* 雅). The succinctness of Yan Fu's principle has made it the most widely followed guideline in literary translation (Editorial Committee 1988: 88–90).

In 1957, Theodore H. Savory authored *The Art of Translation*, in which he put forward the well-known twelve guidelines for the translation of literary works (Chan 2009: 133–134).

Two years later, Roman Jakobson wrote an article entitled 'On Linguistic Aspects of Translation', in which he proposed three types of translation: (1) intralingual translation; (2) interlingual translation; and (3) intersemiotic translation.

The last scholar of this period is Georges Mounin, who in 1955 had authored *Les Belles Infideles*, in which he proposed the idea of 'beautiful but not faithful translation'. In his book, *Theoretical Problems of Translation*, written in 1963, he proposed the idea of a transparent translator whose presence in the translation is totally unnoticed (Xu 1988: 49–53).

The period is characterized by statements of opinions and ideas which are mostly empirical and largely anecdotal and subjective. Translators expressed their views on translation methods and suggestions, not frameworks or major concepts that guided the act of translating.

The emergence of non-philological approaches, turns, and frameworks (1964–1994)

Translation theory in the true sense of the word began in 1964 with Eugene A. Nida, who was known as the 'Father of Translation Theory' because he was the first scholar in modern times to write about the basic theory and practice of translation and to apply that theory to the translation of Scriptures. That theory is known as 'dynamic equivalence translation'.

The year 1965 is generally considered as the beginning of a long search for concepts and ideas that could make translation an academic discipline in its own right. In that year, J.C. Catford proposed the linguistic approach. Catford believes that 'theory of translation is essentially a theory of applied linguistics' (Nida 1964).

In 1972, we have the first framework of 'Translation Studies' proposed by James S. Holmes (Holmes 1972/1987: 9–24, 1988: 93–98). Five years later, in 1978, there was the emergence of the text-linguistic approach in translation

The future of translation technology 261

in Germany, and in Israel, Evan-Zohar proposed the polysystem theory (Even-Zohar 1978: 21–27). In 1980, the deconstructionist theory of translation based on Jacques Derrida appeared (Derrida 1987), and four years later, Katharina Reiss and Hans J. Vermeer developed an action-theoretic and purpose-oriented approach known as 'skopos theory' (Reiss and Vermer 1991).

In 1985, there was the rise of the Manipulation School in Europe. The term 'Manipulation School' was used by Mary Snell-Hornby, of the University of Vienna, to describe a group of translator scholars who view translation as a branch of Comparative Literature. Three years later, Snell-Hornby proposed an integrated approach to translation, attempting to put together concepts from translation-related disciplines to produce a syncretic approach, thus turning translation studies into a discipline in its own right (Snell-Hornby 1988: 22–23).

In 1991, Lance Hewson and Jacky Martin proposed a Variational Approach, which is a two-tier model that first isolates a wide set of paraphrastic possibilities and then goes through a series of selection procedures to produce a final text (Hewson and Martin 1991).

From 1990 to 2004, there were a number of 'turns' taking place in translation circles, including the 'Cultural Turn' proposed by Mary Snell-Hornby in 1990, referring to the shift of emphasis from linguistics to culture and ideology as a shaping force in translation studies; the 'Translator's Turn' proposed by Douglas Robinson in 1991, meaning a new opportunity for the translator to have somatic interactions with a text; and in 1992, the 'Hermeneutic Turn', which was the shift of emphasis from the linguistic to the hermeneutic approach.

Based on the above, we can make the following observations:

(1) Most ideas or concepts in translation studies come from experience in translating religious or literary texts.

(2) Most ideas or concepts in translation studies come from the West.

(3) All theoretical frameworks in translation have been proposed by Western scholars. This being the case, Chinese translators might find them inapplicable, if not totally unusable.

(4) Some translators lack the ability to analyse abstract terms, some of which have become standard terms in the field of translation, such as hermeneutic circle, functional equivalence, etc.

(5) Some translators lack the language competence to put theory into practice, and this leads to the misconception that some theories are not practical.

(6) Some translators have no experience to put ideas into practice, but it is through accumulated knowledge and experience that the workability of some ideas can be fully appreciated.

(7) Some translators find that some problems are pseudo-problems thought up by the theorist and thus have the impression that theory cannot offer much to a translator.

(8) Some translators find that the difficulties they face in translating cannot be solved by reference to translation theories.

262　*The future of translation technology*

Translators find that many of the ideas and concepts in the field are mainly empirical, prescriptive, and most regrettably, unprovable, since they are not based on any systematic documentary analysis.

We are faced with a huge number of terms that come from various people with different educational backgrounds and experience, and from different translators in different periods, working with different language pairs on different text types with different purposes in different cultural sources; it would not be advisable to simply select ideas from certain theories out of context or to apply concepts indiscriminately to translation practice without reference to their sources and contextualized applications.

The rise of corpus-based studies (1995–2003)

The year 1995 witnessed the rise of corpus-based translation studies. The use of corpus in translation has now become a major trend. Over the years, this corpus-based approach has proven to be verifiable, substantiable, and widely practicable. This approach is based on a body of written or verbal data collected for textual and linguistic analysis for translational purposes. It is through the use of corpora that generalizations can be made, concepts formed, and methods created.

The 'technological turn': From 2004 to the present

In 2004, the 'technological turn' in translation emerged. This refers to the wide and frequent application of computers to translation studies and practice. Few scholars would propose any concept or theory without the support of adequate data.

In sum, we can say that translation theory is now technology-oriented or corpus-based. This trend will be with us for a long time to come. Technology has changed the way we create translation theories.

Translation practice: Past and present

Translation practice refers to the act of translation in three major areas: text translation, speech translation, and machine translation (which includes both machine translation and computer-aided transaltion).

Text translations

Text translation refers to the translation of all types of texts, both literary and non-literary. In the last several thousand years, the translation of religious writings has been most dominant in both China and the West.

The earliest translation of religious writings can be traced to 285 B.C., with the work of *Septuagint*, which was the first partial translation of the Bible from Hebrew into Greek that took place during 285–249 B.C. in Egypt (Worth

The future of translation technology 263

1992: 5–19). With the spread of Christianity in the year 30, translation acquired the new role of disseminating the gospels of Christ.

About 350 years later, in 67, Zhu Falan 竺法蘭 translated the 《佛說四十二章經》 (*Sutra in Forty-two Sections Spoken by the Buddha*), which is the first translation of a Buddhist sutra made in China. The beginning of large-scale translations of Buddhist scriptures began in 147 with An Qing 安清. Since then, the translation of Buddhist scripture has been an activity involving more than thousands of translators over a period of 980 years (Editorial Committee 1988: 103).

The case is more or less the same with the translation of the Bible in the West. It started with the translation of the entire Bible into English by John Wycliffe in 1382 (Worth 1992: 66–70). This is generally regarded as the first complete translation of the Bible in English. About 150 years later in 1530, William Tyndale, 'The Father of the English Bible', was the first scholar to translate the Bible into English from the original Hebrew and Greek (Delisle and Woodsworth 1995: 33–35). Martin Luther translated the New Testament in 1521–1522 and the Old Testament in 1534. Another milestone is the publication in 1611 of The King James Version of the Bible, also known as the Authorized Version (Allen 1969).

In the translation of literary works, the case of China is highly illustrative. During the late Qing period, James Legge translated *The Chinese Classics* (1861–1886) and *The Sacred Books of China* (1879–1891). In 1889, Arthur Waley brought a large number of Chinese works to the attention of the English-reading public through his translations (Johns 1968; Morris 1970: 392–393).

In the translation of Western works into Chinese, the first two decades of the twentieth century are of great interest to us. In 1902, Liang Shiqiu 梁實秋 translated many of Shakespeare's plays into Chinese (Yu 1967: 4–6); in 1908, Fu Lei 傅雷 translated a large number of French literary works (Editorial Committee 1988: 221–222); and in 1912, Zhu Shenghao 朱生豪 translated all the plays of Shakespeare (Editorial Committee 1988: 751–752).

From 1920 to 1950, due to political needs, the translation of Marxist-Leninist literature was most popular in China.

It must be noted that what is not recorded may be as important, if not more important, than what is recorded; the translation of practical texts, which is seldom mentioned, is also significant. According to estimations, practical texts account for 96 per cent of the annual translation output in China. The remaining 4 per cent goes to literary translation. In other words, the bulk of text translation is in the area of practical texts, not literary texts. A major difference between literary and practical translation is that in literary translation, translators produce translations in a creative way what is written by their authors, while in practical translation, translators reuse and recycle translations whose source texts are mostly anonymous, which causes no infringement of intellectual property rights.

It must be noted that in text translation, the translation of the latest web information has grown enormously in the last ten years. In the past, text translation was mainly literary, religious, and physical. At present, text translation is practical, virtual, and instant. Technology has changed the texts we translate.

264   *The future of translation technology*

Interpreting

The earliest documentation of interpreting can be traced to 1122 B.C. Official records show that there were official interpreters and translators in the Foreign Affairs Bureau of the Zhou Dynasty to be involved in matters relating to its frontier tribes. This is the first piece of documentary evidence of multilingual interpreting in the world.

The year 1920 is significant, as interpreting in Europe was born because languages other than French were recognized as official diplomatic languages. The major techniques of interpreting were consecutive and whispering interpreting. The year 1945 is also worth mentioning. The Nuremberg Trials were held at Germany from 20 November to 1 October. The Nuremberg Trials were generally regarded as an event that invented simultaneous interpreting (Gaiba 1998).

The fact that interpreting has become more and more technological is demonstrated by developments in speech translation systems.

The use of speech as the fastest and most natural means of input to computers is important in several ways:

(1)   natural – because it requires no special equipment, just a microphone, nor any special training, simply speak out the words;
(2)   convenient – it allows fast and comfortable communication at a rate of 120 to 210 English words per minute without encumbering the hands or eyes; a typist can only reach 100 to 150 words per minute. And speech can be communicated over the telephone, the world's largest network; and
(3)   universal – because everybody can speak.

Speech translation systems, in turn, can be divided into:

(1)   Speaker-dependent system: this refers to a system that is tuned to recognize the speech of a particular speaker;
(2)   Speaker-independent system: This refers to a system that is tuned to recognize the speech of any speaker.

Nowadays, speech translation is widely used. Speech translation is the translation of a spoken text from one language to another. It is a process of automatic speech recognition and production. Well-known speech translation projects include:

(1)   'C-Star' stands for 'The Consortium for Speech Translation Advanced Research'. This project started in 1991 with informal bilateral collaborations between research laboratories interested in Automatic Translation of Spoken Language.
(2)   *Spoken Language Translator*, one of the first major projects in speech translation, began in the second half of 1992 with the aim of producing

The future of translation technology 265

a speech-to-speech translation system between English and Swedish in either direction within the domain of air travel information systems (ATIS).

(3) *Verbmobil* is a speaker-independent and bidirectional speech-to-speech translation system for spontaneous dialogues used with a mobile phone. It is an interpreting machine system that recognizes spoken input in the three languages of German, English, and Japanese, and analyses and translates it into spoken English.

Technology has changed the way we do interpreting.

Machine translation

Machine translation has advanced enormously since its inception in the 1940s. This can be clearly seen from an analysis of the countries that have conducted research and development in machine translation during the last 70 years.

It was not until the years after the Second World War that the climate was ripe for the development of machine translation. The invention of the computer, the rise of information theory, and the advances in cryptology all indicated that machine translation could be a reality. In March 1947, the idea of using machines in translation was proposed by Warren Weaver and Andrew D. Booth, who intended to make use of the newly invented computer to translate natural languages. Historically speaking, their idea was significant in several ways.

The following year witnessed the rise of information theory and its application to translation studies. The role of this theory has been to help translators recognize the function of concepts such as information load, implicit and explicit information, and redundancy (Shannon and Weaver 1949; Wiener 1954). On 15 July, Warren Weaver, now director of the Rockefeller Foundation's natural sciences division, wrote a memorandum for peer review outlining the prospects of machine translation, known in history as 'Weaver's Memorandum', in which he made four proposals to produce translations better than word-for-word translations (Hutchins 2000: 18–20).

The first machine translation system, the Georgetown-IBM system for Russian-English translation, was developed in the United States in June 1952. The system was developed by Leon Dostert and Paul Garvin, of Georgetown University, and Cuthbert Hurd and Peter Sheridan, of the IBM Corporation. This system had the capacity to translate from Russian into English (Hutchins 1986: 70–78).

Russia was the second country to develop machine translation. At the end of 1954, the Steklov Mathematical Institute of the Academy of Sciences began work on machine translation under the directorship of Aleksej Andreevič Ljapunov (1911–1973), a mathematician and computer expert. The first system developed was known as FR-I, which was a direct translation system and was also considered one of the first generation of machine translation systems (Hutchins 2000: 197–204).

266 The future of translation technology

In 1955, Japan became the fourth country to develop machine translation. Kyushu University was the first university in Japan to begin research on machine translation (Nagao 1993: 203–208). It was followed by China, which began research on machine translation with a Russian-Chinese translation algorithm jointly developed by the Institute of Linguistics and the Institute of Computing Technology (Dong 1988: 85–91; Feng 1999: 335–340; Liu 1984: 1–14).

Two years later, Charles University in the former Czechoslovakia began to work on an English-Czech machine translation system (Chan 2009: 132).

Nonetheless, with the publication of the ALPAC Report prepared by the Automatic Language Processing Advisory Committee of the National Academy of Sciences, which concluded with the comment that there was 'no immediate or predictable prospect of useful machine translation', funding for machine translation in the United States was drastically cut, and interest in machine translation waned considerably (ALPAC 1966; Warwick 1987: 22–37). Still, sporadic efforts continued to be made in the area. For instance, an important system was developed in the United States by Peter Toma, previously of Georgetown University, known as Systran, an acronym for System Translation. To this day, this system is still one of the most established and popular systems on the market. In Hong Kong, The Chinese University of Hong Kong set up the Hung On-To Research Laboratory for Machine Translation to conduct research into machine translation and developed a practical machine translation system known as 'The Chinese University Language Translator', abbreviated as CULT (Loh 1975: 143–155, 1976a: 46–50, 1976b: 104–105; Loh and Kong 1979: 135–148; Loh, Kong, and Hung 1978: 111–120). In Canada, the TAUM group at Montreal developed, in turn, a system for translating public weather forecasts known as TAUM-METEO, which became operative in 1977.

During the 1980s, the most important translation system developed was the EUROTRA system, which was able to translate all the official languages of the European Economic Community (Johnson, King, and Tombe 1985: 155–169; King 1982; King 1987: 373–391; Lau 1988: 186–191; Maegaard 1988: 61–65; Maegaard and Perschke 1991: 73–82; Somers 1986: 129–177; Way, Crookston, and Shelton 1997: 323–374).

After 30 years, we now have the very popular online machine translation system 'Google Translate' and more than fifteen cloud-based computer-aided translation systems. According to surveys, 54 per cent of professional translators use online translation systems on a regular basis.

Technology has changed the way we do translation.

The future of translation technology

In the last several decades, translation technology has moved ahead, along with the advances made in various related fields, such as computer science, linguistics, and mobile phonology. As there is no way to predict how technology itself will advance in the future, it is difficult to forecast what the future holds for translation technology. It is believed, however, that some of the themes and directions

The future of translation technology 267

that have emerged in recent decades or even years will continue to exert considerable influence on the development of translation technology, which include the globalization of translation, the creation of multiplicity, the redefinition of translation, the 'networkization' of pedagogy, the modernization of professionalism, the generation of neologisms, the formulation of concepts, the perfection of automation, the enterprisation of translation, the emphasis of practicality, the reorientation in research, and the change of approach.

Globalization of translation: From local to global

For a very long time in the past, translation was bound by locality. Almost every step in the production of a translation was done locally, including the selection and provision of translation services. With the invention of the Internet in 1973 and its popularity in 1983, and since the introduction of web translation systems, translation is no longer confined to any specific physical or national boundary. Translation is globally and instantly done, and translation services are readily available to a very large number of users wherever they are and whenever they need them. The globalization of translation can be clearly seen in (1) the existence of online translation companies that provide round-the-clock translation services in a wide range of languages, which resulted in the formation of the Association of Translation Companies in 1976 to represent the interests of translation purchasers (http://www.atc.org.uk); (2) the creation and usage of online machine translation systems, such as Google Translate; (3) the creation and usage of online computer-aided translation systems, such as Wordfast Anywhere; and (4) the establishment of online computer-aided translation management systems, such as SDL World Server.

It is believed that this globalization trend in translation will continue in the future with wider acceptance and stronger support.

Creation of multiplicity: From textual to multimodal

For a very long time, translation has been a matter of putting one linguistic text into another. But with the recent expansion in computer storage and advances in video technology, other forms of production, such as text-to-speech, text-to-picture, text-to-video, text-to-animation, text-to-diagram, and text-to-graph translations have also been explored. This form of multimedia translation, or 'intersemiotic translation', in Jakobson's terminology, is drastically different from the traditional mode of production.

As human translation cannot be multimodal, machine translation emulates its counterpart by its capacity and storage of different types of images. For the translation of tourist literature, sometime the adage 'a picture is worth a thousand words' is more telling in text-to-picture translation. In the future, we expect source messages to be translated in a more multimodal way.

The world of translation in the future will not be only textual, it will be multimodal. Meanings can be expressed not just by words, but also by different

268   *The future of translation technology*

forms of images and various types of sound. As images are beyond words and beyond cultures, they will be widely used in the future to help tear down the language and cultural barriers that separate so many language communities in the world.

Redefinition of translation: From the traditional to the technological

The first direction concerns the way translation is to be redefined in this digital age. As technology is increasingly used in translation practice and the translation industry, it is deemed essential that technology be given due emphasis in the definition of translation.

Translation has been defined in a traditional way, depending on one's view on the goals of translation, the nature of translation, the practice of translation, and the disciplines related to translation. This has given rise to a number of definitions which are either general or rooted in concepts before the advent of technology. A general and typical definition of translation in a dictionary, for instance, would be 'to transfer from one language to another', which means translating from the source text into the target text. Other definitions are based on different orientations. Translation, for example, has been defined as 'the art of re-expression'. According to Jean Delisle (1988: 3), translation is an art of re-expression based on writing techniques and a knowledge of two languages. Translation is also defined as an act of communication, or, to use the words of Eugene Nida, 'translating means communicating' (1972: 309–316). Basil Hatim and Ian Mason (1997) hold the same view and define translation in terms of communication, saying that translation is 'an act of communication which attempts to relay, across cultural and linguistic boundaries, another act of communication (which may have been intended for different purposes and different readers/hearers)'. To the culturalist, translation is the transmission of culture, an inter-cultural procedure. Scholars such as Susan Bassnett and Andre Lefevere, on the other hand, believe that 'translating is a cultural event and a culture-specific and culture-sensitive process' (Bassnett and Lefevere 1990). Some linguists regard translation as a language acquisition exercise and say that 'translation is a technique of language learning', which is a pedagogical view in the sense that it regards translation as a means of language acquisition. For hermeneuticians (Schmidt 1990: 1–9), 'every act of translating is an act of interpreting'. Interpreting here refers to the way we see things and not the way we say something in a different language. There are scholars who define translation as an act of information transfer. According to Vernay (1974: 237), 'translation is . . . an act which transfers information given in language A into language B in such a way that the amount of relevant information received in language B will be identical with that in Language A'. Related to this view is the definition of translation as a linguistic transfer or a comparative linguistic undertaking. Translation is substituting the linguistic forms of the source language with linguistic forms of the target language. Translation is 'the interpretation of linguistic/verbal text in a

The future of translation technology   269

language different from its own'. This approach to translation deals with translational issues primarily from the perspective of the differences in language structures. There are scholars who regard translation as a semantic transfer, holding the view that translation is 'rendering the meaning of a text into another language in the way that the author intended the text'. Also adopting a linguistic approach, some scholars believe that translation is a semiotic transfer. To them, translation is a process by which the chain of signifiers that constitutes the source-language text is replaced by a chain of signifiers in the target language which the translator provides on the strength of an interpretation. For literary translators, translation is a literary pursuit, a source of personal pleasure, and an engagement in creativity. Those who are more philosophical tend to believe that translation is an ideational transfer, referring to 'the transfer of thoughts and ideas from one language (the source language) to another (the target language) by means of the written word' (Chan and Pollard 1995).

It is clear that under the impact of technology, translation should be redefined in a more technological sense. A simple way of redefining translation is to say that translation is to 'transfer one language into another with the aid of technology' in order that the use of electronic tools or digital devices in translation practice is given due emphasis in the definition. In the future, this technological definition of translation will be generally accepted in the field.

Networkization of pedagogy: From bricks and mortar to bricks and clicks

It has now been widely realized that the use of translation technology is commercially essential and the training of computer-aided translators is professionally necessary. What distinguishes computer-aided translation teaching from the teaching of other translation courses is its pedagogical variety. In other words, there are many ways to train computer-aided translators. Training can be offered by different formal or informal sources, such as academic institutions, government organizations, system developers, user groups, professional bodies, agencies, and online tutorials. Training can be offered within or without physical environments. It is evident that the trend of moving from the traditional bricks and mortar approach to the modern bricks and clicks approach has emerged since the last decade.

One of the most common and formal ways of training technology-competent translators is to study translation technology at academic institutions. A number of tertiary institutions in different parts of the world have offered courses in computer-aided translation to provide qualified manpower for the translation industry. Translation teaching has changed greatly since the introduction of translation technology into translation programmes. The importance of training computer-aided translators is shown, partly at least, by the establishment of the first Master of Arts in Computer-aided Translation Programme by The Chinese University of Hong Kong in 2002 (Chan 2010: 83–154). Government organizations that provide translation services also offer training in computer-aided

270 *The future of translation technology*

translation. The European Union can be cited as an example. In its European Master's in Translation Programme (EMT), the learning of computer-aided translation is included in its curriculum. From the side of system developers, specific training in their systems in the form of online tutorials has been provided by system developers for a long time. Training workshops, particularly online 'webinars', are organized for different levels of users. User groups have forums to exchange views on specific issues on specific systems. Online forums initiated by individual translators in the capacity of user groups have become an informal way of gaining knowledge of computer-aided translation. The online forums provide a platform for system users in different parts of the world to exchange their ideas on the strengths and weaknesses of different computer-aided translation systems and share their experiences on the use of the systems. Translation agencies often provide training to their in-house or freelance translators so that they can work coherently as a team through a network translation management system. It is also becoming commonplace for translators to learn the knowledge and skills of computer-aided translation systems through the online tutorial videos provided by system suppliers.

This networkization of translation teaching is another trend that will be widely practiced for translator training in the future.

Modernization of professionalism: From craftsmen to technologists

The modernization of professionalism in translation will be another area that will be greatly affected by translation technology. It must be recognized that this is closely related to what Anderman and Rogers called the demand for 'intercultural mediators' (Anderman and Rogers 2006: xiii). In the views of Anderman and Rogers, 'the demand for intercultural mediators including translators and interpreters has grown as a result of many recent social, political and economic developments; these include legislative changes, the emergence of supranational organizations, the ease of travel, telecommunications, commercial pressures raising awareness of local needs, migration and employment mobility, and a heightened awareness of linguistic and human rights' (Quah 2006: xii).

Professionally, translators have evolved from craftsmen in the old days to technologists of the present digital age. The growth in the number of technology-competent translators is clearly seen in the increase of computer-aided translators, estimated to be around 200,000 in 2012. With the rapid establishment of computer-aided translation programmes in different parts of the world, the number of computer-aided translators will increase enormously. It is strongly felt that for the sake of professionalization, certification in the proficiency of translation technology is necessary and essential. This certification serves as a testimony to the holder's competence to translate a domain-specific text from a specific language pair, their knowledge of translation studies and translation technology, and their ability to process a text from one language into another through the use of a specific computer-aided translation system.

The future of translation technology 271

The process of modernizing the profession of translation will continue into the future.

Generation of neologisms: From old concepts to new vocabularies

The impact of translation technology on translation studies has been significant. Technology has influenced the development of translation studies in various aspects. It has replaced the old concepts with a new vocabulary based on new developments in the field and has given rise to corpus-based translation studies, which is based on data and statistics.

Technology has brought new concepts and terms to the field. In the past, we talked about loose or even ill-defined terms, such as sense-for-sense translation, free translation, faithfulness, spiritual resemblance, aesthetic translation, and the art of translation. Nowadays, with the use of translation technology in translation practice, we have new terms in our vocabulary, such as localization, interactive systems, controlled language, system sustainability, webpage translation, and translation memory. The emergence of these terms and the related concepts has changed the way translation is discussed and done.

The use of corpora in translation technology has given rise to corpus-based translation studies. It cannot be denied that the use of corpora in translation studies, as in the fields of lexicography and linguistics, is fast gaining momentum and will be a major trend in the future (Baker 1995: 223–243). This is something obvious, as what we get from corpora is verifiable, substantial, and widely practicable, while many of the ideas and concepts in the field of translation are mainly empirical, prescriptive, and cannot be proven, since they are not based on any database or systematic documentary analysis. We have a large number of terms that come from various people, with different educational backgrounds and experience, and from different translators in different periods, working with different language pairs on different text types with different purposes in different cultural situations. Since there are so many different concepts drawn from so many different sources, it would not be advisable to simply select ideas from certain theories out of context or apply concepts indiscriminately to translation practice without reference to their sources and contextualized applications. It is therefore clear that corpus-based research in translation is based on a body of written or verbal data collected for textual and linguistic analysis for translational purposes. It is through the use of corpora that more scientific generalizations can be made, concepts formed, and methods created. Technology, in this sense, has resulted in a drastic change of orientation in translation studies.

Formulation of concepts: From personal subjectivity to data-based objectivity

Translation technology has changed the way ideas and hypotheses in the field have been formed. In the past, concepts could be created without substantiation or proof. Concepts and ideas could be purely subjective and intuitional, relying

272 The future of translation technology

on personal insights. They were therefore mostly empirical, deductive, and unscientific. In recent decades, concepts and principles in translation have been formed through the use of translation corpora.

This change is significant, as translation studies has shifted from personal subjectivity to data-based objectivity. The observations and generalizations based on data will be adequately founded and useful to translation professionals and scholars. The formulation of concepts will be made in this manner for many years to come.

Perfection of automation: From machine translation to machine translation

It is true that machine translation between kindred languages may be, on the whole, acceptable, but it should not be denied that automatic translation between non-kindred languages is still far from satisfactory. That accounts partly for the birth of computer-aided translation as a more reliable way to produce quality translation. With machine translation getting increasingly better and producing quality translations for even non-kindred languages, we begin to rely more and more on machine translation, which accounts for the emergence of hybrid systems in the forms of computer-aided translation systems with the integration of machine translation and machine translation systems equipped with the function of translation memory.

Looking into the future, it is likely that we will rely heavily or even entirely on machine translation. Before then, there might be a period of transition in which computer-aided (human) translation will move to human-aided (computer) translation before we reach the stage of fully automatic machine translation. This means that we have travelled a long way before we return to the starting point, but with a huge difference – machine translation will then be fully automatic high-quality translation (FAHQT), which has been the goal that we have pursued for decades.

Enterprisation of translation: From profession to business

The impact of computer-aided translation on translation business is equally far-reaching. As far as profitability is concerned, computer-aided translation has made it possible for translation companies to translate faster and better with less cost. The use of computer-aided translation management systems has been popular in the West, and it is expected that companies in other parts of the world will follow suit. Some systems target international corporations, others set their target on local business. Both types of systems deserve our study and evaluation.

Translation is a business, an industry. It is part of what is known as 'entrepreneurial humanities'. With the savings in labour cost and faster turn-around time by the use of translation technology, there will be an increase in the number of translation orders, thus creating more income. What is clearly observable is

The future of translation technology   273

that with the aid of translation technology, translation is moving towards enterprisation. It is moving from profession to business.

Emphasis of practicality: From the literary to the practical

One of the major changes that translation technology will bring to the field is the growing attention given to the translation of practical texts. In the past, literary translation was dominant. Both in China and in the West, the translation of religious documents, such as Buddhist scriptures in China and the Bible in the West, and classics dominated the world of translation. Nowadays, we translate mostly practical texts and webpages. According to estimation, practical texts account for 96 per cent of the annual translation output in China. A major difference between literary and practical translation is that in literary translation, translators produce translations of the source texts in a creative and stylistic manner, while in practical translation, translators reuse and recycle translations whose source texts are mostly anonymous, which causes no infringement of intellectual property rights.

The translation of practical writings takes up a very large portion of the work of a translation company. The translation of webpages is also very popular. Computer-aided translation systems are ideal for translating practical and electronic texts. We note that the translation of the latest web information has grown enormously in the last decade. Computer-aided translation systems will continue to serve the function of bridging the language gaps of the source and target texts.

Reorientation in research: From craft to scholarship

Research on translation technology has become a major part of translation studies and practice in recent decades. More research on translation technology is expected in the future.

It is found that during the 58 years between 1948 and 2006, a total of 8,383 works have been published by 5,404 authors in either English or Chinese on 39 areas in translation technology (Chan 2008: xxix). For a very long time in the past, scholars in the field discussed translation from a literary and personal perspective. Nowadays, more and more attention has been given to translation technology. This shift in research direction is drastic and fundamental. The sudden and fast emergence of more than 799 works on translation technology that were published in China in the last few years is a strong indicator of a major reorientation of research areas for scholars in the field. This trend will continue for a long time to come. With computer(-aided) translation gaining more and more interest and attention, more and more academic programmes in this area will be established. It is also expected that more scholars will be able to look into the possibility of putting translation theories into practice through translation technology.

274 *The future of translation technology*

Change of approach: From reactive to proactive

The future of translation technology hinges on whether scholars and practioners in the field will proactively shift their focus from what they are doing now to what they need to do in the future. The field of translation has so far been reactive and backward-looking, with translators concentrating on what they need to do to meet what they are given and what has transpired in the world of translation. Ideas and concepts have been drawn from the past. Methodology has been based on what has conventionally been practiced. Research projects on translation have been conducted in the areas of history, literature, religion, and culture. While admitting that these areas are academically and intellectually important and rewarding, we do see the need of deploying at least some of our efforts to prepare ourselves for the changes which are now taking place on a global scale, and for the transformation in the translation profession in the future, which will drastically change the way translation is done.

This new orientation in translation is in essence a 'proactive approach'. This approach focuses on issues that will meet the expectations of the academic community at large and cater to the specific needs of some regions and domains in particular. A discipline needs to look back on what has happened in the past. But more importantly, it also has to be forward-looking, projecting into the future to see what has to be done. The world is constantly changing, in a state of flux, and in a way drastically and fundamental different from the past. To react to the needs and study the unchangeable past is important. To work on the changeable future is equally important and exceedingly challenging. Seen in this light, this proactive approach has to be based on informative data and reliable statistics, not on intuition, imagination, or personal experience. It has a lot to do with foresight and prediction, but little to do with hindsight. Translation technology can be effectively used to find out more about what the future holds for us and how it can help to meet the challenges ahead. Every discipline must move forward in the best possible way. The proactive approach proposed here is a novel concept and a new orientation. We need to work together to realize it with the help of translation technology.

Conclusion

The territory of technology knows no bounds. If necessity is the mother of invention, technology is the mother of change. Translation technology has brought drastic and fundamental changes to us in the past, and it will continue to do so in the future.

From what we have shown in the above, it can be clearly seen that we have long entered into a digital age in which translation technology plays an important role. With the growing popularity of mobile devices, such as mobile phones, machines and computers, in terms of tools, will be replaced by digital touch-points, and it is likely that mobile translation, which is already popular today, will remain so for a long time to come. The world of translation technology is

The future of translation technology 275

and will be full of inventions to facilitate communication between people in various language communities. Recently, it has been reported in the newspapers that a Word Lens has been developed to provide instant translation of phrases and sentences in the source language without having to photograph them into the mobile phone for machine processing. What seem to be gimmicks nowadays might turn out to be practical tools for us to understand each other in the future. In speech translation, there is considerable success in Google eSpeak, and it also seems that the day of having no barriers in verbal communication among different language communities may not be too far away.

As a growing number of major and minor languages in the world are translated or interpreted with the aid of translation technology, it is likely that we will soon be living in a world without Babel, in which there will be no language and cultural barriers. Everyone on earth will then be living in one world, in a world of peace and harmony, as described in the 'Great Unity' in the *Book of Rites*, a Confucian classic of the Han Dynasty.

Let us move towards a world without Babel as a target for us to achieve in the future. If this seems to be an impossible dream, it might not be inproper to conclude this book with two lines from the lyric of the song 'the Impossible Dream' in the movie *The Man of La Mancha*, originally authored by Don Quixote: 'to dream the impossible dream' and 'to reach the unreachable star'. Dreams, you never know, may come true one day.

References

Allen, Ward (ed.) (1969) *Translating for King James*, Nashville: Vanderbilt University Press.

ALPAC (1966) *Language and Machines: Computers in Translation and Linguistics*, Washington, DC: National Academy of Sciences, National Research Council.

Anderman, Gunilla and Margaret Rogers (2006) 'Series Editors' Preface', C.K. Quah (ed.) *Translation and Technology*, Hampshire: Palgrave.

Baker, Mona (1995) 'Corpora in Translation Studies: An Overview and Some Suggestions for Future Research', *Target* 7(2): 223–243.

Bassnett, Susan and Andre Lefevere (eds.) (1990) *Translation, History, and Culture*, London: Pinter.

Chan, Sin-wai (2008) *A Topical Bibliography of Computer(-Aided) Translation*, Hong Kong: The Chinese University Press.

Chan, Sin-wai (2009) *A Chronology of Translation in China and the West*, Hong Kong: The Chinese University Press.

Chan, Sin-wai (2010) 'A New Curriculum for the Teaching of Translation Technology: The Teaching of a Translation Project Course as a Case Study', Chan Sin-wai (ed.) *Special Issue: The Teaching of Computer-aided Translation, Journal of Translation Studies* 13(1–2): 83–154.

Chan, Sin-wai and David E. Pollard (eds.) (1995/2001) *An Encyclopaedia of Translation: Chinese-English, English-Chinese*, Hong Kong: The Chinese University Press.

Delisle, Jean (1988) *Translation: An Interpretive Approach*, tr. Patricia Logan and Monica Creery, Ottawa and London: University of Ottawa Press.

276 *The future of translation technology*

Delisle, Jean and Judith Woodsworth (eds.) (1995) *Translators through History*, Amsterdam and Philadelphia: John Benjamins Publishing Company and UNESCO Publishing.

Derrida, Jacques (1987) 'Des tours de Babel', *Psyché: Inventions de l'autre*, Paris: Galilée.

Dong, Zhendong (1988) 'MT Research in China', Dan Maxwell, Klaus Schubert, and Toon Witkam (eds.) *New Directions in Machine Translation*, Dordrecht-Holland: Foris Publications, 85–91.

Editorial Committee, *A Dictionary of Translators in China* 《中國翻譯家詞典》編寫組 (ed.) (1988) 《中國翻譯家詞典》(*A Dictionary of Translators in China*), Beijing: China Translation and Publishing Corporation.

Even-Zohar, Itamar (1978) *Papers in Historical Poetics*, Tel Aviv: The Porter Institute for Poetics and Semiotics, Tel Aviv: Tel Aviv University.

Feng, Zhiwei 馮志偉 (1999) 〈中國的翻譯技術：過去、現在和將來〉('Translation Technology in China: Past, Present, and Future'), Huang Changning 黃昌寧 and Dong Zhendong 董振東 (eds.) 《計算機語言學文集》(*Essays on Computational Linguistics*), Beijing: Tsinghua University Press, 335–440.

Gaiba, Francesca (1998) *The Origins of Simultaneous Interpretation: The Nuremberg Trial*, Ottawa: University of Ottawa Press.

Hatim, Basil and Ian Mason (1997) *The Translator as Communicator*, London and New York: Routledge.

Hewson, Lance and Jacky Martin (1991) *Redefining Translation: The Variational Approach*, London: Routledge.

Holmes, James S. (1972/1987) 'The Name and Nature of Translation Studies', Gideon Toury (ed.) *Translation Across Cultures*, New Delhi: Bahri Publications: Pvt. Ltd., 9–24.

Holmes, James S. (1988) 'The Name and Nature of Translation Studies', James S. Holmes (ed.) *Translated! Papers on Literary Translation and Translation Studies*, Amsterdam: University of Amsterdam, 93–98.

http://www.atc.org.uk.

http://www.language-usa.com.

http://www.orangetranslations.com.

http://www.translation-services-usa.com.

http://www.translatorindia.com.

Hutchins, W. John (1986) *Machine Translation: Past, Present and Future*, Chichester: Ellis Horwood.

Hutchins, W. John (2000) *Early Years in Machine Translation*, Amsterdam and Philadelphia: John Benjamins Publishing Company.

Johns, Francis A.T. (1968) *A Bibliography of Arthur Waley*, London: Allen and Unwin.

Johnson, R.I., Margaret King, and Louis des Tombe (1985) 'Eurotra: A Multilingual System under Development', *Computational Linguistics* 11(2–3): 155–169.

King, Margaret (1982) *EUROTRA: An Attempt to Achieve Multilingual MT*, Amsterdam: North-Holland.

King, Margaret (ed.) (1987) *Machine Translation Today: The State of the Art*, Edinburgh: Edinburgh University Press.

Lau, Peter Behrendt (1988) 'Eurotra: Past, Present and Future', Catriona Picken (ed.) *Translating and the Computer 9: Potential and Practice*, London: The Association for Information Management, 186–191.

Liu, Yongquan et al. 劉湧泉等 (1984) 《中國的機器翻譯》(*Machine Translation in China*), Shanghai: Knowledge Press.

Loh, Shiu-chang (1975) 'Machine-aided Translation from Chinese to English', *United College Journal* 12(13): 143–155.

Loh, Shiu-chang (1976a) 'CULT: Chinese University Language Translator', *American Journal of Computational Linguistics, Microfiche* 46: 46–50.

Loh, Shiu-chang (1976b) 'Translation of Three Chinese Scientific Texts into English by Computer', *ALLC Bulletin* 4(2): 104–105.

Loh, Shiu-chang and Kong Luan (1979) 'An Interactive On-line Machine Translation System (Chinese into English)', Barbara M. Snell (ed.) *Translating and the Computer*, Amsterdam: North-Holland, 135–148.

Loh, Shiu-chang, Kong Luan, and Hung Hing-sum (1978) 'Machine Translation of Chinese Mathematical Articles', *ALLC Bulltein* 6(2): 111–120.

Maegaard, Bente (1988) 'EUROTRA: The Machine Translation Project of the European Communities', *Literary and Linguistic Computing* 3(2): 61–65.

Maegaard, Bente and Sergei Perschke (1991) 'Eurotra: General Systems Design', *Machine Translation* 6(2): 73–82.

Morris, Ivan (ed.) (1970) *Madly Singing in the Mountains: An Appreciation and Anthology of Arthur Waley*, New York, Walker, and London: Allen and Unwin.

Nagao, Makoto (1993) 'Machine Translation: The Japanese Experience', Sergei Nirenburg (ed.) *Progress in Machine Translation*, Amsterdam: IOS Press, 203–208.

Nida, Eugene A. (1964) *Toward a Science of Translating*, Leiden: E.J. Brill.

Nida, Eugene (1972) 'Communication and Translation', *The Bible Translator* 23(3): 309–316.Quah, Chiew Kin (2006) *Translation and Technology*, Basingstoke and New York: Palgrave Macmillan.

Reiss, Katharina and Hans J. Vermeer (1984/1991) *Grundlegung einer allemeinen Translationstheotie (A Foundation of Translation Theory)*, Tubingen: Max Niemeyer Verlag.

Schmidt, Dennis J. (1990) *Hermeneutics and the Poetic Motion: Translation Perspectives V: 1990*, New York: Center for Research in Translation, State University of New York at Binghamton.

Shannon, Claude L. and Warren Weaver (1949) *The Mathematical Theory of Communication*, Urbana: University of Illinois Press.

Snell-Hornby, Mary (1972/1988) *Translation Studies: An Integrated Approach*, Amsterdam and Philadelphia: John Benjamins Publishing Company.

Somers, Harold L. (1986) 'Eurotra Special Issue', *Multilingual* 5(3): 129–177.

Vernay, Henri (1974) *Essai sur l'organisation de l'espace par divers systemes linguistiques: Contribution a une linguistique de la traduction*, Munchen: Fink Munchen.

Warwick, Susan (1987) 'An Overview of Post-ALPAC Developments', Margaret King (ed.) *Machine Translation Today: The State of the Art*, Edinburgh: Edinburgh University Press, 22–37.

Way, Andrew, Ian Crookston, and Jane Shelton (1997) 'A Typology of Translation Problems for Eurotra Translation Machines', *Machine Translation* 12(4): 323–374.

Wiener, Norbert (1954) *The Human Use of Human Beings: Cybernetics and Society*, New York: Houghton Mifflin.

Worth, Roland H. (1992) *Bible Translations: A History through Source Documents*, Jefferson, North Carolina, and London: McFarland and Company, Inc., Publishers.

Xu, Jun 許均 (1988) 〈簡論喬治.穆南的翻譯觀〉('On Georges Mounin's Views on Translation'), 《語言與翻譯》 (*Language and Translation*) 1: 49–53.

Yu, Kwang Chung 余光中 (1967) 〈梁翁傅莎翁〉('Shakespeare through Liang Shih-ch'iu'), 《書和人》 (*Books and People*) 66: 4–6.

Index

abbreviation 79, 81, 89, 96, 114, 131; chatroom 130
acceptability 128; ideological 116
accessibility 35, 106, 168
accuracy 75, 102, 126, 128, 142, 216; grammatical 139, 145, 253
acronym 4, 30, 79, 131, 199, 266; detection 232; unknown 131
across 7, 12, 15, 39, 41–5, 47, 51, 57, 68, 71, 76, 84, 103, 124, 171, 221; Across Language Portal 17; Across Language Server 44, 171; Across Language Server 4.0 Service Pack 1 17; Across Language Server 5.0 18, 171–2; Across Language Server v.5 Service Pack 1 19; Across Language Server v.55 23, 80, 84; Across Language Server v.57 172; Across Personal Edition 168, 171–2; crossAuthor 172; crossAuthor Linguistic 172; crossCheck 172; crossDesk 171; crossProject 172; crossTank 99, 171–2; crossTerm 171–2
adaptation 109, 119, 133–5, 139; cultural 133
addition 14, 82, 132
Advanced International Translations (AIT) 14, 17
Advanced Leveraging 16; Advanced Leveraging Translation Memory (ALTM) 10, 193–4
aids 3; authoring 172; machine 2; translation 6, 245–6; visual 90
AidTrans Soft 14

AidTransStudio 1.00 14, 41–3, 45
Alchemy Catalyst 195–6; Alchemy Publisher 42–4, 47, 221; Alchemy Publisher 2.0 17; Alchemy Publisher 3.0 20; Alchemy Publisher Analysis Expert 86; Alchemy's Language Exchange 85
algorithm 4, 8, 112, 218, 251–2, 266; alignment 20; fuzzy research 6; recognition 74
Align Assist 1.5 22; aligner 81; alignment 81–2, 105, 169, 171, 180, 204, 213, 252; alignment box 82; alignment project 82; alignment tool 6, 8, 12, 14, 82, 185, 204; alignment workflow 82; automatic 194, 204, 252; bilingual data 4; clause 252; document 202, 232; fuzzy 252; integrated 8, 14; lexical 252; LF 194; online 212; paragraph 81–2; phrase 81–2, 252; sentence 81–2, 106, 252; statistical 252; terminology 252; text 40, 81–2, 252; word 81, 252
Allen, Jeffrey 129
Al-Shabab, Omar Sheikh 33
Ambassador TMS 180
ambiguity 52, 54, 249; lexical 53, 55, 249; linguistic 249; syntactical 53, 55, 249
An, Qing 安清 263
analysis 18, 32, 49, 86–7, 92, 97, 102, 118, 122, 141, 245, 249, 265; Analysis Agent 103; automatic linguistic 11, 87, 271; componential 32; computer 97; document 11;

280   *Index*

grammatical 5; linguistic 87, 249, 262, 271; manual 97; morphological 87, 107, 249; natural language 87; semantic 87, 107, 249; sentence 9; sentential 87; source 87, 249; syntactical 87, 107, 249; systematic documentary 262, 271; text 30, 87, 249; textual 262, 271; translation 87, 249; translation fee 209; translation memory 215; usage 209

Anaphraseus 16, 41, 45, 47, 123, 168, 172–3

Anchovy 1.0–0 21

AnglaHindi 104

An-Nakel Al-Arabic 9, 11; MLTS An-Nakel Al-Arabic 125

AnyMem 14, 17, 41, 43, 47, 123

Apertium 172, 194, 221–3

AppleTrans 15, 46, 168, 173–4, 196; AppleTrans 1.2 174

application 19, 37, 48, 77, 94, 97, 110, 119–20, 167, 169, 175, 194, 197, 200, 207, 217, 246, 265; browser-based 212; computer-aided translation 174; contextualized 262, 271; corporate mobile 200; cross-platform 174; email-based 182; free 197; fuzzy matching 179; independent 194; IT 246; localized 119; offline 123; single-user desktop 207; software 44; standalone 171; third party 194, 231; web 183; Windows 183, 208

approach 5, 130, 217–18, 220, 250, 259, 267, 274; corpus-based 218; dictionary-based machine translation 128, 220; facsimile 135; function-based 68; hermeneutic 261; hybrid 250; IBM hybrid 220; integrated 261; knowledge-based 219; linguistic 260–1; literal 128; machine translation 218, 220; non-philological 260; philological 259; phrase-based SMT 230; pre-linguistic 259; proactive 274; purpose-oriented 261; statistical 230; syncretic 245, 261; text-linguistic 260; transfer 107; variational 261

AppTek's TranSphere Machine Translation 221–2, 224; TranSphere 224

Araya 41–2, 44, 47, 124, 170, 182–3; Araya XLIFF Editor 183

Arthern, Peter 3

Atlas 35–7, 42, 47, 95–6, 124, 126, 170, 234

author 18, 33, 52–3, 127, 134–5, 137, 142, 245–6, 263, 269, 273; authoring 17, 19, 40, 44, 54; authoring aids 172; authoring system 55; authoring tool 23, 55, 172; controlled 52, 55

Automatic Language Processing Advisory Committee (ALPAC) 1–2; ALPAC Report 266

Automatic Language Processing Systems (ALPS) 3

automation 4, 6, 267, 272; process 18

Autshumato 46–7, 124, 174, 221; Autshumato Integrated Translation Environment (ITE) 1.0 18, 41, 174; Autshumato Project 174

Babel Fish 221, 225

Baker, Mona 134

Balás, Kis 14

Balasubramanian, K. 94

Bar-Hillel, Yehoshua 1

Bassnett, Susan 138, 268

Belazar 194, 221–2, 225

Bell, Roger 31–2

Belloc, Hilaire 132

Benito, Emilio 7

Bly, Robert 34

Booth, Andrew D. 1, 265

Bowker, Lynne 116, 167

box 71–2, 122; alignment 82; dialogue 73, 111, 119; inline 122; inline text 122; list 119; project information dialogue 71; target text 35; translation 104, 122

Brace, Colin 13

Bratcher, Robert G. 135

browser 30, 88, 123, 189, 205, 211, 224, 246; browsing 211; Google Chrome 185, 211; Internet 211; web 16, 41, 69, 123, 183

Index   281

CafeTran 41–5, 47, 124, 170, 221
Casagrande, Joseph B. 140
CatCradle 42
Catford, J. C. 136, 140–1, 260
Cevirmen 104
Champollion, Yves A. 9
change 14, 21, 24–5, 55, 57, 89, 92–3,
    103, 109, 111, 114, 119–20, 134,
    258, 267, 271–4; legislative 270;
    logographical 114; semantic 92–3;
    typographical 114
character 15, 70, 81, 89–90, 99, 106,
    112, 197, 230, 250; alphabetic 115;
    character set 114; double-byte 179;
    simplified 37; simplified Chinese 113;
    special 114, 230; standard Chinese
    113; traditional 37; Unicode 234
check 145; automated quality assurance
    16; automatic 39, 145; automatic
    spell 232; checking 31, 54, 145,
    253; commercial controlled language
    53–4; context 213; controlled
    language 53–4, 253; grammar
    145, 177, 253; in-house controlled
    language 53; number 145; open-
    source spell 197, 208; punctuation
    145; quality 182, 184, 215; quality
    assurance 23, 171, 179–80; space
    145; spell 24, 56, 112, 126, 146,
    214, 231–2; spelling 145, 200, 253;
    style 146, 253; syntax 146, 253; text
    146; translatability 146, 250, 253;
    translation 146; typography 146
CIMOS 8
client 4, 16, 35, 57, 72, 79, 83, 100,
    106, 110, 117–18, 146, 170, 176,
    181, 200, 214–15, 254
code 8, 30, 89–91, 111–12, 180, 203;
    area 115; code list 49; country 115;
    language 49; language-and-region
    49; postal 115; programme 110;
    semiotic 138; source 105, 168, 173;
    sublanguage 49
collaboration 16, 107, 174, 181, 188,
    197, 264; global 254; project 58,
    170, 209
Collaborative Translation Platform
    (CTP) 20
collaborativity 30, 57

communication 6, 22–3, 35–6, 38, 54,
    75, 118, 171, 186, 188, 264, 268,
    275; digital 40; intercultural 115;
    internal 35; Internet-based 131;
    language 37; online 175; reciprocal
    111; simultaneous 187; verbal 275
compatibility 11, 15, 24, 30, 41,
    45, 47–8, 174, 177; language 48;
    systematic 24; translation memory 86
compensation 133; compensation
    by merging 133; compensation by
    splitting 133; compensation in kind
    133; compensation in place 133
competence 254, 270; bilingual 38,
    128, 254; computer-aided translation
    254; cultural 39; language 142,
    261; linguistic 39; multilingual 254;
    professional 38–9; technological
    39, 254; translation 39, 128;
    translator 39, 254
comprehensibility 54, 127, 260
comprehension 30–3, 90, 126, 132;
    source text 31–2
computer 1, 38–9, 41, 53, 55, 69,
    73, 75, 167–8, 219, 251, 253,
    265; computer processing 52, 54;
    computer science 266; computer
    storage 267; computer system 74,
    244; computer technology 218;
    desktop 211
computer-aided translation 1–6, 9, 11,
    21, 25, 30, 33–4, 38–9, 52, 57, 69,
    73–4, 76–7, 81, 88, 97–8, 102, 108,
    120, 132, 144, 167, 186, 194, 220,
    233, 244, 247, 249–54, 259, 262,
    269–70, 272–3; bilingual corporate
    103; bilingual language-pair-specific
    104; browser-based 211; cloud-
    based 24, 211, 266; commercial
    4, 6–7, 25, 198, 246; computer-
    aided translation application 174;
    computer-aided translation company
    4, 14; computer-aided translation
    industry 10; computer-aided
    translation management system 267,
    272; computer-aided translation
    programme 270; computer-aided
    translation project 30; computer-
    aided translation project management

282 *Index*

system 253; computer-aided translation software 17, 167, 203; computer-aided translation studies 244; computer-aided translation suite 210; computer-aided translation system 4–7, 12–13, 24, 30, 34, 38, 40–5, 47–9, 55–8, 60, 68–70, 72, 77–8, 81, 85–6, 88, 95, 98, 100–6, 108, 112, 118–20, 122–3, 144, 167, 171, 175–6, 185, 188, 190, 198, 201, 209, 213, 222, 226, 233, 247–52, 254, 270, 272–3; computer-aided translation tool 13, 20, 37, 39–40, 46–7, 49, 68, 73, 80–1, 96, 99–100, 102–3, 106, 167–8, 173, 176, 178, 180, 182–3, 187–8, 190, 195, 201, 207–14; corporate 103; cross-platform 46, 196; cross-platform standalone 170; customizable 7; custom-specific 103; example-based 103; file-based 105; free 168–9, 171, 172–3, 174, 177, 180–3, 185, 187, 207, 208, 212, 214; hybrid 6, 221; intelligence-based 104; interactive 78, 252; Internet-based 170, 171, 210–11; language-pair-specific 104; language-specific 104; low-cost 168; Microsoft Word plug-in 191; MS Word-based 172; multilingual 108, 192; multilingual language-pair-specific 104; network 102; networked 38; online 189, 267; open-sourced 105, 172, 174, 179, 194–5, 225; paid 167, 175, 196; prediction-based 105; publication-oriented 105; second-generation 104; sentence-based 105; server-based 24, 38, 106, 182, 170, 196, 215, 254; standalone 124, 169, 206; standalone freeware 207; statistical 106; terminology-based 106; text-based 106; translator-based 107; web-based 24, 107, 123–4, 210; web-based bilingual 107; web-based multilingual 108; web browser-based 123; word-based 172

concept 2–3, 16, 23, 30, 33–4, 38, 41, 48, 52, 55, 60, 68, 70, 76, 83, 95, 97, 105, 108, 133, 142, 144, 175, 180, 182, 193, 218, 245, 248, 251, 254, 259–62, 265, 267–8, 271–2, 274; domain-specific 97

concordance 30; automatic term 200; automatic terminology 207; bilingual 87, 97; built-in 97; concordancer 30, 34, 81, 87, 96, 98, 253; concordancing 87, 97, 253; electronic 39; independent 97; linguistic 87; monolingual 97; multilingual 87, 97; system 97; translation memory 200

confidentiality 85, 181, 190, 212

consistency 19, 54, 57, 95, 99, 102, 119, 125, 170, 174, 176, 209, 216, 250; style 102; stylistic 102; terminological 57, 80, 102, 114, 119; terminology 16, 102; translation 99

context 6, 38, 42, 73, 76, 79, 86, 90–2, 94, 99–100, 106, 114–15, 120, 126, 128, 135, 137, 139, 141, 144, 177, 209, 213, 217–18, 250, 252, 262, 271; cultural 140–1; global 100; local 100; original 10; referential 137; social 140–1; translation 97

controllability 30, 52

conversion 35–6, 133, 200; currency 35

Corel CATALYST 10

corpora 213, 218, 254, 262, 271; bilingual 96, 97, 106, 213, 218; corpus 78, 89, 97, 173, 262; corpus evidence 97; domain-specific 96; general 89; online 15; online multilingual 173; parallel 96, 174; pre-existing 218; translation 248, 254, 272

Corporate Translation Management (CTM) 8; Corporate Translation Management 3.5 15

correspondence 95; global 135; linguistic 138; one-to-one 53, 144; sentence-to-sentence 136

cost 4, 40, 54, 60, 99, 117, 120, 128, 176, 185–6, 207, 216, 232, 272; actual 40; labour 272; post-editing 228; translation 102, 177, 216

Crossroad 170, 234

Crowdin 47, 124, 174–5, 185

crowdsourcing 19, 120, 175

C-Star (The Consortium for Speech Translation Advanced Research) 264

Index 283

CULT (The Chinese University Language Translator) 266
culture 90, 110, 115–16, 133–4, 138, 142, 261, 268, 274; receptor 134; source 133–4, 139; source language 133–4; target 139
customizability 30, 55, 179; customization 55–6, 169, 201; editorial 55; engineering 200; individual 200; language 56; lexical 56; lexicographical 56; linguistic 56, 200; machine translation system 57; resource 57; syntactical 56–7; system 55; website 57

Dao An 道安 259
data 5, 23–4, 33–4, 55, 68, 73–4, 86, 96, 106, 177, 185, 212, 218, 230, 233, 244, 271–2; bilingual 96; centralized translation 102; change 83; creation 83; data analysis 34, 68, 86; data application 68; data collection 68, 73; data creation 68, 73; data delivery 68; data editing 34, 68, 120; data exchange 24–5; data format 68; data management 55; data mining 68; data mining system 7; data processing 34, 41, 86–7, 95, 98, 108; data retrieval 34; data reuse 68; data storage 84, 169–70; data type 11; data updating 34; image 43; informative 274; linguistic 251; monolingual 230; parallel 230; public-domain 212; stored 251; text 13; translation 38, 100; verbal 271; written 271
database 5, 16–18, 21, 34, 56–7, 59–60, 76–7, 82–3, 86, 107, 120, 130, 144, 252, 271; bilingual 4, 39, 83, 102; bilingual text 82; Bitext 21–2; central 99; database creation 57; database engine 11; database maintenance 8, 57; database updating 57; electronic 82; exchange 83; external 82; glossary 33, 103; memory 216; multilingual 77; online 123, 246; speech 248; term 39, 59, 181; terminology 76–7, 103, 246; textual 248; translation 5–6, 10; Web SQL 184

date 73, 83, 89, 110, 114, 134–5; change 83; creation 83; date format 114; due 60, 73; project completion 73; project creation 73; system 73
decoder 218; decoding 32, 75; original text 33
definition 76, 79, 82, 85, 89, 94, 96, 108, 134, 167, 171, 175, 268–9; date of 89
Déjà Vu 7–8, 12, 41–5, 47, 51, 86, 98–100, 103, 168, 175–7, 195–6, 221, 229; Déjà Vu 1.0 7, 12; Déjà Vu 2.0 8; Déjà Vu beta v2.0 8; Déjà Vu Interactive (DVI) 8; Déjà Vu TEAMserver 176; Déjà Vu Workgroup 19; Déjà Vu X 11, 79, 86, 98; Déjà Vu X2 19, 21, 68, 71, 80, 84, 121; Déjà Vu X3 Professional 176; Déjà Vu X3 Workgroup 176
Delisle, Jean 31, 33, 268
Derrida, Jacques 261
dictionary 5, 7, 9, 19, 87–8, 91, 93, 95–6, 98, 104, 138, 183, 199–200, 206, 219, 246, 253, 268; abridged 89; advanced learner's 89; alphabetical 88; bilingual 87–8, 96, 104, 179, 218; built-in 198; classified 88; concise 89; customized 9, 56–7, 107, 200, 214; dictionary. com 96; dictionary consultation 3; dictionary database 5; dictionary entry 89; dictionary structure 198; domain-specific 200; electronic 5, 88, 200, 207; elementary learner's 89; etymological 88; external 6; free online 189; general 88, 219; historical principles 88; language-specific 50; monolingual 88, 96; multilingual 87–8, 104; multilingual user 177; multiple-unit 96; multiple-unit online 96; non-system 34, 95; normalization 232; online 30, 88, 96, 146, 206; openoffice 146; paper 88; pocket 89; printed 39; project-specific bilingual 98; pronunciation 88; reverse 89; single large general-purpose 199; single-unit online 96; specialized 88, 104, 220, 232; Standard 95; synonym 89; system 31, 56, 95,

284   *Index*

104; task-specific 97; Technical 95;
thesaurus 89; translation memory 98;
User 14, 95, 200, 232; visual 89
disambiguation 249–50; reference 217;
word 220; word-sense 249
document 12, 15–17, 19, 21, 40–3, 47,
57, 73–4, 83, 98–9, 119, 122, 137,
143, 174–5, 179, 181, 193, 198,
225, 227; blurred 74; creased 74;
document analysis 11; documentation
17, 77, 105, 109, 112, 119, 227,
264; documentation format 17, 20;
document format 7, 11–12, 42,
171, 196, 198, 204, 208, 211, 227;
document formatting 174; document
management 22; existing 248; faded
74; handwritten 74; language 100;
legislative 129; multiple 170; official
95; pre-translated 59; printed 73,
248; project-based 76; project-
specific 76; religious 273; software
119; source 24, 76, 124; tagged 106;
terminology 200; TMX 107, 197;
translated 15; translation 24, 71,
184–5, 188; translation memory 200
domain 52, 55, 72, 79, 83, 90, 97, 104,
177, 189, 232, 249, 251, 254, 265,
274; application 218; denotational
93; domain expert 78; specialized 230
Dostert, Leon 2
Dr. Eye 123, 170, 234
Dryden, John 136, 259

edit distance 129; data 34, 68, 120, 125,
249; editing 33, 42, 73, 120–1, 126,
128, 129, 132, 216, 253; editing
environment 34, 78, 121, 123–4;
editing platform 99, 121; editor 5, 88,
106, 123, 209; full 129; interactive 34,
40, 120, 125, 129, 132, 253; manual
technical 4; maximum 129; minimal
129–30; multi-format translation 171;
online 215; online translation 232;
parallel translation 123–4; platform-
dependent 121; platform independent
121; post 34, 37, 40, 126, 128–30,
132, 181, 200, 251, 253; pre 40, 52,
55, 128, 132, 251, 253; proprietary 6;
rapid 129–30; technical 4, 41;

terminology 188; text 41, 173, 177;
TMX 183; translation 12, 123–4,
198, 208; translation memory 188;
translator 252; universal 8; XLIFF
Editor 124
edition 19, 169, 187, 191, 199, 210–11,
215, 227; academic 190; business
227; cloud 168; corporate 179;
developer 190; educational 187;
enterprise 187–8, 191; free 168, 188;
graduate 179; Internet 22; Internet-
based 209; office 191; personal 179,
187, 227; Pro 227; professional
169; server 168, 205; server-based
179, 191, 209, 216; ServerFive
188; standalone 19, 22, 25, 170,
216; standard 169; team 23, 191;
translation management platform 187;
ultimate 190; university teaching 179
efficiency 10, 58, 116, 174, 177, 193, 202,
216; translation 105; translator's 15
Elanex Translation Inventory 106
emulativity 30, 34
engine 223; automatic 107; hybrid 232;
linguistic analysis 203; MT 20, 106;
online 7; RBMT 230; translation 7
enterprisation 267, 272–3
environment 86, 122, 172; corporate
70; cultural 133; environment
variables 111; GNOME desktop
169, 182; graphic 46; Integrated
Localization 14; international 85;
MS Word 208, 213; network 170;
networked 85, 177; noisy 75; open-
source desktop 182, 234; physical
269; platform-dependent 121–3;
platform independent 121, 124;
plug-in 122; server-based 207; shared
work 57; single 172; single translation
174; standalone 19; text plug-in
122; translation 174, 207; translation
network 85; translation workbench
20; website plug-in 122–3
equivalence 136, 139–40; absolute
93–4; connotative 94; cultural 94,
133, 134; definitional 94; denotative
94; descriptive 94, 134; dictionary
93; direct 134; equivalent 87, 93,
95, 102, 106, 184; explanatory 94;

Index 285

formal 140; functional 134, 142, 261; grammatical 136; lexical 138; linguistic 138; multiple 94; natural 94; nil 139; official 94; one-to-one 134; optimal 87–8, 93, 100, 140; optimal target language 140; phonological 95; poetic 95; potential 87, 93, 96, 140; pragmatic 95; provisional 95, 143; single 95; target cultural 134; target language 140, 143, 220; translation 33, 94, 97, 142
error 55, 119, 125–7, 130, 230, 253, 259; lexical 55; linguistic 127; major 126; minor 126; phrasal 55; referential 127; stylistic 127–8; syntactical 127; terminological 127; typographical 55; typological 127–8
Esperantilo 41, 44, 177; Esperantilo 0.993 177; Esperantilo language 177; EsperantiloTM 47, 124, 177, 234
ESTeam 177–8; ESTeam Translator 177
ETOC (Easy TO Consult) 5
Euramis (European Advanced Multilingual Information System) 21, 182
Eurolang 8; Eurolang Optimizer 7–8, 11–12, 104
EUROTRA 266
Evan-Zohar, Itamar 261
Expert Advisory Group on Language Engineering Standards (EAGLES) 82
explanation 38, 87–9, 94, 97, 132, 134–6, 141, 143, 180, 244, 248
expression 15–16, 39, 55, 60, 77, 87–8, 90–5, 128, 134, 136, 138–9, 141, 233, 249; alternate 90; bilingual 218; elliptical 132; existing 139; facial 93; illogical 219; local 130; set 90, 131; source 95, 138; source language (SL) 94, 134, 143; source-text (ST) 136, 141; target language 139; target text (TT) 136, 141

Felix 41–3, 47, 123
file 41, 59, 72–3, 76, 199, 232; Adobe FrameMaker 8, 17, 44, 211–12, 215; Adobe FrameMaker 7.0 12; Adobe FrameMaker MIF 8, 12, 16; Adobe InDesign 12, 43, 208, 211–12, 215; Adobe InDesign 2.0 12; Adobe

InDesign CS2 15; Adobe InDesign CS5 20; Adobe InDesign CS6 23; Adobe PageMaker 12, 44; Adobe PageMaker 6.6 44; Adobe PageMaker 7 44; ASP 17; AutoCAD 44; CVS 13, 18; desktop publishing 211; DITA 215; electronic 73, 82; eXtensible Markup Language (XML) 179, 190, 214, 227; file format 10, 12–14, 99, 105, 169, 174, 179, 185–6, 190, 194, 198–9, 210–11, 215; file menu 76; filename 41; filename extension 41; file production 202; file type 41, 117, 186, 209; gettext 182; HTML5 227; Hypertext Markup Language (HTML) 10, 12, 16–17, 41–2, 106, 113, 185, 190, 199, 204, 215, 228, 232; Isometry 185; Java 10, 15, 45, 105, 111, 199, 208, 211, 215; localization 175, 196; Microsoft Access 43, 191; Microsoft Excel 11–12, 16, 43, 185, 187–8, 190, 204, 212, 232; Microsoft Excel 2007 192, 206; Microsoft PowerPoint 11–12, 42, 187, 206, 212, 232; Microsoft PowerPoint 2007 192; Microsoft SQL Server 2005 191; Microsoft Visio 215; Microsoft Word 5, 7–8, 10, 12, 17, 49, 122–3, 172, 187–8, 190, 198, 204, 206–8, 210, 212, 232; Microsoft Word 6.0 213; Microsoft Word 2007/2010 21, 24, 41, 185, 192, 213; multiple 125, 232; OpenDocument (ODF) 196, 198, 211, 232; OpenDocument Spread Sheet 192; OpenDocument Text 192; Open Office 16, 45, 199; OpenXML 196; Portable Document Format (PDF) 11–12, 20, 42, 106, 204, 211–12, 215, 232; project 72, 83; Quark 15, 44; QuarkXPress 8, 12; QuarkXPress 5 12; QuarkXPress 7 18; QuarkXPress 8 20; QuarkXPress 8.1 20; QuarkXPress 9.0–9.2 23; RAR 191; RESX 17, 211, 215; Rich Text Format (RTF) 13, 190, 204, 212, 215, 232; Safari 184; SGML 17, 106, 204; source 60, 82, 192, 198, 199; standalone 83; subtitle 43;

286   *Index*

tab-delimited 13; tagged 248; target 82; text 41, 45, 104; TMX 192; translated 60; translation memory 216; TSV 183; TTX 212, 215; TXML 212; TXT 183, 204, 232; Word 16, 248; XHTML 190, 199; XLIFF 1.2 18; XML 192, 199, 204, 215, 227; XML Localization Interchange File Format (XLIFF) 17, 44, 105, 171, 192, 199, 208, 210–11

filter 8, 12, 198, 210, 232; dictionary 198; filtering 86, 169; filter set 79; quick 79; user-defined 79; XLIFF 198

Fluency 35, 41–4, 47, 57, 68, 73, 96, 124, 178, 221, 229; Fluency Chat Server 35; Fluency Enterprise Solutions 179; Fluency Translation Suite 2011 179; Fluency Translation Suite 2013 80, 121, 179

ForeignDesk 7, 12, 168, 179; ForeignDesk 5.7.3 179; ForeignDesk v5.0 9, 13

format 114, 198, 200, 209, 248; address 115; currency 115; date 114; document 171, 198, 204; number 115; original 199; text 197; time 114; TMX 197

Fortis 41–5, 47, 124; Fortis Dictionary Window 96; Fortis Revolution Editor 125

framework 167, 174, 197, 244, 246–8, 254, 259–60; integrated 245; prototypological 245; theoretical 244–8, 254, 261; translation procedure 32

freelancer 10, 22, 59, 69, 210

Free Translation 221

frequency 77, 89, 135, 142–3; frequency data 89; frequency order 77

Fu, Lei 傅雷 263

function 2–3, 8, 12, 14, 18–19, 21–2, 24, 30, 34–7, 51, 60, 68–9, 72–4, 77–8, 81–3, 86, 88, 90, 92, 96–100, 105, 107–8, 111–12, 120–2, 124–6, 137, 146, 167, 169–70, 172, 177, 183, 188, 198, 202, 207–8, 214, 216–17, 219, 232, 250–1, 265, 272–3; batch processing 19; built-in 7, 12; computer-aided translation 101, 200;

database access 191; functionality 8, 10, 19–20, 60, 105, 111, 183, 188–9, 192, 198, 210, 250; leveraging 193; machine 112; machine translation (MT) 14, 36; management 103; project management 20, 40, 167, 190, 194, 208; proofreading 18; quality assurance 214; spell-check 24, 231; terminology management 208; translation memory 106, 199

Fusion 3.1 19, 41, 43, 47, 123, 170; Fusion Collaborate 3.0 18; Fusion One 18

Gábor, Ugray 14

GE-CCT 47, 123, 170, 179

generation 4, 57, 126, 171, 232, 267, 271; target text 52; text 144, 146, 249; translation 101

globalization 7, 21, 109, 110–11, 113, 267; globalization company 10; globalization process 109

Globalization and Localization Association (GALA) 47–8

GlobalSight 41–4, 47, 124, 180–1, 221, 229; GlobalSight SaaS 180–1; GlobalSight TMS 180

gloss 79, 89, 135, 138; extratextual 135; intratextual 138

glossary 21, 76–7, 79–80, 88, 95–6, 105, 107, 135, 138, 174, 181, 184–5, 189–90, 198, 200, 204–5, 208, 212; bilingual 88, 254; centralized 205; customized 105; domain-specific 97; glossary manager 21; glossary memory 216; multilingual 88, 254; specialized 77; user 216

Google 22, 79, 175, 181, 212, 221, 232; Google Chrome 183–4; Google eSpeak 275; Google MT 22; Google Translate 120, 122, 172, 179, 181, 185–6, 194, 206, 211, 215, 222, 225–6, 266–7; Google Translator Toolkit 41–2, 46–7, 120, 124, 168–9, 181–2, 212, 221

grammar 90, 138, 172, 249; context-free 249; dependency 249; functional 249; grammar marker 89; grammar rule 54; grammaticality 126–7;

Index 287

head-driven phrase structure 249; lexical-functional 249; Montague 249; phrase structure 249; simplified 52, 249; source language 136–7, 220; stochastic 249; target language 136, 220; transformational 32; translation 249; universal 249

GRIPS 4, 6

GTranslator 44, 169, 182; GTranslator 1.9.7 182

Hatim, Basil 31–2, 268

Heaney, Seamus 142

Heartsome 7, 46–7, 182–3, 196; Heartsome TMX Editor 124; Heartsome Translation Studio 8.0 22; Heartsome Translation Suite 15, 41–5, 170, 221

Hervey, Sándor 133

Hewson, Lance 261

Heyn, Matthias 6

Higgins, Ian 133

Holmes, James 244, 260

Hongyahu 47, 170, 234

Huajian 7, 12; Huajian IAT 11, 41–2, 47, 123, 234; Huajian Multilingual IAT 15

Hummel, Jochen 4

Hunt, Timothy 39

Hutchins, John 3, 101, 121

IBM701 2; IBM Translation Manager/2 (TM2) 6–7, 12–13, 198, 220, 233

information 3, 36–7, 41, 48, 57, 79, 83, 87–91, 93–4, 96–7, 109, 112, 119, 124–7, 129–30, 132, 134–7, 140, 170, 175, 181, 183, 185–6, 202, 219–20, 231, 246, 268; audio 74; bilingual 182, 219; biographical 175; context 111; explicit 265; global 120; grammatical 90; implicit 265; informational management system 120; information assimilation 37, 217; information dissemination 217; information explosion 127; information interchange 217; information load 265; information management 4; information

technology 4, 24; information theory 265; information transfer 268; informativeness 127; informativity 126; language-dependent 110; language-specific 110; lexical 87, 219, 253; localizable 111; multilingual 258; statistical 87, 253; text 122; updated 119; web 263, 273

input 33, 39, 52, 75, 117, 121, 264; human 121, 167; inputting 253; inputting method 74–5, 253; speech 75; spoken 265

interface 6–8, 16, 19–20, 22, 46, 74, 104, 120, 123, 173, 203, 205, 209; cross-platform web 200; customizable 19; dictionary style 8; editing 123, 183, 192; graphic user (GUI) 111; Java user 214; professional 205; single user 175; user 46, 105, 109, 111, 118–19, 124, 168, 187, 194, 198, 203, 206; Windows DDE 22; WYSIWYG 179

internationalization 109, 111, 115, 117; software 110

Internet 19, 35, 57, 69, 85, 96, 116, 168, 170, 191, 246, 267; Internet address 57; Internet browsing 211; Internet connection 211; Internet Explorer 16, 229; Internet user 109

interpolation 132, 138

interpretation 112, 138, 143, 218, 268–9; back 33; consecutive 264; interpreter 174, 264, 270; interpreting 218, 258, 263–5, 268; interpreting machine system 265; multilingual 264; official 264; simultaneous 264; source text 32; whispering 264

Isometry 124, 183–5, 211; Isometry 2.0 183; Isometry 3 184–5

István, Lengyel 14

iTranslate4 212, 226, 232; iTranslate4eu MT 221–2

Jakobson, Roman 138, 260, 267

Kade, Otto 139

Kay, Martin 3, 38, 169

288 *Index*

knowledge 9, 33, 55, 88, 128, 133, 219, 254, 261, 268, 270; academic 40; computer 110; grammatical 249; knowledge base 16, 218; linguistic 16; specialized 33; translation 39; world 217

Knyphausen, Iko 4

Környei, Tibor 8

label 112; grammatical 253; linguistic 90; translation 95, 143

Lancaster, Mark 7

language 3, 5–7, 11, 13–15, 23–4, 32, 36–7, 41, 48–51, 56, 71–2, 75, 81, 84, 88–91, 93–4, 97, 103, 108–10, 113, 132, 136–9, 141–2, 144–6, 167, 169–70, 174–5, 177, 179, 183–4, 186–7, 190, 196–8, 200, 204, 206, 208–9, 211, 219, 222–3, 225–32, 247, 249–50, 252, 264–70; automatic 72; bi-directional 183; character-based 208; controlled 52–5, 249, 271; double-byte 183; ICQ 131; Indo-European 36, 51, 111; input 55; intermediary 137; ISO 639 196; ISO-639-1 179; kindred 137, 272; language acquisition 268; language background 38; language code 49, 196; language combination 56, 86, 189; language communication 37; language community 94, 134, 268, 275; language detection 72; language industry 193; language intelligence 206; language learning 37, 268; language pair 18–19, 21, 72, 85, 96–7, 104, 138, 170, 174, 177, 181, 189, 199, 222–7, 229–30, 232, 249, 262, 270–1; language processing 13; language service provider (LSP) 4, 9, 69, 110, 171, 215, 233; language structure 269; language system 138; language teaching 137; language technology 9, 178, 216; language usage 97; left-to-right 16; localization 110; maintenance 120; major 36, 49, 105, 217, 275; markup 41; minor 36, 275; minority 217, 223; multiple 8, 12, 103, 110, 170, 232; natural 1, 52, 74, 249–50, 265; net 131;

non-Indo-European 51; non-kindred 272; one-byte 112; output 249; preferred 53; project 71; receptor 32, 127, 131; right-to-left 185; source 6, 32, 55–6, 71, 76, 79, 81, 94, 96, 104, 110, 125, 132–4, 138–9, 141, 143, 268–9, 275; source text 71; specified input 249; specified output 249; strategic 120; target 6, 33, 35, 56, 71, 76, 79, 82, 93–4, 99, 104, 110, 113, 125–7, 132–3, 136, 138–9, 141, 143, 219–20, 229–30, 268–9; target text 71; two/three-byte 112; unknown net 131; WordBasic 213

LEC 221, 226–7; LEC Translate 222, 226–7

Lefevere, André 138, 268

Legge, James 263

Levy, Jiri 140

lexicography 91, 248, 253–4, 271; computational 254; corpus 254

lexicon 15, 79–80; bilingual 220; controlled 52, 249; phrasal 254; topic-specific 10; translated 79; translation 254

Liang, Shiqiu 梁實秋 263

license 16, 69, 190, 210; GNU GPL 16; initial 176; licensing 69, 169; licensing management 209; server 210; Wordfast 16

Linear B Searchable Translation Memories 106

Lingo 41–2, 44

Lingotek 41–5, 47, 185, 229; Lingotek Collaborative Translation Management System 185; Lingotek Collaborative Translation Platform 24, 46, 125, 185–6, 221

Lingua et Machina 15

linguistics 245, 261, 266, 271; applied 260; computational 6, 126; descriptive 137

locale 79, 113; source 83; target 83

localizability 118; localizability test 118

localization 16–17, 56, 98, 108–10, 112–16, 118, 120, 183, 185, 271; built-in 98; cultural 115; image 189; independent 98; in-house

Index 289

117; linguistic 113; localization company 120; localization engineer 117, 119; localization group 117; localization industry 109–10, 119, 198; Localization Industry Standards Association (LISA) 20, 24, 47–8, 83; localization language 110, 120; localization manager 118; localization memory store 9; localization plug-in 10; localization process 117, 189, 200, 202; localization project 109, 115, 117–18, 196, 202; localization project management 117; localization project team 116; localization software 9, 113–14; localization specialist 110, 117; localization system 34, 119; localization team 117; localization technology 17; localization tool 109; localization workflow 20, 118, 202; post-localization 118; pre-localization 117; reverse 120; software 108–9, 111–13, 115; visual 17; web 42, 108–9, 111, 115, 120; webpage 42

Locke, William N. 1

Logic-Based Machine Translation (LMT) 12

LogiTerm 42–3, 47, 123, 186; LogiTerm 5.2 21, 186; LogiTerm Pro 186; LogiTerm Web 186–7; LogiTerm We Extension Module 186

Logoport 11, 195, 209

Logos 221

LogoVista 11, 123, 125, 170, 227, 234; LogoVista PRO 2013 22

LongRay CAT 47, 123, 186, 221; LongRay CAT 3.0 19, 186

Loughridge, Michael 133

Lucy LT 221–2, 227; Lucy LT KWIK Translator 228

Luther, Martin 263

machine translation (MT) 1–3, 6–7, 9, 12, 30, 34–5, 37, 53, 55, 81, 87, 98, 108, 126, 129, 136–7, 144, 146, 177, 180, 185, 207, 212, 216–17, 219–20, 230–1, 233–4, 248–9, 253–4, 258–9, 262, 265–6, 272; case-based 217; concept-based

217–18; context-based (CBMT) 218; corpus-based 218; data-driven 218; example-based (EBMT) 7, 15, 103, 175, 177, 218; free 231; fully automatic 272; general-purpose 55; hybrid 232; instant 9; instant text 232; interactive 3, 252; interlingua-based 219; internal 205; knowledge-based 14, 219; logic-based 6, 220, 233; machine-aided translation 2; machine translation engine 106, 112, 167, 174–5, 177, 179, 181, 209, 211, 215, 218, 221, 226, 233; machine translation industry 232; machine translation output 126; machine translation provider 232; machine translation quality 55; machine translation services 231; machine translation system 3, 7, 11, 34–5, 52, 55–6, 58, 81, 98, 100, 105–7, 118, 120, 126–8, 130–1, 167, 172, 174, 182, 186, 194, 199, 202, 207, 217–20, 222, 226, 234, 246, 249–52, 254, 265, 272; machine translation technology 6–7, 200; machine translation tool 172, 217; memory-based 105, 107, 218–19; n-gram-based 219; online 179, 206, 221, 233; open-source 222; Pangloss Mark III 218; rule-based (RBMT) 207, 219, 224; shake-and bake 220; statistical (SMT) 218, 220, 224–5, 230; statistics-based 218; third-party 228; transfer-based 105, 220, 227; translation memory-based 107; word-for-word 206

MadCap Lingo 16, 41, 43–4, 47, 125; MadCap Lingo 2.0 18; MadCap Lingo 3.0 18; MadCap Lingo 4.0 20; MadCap Lingo V9 124

Manson, Andrew 16

marker 91, 122, 136; grammar 89; grammatical 136; lexical 136; part-of-speech 91; segmentation 122; stylistic 136

Martin, Jacky 261

Mason, Ian 31–2

match 5, 86, 98–9, 103, 122, 181, 206, 220; character-string-based

176; context 17, 19, 24, 99, 175; deep 193; dictionary 208; dual 209; exact 38, 83, 85, 98–9, 103–4, 106–7, 120; full 3, 4; fuzzy 5, 33, 77, 83, 85, 98–100, 103–5, 120, 122, 176, 177, 179, 194, 208, 209, 232, 252; glossary 208; greatest 99; guaranteed 98–9; Guaranteed Matching 99; in-context 99; In Context Exact (ICE) Matches 99; in-context perfect 99; Leveraged Match 100; linguistically enhanced 176; low-score 177; machine translation 122, 181; matching 34, 99, 106, 133, 138, 170, 216, 218, 252; matching percentage 179; matching rate 199; match propagation 194, 208; match rate 85, 122; match retrieval technique 176; no 120; 100% leveraged 99; perfect 5, 99; PerfectMatch 16, 24, 99; phrase 106; target-language 209; translation 124; translation memory 214; word 106

meaning 32–4, 53, 88–91, 97, 126–7, 135, 140, 143, 267; affective 91; associative 91; basic 91–2; change of 93; cognitive 91; collocational 91–2; combinatory 92; connotative 92; contextual 92, 94; core 91–2; denotative 91–2; derogatory 92; designative 92; dictionary 93; emotive 91–2; evaluative 92; fuzzy 92; grammatical 33; identical 142; intended 33, 141; lexical 33, 92, 94; literal 93; narrowing of 93; new 93; one-word one 53; original 94; pragmatic 95, 140; primary 93, 138; prosodic 93; referential 92–3; reflected 93; rhetorical 33; shades of 93; social 91, 93

Melby, Alan 3, 130

MemoQ 14, 41–4, 47, 51, 124, 168, 187–8, 196, 221, 229; MemoQ 2.0 16; MemoQ 3.0 17; MemoQ 4.0 20; MemoQ 4.5 20; MemoQ 4free 188; MemoQ 6.0 23; MemoQ 6.2 23, 68, 71, 80, 84, 121; MemoQ server 14, 188; MemoQ Server 2014 189; MemoQ Server Enterprise 188; MemoQ ServerFive 188

MEMOrg 41–3, 189; MEMOrg 2.0 189; Online MEMOrg Translation Memory (MEMOrgTM) 189

MemorySphere 106, 221

Memsource 41, 43, 47, 190, 221, 229; Memsource Cloud 22, 46, 123, 168, 190–1; Memsource Cloud 2.0 22, 190; Memsource Cloud 2.8 23; Memsource Cloud 4.3 190; Memsource Editor 22–3, 123, 190; Memsource Personal 168; Memsource Plug-in 22; Memsource Server 22, 168; Memsource Web Editor 125, 190

message 32, 37, 111, 116, 126, 140–1, 170, 175, 182, 198, 227; alternative 35; default 111; instant 227; message content 141; message dissemination 37; message table 182; source 126, 267; source text 36, 136

MetaTexis 41–5, 47, 105, 107, 123, 190, 192, 221; MetaTexis 1.0 11, 190–1; MetaTexis 2.0 11, 13; MetaTexis 3.0 19; MetaTexis 3.17 191; MetaTexis for Word 191; MetaTexis Server 191

method 3, 18, 34, 37, 52–3, 74, 88, 95, 103–4, 114, 126, 128, 132–3, 136–9, 141–5, 171, 176–7, 245, 250–2, 259, 262, 271; block-out 132; classification 167; common 132; copy-and-paste 74; corpus-based 259; data-capturing 74; general 132; human translation 132; image-conversion 136; inputting 74–5, 253; key-in 74; keying-in 105; machine translation 219; methodology 250–1, 274; modification 139; partial translation 136; teaching 246; translation 97, 120, 132–5, 138–9, 141, 143–4, 260; transparent 139

Microsoft Bing 172, 175, 179, 186, 221–2, 228; Bing Translator 225, 229; Microsoft Translator 211–12, 228–9

MindReader 6

Moses 221–2, 227, 229–30

Index 291

Moumin, Georges 135, 260
MT2007 16, 47, 169, 191–3, 234
Multiconcord 87
Multicorpora 229
Multi-Lingual Translation System
 (MLTS) 107, 170, 234
Multilizer 14
MultiTerm 5, 13; MultiTerm 2 6;
 MultiTerm Dictionary 13; MultiTerm
 Lite 13; MultiTerm Pro 13;
 MultiTerm Professional 1.5 8
MultiTrans 7, 12, 41–4, 47, 103, 123,
 192, 195, 221; MultiTrans 3 10,
 13; MultiTrans 3.5 11; MultiTrans
 3.7 14; MultiTrans 4 14; MultiTrans
 Prism 21–2; MultiTrans Prism
 5.5 21; MultiTrans Prism 5.6
 193; MultiTrans Prism Blue 194;
 MultiTrans Prism Enterprise Server
 193; MultiTrans Prism Red 194;
 MultiTrans Prism Yellow 194
Munday, Jeremy 244, 246

Nagao, Makoto 218
name 48, 70, 80, 82, 84, 113, 127,
 130–1, 136–7, 172, 222, 225–7;
 art 131; bilingual 250; command
 111; file 41; geographical 143;
 group 131; login 86; multilingual
 250; name entity 250; name
 transliteration 139; object 131;
 personal 130–1; place 130–1,
 140; project 71, 121; proper
 127, 130–1, 134, 137, 143, 250;
 trademark 131; translated 139; user
 70; variable 111
networkization 267, 269
Newmark, Peter 139, 142
Nida, Eugene 31–2, 91, 132, 136,
 260, 268
note 79, 83, 90, 135; cultural
 135; linguistic 135; textual 135;
 translational 135

Okapi Framework 42–5, 194
OmegaT 7, 10, 41–2, 45–7, 49, 51,
 71, 121, 125, 168, 174, 194–8, 207,
 221, 225, 229; OmegaT 2.6 80, 84;
 OmegaT 3.0 68

OmegaT+ 41–2, 45, 47, 125, 196–8;
 OmegaT+ 1.0M3.1 196
omission 127, 139–40, 142; general
 140; grammatical 140
Open Language Tools 42, 44–7, 125,
 198; Open Language Tools 1.3.1 198
OpenOffice.org 194, 215; OpenOffice.
 org Writer 172
OpenTM2 20, 47, 125, 198–9;
 OpenTM2 v 0.9.5 199
OpenTMS (Open Source Translation
 Management System) 47, 199
OpenWordfast 41, 172
operating system 6, 10, 14, 41, 45–6,
 69, 73, 111, 167–72, 177, 183, 189,
 192, 196, 204, 224; Android 185,
 208; Apple 46; computer 47; DOS
 5; DOS operating system 12; IBM
 47; interface-based 46; Linus 167,
 172, 174, 177, 182–3, 185, 190,
 194, 198, 208; Macintosh 190; Mac
 OS 46, 167, 169–70, 172–4, 185,
 194, 198; Mac OS 10.3 174; Mac
 OS X 46; Microsoft 9, 22, 45, 233;
 Microsoft 2003 11; Microsoft Office
 208, 211, 215, 229; Microsoft Office
 2003 12, 22; Microsoft Office 2007
 16, 20; Microsoft Windows 7–8, 12,
 24, 45, 167, 170–2, 177, 183, 185,
 190, 192, 194, 196, 198–9, 204,
 206, 210; Microsoft Windows 2000
 14, 208; Microsoft Windows XP
 69; operating system customization
 services 47; operator 121; OS/2
 operating system 12–13, 47; Solaris
 183, 198; Unix 172, 182–3; Unix-
 based 182; Unix-based graphical
 interface 46; Unix-like 208; Windows
 2.0 7; Windows 7 174, 208; Windows
 8 22–3; Windows 95 8, 208;
 Windows 98 208; Windows 2003
 Server 14; Windows DDE interface
 8; Windows NT 208; Windows Vista
 16, 24, 174, 208; Windows XP 174;
 Windows XP Home 14; Windows XP
 Professional 14
OSCAR (Open Standards for
 Container/Content Allowing Reuse)
 47–8, 83

292 *Index*

output 39, 52, 57, 95, 102–3, 105–6, 121, 126, 128–30, 145, 186, 217, 233; machine 10, 126, 128; machine translation 126, 128–9; output quality 227; quality 52; translation 36, 227, 263, 273

ParaConc 87, 97
Passolo 195
PC-Transer 125, 234
PeTra 207, 234; PeTra 3.0 207
phrase 5, 57, 77, 81–2, 88–9, 91–2, 99–100, 105–6, 114, 125, 132–3, 140, 143, 145, 218, 275; example 89; loan 133; noun 203; phrase memory 216; set 106; source language 97; target 230; target language 97; verb 203
platform 22, 101, 123, 169, 171, 175, 185, 201, 211, 222, 224, 270; application 17; central database server 172; central software 171; cloud 231; cloud-based 171; cloud-based translation productivity 208; computer-aided project 17; editing 99, 121, 216; Internet-based collaborative translation 174; MS-DOS-based 46; multilingual maintenance 33; online 189; online service delivery 107; online work 205; open-source computer-aided translation 105; real-time translation memory 209; software 171; standalone computer-aided translation 18; translation 216
Poedit 44
Pootle 41–2, 44–5
Popovic, Anton 138, 142
pre-translation 22, 37, 98–9, 179, 181, 199; automatic 99; corpus-based 11; pre-translation phase 98; pre-translation server 8, 105
procedure 31–2, 118, 133, 139, 141–2, 251; application processing 202; cultural 268; eight-stage 34; intercultural 268; localization 116, 118–19; quality control 118; selection 261; technology-oriented translation 31, 87, 253; three-stage

32–3; translation 31–4, 52, 134, 139, 143
process 31, 55, 68–9, 75, 81, 86, 98, 109, 113, 115–16, 120, 141, 143, 175, 180, 183, 199, 216, 250, 252, 264, 269–71; computational 55; computer 52, 54, 74; data 34, 41–2, 86–7, 95, 98, 108; filtering 86; globalization 109; human language 223; installation 168, 191; internationalization 115; language 13; language-related 48; linguistic 32; localization 23, 117, 189, 200, 202; machine 30, 49, 55, 86, 128, 253, 275; mechanical 36; parallel text 254; parsing 217; post-editing 200; process automation 18; process efficiency 177; processing 13, 41, 43, 59, 120, 214, 250, 252; processing speed 11; processor 69; speech 75, 249; terminology 76; text 46, 122; transfer 32; translation 1, 21–2, 32, 42, 73, 109, 124, 137, 141, 167–8, 172, 174, 179, 181, 192, 194, 199, 207, 209, 216, 218, 232, 245; word 3, 8, 105, 112
production 38, 40, 55, 57, 73, 95, 129, 136, 140, 142, 251, 267; computer-aided translation software 17; file 202; in-house 5; pre-press 117; productivity 11, 16, 30, 38–40, 105, 174, 176, 181, 201, 251; speech 249, 264; system 108; translation 38, 57, 99, 193; translation software 7
profession 102, 128, 258, 271–3; professional 60, 169, 193, 195, 272; professionalism 40, 267, 270; professionalization 270; translation 176, 207–8, 248, 254, 271–2, 274
profile 33, 57, 70–1; named 232; profile setting 57, 70; project setup 71; project wizard 71; translator 182; workflow 181
profitability 39, 254, 272; translation 102
programme 15, 110–12, 169–70, 172, 177, 198, 203, 213, 218, 248; academic 273; application 45; computer-aided translation 270;

Index 293

cross-platform 183; desktop publishing 43; external 213; freelance 168; internationalized 111; Java 194, 196, 198–9, 207, 251; Java 1.5 199; presentation 42; professional 16; programme code 110; programmer 7, 16, 111, 168; programme size 208; programming 5, 251; programming guideline 111; programming language 111, 251; standalone 179; translation 201, 269; translation memory 8; translator training 171; VBNet 251
project 4, 8, 18–19, 23, 56–60, 69, 77, 79, 83, 102, 104, 146, 170, 181, 211, 213, 251; amateur 168; collaborative 214; computer-aided translation 30; document 175; large-volume translation 38–9, 110; local 189; multiple-language 106; online 189; open-source 20, 230; project administrator 56; project analysis 10, 102; project collaboration 58, 170, 209; project creator 72; project delivery 16; project domain 72; project evaluation 102; project execution 117; project file 33; project location 72; project management 6, 8, 10, 12, 17, 20–1, 24, 40, 57, 60, 109–10, 167, 169–70, 180, 182, 188, 202, 208, 253; project management system 22, 189; project management tool 8, 12, 15; project manager 8, 20, 56, 58–60, 86, 102, 107, 117–18, 146, 175, 181, 188; project name 71; project plan 118; project planning 102, 117; project preparation 102; project setting 73; project strategy 117; project team 118; project template 189; project user 56; project wizard 16; project workflow 117; real-time 209; research 274; server 14, 16; software 175; translation 4, 17, 38–9, 57, 59–60, 86, 96, 102–3, 105, 124, 175, 186, 201, 204, 211, 253
ProMemoria 13, 125, 170, 221
PROMT 7, 11–12, 15, 20, 47, 123, 125, 170, 221–2, 230–1, 234; PROMT 7.0 15; PROMT 8.0 17;

PROMT 9.5 200; PROMT 10 200; PROMT Cloud 200; PROMT Dictionary Editor 200; PROMT Expert 12; PROMT-Idiom XLIFF Connector 200; PROMT Industry Products 200; PROMT Translation Server 10 200; PROMT Translation Server 10 DE 200; PROMT Translation Server Developer Edition 200; PROMT Translator 230; PROMT v7.8 199; PROMT XT 12; PROMT XT Export 13

QTerm 14
quality 10, 19, 55, 74, 77, 88, 105, 118, 128–9, 137, 146, 170, 176, 181, 193, 214, 216–17, 227, 233, 251; expected 129; output 227; quality assurance 23–4, 126, 145, 214; quality assurance team 119; quality assurance tool 21, 31, 184, 209; quality control 142; quality delivery 118; quality management 118; translation 39, 102, 105, 216, 227, 232
QuickPlace 19

readability 54; reader 135, 137, 140, 268; readership 94, 129, 134, 140; source language 133; target 134, 138–9; target language 133, 140
Reiss, Katharina 261
repetition 57, 119, 141, 143; external 119; internal 18, 119; Repetitions Processing 3; textual 119
reusability 4–5, 54, 144, 250–1; reuse 251
Reverso 211, 221–2, 230; Reverso Expert 231; Reverso Pro 5 231
revision 96, 126, 129, 141–2; post-translation 126; reviser 128
rewriting 120, 135, 138, 142; automatic 53, 55; rewriting system 53
Robinson, Douglas 261
Romanization 143; Hanyu Pinyin 37, 131; Romanization rule 139; Romanization system 36, 94, 250; Wade-Giles 37, 131

294 *Index*

Sakhr CAT Translator 104, 170
Savory, Theodore H. 260
SDL 9–10, 20, 39, 99–100, 103, 201, 231–2; SDL Align 11; SDL Analyse 11; SDL Apply 11; SDL Automated Translation 221–2, 231; SDL BeGlobal 231; SDL EasyTranslator 232; SDL Edit 11; SDL Maintain 11; SDL MultiTerm 18, 78, 201; SDL MultiTerm 7 Extract 78; SDL MultiTerm Convert 78; SDL OpenExchange 20; SDL Passolo Essential 18; SDL Project Wizard 11; SDL Server 2009 19; SDL Studio GroupShare 201; SDL Studio GroupShare 2014 SP1 201; SDL Termbase 11; SDL TMS 201–2; SDL TMS 2011 SP4 202; SDL TMS 2013 201; SDL-Trados 41–4, 47, 51, 78, 168, 170, 188, 201, 221; SDL-Trados 2006 15, 177, 195–6; SDL-Trados 2007 Synergy 15–16, 18–19, 59–60; SDL-Trados 2015 58; SDL-Trados Studio 125, 201, 229, 231; SDL-Trados Studio 2009 18, 20; SDL-Trados Studio 2011 24, 80, 121; SDL-Trados Studio 2011 Alignment Editor 82; SDL-Trados Studio 2013 84; SDL-Trados Studio 2014 68, 71, 201; SDL-Trados WinAlign 6, 9, 12–13, 18; SDL Webflow 10; SDL Workbench 10, 125; SDL World Server 24, 180, 201–3, 267; SDL World Server 2011 202; SDLX 7, 9–10, 12–13, 86, 125, 195, 201, 221; SDLX 1.03 10; SDLX 2.0 10; SDLX 4.0 10; SDLX 2004 14; SDLX 2005 15; SDLX AutoTrans 11, 221; SDLX Translation Suite 4 11
search 8, 21, 75, 79, 216, 260; alphabetic 79; auto-concordance 11, 79, 183, 199; automated 11; character-based fuzzy 184; concordance 79; concordancing 124; entry 79; fuzzy 8, 17, 79, 172; online 10; real-time terminology 209; real-time translation memory 209; search bar 79; search engine 55; search filter 79; search speed 188; terminological 97;

terminology 124; translation memory 124, 169; wildcard 79
security 86, 107; administrative 86; computational 86; user-based 86; web 11
segment 12, 21, 81, 104, 122, 124, 146, 177, 188, 204, 220, 230, 252; automatic 81; automatic text 105; customizable 208; manageable 81; new 83; segmentation 76, 81, 252; segmentation marker 122; segmentation rules 48; Segmentation Rules eXchange (SRX) 16, 24, 48; segment memory 216; segment pair 82; sentence 105, 252; sentence-based 185; source 83, 122, 189, 204, 252; source-language 82; target 78, 83, 204; target-language 82; text 172, 252; translated 3, 16, 39, 122, 125, 175, 189; translation 179; word 252
sentence 4–5, 37, 39, 53, 57, 77, 81, 83, 92–3, 96, 98–100, 103–6, 114, 125–6, 130, 132, 138, 140, 142, 144–5, 193, 202, 216, 227, 253, 275; bilingual 5; complete 106; complex 53; decontextualized 105; example 96; identical 216; input 99, 219–20, 230; long 53, 138, 142; repeated 99; segmented 106; sentence analysis 9; sentence length 53; sentence memory 216; sentence pattern 5; sentence separation 81, 252; sentence structure 53; short 53; source language 220; source-text 82; stored 99, 125; target 38, 220; translated 84, 211, 252
Serebryakov, Alexander 6
Sheikh Al-Shabab, Omar 135
Sheridan, Peter 2
Similis 15, 41–2, 45, 106, 123, 168, 203–5; Similis Freelance 205; Similis Libellex 205; Similis LSP 205; Similis Manager 204; Similis Server 205; Similis Translation Tool 204; Similis v1.4 15
Snell-Hornby, Mary 244–5, 261
Snowball 47, 123

Index 295

Snowman 41–3, 47, 88, 121, 170, 206, 221; Snowman 1.0 19; Snowman 1.27 22; Snowman 1.3 71, 80, 84; Snowman Collaborative Translation Platform 22; Snowman V.1.33 68, 206
Softissimo 211
software 2, 7–10, 13, 16, 22, 36, 42, 44, 46, 53, 55, 69, 105, 107, 110–15, 117, 119, 122–3, 167–8, 170, 177, 179–80, 182–3, 188, 190, 192–4, 197–8, 200–2, 207, 210, 224; computer 167; computer-aided translation-related 101; controlled language 54; cross-platform 46; foreign language 115; free 168; free open-source 223; localized 98, 119; machine translation 199; open-source (OSS) 168, 179; paid 169; rule-based 199; software application 117, 119; Software-as-a-Service (SaaS) 20, 180, 185, 207, 211; software developer 110–11, 117, 120, 207; software documentation 119; software engineering 109; software license 10; software localization market 4; software producer 120; software product 109–10, 112, 114, 117; software supplier 116; software user 111; subtitling 113; third-party 43; translation software 5–7, 9, 12–13, 36, 77, 246; translation software industry 227
Sokolova, Svetlana 6
source text 33, 37, 39, 52–3, 55, 76, 81–2, 87, 95–7, 99, 102, 104, 106–7, 122, 124–8, 130, 134–41, 143, 146, 175, 177, 181, 185, 218, 248–9, 252–3, 263, 268, 273; finalized 109; source text comprehension 31, 33; source text interpretation 32; source text message 36; source text selection 34; source text translation 34
speech 75, 264; automatic 264; Automatic (ASR) 75, 264; bidirectional 265; connected 75; continuous 75; interactive 252; isolated-word 75; Plain 224; shifts in part of 142; speaker-dependent 264; speaker-independent 264;

speech generation 75, 249; speech input 75; speech process 249; speech processing 75; speech production 249; speech recognition 74, 249; speech recognition system 73–4, 249; speech synthesis 75, 249; speech technology 39, 74; speech-to-speech translation system 265; speech translation 74–5, 249, 258, 264, 275; speech translation project 264; speech translation system 75, 249, 264
SPIDER 6
Spoken Language Translator 264
Standard Generalized Markup Language (SGML) 6
Steiner, George 33
Sumita, Eichiro 5
Swordfish 41–7, 125, 170, 221; Swordfish 1.0–0 18; Swordfish II 21
Synthema WebCAT 206
system 3, 5, 7–9, 11–17, 19, 24–5, 33, 35–7, 39–42, 44, 46, 49, 57, 68–72, 78, 83, 95, 101, 104, 106, 121–2, 130, 169, 247, 272; API 186; automatic translation 127, 227; bilingual 108; built-in 221; client-server 172; closed 35; cloud-based 46, 56, 68–9; cloud-based translation 190; collaborative translation 201; commercial 6–7, 25, 167, 212, 217; commercial translation 217; cross-platform 167, 170, 211; cross-platform web-based 199; customer-specific 105; direct translation 265; experimental 217; free 168, 171, 213; free machine translation 225; hybrid 98, 100, 167, 220–1, 224, 230, 233–4, 272; interactive 271; interactive bilingual 252; Interactive Hybrid Strategies (IHSMT) 217; interactive multilingual 252; interactive text-editing 252; interactive translation 252; Internet-based 170; language-specific 167; Microsoft Machine Translation 225; MT 127; MT-TM hybrid 7; multidirectional 217; multilingual 105, 177; multiplatform 190; network-based 167, 170; networked

296 *Index*

169–70, 217; occasional user 217; online 233; online translation 120, 222, 230, 233, 266; open-source 105, 167; paid 167, 169, 171; plug-in 182; RBMT 230; sentence-based 106; server-based 69, 169–70, 201, 253; SMT 228–9; standalone 69, 167, 169, 177; statistical online 225; system commercialization 4–5; system developer 244, 269–70; system development 6, 168; system provider 103; system requirement 69; system supplier 270; system sustainability 271; text-based 106; translation 73, 77, 145, 215, 230; transliteration 131; Unicode-compliant 167; unidirectional 217; web-based 253; web-based customer-specific 108; web translation 267; writing 253

Systran (System Translation) 14, 22, 47, 105, 125, 170, 221–2, 225, 232–4, 266; Systran 5 233; Systran 7 232; Systran 7 Premium Translator 232; Systran 8 232; Systran Enterprise Server 5 233

Taber, Charles 31–2

tag 21; ALT (alternative tag) 35; IMG (inline image graphic tag) 35; on-the-fly 10; part-of-speech 253; statistical 253; TagEditor 14; tagger 253; tagging 249, 253; tag protection 6, 105

target 23, 83; target text 32–3, 52, 57, 81–2, 94–5, 97, 125, 127, 129, 134–7, 141, 145–6, 218, 233, 252, 268, 273; target text assessment 33; target text conventions 33; target text formulation 31; transcribed 75

TAUM-METEO 266

TCAT 2.0 22

TCloud 123

team 107; Team Server 19; translation 57, 60, 101, 141, 144, 170, 186, 210, 254

technique 133, 145, 177, 249–52, 264, 268; knowledge engineering 219; matching retrieval 177; probability

based 220; translation 132, 136, 138, 140, 142; writing 268

technologist 14, 187, 270; RBMT 232; rule-based 225; SMT 232; technology 38, 75, 110, 219, 258, 262–3, 266, 268–9, 271, 274; technology revolution 258; telecommunications 116; video 267

term 5–6, 10, 16, 22, 30, 33, 39, 60, 76–9, 95, 114, 138, 140, 262, 271; abstract 261; automatic 179, 183; automatic bilingual 78; automatic monolingual 78; brand 170, 216, 233; cultural 94, 97, 134–5; culture-specific 141; default 78; high-end 48; industry 170; input 77; local 131; new 78; rhetorical 141; source 79, 94, 134–5; source-language 143; standard 261; technical 88; term bank 77; termbase 9, 48, 59–60, 78, 119, 123, 125, 170, 210; termbase creation 34; Termbase eXchange (TBX) 24, 48, 171; termbase maintenance 190; termbase management 40; term creation tool 21, 77; term database 40, 59; term database management 40; term exchange 48; term extraction 78, 200; term extraction tool 21, 77; term manager 77; term recognition 183; term type 79; translated 18, 76, 78

terminologist 60, 78; automatic 204; bilingual 15, 88, 106, 204; centralized 170; customer-specific 60, 80; independent 77; multilingual 88; multiple 80; pre-established 114; proprietary 12; specialized 77; standard 79; system 77; terminology 56, 72, 76–80, 88, 172, 188; terminology acquisition 76, 252; terminology bank 76–7; terminology creation tool 77; terminology database 8, 12, 33–4, 41, 48, 57, 60, 69, 73, 77, 79–80, 103–4, 107, 116, 120, 172, 199, 201, 207, 211, 216, 234, 252; terminology database structure 79; terminology development 118; terminology extraction 76, 252;

Index 297

terminology extraction system 12; terminology maintenance module 8; terminology management 6, 11–12, 21, 76–7, 180, 194, 198, 214, 252; terminology management system 77, 105, 118, 198, 252; terminology management tool 5, 118–19, 179, 194, 198; terminology processing 76, 252; terminology recognition 76, 172, 252; terminology report 79; terminology system 39, 171; terminology tool 14, 208; terminology translation 76, 252; Terminology Wizard 207

TermStar 6; TermStar NXT 21

text 3, 6, 15–16, 22–3, 34–7, 41–2, 48–9, 52–3, 55, 81, 86, 128, 134, 203, 209, 225, 248, 251, 253, 261; alternative text 35; automatic 11, 188; bilingual 248; colloquial 248; comparative 248; controlled 52; controlled language 52, 253; controlled source 52; controlled target 52; descriptive 53; domain-specific 270; electronic 73–5, 248, 273; generated 128; handwritten 74; highlighted 36; immediate 135; input 33, 52, 55, 103, 107, 121, 250; linguistic 267; literary 259, 261, 263; machine-translated 129; machine translation 126; main 135; original 39, 126–7, 137; output 55; parallel 218, 248; parallel aligned 254; plain 185, 196, 198, 206, 208, 212, 227; practical 263, 273; pre-translated 106; printed 74; procedural 53; project-specific 76; quality 52; religious 259, 261; repetitive 24, 119; scanned 253; source language 52, 74, 138, 140, 220; spoken 75, 249, 264; standard 18; stenographed 75; target language 140, 143; text aligner 188; text alignment 11, 40; text alignment tool 9; text chunk 230; text chunking 249; text clustering 249; text creation 76; text data 13; text file 7; text format 37; text importation 76; text length 128; text parsing 33; text processing system 41; text quantity 128; text

readability 33; text reformulation 32; text summarization 249; text type 31, 97, 128, 217, 245, 262; translated 33, 35, 135, 218; translation 122, 124, 138; Unicode 208

theory 137, 245, 259–62, 265; area-restricted 245; deconstructionist 261; general 245; information 265; medium-restricted 245; partial 245; polysystem 261; problem-restricted 245; rank-restricted 245; skopos 261; text-type restricted 245; time-restricted 245; translation 40, 244–5, 258–60, 273

TinyTM 207; TinyTM 0.1 207

TM-database 41–3, 47, 125, 207–8, 221; TM-database v1.82 207

Toma, Peter 266

tool 3, 5, 8, 12, 23, 39, 48, 55, 73, 77–9, 81, 87, 96–7, 103, 109, 112, 129, 145–6, 167, 169, 171, 173–4, 176, 181–3, 188, 191, 196–7, 208, 211, 246, 251, 274–5; assimilation 170; authoring 16, 55, 172; auto-alignment 185, 194; built-in 30; communication 171; computer 167; computer-based 167; controlled authoring 55; cross-platform 18, 194; dissemination 170; document-based 182; drafting 44; electronic 269; electronic translation 169; free 22; independent terminology creation 77; in-house translation 178; Internet-based 167; localization 109, 202; management 20; multi-format alignment 21; online 189; phrase-chunking 203; pre-editing 55; production 202; productivity 20; professional translation 8; project-based 182; quality assurance 21, 31, 184, 209; quality checking 215; server-based 167; source authoring assistance 172; standalone 14; system terminology creation 77; term creation 77; term extraction 21, 77; text processor 5; toolbar 30, 122, 168; translation 8, 20, 40, 47, 104, 106, 169, 185; web translation 36–7

Toury, Gideon 244, 246

298 *Index*

Trados 4–10, 12–15, 25, 86, 108, 176–7, 195–6, 199, 203; Trados 5.0 10; Trados 5.5 10; Trados 6 11; Trados 6.5 11–12; Trados 7 Freelance 14; Trados Workbench 11, 191
Tr-AID 168, 208; Tr-AID 2.0 13, 208
TransAssist 107
TransCheck 146, 253
transfer 32–3, 52, 107, 116, 126, 128, 134, 140–1, 220, 269; direct 134; ideational 269; information 268; interlingual 91; linguistic 268; meaning 33; multimodal 98; semantic 269; semiotic 269; text 96; transfer approach 107; transference 93, 143; transfer process 32
TransFlow 18
Transit 4–5, 41–4, 47, 55, 125, 188, 209, 221; STAR Transit 195; Transit 1.0 5–7; Transit 3.0 13; Transit NXT 18, 209; Transit NXT Service Pack 3 20; Transit NXT Service Pack 4 21; Transit NXT Service Pack 6 23
translatability 54, 249–50; inter 250; machine 250; translatability checker 146, 250, 253
TranslateCAD 44
translation 2, 4, 31, 37–9, 57, 60, 93, 98, 109, 126, 135–6, 140, 143, 167, 175, 250, 252, 258–60, 267, 272–4; aesthetic 271; alt-tag 34; approximate 94, 133; automatic 98, 105–7, 177, 234, 272; back 142; Bible 259; bilingual 88; bottom-up 133; Buddhist 259; chat 35; chatroom 35; clause-for-clause 139; clipboard 35; collaborative 211; collective 38; communicative 139; context-bound 140; controlled 52; controlled language 54, 249; controlled target language 52; crowdsourcing 175, 185, 216; custom 136; decontextualized fragment 114; definitional 134; diagrammatic 134; document 109, 112, 114; documentary 119, 248; double 134; draft 37, 121; dynamic equivalence 260; email 36; ethnographic 134; existing 39; foreign language 36;

formulation 135; fragment 114; free 135, 259, 271; free online 226; full text 253; fully automatic high-quality (FAHQT) 31, 126, 272; generic 136; gist 36, 127, 136; gloss 136; grammatical 136; graphological 136; human 2, 31, 33–4, 36–7, 52, 87, 102, 128, 132, 144, 146, 249, 253, 267; human-aided (computer) 272; Human-Aided Machine (HAMT) 167; idiomatic 127; indicative 137; indirect 137; individual 57; information 137; informational 127, 137; interactive 177; interactive speech 252; interlinear 137, 143; interlingual 260; intermediate 137; Internet 252; intersemiotic 138, 143, 260, 267; intracultural 138; intralingual 138, 260; language 38; lexical 138; literal 137–9, 143, 259; literary 39, 245, 260, 262–3, 273; loan 139; Machine-Aided Human (MAHT) 167; manual 31; mobile 274; morpheme-for-morpheme 139; mouse 37; multilingual 88, 100, 104; multimedia 267; multiple 114; non-literary 262; oblique 139; offline 190, 217; online 37, 217, 251–2; outline 136; paragraph-to-paragraph 136; parallel 140; parenthetical 140; partial 140, 143; past 40, 107; phonological 140; phrase-for-phrase 139; place-name 140; poetry 95, 138–9; practical 39, 251, 263, 273; pragmatic 140; pre-dictionary 135; previous 125; professional 39, 129, 135, 217, 251; proper 136; proper-noun 131; quality 52, 272; raw 128; real-time 10; restricted 136, 138, 141; rough 36, 127, 136–7; second-hand 137; semantic 94, 139; sense-for-sense 271; sentence 37, 142; sentence-splitting 142; sentential 37; software localization 114; source-equivalent 142; source-oriented 142; source-text-biased 137; speech 248, 262; stylistic 142; suggested 83, 125; summary 143; target language 143; target-language-biased 135; team 57,

Index 299

119; text 41, 248, 258, 262; text-to-animation 267; text-to-diagram 267; text-to-graph 267; text-to-picture 267; text-to-speech 267; text-to-video 267; under 143; web 37, 42, 170, 217, 252; web localization 114; webpage 33, 227, 271; word 143; word-for-word 104, 137, 139, 143, 265

Translation Brain 47, 234

translation management 102; computer-aided 267, 272; corporate 8, 15, 103; global 258; network 270; open-source, server-based 180; Translation Management System (TMS) 21, 23, 101, 103, 185, 194, 202, 216, 253; translation management technology 216

translation memory (TM) 2–5, 9–10, 12–13, 15, 20–1, 33, 39, 56, 60, 72, 82–3, 85–6, 97–8, 105–7, 109, 122–3, 146, 167, 171–3, 175, 177, 181, 188, 194, 197, 199, 202, 204, 206, 208, 210–12, 216, 219–20, 232, 234, 252, 268, 271–2; active 85; Arabic 14; background 85; bilingual 106; browser-based 185; centralized 144, 170, 201, 205, 246; cross-platform 172; current 85; customized 105; desktop 108; eXtensible Markup Language (XML) 16–17, 47, 106; file-based 85; first-generation 3, 203, 204; free 10, 171; integrated 15; interactive 105; literary 269; master 85; multiple 194; multiuser 14; open-source 177; read-only 85; real-time 209; regular 85; second-generation 203; sentence-based 209; server-based 85; server-based centralized 216; TextBase 15, 103; third-party 198; 32-bit 8; TMX Certification 14; TMX-format 199; Trados TXT 18; translation memory analysis 215; translation memory data 48, 95, 107, 177; translation memory database 4, 8, 34, 38–9, 41, 47, 55, 57, 59, 73, 76, 81–5, 100–1, 103–4, 106–7, 114, 116, 119–20, 125, 146, 169, 175, 183, 199, 207,

214; translation memory database management 40; translation memory database tool 9; translation memory engine 6, 199; Translation Memory eXchange (TMX) 15, 17–18, 20–1, 24, 47, 83, 107, 119, 171, 177, 252; translation memory format 47; translation memory manager (TMM) 14; translation memory platform 209; translation memory programme 8; translation memory propagation 83; translation memory server 57; translation memory software 7; translation memory system 7, 14, 81–3, 106, 172, 176, 189, 195, 203, 213, 216, 234, 252; translation memory technology 4, 7, 103, 175, 201; translation memory tool 5, 7–8, 103, 118–19, 168, 174, 179, 196, 208, 229; translation memory workbench 198; Very Large Translation Memory (VLTM) 16, 85, 212; visual 17; web-based 16; web-enabled 14; working 86; XHTML 16

translation practice 4, 37, 97, 169, 246, 258, 262, 268–9, 271

translation studies 97, 244–8, 260–2, 265, 270–3; applied 245–6; applied computer-aided 253–4; computer-aided 246–8; computer-related theoretical computer-aided 250; corpus-based 271; descriptive 244, 246; function-oriented descriptive 245; function-specific practical computer-aided 252; goal-related theoretical computer-aided 251; language-related theoretical computer-aided 249; medium-related theoretical computer-aided 248; practical computer-aided 251; process-specific practical computer-aided 253; product-oriented descriptive 245; pure 244; system-specific practical computer-aided 251; theoretical 244; theoretical computer-aided 248–9

Transolution 42, 44–5, 105, 210; Transolution 0.4b8 210

Transoo Editor 125

300 *Index*

TransSearch 42
Trans Suite 2000 7, 12–13, 221
TransType 105
Transwhiz 7, 12, 47, 105, 125, 170, 234; Transwhiz 9.0 15; Transwhiz 10 17; Transwhiz Power 11
TraTool 14, 47, 125
Tsutsumi, Yutaka 5
Tyndale, William 263
Tytler, Alexander Fraser 260

Unicode 49, 106, 111, 172, 179, 186, 190; Unicode 3.0 13; Unicode UTF-8 194
unit 35, 59–60, 81, 84, 87, 90, 105, 115, 126, 132, 139–41, 172; bilingual 219; grammatical 53, 143; lexical 94, 143; multiword 90; operational 142; predefined 81; service 180; source language 140; sub-segment aligned 203; textual 135–6; translation 21, 23, 59, 72, 81, 84–6, 105, 125, 133, 169, 204, 234, 250
usability 109, 168, 188, 192, 198, 212, 250; alignment 18; bilingual word 97–8; grammatical 127; target language 139; usage 97, 213
user 8, 12, 16, 18, 21–3, 34, 36–7, 39, 42, 52, 55–7, 68–72, 78, 83–4, 86, 95, 106, 122, 124, 146, 167–71, 173, 179, 181–2, 194, 204, 212, 214, 216, 232, 267, 270; ad hoc 169, 177; advanced 169; authorized 175; average 233; commercial system 247; computer 168; concurrent 19, 69; corporate 68, 186, 192, 233; end 129; general 186, 205; home 200; human 72; intuitive 194; licensed 69; machine translation 127, 137; named 69; non-frequent 168; non-TM 195; occasional 258; registered 106–7, 170; software 111; standalone version 35; system 95, 270; target 36, 89, 99, 113, 118, 128, 253; translation-memory 176, 196; user administration 180; user group 269–70; user interface 46, 109, 111

vendor 40; freelance 40; language-service 120; localization 110, 117; multi-language 110; single-language 110; vendor control 254
Verbmobil 265
Vermeer, Hans J. 261
Vernay, Henri 268
version 5, 7–12, 14–18, 21, 23–4, 36, 41–3, 46–7, 101, 109, 113, 136–7, 142, 168, 171–2, 174, 176–7, 179, 182–6, 188–93, 196, 198–202, 205–11, 213–14, 231–2; beta 15; client-server 105; elite 11; free 22, 185, 188, 232; literal 34; network 101; official 11, 47; open source 20, 45; paid 226; professional 11, 101, 199; server-based 179; standalone 15, 101, 205, 216; standard 48, 206; translated 137; trial 19, 101, 188; version control 23; versioning 21; web-based 183
Virtaal 44
Visual Localize 114
Visual Transmate 123
vocabulary 88, 98, 271; active 87; basic 53; controlled 53; general 127; new 271; specialized 252; vocabulary size 75

Waley, Arthur 263
Weaver, Warren 1, 265; Weaver's Memorandum 1, 265
web 96, 106–7; audible 41; bilingual 33; corporate 203, 205; localized 98; multiple-language 116; official 69, 172, 174, 176, 180, 182, 184, 186–7, 190, 207–10, 212, 216, 230; visual 41; web access 19; web address 69; web application 183; web browser 16, 41, 69, 123, 183; webpage 16, 33, 37, 41, 59, 69, 73, 98, 109, 115, 170, 216, 225–7, 230, 248, 273; webpage translation 33, 37, 175, 271; website 22, 34, 47, 109, 115, 170, 175, 183, 186, 188–9, 192–4, 196, 198, 207, 210–12, 223, 226–7, 229, 231–3, 246; web translation 42, 170, 217, 252; web translation service 225; web translation system 267; web translation tool 36–7

Index 301

WebCat 207
WebTerm 6
WebWordSystem 46–7, 123, 210; WebWordSystem Public Area 211
Wilss, Wolfram 31–2
window 125; bubble 209; single 125
word 5, 8, 16, 22, 36, 53, 55, 75–9, 81–2, 85–6, 88–97, 102, 104–5, 113, 120, 127, 130–2, 134–43, 145, 184–6, 209, 250, 253, 258, 260, 264, 267–8; ambiguous 56; appreciative 92; approved 53; borrowed 139; do-not-translate 130; do-not-use 171; empty 5; fuzzy 92; highlighted 90; isolated 75; loan 133, 139; measure 132; mistranslated 130; neutral 92; new 60; Not Translated (NTW) 130; omitted 130; onomatopoeic 95; orthographic 144; restricted 171; selected 79; single 77; source-language 94, 139, 143–4; source language cultural 94, 133; source-text 81; specialized 76–7; target language cultural 94, 133; unfound 131; word boundary 81; word chunk 106; word class 141; word combination 56; word game 96; wordlist 77; word-order 137; word origin 96; word processing 105; word processor 8, 112; word selection 3; word usage 171; written 116, 269
Wordbee 46–7, 125, 211, 229; Wordbee Translator 146, 211, 221
Wordfast 7, 9, 11, 18, 41, 43–4, 49, 51, 57, 78, 80, 83, 85–6, 105–6, 146, 170, 172, 177, 195–6, 203, 229; Wordfast 3.22 13; Wordfast 4 11–12; Wordfast 5.5 16, 24; Wordfast 5.90 24; Wordfast Anywhere 19, 123, 125, 168, 211–13, 221, 233, 267; Wordfast Classic 18, 46–7, 49, 68, 80, 83–4, 123, 169, 172, 211, 213; Wordfast Classic 3.34 13; Wordfast Classic 6.03t 71, 121; Wordfast Classic v6.0 21, 46, 68, 80, 84; Wordfast PlusTools 9; Wordfast Pro 18, 47, 69, 125, 188, 211; Wordfast Pro 2.4 19; Wordfast Pro 3.0 23; Wordfast Server 211; Wordfast

Translation Studio 18, 211; Wordfast v3.0 10
WordFisher 7–8, 12, 41, 168, 213–14; WordFisher 4.2.0 13
WordSmith 77, 87
workflow 19, 21, 23, 59, 106, 175; automated 214; customizable 21; localization 20, 118, 202; management 171; multilingual 14; online 23; project 117; translation 20, 23, 185–6, 202, 231; web-based 172; workflow automation 189; workflow control 24; workflow management 8, 18, 171, 193; workflow management tool 194; workflow profile 181; workflow technology 216
workstation 6, 12, 209; independent 123; personal 101, 258; personal translation 101, 105; standalone 224; translation 105; translator's 8, 217
WorldLingo 212, 221–2, 229, 232–3
Wycliffe, John 263

Xpro7 7, 14, 234
XTM 41–5, 47, 49–51, 56, 68–72, 77, 83–4, 97, 99–100, 121, 214–15, 221; server-based XTM Suite 215; XTM 5.5 21; XTM Cloud 20, 23–4, 46, 80, 215, 229; XTM Suite 69; XTM Suite 6.2 23; XTM Suite 7.0 23; XTM v7.3 68; XTM Workbench 21
Xuanzang 玄奘 259

Yahoo 221, 225; Yahoo! Babel Fish 222, 224–5, 229, 232
Yan, Fu 260
Yaxin 41, 43, 51, 68, 100, 103–4, 107; Yaxin CAT 7, 9, 12, 33, 47, 170, 215; Yaxin CAT 2.0 15; Yaxin CAT 3.5 15, 68; Yaxin CAT 4.0 17, 71, 80, 84, 121; Yaxin CAT Software 216; Yaxin CAT v1.0; Yaxin CAT v2.5 Bidirectional (English and Chinese) 10
YOOmanage 216

Zhu, Falan 竺法蘭 263
Zhu, Shenghao 朱生豪 263